Parenting Evaluations for the Court

Care and Protection Matters

Perspectives in
Law & Psychology

Sponsored by the American Psychology-Law Society / Division 41 of the American Psychological Association

Series Editor: Ronald Roesch, *Simon Fraser University, Burnaby, British Columbia, Canada*

Editorial Board: Jane Goodman-Delahunty, Thomas Grisso, Stephen D. Hart, Marsha Liss, Edward P. Mulvey, James R. P. Ogloff, Norman G. Poythress, Jr., Don Read, Regina Schuller, and Patricia Zapf

Parenting Evaluations for the Court

Care and Protection Matters

Lois Oberlander Condie

Children's Hospital, Harvard Medical School
Boston, Massachusetts

and

Doctor Franklin Perkins School
Lancaster, Massachusetts

KLUWER ACADEMIC / PLENUM PUBLISHERS
NEW YORK/BOSTON/DORDRECHT/LONDON/MOSCOW

Library of Congress Cataloging-in-Publication Data

Condie, Lois Oberlander, 1961–
    Parenting evaluations for the court: care and protection matters/Lois Oberlander Condie.
      p.   cm.—(Perspectives in law & psychology; v. 18)
    Includes bibliographical references and indexes.
    ISBN: 0-306-47486-7
    1. Psychology, Forensic—United States. 2. Evidence, Expert—United States. 3. Child abuse—Evaluation. 4. Child welfare—Evaluation. I. Title. II. Series.

KF505.5 .C66 2003
347.73'67—dc21

2002042766

ISBN 0-306-47486-7

©2003 Kluwer Academic / Plenum Publishers, New York
233 Spring Street, New York, New York 10013

http://www.wkap.nl/

10 9 8 7 6 5 4 3 2 1

A C.I.P. record for this book is available from the Library of Congress

Permission for books published in Europe: permissions@wkap.nl
Permission for books published in the United States of America: permission@wkap.com

Printed in the United States of America

Preface

The impetus for this book came from the applied clinical work and research of a group of professionals at the University of Nebraska Department of Psychology, the University of Nebraska Law School, the University of Virginia Law School, the University of Massachusetts Medical Center, and Harvard Medical School. Combining the research methods of psychology with the concerns of the law, this volume explores important aspects of the care and protection system. It is based on a review of critical issues in care and protection regulations, laws, and procedures concerning the well being of children whose parents face the scrutiny of the child protective services system. It will be of special interest to forensic mental consultants and evaluators, attorneys, judges, child protective system administrators and workers, and policy makers. Applied researchers will find that the book provides valuable insights into the complexity of the psychological aspects of the care and protection system.

Psychology and law subsumes many specialty areas. Children and the law is a specialty that is coming of age in terms of its heavy emphasis on scientific integrity, forensic relevance, and standards of practice. This book builds upon the work of clinical psychologists and psychiatrists, developmentalists, and forensic mental health experts who are concerned with the relevance of the mental health professions to care and protection matters. It is intended as an introductory overview to consultation and forensic evaluation in the subspecialty of children and law, with an emphasis on children whose parents are involved with the care and protection system and parents who potentially might face termination of their parental rights. Although termination of parental rights cases are the predominant focus of the book, attention also is given to consultation and evaluations for service planning purposes, the impact of maltreatment on children, diagnostic and treatment planning purposes, issues of family process, amenability to treatment, potential family reunification, and post-termination pre-adoption questions.

One purpose of this book is to increase the legal relevance of forensic consultation and evaluations in care and protection matters. The proposed assessment models are based on an analysis of common features of regulations and statutes relevant to parental rights termination. Questions of the care and protection of children frequently require courts to make legal decisions about children based on legally defined infringements by parents of their caregiving responsibilities. In recent decades, courts have turned increasingly to mental health professionals to assist them in considering a range of factors that are relevant to statutes governing the care and protection of children and termination of parental rights. At the same time, the legal system has challenged the role of experts by setting high admissibility standards for scientific integrity and objectivity in forensic consultation and assessment practice. The purpose of this book is to lay a foundation for solid conceptual and methodological approaches for use by mental health professionals in making an effective response to relevant legal standards and to the needs of individuals about whom the law makes care and protection decisions.

The second purpose of this book is to promote the scientific integrity of forensic consultation and assessment in care and protection matters. During the last three decades, research has produced findings that are advancing the subspecialty in a number of ways. Although there is much applied research to be done, it is possible to use leading theories and research findings to advance the standards of practice for psychological consultation in care and protection matters. This book was written to provide examples of ways to integrate theory and research into practice. It offers conceptual models for consultation and assessment of parenting concerns that reach the level of state scrutiny, and consultation and assessment of the impact on children. It is hoped that this book will further enhance both research and practice in the subspecialty of children and the law.

This work is the product of my association with many individuals over the course of my career. It represents the culmination of research with Dr. Gary Melton, a post-doctoral fellowship with Dr. Tom Grisso, and grant funding on a project early in my career from Dr. John Monahan. Each of these associations provided the framework for my research and clinical consultation that naturally segued into this topic. It also is an extension of clinical work with Ms. Bev Amazeen, the Honorable Jay Blitzman, Dr. Linda Cavallero, Dr. Geri Fuhrmann, Attorney Margaret Geary, Attorney Barbara Hannigan, Mr. Mark Horwitz, Ms. Susie King, Dr. Peter Metz, Ms. Felicia Rao-Hagberg, and Attorney Thomas Stylianos.

This book was strongly influenced by my association with Dr. Linda Forsythe, Dr. Steven Nickman and the members of the Adoption Study Group at Massachusetts General Hospital. Their seminal work and presentations in this area of study provided me with a rich source of data, articles, theories, and professional consultation. I am grateful to individuals who reviewed early drafts of chapters of this book, including Dr. David Doolittle, Ms. Jessica Geier, Dr. Alan Tomkins, and Dr. Vicky Weisz. I am grateful for the expert assistance of Dr. Ronald Roesch in his capacity as editor of this Kluwer-Plenum series. Finally, a warm thanks to Dr. Don Condie and Dr. Alan Goldstein, who listened to and provided feedback on my ideas and concerns as I completed this project; and to Ms. Emma Condie, who made meaningful most of what I know about developmental psychology.

Contents

1

Introduction to Care and Protection Evaluations

This introductory chapter describes the landscape of psychology, law, ethics, and standards of practice for forensic mental health evaluations in care and protection matters. Parenting involves a broadly defined set of skills and abilities embedded in cultural and other contextual features. Measures for child safety within families, within cultural groups, and within legal definitions and statutes, vary across jurisdictions. However, statutorily defined infringements of parenting responsibilities also contain some common elements across jurisdictions. Most statutes address physical abuse, sexual abuse, and physical and emotional neglect. The breadth and specificity of definitions vary widely, as will be illustrated in later chapters. Some statutes increase specificity by adding inclusionary or exclusionary criteria based on child developmental trajectories, sometimes incorporating developmental principles or constructs into statutory language. Definitions in state statutes show some correspondence to mental health and social service definitions of child maltreatment, but there are many differences in constructs and definitions across the legal, social services, and mental health systems.

The decision-making process used by courts in determinations of whether to assume jurisdiction over a care and protection matter has evolved over the past century. Societal developments have influenced judicial judgments concerning the nature and seriousness of harm that merits jurisdiction, the weight accorded to children's right and the rights of parents, and the responsibilities of the child protective services system after jurisdiction is assumed. Courts face more and more nontraditional familial structures and dynamics, challenging traditional notions of family functioning and family safety. Mandated reporting requirements have influenced the variety and frequency of maltreatment concerns that enter the legal and child protective services system. Each of these factors has influenced the court's interest and willingness to turn to forensic evaluation and consultation. Conducting parenting evaluations in the context of care and protection matters requires a broad foundation of theoretical knowledge and forensic clinical assessment skills. A realistic appraisal of cases dynamics and the reasonableness of referral questions requires knowledge of the history of the child protective services system, and how the current evaluation context is similar to and different from past concerns about families and child safety. Evaluators must be familiar with relevant statutes, case law, ethical codes and practice guidelines, and research relevant to evaluating parents and children in the context of court proceedings.

The first two chapters of this book cover foundations of forensic psychology and its application to the legal and social service systems in care and protection matters. Content includes legal tension between children's rights and the rights of parents, the role of state intervention in the lives of families, legal and regulatory exceptions to family privacy, the ethical contours of evaluations, and existing guidelines for practice. Chapter three addresses the need to frame referral questions in a manner conducive to good assessment practice and legal concerns for evaluations. Typical problem questions are addressed, along with suggestions for avoiding or redefining problem referral questions. Chapters four through seven cover theory and empirical research relevant to parenting evaluations for the court. Foundational issues include the psychology of parenting, theories and associated features of parenting behavior, child development and the parenting needs of children, and research on the impact of child maltreatment on children, families and society. Multicultural issues in parenting and child maltreatment are reviewed. Specific issues related to parental self report, children's competence as reporters of maltreatment, children's suggestibility, embellishments, and minimization are addressed. Chapter eight addresses evaluation methodology for caregivers and children. Interview and assessment methods for parents and children are reviewed, along with the relevance to parenting evaluations of risk assessment, the assessment of malingering and dissimulation, and parental amenability to rehabilitation. The final chapter gives suggestions for report preparation, report organization, and strategies for interpretation. Research relevant to interpretive points is described, providing the reader with ready access to recent research developments on issues that commonly are the subject of direct and cross-examination. Pragmatic issues relevant to testimony preparation are reviewed.

LEGAL AND REGULATORY ISSUES IN CARE AND PROTECTION CASES

A Prototype of Current Child Protective Service System Statutes and Regulations

Each state has statutorily defined jurisdiction over strengthening and encouraging family life for the protection and care of children (Kantrowitz & Limon, 2001). States have the authority to encourage the use by any family of available resources to promote the safety of children. State statutes governing care and protection matters contain provisions for mandatory reporting of maltreatment, specifying who is required to make mandatory reports, what conditions must be reported, and the level of identifying information and of confidentiality in the state's central registry of reported information (Kalichman, 2000). When families fail to protect and care for children, as defined by statute, states have the authority to provide substitute care of children (Goldstein, 1999). The state's goal is to ensure the rights of children to sound physical, mental, and moral development. The prevailing standard for the care and protection of children is the *best interest* standard, described more fully in subsequent chapters. Factors that court may consider in making best interest determinations include precipitating factors, previous living conditions, the current status of factors and precipitating conditions, and an assessment of the likelihood of their amelioration or elimination. Courts may consider the child's fitness, readiness, abilities, and developmental level. Courts may intervene, giving orders for specification or modification of service plans designed to meet the needs of the child within a particular placement or within the child's family. The court may request written documentation or evidence of the effectiveness, suitability and adequacy of services and placements provided to the child. The court also may request information relevant to the child's prognosis. The court may require that services be provided in a timely manner in order to facilitate permanency planning for the child (Kantrowitz & Limon, 2001).

Statutory definitions of jurisdiction or custody usually include the power to determine the child's placement, medical care and educational care (Goldstein, 1999). They contain provisions for emergency placements for children, usually of about three days. The child might then be returned to the parents if the matter is resolved, or the case will go to a hearing for evidence relevant to whether the state should assume jurisdiction (Melton, Petrila, Poythress, & Slobogin, 1997). States assume automatic jurisdiction over children born to incarcerated mothers or adolescent mothers committed to the juvenile justice system. The child protective service system, usually in consultation with the commissioner of the state's correctional department, then makes provisions for placement of the child (Kantrowitz & Limon, 2001). When jurisdiction of any child is assumed, the state is granted power to place the child in foster or residential care, to control parental or other caregiver visits to the child, and to consent to military enlistments, marriages and other contracts usually requiring parental consent. There is a provision for a hearing if the parent objects to the decisions of the child protective service system or the judge (Goldstein, 1999).

Evidence in support of assuming jurisdiction may include an investigation of the facts related to the safety of the child, and it includes a mechanism for subjecting investigators and investigation records to cross examination (Goldstein, 1999). Evidence might also include the testimony of foster parents or pre-adoptive parents if the child has been in placement for a specified duration, usually six months or more. It may include the testimony of the child if the court determines that a child is competent and willing to provide testimony (Kantrowitz & Limon, 2001). Under certain circumstances, state care and protection statutes are linked to criminal codes and jurisdiction results in an automatic referral to the criminal justice system. Administrative regulations specify the roles and responsibilities of child protective service system officials, and procedures for petitioning for jurisdiction, disposition requests and pretrial motions (Goldstein, 1999).

In care and protection matters, children usually are appointed their own counsel (Melton et al., 1997), with indigent funding, for individual representation in care and protection matters. A child may not independently petition the court for care and protection jurisdiction. Placement in foster care with biological relatives is encouraged. Separation of siblings is discouraged. When separation of siblings takes place, sibling visitation is provided for by statute. Court jurisdiction of sibling visitation is retained even after adoption of the siblings into separate homes. Children cannot be removed by foster parents or by residential transfer from one state to another while in state custody, unless a specific arrangement is made for an interstate compact (Kantrowitz & Limon, 2001).

Statutory provisions for child protective service departments or agencies include the power to visit, supervise, and license foster homes and placement agencies. It includes authorization to remove the child from a placement if the child's safety is compromised in any way. There are specific requirements for transfer of information about the child from one placement to another when changes in placement are made. Child protective service departments have the responsibility (including financial responsibility except where partial or full parental reimbursement is required) for providing foster care. Visitation by parents can be barred if there is a risk to child safety or under specific circumstances such as the parent's conviction of murder in the first degree. There sometimes are provisions for visitation by extended family members such as grandparents, unless such visitation is not in the child's best interest (Goldstein, 1999; Kantrowitz & Limon, 2001).

Permanency hearings are conducted according to statutory time lines, usually every 12 months (Melton et al., 1997). Foster parents and pre-adoptive parents are given notice of hearings and they are allowed to attend hearings and to be heard; however, they are not given standing as a party to the hearings (In re Harley C., 1998). Foster parents also have no standing in seeking visitation rights (In the Interest of G.C., A Minor Child, 1997). Statutes provide for voluntary surrender of parental custody of children for the purpose of consenting to adoption. The child protective service system can consent to adoption only when it is expressly included in an order of the court, following termination of parental rights (Goldstein, 1999). If a child remains in foster placement for a specified duration after the court has released the child for adoption, there are provisions for notification of foster care and adoption agencies of the child's eligibility for adoption. If termination is not granted, other dispositional options include returning the child to the parent, a referral for legal guardianship, or placement in another planned permanent living arrangement (such as permanent foster care). In the case of a child who reaches mid- to late-adolescence (usually at around age 16), provisions are made for an eventual transition from foster care to independent living (Kantrowitz & Limon, 2001).

REQUESTS FOR FORENSIC ASSESSMENT

Referral questions in care and protection matters cover an array of topics and they may be introduced in the initial phase, the mid-phase, or the termination phase of care and protection proceedings (Grisso, 1986). Although evaluation requests take many forms, there are four main reasons that evaluations are requested or ordered by the court. The first reason is to evaluate the caregiver's need for services just after the court has assumed jurisdiction of the child. The second reason is to evaluate the current risk that the parent poses to the child. A risk assessment might be requested early in the process to help the child protective service agency determine if the parent can resume physical custody while the state provides indicated services. It might be requested later in the process to facilitate dispositional planning relevant to whether it is safe to close the case and return a child home. The third reason is to assess the child's current functioning and treatment needs. The fourth reason is to gather data relevant to judgments about the caregiver's amenability to interventions. The fourth question might be posed early in the process as part of a treatment planning referral, or it might be posed late in the process as part of an evaluation request when a caregiver is facing possible termination of parental rights. Related questions include the child's capacity to provide an account of the maltreatment, the child's reaction to maltreatment, the child's attachment to substitute caregivers and the child's readiness for adoption.

An evaluation is used to gather relevant information to assist child protective service workers in administrative decisions and the court in judicial decisions over whether continued services are merited with a goal of reunification, or whether the case merits termination of parental rights. A quality evaluation report provides useful probative data to facilitate decisions of legal strategy that must be made by attorneys and judicial decisions made by the court (Grisso, 1986). Regardless of the actual referral question or questions, most evaluations in care and protection proceedings either directly or indirectly address safety issues in the parent-child relationship. Evaluations take place in the context of the best interests of the child standard that is in effect in virtually all jurisdictions (Melton et al., 1997).

THE CONTEXT WITHIN WHICH EVALUATION REQUESTS ARE MADE

THE REFERRAL PROCESS

Most forensic evaluation requests occur after a care and protection petition has been granted by the court. Referrals are most common near the beginning of a care and protection matter, focusing on helping the families and the system identify goals and recommendations. Referrals also are common when there is a decision to seek termination of parental rights. Although there are exceptions, families with this level of court scrutiny typically have partially or fully resisted the initial phase of services offered by child protective service agencies. The quality of services provided by child protective service agencies varies from state to state and within jurisdictions. Families who resist services are quite heterogeneous. State statutes and social service regulations typically provide standards for areas of inquiry in care and protection evaluations, especially when the evaluation is centered on the question of whether all reasonable attempts at family reunification have been exhausted. The proliferation of evaluation referrals in care and protection cases led to the recent development of guidelines for practice, *Guidelines for Psychological Evaluations in Child Protection Matters*, published in 1998 by the American Psychological Association, Committee on Professional Practice Standards.

Referrals for evaluations come from different sources, including the court, the child protection agency, the attorney for the child, the guardian *ad litem*, or the attorney for the parents (in some cases each parent is assigned an attorney). Regardless of the referral question, it is important to be aware of state statutory or case law requirements that govern care and protection proceedings (Grisso, 1986; NCCAN, 1988). Rarely is the referral question so comprehensive that it subsumes all elements of the statute governing parental rights termination cases; however, because of the breadth of state statutes, the band of behaviors that constitute parental breaches of responsibility, and the repertoire of behaviors that generally are associated with parenting, comprehensive evaluation questions are not unusual.

After allegations are supported, the court or attorneys may call upon forensic evaluators to assess the impact of child maltreatment on a particular child. They may request a consultation to determine the best approach to treat the child or the best approach to provide rehabilitation for the parent. Care and protection statutes sometimes contain time limitations that allow greater predictive validity because short-term projections are indicated rather than projections over the potentially long span of a parent-child relationship. Under statutes where cases can lay dormant or become protracted, the issue of predictive validity is of greater concern. Protracted cases also are complicated by the secondary and sometimes primary attachments that the child might make to substitute caregivers. Substitute attachments are an important consideration, but they do not necessarily preclude a successful reunification between the parent and the child.

ARE CARE AND PROTECTION EVALUATIONS FORENSIC?

Care and protection evaluations are just beginning to come of age as an activity falling under the rubric of forensic specialization. Courts and referring parties are beginning to recognize the advantages of retaining evaluators with forensic assessment experience. In the early 1990s, when I first began conducting research on standards of evaluation practice in cases involving allegations of child maltreatment, a subset of survey responders questioned the wisdom of being classified as forensic evaluators. Their identity was closer to that of a child psychologist, a child development specialist, or a psychotherapist. Their grasp of the foundations of forensic assessment in care and protection matters, such as unique ethical concerns, suggestibility in children's recollections, embellishments, false allegations, and dissimulation in maltreating parents, was limited (Oberlander, 1995b).

On the other hand, forensic training by itself is not sufficient for competent evaluation practice in care and protection matters. Forensic evaluators with little understanding of child development, theories of parenting behavior, parent-child attachment, the impact of maltreatment, and treatment outcome studies are at risk of producing reports with technical correctness but little clinical sophistication. Because most care and protection matters involve children under the age of six, competent practice requires expertise in the linguistic capacities, developmental trajectories, and the diagnosis and treatment of very young children. Currently, evaluations in care and protection matters probably are best described as forensic because of the legal pretext and the special aspects of evaluations that traditionally are viewed as forensic (such as addressing legal standards). Although the term *forensic* can apply to any evaluation that is conducted specifically to assist the court in decision making about a case, the term more often is reserved for evaluations that are designed to help the court address a specific *legal standard* (Grisso, 1998). In care and protection matters, the legal standards typically are found in statutory definitions of abuse and neglect and statutory criteria for termination of parental rights. There is no single approach to examining family systems in which child maltreatment is so severe it results in the filing of a care and protection petition. In order to produce reports that have utility for children, families, child protective service systems, and the court it is necessary to understand the legal and ethical context of assessment in care and protection matters.

Individual Responses to Cases

Case Dynamics

Judges, attorneys, investigators, child protective service workers, and forensic evaluators are met with a high level of caregiver ambivalence in care and protection matters. Many caregivers involved with the child protective service system feel challenged, threatened, disbelieved, embarrassed, and scrutinized. When allegations reflect misrepresentation of their behavior, they struggle with understandable anger and concern. When allegations reflect factual conditions, they struggle with the challenge of facing difficult realizations concerning their parenting and their risk of harm (Oberlander, 1998). Parents in care and protection matters present with complex compromises to personal functioning, usually involving a multiple array of diagnostic, social, financial, and behavioral concerns. Because of pre-existing parenting problems and because of the unavoidably confrontational approaches that usually are involved when parents are informed of the removal of children from their care, it frequently is complicated for caregivers to prioritize the importance or primacy of their children's needs as they move through their own emotional and personal upheaval in responding to the allegations of maltreatment. As a result, it is difficult for some of them to move beyond the immediate circumstances and accept recommendations in service plans, adhere to the plans, and follow the necessary steps to regain custody of their children. In some circumstances, poor cooperation is a reflection of compromised functioning or priorities, but in other circumstances it reflects the parent's response to poor planning and execution of service plans (Crenshaw & Barnum, 2001). Because child protective services systems tend to be reactive rather than proactive (Melton, 1987, 1994), it is difficult for service systems to view the caregiver as an ally or collaborator rather than an adversary. It is equally difficult for the parent or caregiver to view the child protective service system as a mechanism of support. When parents seek voluntary services, they are more likely to view the system as an ally; however, most parents involved in care and protection actions do so involuntarily, and even voluntary requests sometimes evolve into involuntary jurisdiction. Some parents progress through the system, meeting all requirements, benefiting from services, and regaining custody of their children. Others find it more difficult.

Case Complexities

More than most forensic assessment referrals, care and protection evaluation referrals take place in a highly emotional context. Individual reactions to cases usually involve a reasonable degree of objectivity across professions, but cases challenge deeply entrenched personal beliefs about the status and safety of children in families and society.

JUDGES. Because of the fundamental goal of the child protective services system, that of child safety, many judges, attorneys, case managers, caseworkers, and evaluators struggle with professional and personal reactions to care and protection cases (Onheiber, 1997). For example, although judges are prepared to apply statutory criteria to their judicial decisions concerning retention or termination of parental rights, the experienced judge knows that a strong understanding of the law and the rules of legal procedures is not tantamount to awareness of the vicissitudes, volatilities, and idiosyncrasies of maltreatment behavior, parental responses to service plans, and parental amenability to treatment. Judges are well aware of the high level of tension associated with termination of parental rights cases. They are familiar with both the constitutional and the emotional weight of the decision to terminate the relationship between a parent and a child. Judges also know that the minimal level of competence required to retain parental rights often belies the wishes and attempts of child advocates to keep children safe from *any* harm, not just harm that is defined by statute or case law.

ATTORNEYS.   Attorneys are prepared to defend parents or children in court; however, the rights of parents and the rights of children (to the extent they are manifest) sometimes are in direct conflict with one another (Melton et al., 1997). Attorneys must directly face the emotional tension that is inherent in care and protection matters and in the adversarial process. They are prepared to call upon forensic evaluators to assist the court in gathering data relevant to the court's decision to preserve or terminate parental rights, but their use of an evaluator is based on decisions of legal strategy, not child advocacy. The experienced attorney avoids referral questions that compromise the role of the evaluator; however, determining when forensic mental health consultation is indicated, framing suitable referral questions, and judging the merits of particular legal strategies sometimes are complex endeavors in the myriad of cases that are seen in care and protection matters.

CHILD PROTECTIVE SERVICE WORKERS AND CASE MANAGERS.   Child protective service workers and case managers are skilled in the management of heavy caseloads that require careful investigation strategies and detailed documentation requirements (Onheiber, 1997). They must face the stress of daily management of vulnerable children with a complex array of problems, caregivers who challenge their approach to cases, the sometimes tiresome bureaucratic features of cumbersome state systems, and possible vicarious trauma reactions because of daily exposure to the physical and emotional pain and suffering of maltreated children (Oberlander, 1998). They face the challenge of forging positive professional relationships with a variety of individuals, including parents, children, foster parents, service providers, administrators, attorneys, and judges. The decision to introduce a forensic mental health evaluator to the list of individuals with whom they must interface often is beyond their personal control. Whether the forensic mental health evaluator is a welcome addition to the case or another source of tension depends upon case dynamics, whether the case worker's input is requested in crafting referral questions, and the worker's view of the relevance of forensic mental health evaluation to a particular case.

FORENSIC EVALUATORS AND CONSULTANTS.   The evaluator in care and protection cases must have foundational competencies across many domains of the profession (Azar, 1992). He or she must then apply the integration of those domains to referral questions that are raised in the context of service system goals and legal processes that might change as a case progresses through legal or regulatory steps. Referral questions that are raised in care and protection cases usually are broad compared to other forensic evaluation questions, challenging the evaluator to develop comprehensive evaluation skills, skill in narrowing the scope of referral questions when possible, and skill in adhering to brief evaluation questions that are raised in the context of complex system, family, and individual dynamics (Oberlander, 1998).

ETHICS IN EVALUATION PRACTICE

Ethical standards refer to basic philosophical notions and norms about the appropriateness of conduct within a professional sphere (Koocher & Kieth-Spiegel, 1990). Psychologists turn to the *Ethical Principles of Psychologists and Code of Conduct* (2002), *Standards for Educational and Psychological Testing* (2000), and *Record Keeping Guidelines* (1993). Other professions have developed related ethical standards (e.g., *Ethical Guidelines for the Practice of Forensic Psychiatry*, American Psychiatric Association, 1995). The value of ethical standards as applied to every day practice (and, by extension, parenting evaluation practices), is not inconsequential.

The next section reviews essential ethical concerns, with emphasis on issues relevant to practice in the legal arena. Forensic evaluators are aware that potential conflicts sometimes arise between the law, the ethics of the profession, and guidelines for practice (Melton, 1984a, 1984b). Most evaluators who accept care and protection referrals are aware of the broad brush approach to ethical standards on issues specific to children, and, by extension, children in the legal system. Guidelines for practice provide useful strategies and approaches to evaluations, but they only broadly touch upon on the complexities of concerns such as appropriately responding to a child's request to "take back" reported maltreatment information after a reminder of the limits of confidentiality (Oberlander, 1999).

To complicate the issue further, the Constitution, statutes, and regulations were written with adults in mind. Cases involving children typically are treated as exceptions to the rule when considering the applicability of constitutional rights, federal and state statutes, case law, and administrative policies and regulations to children. The legal autonomy of children often is precluded by developmental concerns about giving them standing (Weithorn, 1984). The next section provides a structure for thinking about ethical issues and dilemmas in the legal context of parenting evaluations for the court. Suggestions are given for minimizing the potential for ethical complexity in cases by anticipating possible permutations of ethical questions. The best course of action to resolve a particular ethical dilemma depends upon the features and context of the case. Evaluators should follow basic procedures to address ethical concerns: seeking consultation, and carefully considering the impact of their actions on children, parents, the court, society and the profession.

ETHICAL STANDARDS AND GUIDELINES FOR PRACTICE

Ethical issues in forensic settings differ from those in clinical or other settings (Ogloff, 1999). The main issues include whom the client is, the role of the mental health expert, informed consent, confidentiality and privilege in forensic assessment, standards of record keeping specific to forensic practice, professional responsibility, competence and specialization, and maintaining relevance to legal standards. For answers to questions of ethics in practice, psychologists turn to the *Ethical Principles of Psychologists and Code of Conduct* (hereinafter referred to as the Ethics Code; American Psychological Association, 2002). The most recent version of the Ethics Code was published in 2002 (there were nine previous versions). The Ethics Code contains Ethical Standards, or enforceable rules for the conduct of psychologists. They were written broadly for applicability to the varied roles of psychologists. The Ethics Code is used by the American Psychological Association, state psychology boards, courts, and other public bodies to enforce rules, procedures, and standards of professional conduct relevant to the practice of psychology. Compliance with or violation of the Ethics Code is not isomorphic with legal liability; however, rulings based on the Ethics Code may be admissible as evidence in civil and criminal proceedings, depending upon the circumstances of the legal matter.

The Introduction of the Ethics Code states that psychologists must meet the standard of conduct established by the Ethics Code if that standard is higher than required by law. If there is conflict between the Ethics Code and the requirements of the law, then psychologists are required to take steps to resolve the conflict in a responsible manner. If an ethical problem arises that is addressed by neither the law nor the Ethics Code, psychologists are obliged to consider other professional materials (some of which are described below), to seek consultation, and to consider their own conscience (American Psychological Association, 2002). Although the

Ethics Code is broad, it is not exhaustive. The ethical issues that are unique to forensic psychology cover a spectrum of issues that are more comprehensive than the issues addressed by the Ethics Code (Committee on Ethical Guidelines for Forensic Psychologists, 1991). Forensic psychologists are obligated to seek training and guidance in anticipation of ethical concerns that are unique to the specialty. Most forensic psychologists turn to additional resources to guide their practice (Ogloff, 1999).

In particular, psychologists in forensic practice consult the *Specialty Guidelines for Forensic Psychologists* (hereinafter referred to as Specialty Guidelines) published in 1991 by the Committee on Ethical Guidelines for Forensic Psychologists. The Specialty Guidelines were prepared and authored by a joint Committee on Ethical Guidelines of Division 41 (American Psychology-Law Society) and the American Academy of Forensic Psychology (A division of the American Board of Professional Psychology). The Specialty Guidelines (1991) are consistent with the Ethics Code. They were designed to amplify it and to improve the quality of forensic psychological services. They are "an aspirational model of desirable professional practice" by psychologists who provide expertise to the judicial system (Committee on Ethical Guidelines for Forensic Psychologists, 1991, p. 656). The Specialty Guidelines and other guidelines discussed below have not been formally adopted by the American Psychological Association. However, the American Psychological Association encourages professionals to turn to them for their educational and training value to psychologists, courts, and other professional bodies. Survey data have suggested many psychologists have a less than optimal understanding of the principles of law and ethics that have a daily affect on the practice of psychology (Otto, Ogloff, & Small, 1991).

For more specific guidance, forensic psychologists who work with children and families consult the *Guidelines for Psychological Evaluations in Child Protection Matters* published in 1998 by the American Psychological Association, Committee on Professional Practice and Standards. Although they are not directly relevant to child protection matters, the *Guidelines for Child Custody Evaluations in Divorce Proceedings* (published by the American Psychological Association in 1994) also are a useful resource. Other resources that evaluators find useful are those published by the American Professional Society on the Abuse of Children, including the Guidelines for Psychosocial Evaluation of Suspected Sexual Abuse in Young Children (1990). For questions specific to psychologist assessment, the *Standards for Educational and Psychological Testing* (1985) contain guidance for evaluating the reliability, validity, scaling, and applicability of tests to particular populations. The Guidelines for Computer Based Tests and Interpretations

(1987) contain useful information relevant to computerized psychological assessment. The Guidelines for Providers of Psychological Services to
Ethnic, Linguistic, and Culturally Diverse Populations (1990), contain valuable information to promote cultural sensitivity, reliability, and validity in
psychological assessment of specific populations.

WHO IS THE CLIENT?

In clinical practice, the identification of the client usually is obvious.
An individual voluntarily seeks the services of a psychologist and is identified as that psychologist's patient or client. In forensic evaluations, by
contrast, the psychologist's obligation is to an attorney and by extension to
the court. Because examinees typically assume their status is one of patient
or client, forensic evaluators must inform examinees of their actual status
(Ogloff, 1999). The issue is similar for children. When children are involved
in an assessment in non-forensic contexts, the psychologist has an obligation to the child and to the child's parents, who must consent to the evaluation. In care and protection matters, the client is the referring attorney,
not the child or the child's parents. The child often is in the legal custody
of the child protective service system. Even if the parents retain physical
custody, it is the legal custodian who has the power to initiate or consent to
evaluations (Koocher & Keith-Spiegel, 1990). If the legal guardian, the child
protective services system, refuses consent for an evaluation of a child, in
some cases the refusal will be over-ridden by court order. In that circumstance, either the referring attorney or the court is the client, depending
upon the phrasing of the court order. In forensic assessment, the role of
"examinee" is not equivalent to the role of "client" (Committee on Ethical
Guidelines for Forensic Psychologists, 1991; Ogloff, 1999).

CONFIDENTIALITY AND PRIVILEGE

Confidentiality is an ethical duty between client and patient. Privilege
is statutory protection, owned by the examinee, of confidential communications. In forensic evaluations, the examinee usually is not the contracting
agent, the client, or the patient. Therefore the psychologist owes no duty
of confidentiality to that person. That fact must be made known to the examinee through the process of informed consent, described below. The
evaluator must not begin the evaluation until he or she has notified the examinee of the limits of confidentiality (Grisso, 1998; Ogloff, 1999). A typical
warning of the limits of confidentiality includes a description of the referral

question, identification of the referring or contracting party, the nature of the evaluation, a warning that the information revealed by the party cannot be held in confidence, the identification of all parties who will receive a copy of the report, and instructions that the party being evaluated has a right to know the *contents* of the report, but that there may be restrictions to obtaining an actual copy of the report (some courts prohibit parties who are evaluated from receiving a copy of the report for themselves). The Ethics Code encourages psychologists to provide an explanation in language that is reasonably understandable to the client or his or her representative (American Psychological Association, 2002).

A comparable warning should be given to all collateral contacts. The wording might need modification for non-professional collateral contacts so that it is understandable and so the individual is not unsettled by the complexities of the legal process. Non-professional collaterals should be told they have a choice about providing information or answering particular questions. In the case of professional collaterals that owe the examinee a duty of confidentiality and privilege, the examinee owns privilege. As long as a release is properly executed, the professional has a duty to provide the requested information. In the occasional circumstance where a misinformed professional declines to provide information in response to a release, believing they own the privilege, consultation or legal assistance helps to clarify the professional's duty. The assistance of the referring attorney in obtaining records sometimes resolves the issue (Oberlander, 1998, 1999). With respect to privileged communications between a psychotherapist and a child, some state statutes authorize the psychotherapist to invoke privilege on behalf of the child and to decline any requests for information. The psychotherapist uses a formal mechanism to invoke privilege, usually via a limited purpose guardian *ad litem*. The court is petitioned, via the child's limited purpose guardian *ad litem*, for permission to refuse to release the records. The court, weighing the child's confidentiality needs against the probative value of the information, might authorize full release of records, limited release of specific information, *in camera* release, or no release (Oberlander, 1999).

When the evaluation includes a child, the child should be given a notification of the limits of confidentiality appropriate to his or her age or level of development. The Ethics Code suggests minors should be notified of the limits of confidentiality to the extent feasible (2002). The evaluator may wish to ask how much the child has been told about the legal proceedings. The evaluator also may wish to request this information from the child's attorney, depending upon the nature of the referral process. Children often have been given some information by foster parents, child protective service workers, or legal representatives. It is important to ask what the child knows about the evaluation when giving an explanation of the evaluation. When notifying children of the limits of confidentiality, evaluators must determine whether to make a full disclosure of the purpose of the evaluation (for the sake of protecting children's rights) or explain it in a limited manner (for the sake of protecting children from distress). In cases where the evaluator will make recommendations about the child's placement options, children should be protected from feeling as though they have influence over where they will live and who will take care of them (Stahl, 1994). Children should be protected from feeling as though they must choose between a parent and a foster parent. Advocacy or promises of protection from further maltreatment should be avoided in notifications of the limits of confidentiality (Oberlander, 1995b).

Access to the Report

Although the Specialty Guidelines (1991) provide for the release of forensic reports as long as permission is received from the client and his or her legal representative, it is important to be aware that such releases are permissible only if they do not violate attorney-client privilege and only if the court does not bar release of documents that have been introduced into evidence. Depending upon how the court and the rules of attorney-client privilege define access to the report, children and their parents might or might not be able to request a copy of the evaluation report or sign a release for the psychologist to provide a copy of the report to a third party. Because the parents were not the source of hiring or contracting with the psychologist, they have no right to confidentiality that the law and ethical obligations would require in private matters (Koocher & Keith-Spiegel, 1990; Ogloff, 1999). Confidentiality extends to release of the report to other parties. When the court puts a bar on such release, as might be the case after the evaluation is introduced into evidence, because it addresses legally sensitive matters, or because it contains information about more than one participant in the evaluation, it is the court who authorizes release and not the party or parties who were evaluated. Legal proceedings, although usually public, contain sensitive written evidentiary material that the court may choose to keep semi-private. That is, the forensic evaluation report, although entered into evidence, usually does not become part of the court record that is made available to the public (Oberlander, 1998).

When an evaluation is court ordered, only the court can place limitations on the use or release of the forensic evaluation report. The rules are different when an evaluation is initiated by an attorney, especially if it is initiated *ex parte*, or without the knowledge of the opposing party. The evaluation results typically belong to the referring attorney if the evaluator's opinion is successfully quashed (that is, legally hidden from discovery). Under those circumstances, most attorneys will request verbal feedback. After receiving verbal feedback from the evaluator, they determine whether they wish to introduce the information into evidence. If they decide against doing so, they usually will request that the evaluator refrain from placing the results in the form of a written report.

Although the court recognizes and has the capacity to enforce the privacy of documents contained in court records, psychologists may find that state statutes relevant to privilege may be in conflict with rules of evidence governing care and protection matters. When a psychologist receives a release of information form requesting a copy of the forensic evaluation report, the best strategy is to refer the party requesting the document to the court, instructing them to obtain a court order for the release of the report. (In most instances, the judge will prohibit release of the full report.) At this point, the psychologist is protected from seeking further resolution of the conflict because the court resolves the conflict by making a ruling specific to the case. The Ethics Code provides for limitations in disclosure of information even when the client has consented to release. It states that confidential information may not be disclosed (even with client consent) where it is prohibited by law (American Psychological Association, 2002). Another way to avoid conflicts between policies governing releases of information and court orders is to notify the examinee in advance of possible limitations to releases of the reports.

Payment for Services

Evaluations in care and protection matters have different funding mechanisms depending upon the level of resources devoted to indigent parties in legal proceedings. In some states, evaluation fees are paid in a similar manner to legal fees for indigent defendants. Most health insurance companies, including public insurance, will not reimburse evaluators for matters that are deemed legal rather than medical. Some state agencies may award contracts to individuals or agencies for evaluation services. Others might pay on a fee-for-service basis. Private pay cases are exceedingly rare in care and protection matters. Regardless of who is responsible for payment, fees and financial arrangements should be clear to the parties being evaluated, the referring party, and the court. The Specialty Guidelines (1991) discourage forensic psychologists from providing expert testimony or other services on the basis of contingent fees.

Informed Consent

Even though forensic evaluations are not initiated by the examinees, the examinees are entitled to informed consent. Informed consent includes a notification of the limits of confidentiality, as described above. Informed consent doctrine requires that the examinee consent to the evaluation voluntarily, knowingly, and intelligently. *Voluntariness* requires that examinees are not forced, coerced, or manipulated to consent to the evaluation. A *knowing* consent to an evaluation requires that the examinee must be given a full disclosure of the nature and purpose of the evaluation, the risks and benefits of the evaluation, and the risks and benefits of any alternatives to the evaluation. An *intelligent* consent to an evaluation requires that the individual have the mental abilities or capacity to make a reasoned decision as to whether or not to participate in the evaluation. It focuses on the examinee's capacity to balance the risks and benefits of the evaluation, but not on the rationality or logic of the decision. In situations where examinees cannot provide informed consent due to limitations in any of the above capacities, the limitations should be described to the referring party. Depending on the nature of the limitations, the referring party might seek legal designation for another individual to render substitute legal judgment (Ogloff, 1999).

The Specialty Guidelines (1991, p. 659) encourage psychologists to inform clients of "the purpose of the evaluation, the methods used, and the intended use of the report or other services." In cases where the evaluation is conducted pursuant to court order, the notification extends to the examinee's attorney. If the client's attorney objects to the evaluation, the psychologist should notify the court and then proceed as directed by the court. If the court directs the evaluator to proceed, even when the attorney objects and the examinee refuses to be evaluated, the psychologist must clarify the impact of limited data on the reliability and validity of the report and any subsequent testimony. They should appropriately limit the conclusions and recommendations (American Psychological Association, 2002). For attorney-initiated referrals, if the examinee is unwilling to be evaluated, the psychologist should contact the referring attorney for advice about whether to provide any further services.

Maintaining Records

The Specialty Guidelines (1991) suggest that forensic psychologists must document and prepare data with a level of quality and detail that satisfies reasonable judicial scrutiny. The guidelines suggest that evaluators should provide the best documentation possible when they work with foreknowledge that their services will be used in court. Standards for record keeping in forensic cases are not the same as standards for medical or clinical records. A higher standard of maintaining confidentiality of records usually is kept in order to safeguard forensic reports from inappropriate release. Sometimes forensic evaluations take place in a clinic or hospital as part of a larger mental health program. When the same medical record number or procedures are used for forensic and non-forensic matters, the agency faces a confidentiality problem when the entire medical record is sought by another individual or agency for reasons having nothing to do with the forensic matter. However, shielding the forensic report from a medical record without specifying the rationale in policy also raises the risk of liability when complete medical records are requested but not provided. Agencies are advised to adopt a uniform policy for forensic records after considering medical record keeping requirements, accountability requirements, insurance requirements, forensic record keeping requirements, and after consulting with legal counsel for the agency. When documentation in addition to the forensic evaluation report (e.g., encounter forms and progress notes) are required to meet accreditation standards or to bill for services, agencies must be careful to set forth policies that meet agency documentation requirements while also protecting forensic cases from confidentiality problems.

Professional Responsibility

The Ethics Code (American Psychological Association, 2002) encourages psychologists to engage in conduct that does not compromise their professional responsibilities or reduce the public's trust in the profession. When considering an appropriate course of action, evaluators who face ethical concerns should seek appropriate consultation, considering the impact of their actions on the parties they are evaluating. Psychologists also should consider the impact on the public, the profession, and themselves (Oberlander, 1999). Care and protection matters, especially those that reach the stage of courtroom hearings, are by definition public matters. Although the public might be excluded from matters relating to children, a public record is nonetheless created. The impact of a breach of ethics on the involved parties and the mental health professions becomes compounded by the possible publicity of cases.

The court sometimes is unaware of the psychologist's need to avoid multiple relationships. Evaluation orders might be issued, for example, that include a request for both an evaluation and a mediation or treatment role. Evaluators should decline such referrals in whole or in part, explaining the need to engage in a single role in order to maintain objectivity.

In the evaluation of children, extended periods of time might be necessary to establish sufficient rapport to gather valid interview or assessment data; however, evaluators should be clear about the boundaries of the evaluation even when clients request a transition to treatment or some other service (Oberlander, 1995a, 1995b). The Ethics Code recognizes that a prior relationship with a client does not preclude the provision of other services at a later date; however, the psychologist must consider ways in which the prior relationship might compromise objectivity. The Specialty Guidelines (1991) encourage forensic psychologists to disclose factors that might influence a referring party's decision to contract with the forensic psychologist, especially those that might produce a conflict of interest. In some communities or situations where the supply of mental health professionals is limited, it may not be possible to avoid multiple relationships. In such cases, the Specialty Guidelines encourage the psychologist to take reasonable steps to minimize possible negative effects on confidentiality, the rights of clients, and the evaluation process. Evaluators who must transition to other roles should be certain the legal matter has ended and they should be clear that they would not return to the role of forensic evaluator after assuming another role. Similarly, treatment providers, mediators, or case consultants should not offer forensic evaluation services in cases involving their clients.

TRAINING AND SPECIALIZED COMPETENCE

The Ethics Code (American Psychological Association, 2002) requires psychologists to practice within the boundaries of competence. Competence may be attained through education, training, supervised experience, or appropriate professional experience. Psychologists are encouraged to seek continuing education to maintain competence. The Specialty Guidelines (1991, p. 658) reinforce the Ethics Code by stating the psychologist is obligated to "maintain current knowledge of scientific, professional and legal developments" within their areas of expertise. Families who come to the attention of the child protective service system often represent diverse groups. Competence in forensic assessment includes a reasonable level of understanding of differences of age, gender, race, ethnicity, national origin, religion, sexual orientation, disability, language, or socioeconomic status. The Ethics Code encourages psychologists to gain competence in the awareness of human differences and how those differences might influence evaluation results.

Forensic psychology has achieved specialty status with the American Psychological Association. Board certification in forensic psychology is offered by the American Board of Professional Psychology through its affiliate, the American Board of Forensic Psychology. Some states require state certification or designation in order to practice forensic psychology for governmental entities such as correction departments or departments of social services. Consultation in care and protection matters can be thought of as a subspecialty combining psychological assessment of children and adults, clinical child psychology, forensic psychology, and developmental psychology. The quality of assessment, consultation, and report writing typically is best if evaluators are cross-trained in each of these areas. The Specialty Guidelines (1991, p. 658) encourage training in the areas that form the factual bases for qualification as an expert on specific matters and a "fundamental and reasonable level of knowledge" of relevant legal standards.

Multimodal Assessment

It is good practice to use more than one method of assessment in order to increase the validity of evaluation results. The Ethics Code (2002) suggests psychologists should use techniques sufficient to provide appropriate substantiation. In parenting assessments, the constructs or behaviors assessed vary widely depending upon the circumstances and the nature of the referral question. It is important to use assessment techniques for the purpose they were designed and to refrain from misuse or over-interpretation of data. It is equally important to refrain from disregarding or minimizing assessment results when the data are consistent across different forms of assessment. The Ethics Code (2002) provides general guidance about psychological assessment. The Testing Standards (1985) contain specific information that helps a psychologist to evaluate the validity and reliability of a specific instrument for a specific purpose.

When choosing which tests to include in an assessment battery, relevant considerations include the population on which the test was standardized, reliability, validation, outcome studies, proper applications of the tests, limitations in the predictions that can be made about individuals, and whether the constructs measured by the test are applicable to the set of behaviors of interest to the court. When using computerized interpretations, it is important to consider how the scores apply to the individual. Some computerized scoring systems offer interpretive aids. It usually is not helpful to the court when a psychologist merely includes the computerized interpretive summary in the report without discussing the degree to which the computerized interpretation applies to the individual (Matarazzo, 1986). Use of computerized interpretations in the body of reports disrupts the flow and organization of the report. In addition, the language of computerized interpretations, often is enigmatic to attorneys, judges, and clients. More importantly, when computerized interpretations are used verbatim, it signifies the evaluator's failure to fully analyze and integrate different forms of assessment data (Snyder, 2000). It is best to integrate, interpret and discuss the results in language that the parties to a proceeding will understand (Matarazzo, 1986). Regardless of whether a computerized interpretation system is used, the psychologist retains the responsibility for appropriate interpretation (Ethics Code, 2002).

THE UTILITY OF FORENSIC ASSESSMENT IN CARE AND PROTECTION CASES

THE BENEFIT OF EVALUATIONS

Children benefit from care and protection evaluations because they assist decision-makers in identifying appropriate recommendations for services and placement. Families benefit because child safety is prioritized and patterns of family dysfunction are identified and addressed in a reasonable fashion. Child protective service systems benefit because they have added information that assists in service planning, judgments about progress in rehabilitation, judgments about risk, and goal-setting for closing cases, proceeding with reunification plans, or modifying goals toward possible termination of parental rights. Child protective system attorneys benefit from data that helps them choose appropriate legal strategies for the case. Attorneys for parents benefit because the caregiver's potential incapacities are illustrated and attorneys then can urge their clients to seek appropriate means to address the problem, which then might eventuate in reunification. They also might choose to highlight extenuating circumstances identified in the evaluation process. The courts benefit when the risk factors and causal links to child maltreatment are identified in a legally relevant manner that facilitates judicial decision-making concerning case status and case goals.

An evaluation might be requested in order to aid the process of developing a service plan for the caregiver, the child, or both. The referring party may wish to measure the impact of child maltreatment or the child's response to interventions addressing the impact. They may wish to determine progress in rehabilitation for the caretakers or for the child. They may request an evaluation of the suitability of the child for a particular placement. They may request an evaluation of a substitute caregiver (or the relationship between the child and the caregiver) who is willing to serve as a potential adoption resource. They may want assistance in gathering data to determine whether the filing of a parental rights termination petition is merited (or alternatively whether a return of the child to the custody of the caregiver is merited). When a petition is filed for termination, it is common for child protective services to request an evaluation in order to organize, describe, and bolster the data or evidence in support of the petition. Evaluation data should not be viewed as synonymous with evidence in support of termination; however, there may be some corollary findings that constitute both evaluation results and legal evidence (Oberlander, 1998).

THE IMPACT AND CONSEQUENCES OF EXPERT OPINIONS IN CARE AND PROTECTION MATTERS

The task of accepting referral questions, addressing them in evaluation reports, and preparing for court testimony should take place within the rules of admissibility of evidence. In care and protection matters, there are rules against invading the province of the jury to assess witness credibility. There also are limitations on the rule against invading the province of the jury. For example, the court has made a distinction between making credibility judgments about a particular witness and providing expert witness on the unreliability of child witnesses in general. There is a rule against telling the jury what they already know. Expert testimony is inadmissible unless it assists the trier of fact. However, telling the jury what it already knows is permissible if the expert provides an empirical base for information that supports what is commonly known. For example, a jury might understand that children are suggestible in some circumstances, but they might not be aware of or fully understand the scientific basis for that information (Sagatun, 1991).

Expert testimony must be scientifically valid. Under *Daubert* (1993), district courts act as a gatekeeper, determining whether the expert's data is admissible, reliable, and relevant (Kovera & Borgida, 1998). The details of *Daubert v. Merrell Dow Pharmaceuticals* (1993) are reviewed later. Most courts follow *Daubert* in establishing rules for the validity and reliability of scientific techniques and expert testimony. The expert testimony must fit the facts of the case. It must be tied to the facts of the case so that it will sufficiently aid the jury in resolving the dispute. If research or techniques used by the expert lack relevance to the legal standards of the case or touch upon tangential details, the information might not meet admissibility standards (Walker, 1990). For example, an evaluator cannot testify that trauma from suspected sexual abuse caused posttraumatic stress disorder in a case in which the initial evidentiary hearings for state jurisdiction supported only allegations of neglect or physical abuse. Such testimony probably would be barred. Similarly, in a risk assessment matrix, it might be questionable for an evaluator to consider a parent's failure to address his or her risk of sex offending if child protective services neglected to highlight the issue on the parent's service plan. The failure certainly might be relevant to risk, but the burden of fixing the mistake in the administrative aspects of the case would probably rest with the child protective services agency, not the parent. The case would have to be managed in a different way in order for such data to meet admissibility standards, otherwise the court might not find the psychologist's risk analysis admissible or persuasive. For example, in *DSS v. Lail* (1999), a termination of parental rights ruling was overturned on appeal because the removal hearing showed no evidence that the state had provided the family with a treatment plan despite the fact that the case went to numerous hearing over a period of five years and despite that fact that the children were kept in state custody during that five-year period. In summary, the data must fit the facts of the case, but they also must factor in the state's requirements (or failure to set relevant requirements) for the parent.

Psychological research on the effectiveness of *Daubert* (1993) safeguards suggests that unreliable testimony and data nonetheless find their way into courtrooms. Psychologists who assume the role of expert witness should restrict their testimony, despite admissibility rules, to data and conclusions that are warranted at the time of court testimony. Hearings are not the appropriate forum to propose novel hypotheses or assert personal opinions. Psychologists should consider the consequences of testimony, making sure that opinions are solidly based in supporting research. When research is not available, appropriate caveats should be stated candidly. Psychologists should not fall prey to the spin that attorneys might wish to place on the data or results. They should make a full disclosure of the limits of data and testimony without fear of appearing tentative (Lavin & Sales, 1998). The profession benefits from appropriate caution and suffers from public sentiment about dueling experts (Cutler & Penrod, 1995).

SUMMARY

1. Parenting competencies represent a broad band of behaviors embedded in a broad constitutional framework of family privacy and children's rights.
2. Legal and administrative standards for jurisdiction and permanency planning influence the nature of requests for care and protection evaluations.

3. The expanse of questions that might be raised in care and protection matters is broad in contrast to other legal competencies. Training is needed across many content domains of professional practice.
4. Professional and personal responses to care and protection matters typically are not insignificant in their impact on the conduct of professionals, children, and families in any give case. Quality practice is enhanced by a repertoire of personal and professional responses to possible vicarious influences on professional practice.
5. Ethical standards and guidelines for practice provide a basis for methodological approaches to complex factors in care and protection matters, including client status, confidentiality and privilege, access to reports, informed consent, and professional competence and responsibility.

2

Parental Rights, Children's Rights, and State Intervention

Societal responses to the social problem of child maltreatment have taken many forms. The legal system represents the most formal response mechanism. The legal system is bound by relevant federal or state statutes governing care and protection matters. The administrative law corollary to the judicial system is the child protective services system and its accompanying regulations. The nature and breadth of child safety and protection depends upon the definitions and procedures for identifying, investigating, intervening, and making decisions about family reunification or separation. There are broad constitutional rights that envelope legal and social service approaches to child safety and protection. Far-reaching issues ranging from family privacy to children's rights are adjudicated in the broad view of care and protection cases. Social system regulations, including the child protective services and child welfare legislation and regulations add layers of definitional and procedural complexity to care and protection matters. Child abuse reporting requirements and associated statutes and regulations influence the frequency and nature of cases entering the child protective service system. Procedural regulations govern the flow of cases through the system. Child protective service system policies emphasize the relative weight given to family reunification or child safety. Policies influence decisions about the clinical and legal goals of cases. Although policies and regulations might influence internal system goals for specific cases, procedural regulations do not govern the actual termination of parental rights. Termination is a legal system function. Statutes governing termination of parental rights define the outer limits of time frames for cases. Statutes govern the outer behavioral limits of parental misconduct relevant to original breaches of parenting responsibilities. They often specify legal consequences for minimal or no parental efforts at appropriate rehabilitation. Case law clarifies definitional and legal procedural issues, and the scope of parental rights termination statutes.

This chapter reviews legal and regulatory information relevant to parenting evaluations for the court. It describes constitutional issues, the influence of mandated statutory reporting requirements, and the child welfare service screening and investigation regulations and procedures. This chapter describes issues that arise from the inherent difficulty of reaching definitional clarity and cogency in statutes and regulations governing child maltreatment. Limits in the law's capacity to define, identify, and monitor abuse and neglect in families are described. The interplay between pragmatic issues, such as requests for evaluations and judicial and social service uses of evaluation reports, are contrasted with complex philosophical issues such as the rights of parents and children to participate in or refuse evaluations, children's legal rights in the evaluation process, and the relevance of the best interest standard to data interpretation and conclusions in evaluations. The complexity of the legal rights of children in the context of care and protection evaluations stems from their anomalous status as agents who are neither fully independent of nor fully dependent upon their caretakers. In the legal system, definitions and protections of children's rights have seen fruition in contrasting cases within which children have demanded both more autonomy and more protection. Most disputes involving children feature the state as an agent in some capacity, purporting to serve the best interests of children. There is little consensus over whether (or the extent to which) children should prevail over the competing interests of the state or the family.

CONSTITUTIONAL ISSUES, STATE STATUTES, AND CHILD PROTECTIVE SERVICE REGULATIONS

FAMILY PRIVACY

The meaning of the word *family* depends upon the field of law within which the word is used. It conveys a relationship among individuals, blood or otherwise, living in the same household and subject to the rules, management, support structure, and control of the head(s) of household (Black & Garner, 1999). Family privacy stems from the general legal construct of *privacy*, the nature of which is well established but relatively novel in constitutional law. Examples of constitutional privacy issues include abortion, marital rights, family rights, sexual activity, the right to privacy, and the right to die. With only one exception, all Supreme Court privacy cases were decided within approximately the past 35 years (Spaeth & Smith, 1991). *Common law* refers to legal principles that derive from sources related to constitutional issues but that are not always formalized by legislative enactment. *Statutes* refer to laws enacted at local, state, and federal levels. *Case law* refers to legal precedents issued by the courts on a case by case basis. *Administrative law* refers to regulations that originate in the executive branch of the government, such as rules and procedures for social service systems. Aspects of family rights and family privacy thread throughout all of these sources of law.

Constitutional Protection of Family Privacy

Constitutional protection of family privacy is not manifest in the U.S. Constitution. It is assumed in the law based on the traditional structure and function of families in American society. The right to *privacy* and hence to family privacy exists in the penumbras and emanations from those guarantees. The penumbra doctrine of the U.S. Constitution is based in the *implied powers* of the federal government. It is predicated on the Necessary and Proper Clause of the U.S. Constitution. The penumbra doctrine permits one implied power (family rights) to build upon another implied power (privacy rights) (Black & Garner, 1999). In privacy cases, the Supreme Court has ruled that the Bill of Rights has a broader scope than its language suggests. These penumbras are what the Supreme Court has termed *zones of privacy* (Spaeth & Smith, 1991). Examples of landmark cases relevant to family privacy include *Meyer v. Nebraska* (1923), *Pierce v. Society of Sisters* (1925), *Griswold v. Connecticut* (1965), *Loving v. Virginia* (1967), *Roe v. Wade* (1973), *Matthews v. Lucas* (1976), *Lassiter v. Department of Social Services* (1981), *Santosky v. Kramer* (1982), and *Palmore v. Sidoti* (1984).

The Constitutional Source of Family Privacy

Family privacy also might be described as *family autonomy* as interpreted by the U.S. Supreme Court. The privacy or family autonomy rights that the Supreme Court has found to be fundamental have tended to be in the related areas of sex, marriage, child bearing, and child rearing (Emanuel, 1999). The Supreme Court usually relies on the doctrines of *substantive due process* and *fundamentalness* in its decisions to review cases related to family privacy and family autonomy. However, the Supreme Court sometimes has found a liberty interest that is protected by the due process clause of the Fourteenth Amendment (*Roe v. Wade*, 1973).

U.S. Supreme Court cases involving child and family privacy first emerged in school systems, but they were based on parental childrearing rights. In *Meyer v. Nebraska* (1923) the Supreme Court struck down a state statute that prohibited teaching foreign languages in elementary school and that forbade teaching any subject in a language other than English. The Court held that the law unreasonably infringed on the liberty of parents to secure instruction for their children, the liberty of teachers to teach, and the liberty of students to acquire knowledge, all of which violated the due process clause of the Fourteenth Amendment. In *Pierce v. Society of Sisters* (1925, p. 510), the Supreme Court voided a state statute requiring children to attend public school and thereby preventing attendance at private or parochial schools. The Court's decision was based on the liberty of parents and guardians to raise and educate their children.

1960s and 1970s U.S. Supreme Court Privacy Cases

In the 1960s and 1970s, privacy cases addressed permissible autonomy related to sexual conduct and the decision to bear children. In *Griswold v. Connecticut* (1965), the Supreme Court voided a state statute that forbade the use of contraceptives and that made it a criminal offense to use contraceptives. The statute also forbade aiding or counseling others about contraceptive use. (The defendants were the director and the medical director of a local Planned Parenthood Association who were convicted of counseling married persons in the use of contraceptives.) In voiding the statute, the Court did not make explicit any use of the substantive due process doctrine. The Court instead found that several Bill of Rights guarantees protected the privacy interest by creating a penumbra or zone of privacy. The Court concluded the right of married persons to use contraceptives fell within this penumbra. Developments since *Griswold* extend the family privacy reach to all persons, single or married. No person may be subjected to undue interference with decisions on procreation. Much of the expansion of the meaning of *Griswold* was articulated in *Eisenstadt v. Baird* (1972), a case that voided a state statute that permitted distribution of contraceptives only to married persons. The Court invoked an equal protection argument as well as substantive due process, stating the right of privacy is an individual right and that individuals should be free from government intrusion when they make a fundamentally personal decision of childbearing.

The court invoked the Equal Protection Clause (Emanuel, 1991) in *Loving v. Virginia* (1967), voiding state laws prohibiting interracial marriage. The Commonwealth of Virginia rebutted by contending that the statue applied equally to blacks and whites. The Court held it was a deprivation of liberty and a denial of equal protection. The Court held the statute had only invidious and discriminatory purposes. In *Roe v. Wade* (1973, p. 113), the right to family privacy was found to be part of the liberty, guaranteed by the Fourteenth Amendment "broad enough to encompass a woman's decision whether or not to terminate her pregnancy."

Illegitimacy laws were challenged in the 1960s and 1970s. The challenges were based more on autonomy than privacy. For example, in *Levy v. Louisiana* (1968) the U.S. Supreme Court struck down a Louisiana law that barred children born out of wedlock from suing for the wrongful death of their mother, encouraging states to refrain from punishing children on the basis of out-of-wedlock births. *Matthews v. Lucas* (1976) upheld a provision of the Social Security Act requiring illegitimate children to show documentation of dependency on their deceased father in order to qualify for survivor's benefits. The Court held that the regulation did not unconstitutionally discriminate against illegitimate children because it reasonably related to a permissible government purpose. In *Trimble v. Gordon* (1977), the Court used an equal protection argument as the basis for scrutinizing an Illinois statute preventing non-marital children from inheriting intestate from their putative fathers. The Court did not hold that birth classifications are inherently suspect, but the Court put states on notice that they must present a persuasive justification for such laws in the future.

Recent U.S. Supreme Court Cases on Family Privacy

Other Supreme Court cases have addressed the rights of parents in the context of legal proceedings relevant to custody and parental fitness. In *Lassiter v. Department of Social Services* (1981), the Court upheld a state's refusal to appoint a publicly funded attorney to represent an indigent mother in a battle for custody of her child. The mother previously was convicted of second-degree murder. The Court held that the state's invasion of her rights was not intrusive enough to compel the Court to hold that the appoinment of counsel to indigent parents is mandated by the Constitution. However, the Court concluded a state was free to provide counsel to indigent parents if it wished. In *Santosky v. Kramer* (1982), the Court held that due process required clear and convincing evidence of a state's allegations of parental unfitness before a state could remove a child permanently from the custody of an abusive or neglectful parent. The standard prior to *Santosky* was a fair preponderance of evidence. The Court held the preponderance standard provided insufficient protection of the fundamental rights of parents in the care, custody and management of a child. In *Palmore v. Sidoti* (1984), two white parents were divorced and physical custody was granted to the mother. After the mother married a Black man, the Florida court transferred custody to the father, fearing the child would suffer the effects of peer pressure and social stigmatization. The Supreme Court unanimously reversed the Florida ruling (using the equal protection clause as its basis), acknowledging that the biases might be real, but the law cannot give weight to prejudices. The Court ruled that yielding to private prejudices was not an appropriate means of accomplishing the goal of the best interest of the child.

CHILD WELFARE AND SAFETY

The Best Interest Standard

States must balance the constitutionally protected rights of parents and the privacy rights of families with the state's interest in protecting children from maltreatment. Advocates of parental rights prefer a high threshold for state jurisdiction, but with ease of termination once that threshold is crossed. The argument is based on the concept of psychological parent, recognizing a child's need for continuity of parenting relationships. It also is based on the argument that the state is not equipped to meet the emotional needs of children through broad interventions of foster care, residential care, or other state-sponsored care (Goldstein, Freud, & Solnit, 1979; Goldstein, Solnit, & Freud, 1996). Proponents of parental rights emphasize the state's role in family preservation. They advocate for state jurisdiction only under the most imminent, serious, and clearest harm to the child. Advocates of children's rights argue the state's primary interest is in the best interest of children and the socialization of children to become productive citizens. They believe a child has an independent interest in liberty, privacy, and his or her care and relationships. They tend to prefer a lower threshold for initial intervention, with broad discretion and considerable resources for child protective services. They prefer to err on the side of ensuring child protection, with a low threshold for intervention and high levels of intervention once the threshold is crossed (Melton et al., 1997). Greater emphasis on children's right has resulted in greater legal representation for children. In most states, children are appointed counsel and the also might be appointed a guardian *ad litem* (46 states require that a guardian *ad litem* be appointed) (Dyer, 1999). In care and protection matters, the role of the child's attorney is to advocate for the child's expressed interests. The role of the guardian *ad litem* is to advocate for the child's best interests.

A description of the *best interest* doctrine is contained in *Chapsky v. Wood* (1881) in which the legal system first acknowledged the best interests of the child. *Chapsky* was an 1881 case in which custody of a child was awarded to an aunt who had cared for the child for many years. The biological father sought to reclaim custody from the maternal aunt who had care for the child since infancy after the death of the biological father's wife. In upholding the decision to leave the child in the aunt's care, the *Chapsky* court recognized the psychological ties that bind children to nonparents (a full century before the construct of *psychological parent* was introduced in the behavioral sciences literature). The *Chapsky* (p. 652) court wrote:

> The affection which springs from the natural relation between parent and child is stronger and more potent than any which springs from any other human relation and from it...arises the reciprocal right to custody....it is an obvious fact, that ties of blood weaken, and ties of companionship strengthen, by lapse of time; and the prosperity and welfare of the child depend on the number and strength of these ties, as well as on the ability to do all which the promptings of these ties compel.

Indirect Constitutional Protections

Between 1800 and 1900, the plight of neglected, homeless, abused, and abandoned children influenced the legislative enactment of benevolent laws. The legislative evolution was accompanied by the establishment of orphanages for unwanted or abused children (Nurcombe & Parlett, 1994). More contemporary law has established a triad of children's rights that weighs the interests of the child, the interests of the parent and the interests of the state. Courts tend to base their decisions on case law reflecting the current view of the proper balance of that triad (Nurcombe & Parlett, 1994). Under the doctrine of *parens patriae*, all states have the right to intervene in cases where a child is at risk of harm due to parental misconduct. However, the Supreme Court has stopped short of giving children substantive rights to due process protection from child abuse. In *DeShaney v. Winnebago County Department of Social Services* (1989), the court ruled that the state has an obligation to protect children from abuse under limited circumstances (as statutorily defined). In *DeShaney*, children were denied the affirmative right to individual autonomy in seeking legal recourse to protect their safety. Stated another way, children could not seek legal protection from abuse that extended beyond (or more broadly than) existing state definitions of child maltreatment or statutory provisions for intervention.

Children's rights to safety and protection have been protected in indirect ways by the Supreme Court. For example, in *Baltimore City Department of Social Services v. Bouknight* (1990), a case in which a mother attempted to refuse an evaluation of her child in the context of suspected child maltreatment, the court indirectly treated the child as an independent agent for the purposes of seeking an evaluation (or for freely expressing the child's words) in the context of a care and protection matter. The Supreme Court found that an order for a mother to present her child for an evaluation of suspected child maltreatment did not violate the mother's Fifth Amendment protection from self-incrimination. In *Smith v. Organization of Foster Families for Equality and Reform* (1977), the Court indirectly addressed the child's attachment to psychological parents. The Court avoided the novel issue of the rights of foster parents, but it upheld a New York lower court ruling of inadequate foster care removal procedures. The lower court held that the procedure of removing foster children from a foster home, after at least one year of residence, without a hearing, was inadequate. The lower court found the procedure inadequate because it denied foster children an opportunity to be heard before suffering the loss of their foster families. Federal regulations have an impact on children's rights or their entitlements. The state must certify and supervise foster placements and residential placements for children. Children are provided with entitlements that emanate from juvenile or family law codes, federal foster care laws, the Social Security Act and the Education for All Handicapped Children Act (Nurcombe & Parlett, 1994).

Statutory Trends

Recent trends in state statutory law include efforts to keep children on a "fast track" toward adoption once they have been deemed eligible for adoption. Placing priority on children's sense of the passage of time, state statutes governing termination of parental rights have been modified in many states to include limitations in time frames for active care and protection petitions (examples include but are not limited to California Family Code ss. 7800–8801, Massachusetts c. 210, s. 3, Michigan 712A, 19b, Pennsylvania 23 Pa.C.S.A. s. 2511, Texas Family Code c. 15 ss. 15.01–15.051, Washington RCW 13.34.180). Support for state efforts to petition for a release of a child for adoption as quickly as is feasible in termination cases is seen in national legislation. The Adoption and Safe Families Act of 1997, signed into legislation on November 19, 1997, provided financial incentives for states that demonstrate progress in moving children from foster care to adoption. In cases with aggravated circumstances, it removed the federal requirement that states must make reasonable efforts toward reunification of children with birth parents. Aggravated circumstances are defined by state statutes, but (according to the federal act) may include abandonment, torture, chronic abuse, and sexual abuse.

State law designed to protect children from parents who abuse or neglect them usually has at least three facets: definitions of child abuse and neglect (which may be found in state statutes, child protective service regulations or both), criminal codes, and statutes governing termination of parental rights. Definitions of child maltreatment relevant to determining whether allegations are serious enough and well-founded enough to merit the right of child protective services to intervene and open a care and protection matter may differ from definitions that are relevant to termination of parental rights. That is, definitions governing the threshold for jurisdiction or intervention sometimes differ from definitions governing the threshold for termination. The differences are reflected in the higher threshold that usually is required for termination compared to intervention.

Across jurisdictions, state statutes governing termination of parental rights are similar in many ways, but there are some important differences among them. The content of the relevant statute frequently has bearing on the way that referral questions are crafted. Evaluators who practice in federal jurisdictions such as military installations and with Native American populations must conform evaluation practices to the use the federal statute for those populations (rather than the state statute). In the case of a Native American child, state statutes are superceded by special provisions designed to comply with the Indian Child Welfare Act. Examples of special provisions include written notification to the child's tribe in a manner provided by the Indian Child Welfare Act, transfer of the proceedings to the Indian child's tribe (the tribe may decline jurisdiction), provision for payment of fees and expenses of attorneys by the Secretary of the Interior, and specification of who is deemed a qualified expert witness. Experts must have personal knowledge about the child's tribe and its customs related to raising a child and the organization of the family. The expert must have extensive knowledge of the social values and cultural influences of the tribe.

Broadly speaking, statutes usually address grounds for termination, issues that the court should consider before returning a child to the custody of his or her parents, and procedural issues (Kantrowitz & Limon, 2001). Grounds for termination typically invoke or contain statutory definitions of different forms of abuse and neglect. They describe the breath of maltreatment that is relevant to the statute. Issues the court should consider before returning a child to the custody of his or her parents typically contain factors relevant to the caregiver's involvement in and response to relevant interventions. Some statutes address the availability of relevant interventions. In "fast track" statutes, time frames are specified within which rehabilitation should have occurred with success. They may vary with the child's age. Procedural issues include requirements for notice of impending hearings, the right of appeal, the right to counsel (for parents and for the child), the rights of putative fathers, and time frames for completing termination litigation. The standard for termination (clear and convincing evidence) was determined by the U.S. Supreme Court in *Santosky* (see above). States may elect to use the even higher standard, beyond a reasonable doubt. So far, only New Hampshire has elected to do so (Oberlander, 1998). Some states specify time limitations for an automatic shift in the burden of proof from the state to the parents (the burden of proof initially lies with the state).

Features of State Statutes

In state statutes, grounds for termination might include the following factors: parental incapacity to care for the child (by reason of mental illness, substance abuse, neglect of needed care for medical illness, or mental defect), extreme disinterest in or abandonment of the child (including failure to visit or communicate with a child in state custody, failure to provide a home when financially able to, and infant abandonment, especially with no identification of the infant for a specified period of time). Other grounds include extreme or repeated abuse or neglect, conviction of a crime carrying a sentence of long-term incarceration with early parole unlikely, failure of the parent to improve in response to child protective service interventions (in some states, services must be specified in a plan and services must be reasonably available and provided pursuant to the plan), parental payment (unless indigent) for a portion of the cost of state-sponsored care of the child, and limitations on the length of time the child remains in state-sponsored placement (this might be based further on the age of the child, with specified differences in how the case will proceed based on the length of time children at different ages are in foster care or other care). Most states have provisions for an expedited process of early termination under certain conditions of severe maltreatment (Oberlander, 1998).

With respect to statutorily specified issues concerning a child's possible return to parental care, attention might be given to the child's significant relationships with parents, siblings, foster parents and potential adoptive parents. With respect to the readiness of substitute caretakers to assume parenting responsibilities, some state statutes manifestly emphasize the child's relationship to substitute caregivers. In other states, such provisions may be found in case law (*Troxel v. Granville*, 2000). Even when parents improve and address maltreatment behaviors of concern, states might have the latitude to go forward with termination on the basis of the quality and strength of the child's relationship to substitute caregivers (Oberlander, 1998).

Some states allow children to express their own preference after they have reached a certain age (usually ranging between 10 and 14). For example, in California, the court can consider a child's preference if the child is age 10 or older. The age for consideration of a child's preference is 12 in Massachusetts and Wisconsin. Seven states (Hawaii, Louisiana, New Mexico, New York, Texas, Virginia, and West Virginia) consider preference for children who are 14 or older (Dyer, 1999; Oberlander, 1998). The availability of alternative placements might be a specified as a legally relevant consideration for children who are regarded as difficult to adopt. Options might include permanent guardianship, permanent foster placement, and other forms of long-term care such as group homes. Some state statutes provide for open adoption in termination cases, provided that preliminary conditions are met (Oberlander, 1998).

States might include different permutations of the above conditions. Some states have age limits for child protective services jurisdiction. For example, in Massachusetts any child can be adjudged in need of care and protection; however, children age 12 or older must consent to adoption even in cases where their parent's rights have been terminated. Some states have age thresholds for providing notice to the child that a termination hearing will take place. In Michigan, children must be advised if they are age 11 or older. When adolescents begin to age out of the child protective service system, states might consider other avenues for parent-child separation (Oberlander, 1998).

Some states specify and exclude conditions that are deemed beyond the control of the parent because of impoverishment or lack of availability, such as inadequate housing, inadequate furnishings, low income, inadequate clothing, and inadequate medical care. For example, a parent cannot be deemed neglectful if he or she has an apartment with insufficient space, especially if that same parent was denied or placed on a waiting list for a larger apartment by the housing authority. Exclusions based on impoverishment sometimes are challenging for investigators who must determine whether a dangerous household condition or situation is a function of limited resources or a reflection of parental behavior associated with child neglect (Goldstein, 1999).

Incarcerated parents present a challenge to child protective service systems because of the length of forced separation imposed by criminal justice system sanctions. Incarceration alone rarely is grounds for termination unless it is protracted. Some states specify categories of crime that can result in termination of parental rights regardless of length of incarceration of the parent. Examples include murder, manslaughter, aiding or soliciting suicide, aggravated assault, rape, gross sexual misconduct, gross sexual assault, sexual abuse of minors, incest, kidnapping, and promotion of prostitution (Goldstein, 1999).

CHILD ABUSE REPORTING REQUIREMENTS

Mandatory Reporting Requirements

Mandated reporting statutes were developed to expedite the identification of maltreated children by the child protective services system. They serve a prevention function, promoting early service provision to families in need (Kalichman, 2000). The fruition of mandated reporting occurred in the late 1960s, with a broadening of definitions in the 1970s and 1980s. For example, although initial model legislation specified that *serious* injury should be reported, most states dropped the term *serious* in their definitions of child maltreatment as it applied to mandated reporting requirements for suspected child maltreatment (Kalichman, 2000; NCCAN 1979, 1989). The unintended result of mandated reporting was an overburdened child protective service system. There is much concern about the broad reach and the vagueness of mandated reporting statutes; they typically provide little clarification concerning *when* reporting is required. Reporters must have *reason to believe* or *reasonable cause to suspect abuse*, but they typically are not required to have specific knowledge or any degree of certainty that abuse has occurred or will occur (Kalichman, 2000).

Precursors of Mandatory Reporting

The child welfare movement was initiated in 1875 when the New York Society for the Prevention of Cruelty to Children was formed. The first national agency with a goal of child protection appeared in the late 1870s, when the American Humane Association was formed. In 1935 the Social Security Act provided the first semblance of funding for the protection of homeless and neglected children. Although these agencies drew some attention to the social problem of child maltreatment, it was not until the middle 20th century that it was given significant attention. In the 1950s there was growing interest in the problem of child homelessness and neglect. In the 1960s, there was an upsurge of interest in both abuse and neglect. The political climate of the 1960s provided the impetus for the inception of national legislation. Although any citizen could report child abuse, the first formal reporting legislation was passed in the 1960s, on the heels of some of the historically most influential pediatric publications documenting the physical effects of child abuse. Pediatricians began highlighting the problem of the impact of child abuse in clinical reports, at an American Academy of Pediatrics symposium (Levine & Levine, 1992), and the seminal publication of Kempe Silverman, Steele, Droegmemueller, and Silver in 1962, in which *battered child syndrome* was introduced.

Kempe et al. (1962) characterized *battered child syndrome* as injury to the skeleton, poor skin hygiene (suggestive of neglect), multiple soft tissue injuries, and malnutrition. They described radiologic and clinical features of child abuse, findings that often were discrepant from information provided to explain the child's condition. They described their hypotheses concerning the reluctance of pediatricians and other physician and health care providers to report child abuse and neglect. They speculated that reluctance to report was due to unwillingness to consider abuse as a causal factor, and role conflict in relinquishing the role of helper or healer for something more consistent with police officer or investigating attorney. Their recommendations for mandated reporting policies are reflected in contemporary reporting statutes (Kalichman, 2000).

Mandatory Reporting Statutes

In 1963, The Children's Bureau of the National Center on Child Abuse and Neglect (NCCAN) proposed a model reporting statute. In 1965, the American Medical Association proposed its own model statute. Another statute was proposed by the Program of State Governments (Kalichman, 2000; NCCAN, 1979, 1989). In a swift proliferation of legislative activity, by the late 1960s, all 50 states had enacted mandated reporting requirements for suspected child abuse. Many early statutes applied only to physicians. Legislative changes broadened the range of professionals and the types of maltreatment subsumed under mandated reporting requirements. Definitions were broadened from non-accidental physical injury to emotional abuse, nutritional problems and failure to thrive, and sexual abuse and exploitation. Most states now use a close approximation of the 1974 and 1988 definitions (Kalichman, 2000). The Child Abuse Prevention and Treatment Act of 1974 set subsequent definitional standards for mandatory reporting statutes. Section Three of that act defined maltreatment as:

> The physical or mental injury, sexual abuse, negligent treatment, or maltreatment of a child under the age of 18 by a person who is responsible for the child's welfare under circumstances which indicate the child's health or welfare is harmed or threatened thereby as determined in accordance with regulations prescribed.

The definition of maltreatment was further broadened in 1988 with the passing of the Child Abuse Prevention, Adoption, and Family Services Act of 1988, wherein maltreatment was defined (in Section 14) as:

The physical or mental injury, sexual abuse or exploitation, negligent treatment, or maltreatment of a child by a person who is responsible for the child's welfare, under circumstances which indicate the child's health or welfare is harmed or threatened.

Mandated Reporters

In all states, mandated reporting requirements apply to physicians, teachers and other school personnel, nurses, psychologists, social workers, psychiatrists, and other counselors. Some states include pharmacists and religious leaders. Some states even include commercial film developers because they are in a position to identify photographers of child pornography. Immunity from liability due to breaching confidentiality or participating in judicial proceedings is provided in almost all states. Decisions not to report suspected child maltreatment place professionals at risk for professional sanctions and legal sanctions such as fines, jail sentences or civil suits (Kalichman, 2000). The onset of reporting requirements and the broadening of types of child maltreatment, the broadening of categories of professionals who serve as mandated reporters, the low threshold for when to report (*reason to believe* or *reasonable cause*) and the removal of the qualifier of *serious* abuse led to a steady expansion of reported cases from the 1960s through the 1980s. The expansion led to a further reporting increase in the 1980s with additional public concern over and criminal prosecution of sexual abuse cases. There is considerable dialogue concerning child maltreatment definitional issues and *what* is required to be reported. The scope of definitions is described below. Kalichman (2000) provides a history of definitions of child maltreatment in reporting statutes.

SCREENING AND INVESTIGATING PARENTING BREACHES

The Stages of Care and Protection Matters

The first stage of a care and proceeding matter is the identification of abuse or neglect. The most important development in the identification of child abuse and neglect is mandatory reporting as described above. When a professional (or a citizen reporter) has reasonable cause to suspect child abuse or neglect has occurred, the report is given to the designated reporting center. The initial state intervention or response to the report is to screen it out and take no action, or to screen it in. For reports that are screened in, the state can take an emergency action to remove custody if deemed necessary and to conduct an investigation (Melton et al., 1997). Most states have a specified time limit within which the investigation must take place.

Once the report of child maltreatment has been investigated, the second step usually involves a formal petition to the court alleging that a child was abused or neglected. A hearing is usually held within 48 hours after an emergency removal of the child from the home (Nurcombe & Parlett, 1994). A hearing takes place concerning whether the state has a legally sufficient basis for assuming jurisdiction over the child and family (Kantrowitz & Limon, 2001). Jurisdiction may or may not involve assuming or continuing the state's physical and legal custody of the child. For example, if two parents are the subjects of a petition, but one parent promptly separates and shows the immediate capacity to provide a safe home, the state might assume legal jurisdiction (to ensure the child's safety beyond the immediate crisis) without assuming physical custody (Oberlander, 1998). A civil protection order may be sought as an alternative to the child's removal from the caretaker's custody (Nurcombe & Parlett, 1994).

Some states have a two-part approach to hearings, with the first hearing, a temporary custody hearing, addressing evidence that supports an emergency removal and the second hearing, a final adjudication hearing, addressing evidence that supports the retaining of state jurisdiction (Kantrowitz & Limon, 2001). Soon after a temporary custody hearing in which the state assumes jurisdiction, there typically is a separate adjudication hearing on the merits of the case before the state can retain jurisdiction. The state files or renews the petition alleging that the child was in fact maltreated. This civil proceeding to adjudicate maltreatment charges is held in juvenile or family court wherein the state must prove by clear and convincing evidence that it should retain jurisdiction on the grounds that the child remains in danger. A criminal proceeding also may be held before or after the civil proceeding. The objective of a civil proceeding is to protect the child and to arrange a placement. In civil hearings, parents have no right to counsel or to a jury (although state law may provide for either). The objective of a criminal proceeding is to determine if the accused perpetrator of child maltreatment is guilty and to mete out punishment. The accused has the right to counsel and to a jury (Nurcombe & Parlett, 1994).

If a legally sufficient basis is found for state jurisdiction, the third phase is a dispositional phase (Melton et al., 1997). In some states, the filing of a *care and protection petition* is synonymous with the dispositional phase. In other states, there are provisions for a temporary period of time within which parents are given the opportunity to demonstrate their willingness to address the issues of concern prior to a formal filing of a care and protection petition. The dispositional inquiry usually follows the *best interest* standard, as legally defined, in which the court has broad regulatory and statutory discretion in determining the conditions the parent(s) must meet in order bring their parenting of the child to the minimal standard of care required by the state. The overriding concern in establishing the conditions is the safety of the child; however, the *best interest* standard is broad and may subsume other child welfare issues related to quality of care (Dyer, 1999; Melton et al., 1997). Within the third step, or the dispositional inquiry, there may be a distinction between child protective service jurisdiction that involves an oversight or supervision as defined by social service regulations (setting of conditions and monitoring parental compliance with service plans) and a more formal legal mechanism of jurisdiction. Legal jurisdiction specifies the minimal parenting standards that must be met within a statutorily defined time frame in order for parents to avoid further court jurisdiction and a hearing relevant to termination of parental rights (Kantrowitz & Limon, 2001).

The final step depends upon the court's view and the social service system's view of the caregiver's status after time has passed. The final step is regarded as jurisdictional, but the word jurisdiction carries a different meaning than it does in the dispositional phase. It involves filing a formal petition for termination of parental rights (Melton et al., 1997). However, even after filing a formal petition, some social services agencies may still set forth an internal case-specific goal of service provision and/or family reunification during the pendency of the termination proceedings. Or the goal may change back and forth from reunification to termination depending upon the progress of the caregiver(s) in remedying the behavior or conditions of concern. Even when the agency goal is strongly one of reunification, a formal petition for termination may be required because of time limitations in statutes. More often, termination petitions are filed because of lack of sufficient parental progress (Melton et al., 1997). Child protective service regulations provide more agency discretion at the outset of a case compared to later on. Fast track legislation reduces the amount of discretion states have in working toward reunification after the passage of a specified period of time, usually based on the duration of the child's out-of-home placement (Dyer, 1999; Oberlander, 1998). Statutory time frames might not mirror real time insofar as there might be legal reasons for case continuances that would modify or effectively extend the time frame. Judges are unwilling to hold parents accountable for delays that are due to procedural issues, judicial docket scheduling problems or other reasons that are out of their control (Oberlander, 1998).

Supported Investigations

In order for an allegation of child abuse or child neglect to be supported, the allegation must be verified according to regulatory standards. Some initial reports to child protective services are screened out. A call might be screened out because the allegation does not meet the reporting regulations (Kalichman, 2000). For example, the allegation of child maltreatment must be made against a caretaker (a parent, a guardian, a child care worker, a residential school staff member) in order to fall within child protective services jurisdiction. An allegation of child maltreatment by a non-caretaker (such as a neighbor who was not providing child care) would be screened out (the caller might be referred to the police, who would have jurisdiction over the matter). An allegation of child maltreatment by a minor would be screened out because minors by definition are not caretakers (the caller might be referred elsewhere). Other calls might be screened out because they do not meet the definitional threshold for maltreatment. For example, a call alleging that a parent made a vague threat to someday harm a child might be screened out. A call alleging a parent made a threat to severely injure an identified child in a specific manner probably would be screened in (Kantrowitz & Limon, 2001; Oberlander, 1998).

The investigation phase usually must begin within 24 hours and must not extend beyond roughly a 10-day period (states vary in the specified investigation duration). It involves the assignment of an investigation worker to interview relevant parties, interview the parent(s) or other relevant caretakers, interview the child about whom the allegations were made, interview siblings, and review relevant records. Teachers, school administrators, other family members and neighbors might be interviewed. Although investigation procedures are idiosyncratic to the content of the allegations, most agencies have attempted to standardize investigation questions and procedures to the degree possible. The goal of the investigation is fact finding for evidence of child maltreatment and risk of future child maltreatment (Pecora, 1991). The risk assessment phase of investigations involves consideration of factors such as parenting skills, frequency and severity of maltreatment, the perpetrator's access to the child, the child's age and related capacity for resilience and self protection, recency of maltreatment, and the potential recurrence of parental stress conditions deemed relevant to the maltreatment (Kalichman, 2000).

Some states have an additional requirement of notifying law enforcement agencies of screened in reports. Other states require notification of law enforcement agencies only after the investigation results in a supported report (Kalichman, 2000). In some circumstances, the supported investigation will be followed by a criminal investigation or the filing of criminal child abuse charges. According to the U.S. Department of Health and Human Services (1988), approximately half of all reports of child maltreatment are supported upon investigation. There is little data available on the reliability and validity of investigation outcomes with respect to either establishing evidence of child maltreatment or correctly identifying risk of future child maltreatment (Pecora, 1991). Typically, there are four investigation outcomes: (a) supported (or substantiated), (b) supported (or substantiated) with perpetrator unknown (see description below), (c) not supported (or unsubstantiated), and (d) inconclusive (Kalichman, 2000; Pecora, 1991).

Care and Protection Petitions

A care and protection petition is a formal written legal request for court jurisdiction over the outcome of the case. A petition is the functional equivalent of a *complaint* at law and it must include the facts and circumstances relied upon as a cause for legal action (Black & Garner, 1999). In all states a petition is mandatory at some stage, as specified in either the statutory requirements or child protective service regulations (Kantrowitz & Limon, 2001). States vary in the specificity of criteria for when and under what conditions a care and protection petition must be filed. The party bringing the petition before the court, usually child protective services, is referred to as the petitioner. The parent or caretaker against whom the petition is filed is referred to as the respondent. Some states allow parties in addition to child protective services (for example, a relative or another concerned person) to file a petition (Oberlander, 1998). Although their success is rare, termination of parental rights petitions sometimes are filed in the context of other proceedings, such as divorce custody or paternity suits (Kantrowitz & Limon, 2001).

Care and Protection Petitions and the Relevance of Criminal Court

In many jurisdictions, specific effort has been made to link child maltreatment statutes and regulations to criminal codes. Conduct defined as child maltreatment by child protective service statutes and regulations is concurrently defined as criminal conduct in the state's corresponding criminal codes. Some child protective service regulations require a referral to law enforcement and to the district attorney for certain categories of child maltreatment. Some statutes governing termination of parental rights make it necessary for a criminal conviction of certain categories of child maltreatment (usually criminal acts of sexual abuse as codified) in order for the court to terminate parental rights. Where referrals are discretionary, there may be less correspondence between child protective service regulations and criminal codes (Dyer, 1999; Kalichman, 2000).

When an act of child abuse or neglect, as defined by child protective service regulations or statutes relevant to state jurisdiction and custody, carries the potential for an eventual finding of criminal conduct, it can have a substantial impact on the willingness of the parent or other caretaker to cooperate or work collaboratively with child protective services at the outset of jurisdiction. The looming risk of criminal prosecution has a chilling effect on the degree to which the person against whom allegations are made is predisposed to participate in the investigation process or the development of a service plan (Oberlander, 1998). For that reason, many child protective service agencies have broadened their possible findings to include "supported" or "substantiated" with "perpetrator unknown" in order to assume jurisdiction when maltreatment is apparent, without having to rush through the investigation phase in identifying the perpetrator. In perpetrator unknown cases, because the person against whom an allegation is made must be a caretaker, there also must be a corresponding finding of neglect (or failure to protect) on the part of the custodial caretaker(s) (Kantrowitz & Limon, 2001; Oberlander, 1998).

When corresponding criminal codes are invoked, the child protective services system works in concert with law enforcement agencies to gather appropriate evidence. There is potential for role conflict, however. The child protective services goal is to assume jurisdiction and to identify appropriate services for the parties in order to facilitate the construction of a relevant service plan and to promote eventual family unity. The law enforcement goal is the identification and conviction of the appropriate defendant in order to impose legal consequences. Defendants understandably rely upon attorney advice not to disclose incriminating facts, but the social service system relies upon perpetrator acknowledgement of child maltreatment to gauge the candor of admissions of responsibility, to make judgments about amenability to treatment, and to identify appropriate interventions (Oberlander, 1998).

Individuals in the dual role of criminal defendant and suspected perpetrator of child maltreatment on the civil side might suffer more severe repercussions from statutory time limits because they typically prefer to wait until the criminal matter is resolved before they make acknowledgements of child maltreatment to child protective service authorities. Child protective service system workers have the onerous task of encouraging acknowledgments even under the threat of criminal prosecution. They must try to discern whether the lack of acknowledgment is related to the pending criminal matter, clinical denial, innocence, or another factor. The advantage to invoking the powers of both systems is the symbolic value of societal disapproval of child maltreatment, consequences for perpetrators that enhance the victim's appraisal of vindication and safety, and the weight of the punitive sanctions of the criminal justice system in punishing perpetrators and in discouraging further acts of child maltreatment (Oberlander, 1998).

EXAMPLES OF TERMINATION CRITERIA IN STATE STATUTES

Criteria governing termination of parental rights are based on abuse or neglect (neglect includes abandonment). Abuse or neglect usually constitutes the initial breach of parenting responsibilities; however, other conditions serve as potential termination criteria if they are causally related to a respondent's failure to use or benefit from relevant child protective service interventions. Those conditions include mental illness, mental deficiency, substance abuse, severe personality factors related to an unstable lifestyle, and parental unavailability through long-term incarceration (Grisso, 1986). The presence of any of these conditions by themselves is insufficient for a finding of termination of parental rights. Most courts recognize those conditions rarely fully explain the parenting breach. Statutes typically specify that there must be a relationship between those conditions and any problems or deficits related to the initial breach of parenting responsibility in order for the court to consider criteria in the termination statute relevant to those conditions (Dyer, 1999; Grisso, 1986). Where statutes are silent on the relationship between those conditions and parenting behavior, case law usually establishes precedent for such a relationship (Oberlander, 1998).

To illustrate the court's interest in the link between the parenting breach, the causal condition or conditions, and the failure of the parent to use or benefit from services, consider the following case examples. In the Hawaii case of *In re: Doe Children* (1997), a mother's rights were terminated on the grounds that her mood disorder caused her children to fear her and caused her to act in detriment to the children's best interests. In the North Carolina case of *In re: Montgomery* (1984), the rights of a mentally retarded couple were terminated based on neglect of their children only after it was determined that they were incapable of caring for their children. In the Minnesota case, *In the Matter of B.S.M.* (1997), a father's rights were terminated because he had a chemical dependency, active alcoholism that affected his availability as a parent, problems with the law related to his substance abuse, he presented no evidence that his substance abuse problems were remitting, and he had not seen his son for eight years or contributed financially to his care.

Even when caretakers adhere to their service plan, if their progress is insufficient, most courts (in 34 states) have a statutory obligation to consider termination based on the length of time the child has been in an alternative placement (Dyer, 1999). Some statutes may provide further specification based on the age of the child. For example, in Massachusetts, if a child age four or older has been in placement for 12 of the last 15 months and sufficient parental progress is not expected prior to the cessation of the 15-month period, the court may consider the child's duration in placement as a criterion for termination. If a child is younger than age four, the court can consider the child's duration in placement after only six months, if parental progress is not reasonably expected at the cessation of a 12-month period. The statute also contains a criterion in which the court can consider the child's relationship with the substitute caretaker if the separation from the parent has been *lengthy*. It does not clarify what is meant by *lengthy* (Massachusetts c. 210, s. 3). Michigan allows the court to consider the duration of the child's placement after a two-year period, regardless of the child's age (Michigan 712A, 19b). Pennsylvania allows the court to consider duration of the child's placement after a 12-month period, regardless of the child's age (Pennsylvania 23 Pa.C.S.A. s. 2511).

Most state statutes specify an obligation for child protective services to offer services intended to correct the conditions that led to the parenting breach. Those services must be reasonably available on a consistent basis. For example, the Washington statute specifies that "all necessary services, reasonably available, capable of correcting the parental deficiencies within the foreseeable future have been offered or provided" (Washington RCW 123.34.180). Many states require that a parent with sufficient resources must provide financial support for a child in placement. Failure to do so is included as a criterion for termination. Some states have unique elements in their statutes. For example, the Texas statute specifies that a child's failure to be enrolled in school or his or her absence from home without parental consent serves as a criterion for termination.

Some state statutes include provisions for termination of the rights of fathers who (with knowledge of the pregnancy) abandon mothers at the time of the pregnancy and continue the abandonment after the child's birth. However, it should be noted that most states draw a distinction between actions brought by the state and actions brought by the abandoning parent. Case law in most states specifically disallows fathers to petition for termination of parental rights solely on the basis of an unwanted child. The court is more likely to rely upon paternal abandonment of an unwanted child if a party other than the father brings forth a petition that relies upon that criterion (Oberlander, 1998). The Supreme Court of the State of North Dakota (*In the Matter of Adoption of J.M.H.*, 1997) upheld the termination of a father's rights because he made no post-divorce effort to visit the children, threatening the child with serious bodily harm, and incurring eight or nine felony convictions. The court does not allow either parent to petition for termination of parental rights in the midst of a custody dispute. In *Davenport Bost v. van Nortwick*, 1994, the court refused to grant a mother's petition for termination of the biological father's parental rights. In her petition, the mother alleged the father's visitation was sporadic because he had a history of alcohol problems.

MALTREATMENT DEFINITIONS AND THE BREADTH OF STATE INTERVENTION

Typically, an act of abuse alone is insufficient to meet the threshold of most legal definitions of child maltreatment. Most definitions require a finding of *harm* or *risk of harm* (Melton et al., 1997). States vary in the level of specificity, breadth, scope and severity of harm (or risk thereof) required to meet the threshold for state jurisdiction and intervention. Some definitions are vague, while other definitions have more specificity or criteria that clarify the definitional scope. Regardless of the specificity of definitions, some measure of legal and clinical ambiguity is inevitable. The term clinical here denotes both mental health vagaries and medical vagaries of definitions of child maltreatment. For example, the term *failure to thrive* in pediatric medicine might describe physical abuse, physical neglect, or both.

Definitional problems result from the lack of consensus over the scope and overall policy framework for addressing child maltreatment. There is disagreement over the proper balance between the rights of parents and the state's interest in the protection of children. Those disagreements are seen at the entry phase of cases and at the dispositional phases. A second source of problems with definitions of maltreatment lies in the relative lack of consensus among mental health professionals, pediatricians and other physicians over the nature and etiology of child maltreatment (Dubowitz, 1999; Zuravin, 1991a). Although there is somewhat more consensus about the impact of child maltreatment, there remain some divisions within the professions over the ability of professionals to detect and describe the long-term impact of child maltreatment (Zuravin, 1991a).

DEFINITIONS OF CHILD MALTREATMENT

Definitions of child maltreatment fall roughly into the categories of physical abuse, physical neglect, emotional abuse and emotional neglect (with relatively little pragmatically useful differentiation between what constitutes emotional abuse and what constitutes emotional neglect), sexual abuse and other types of sexual child maltreatment (such as sexual exploitation). Abandonment of children usually is subsumed under the category of physical neglect, emotional neglect, or both. Virtually all jurisdictions have statutory or regulatory provisions for state intervention to protect physically abused and physical neglected children (Kalichman, 2000). Because there is less consensus over definitions of emotional abuse and neglect, fewer states have specific definitions of or provisions for the protection of emotionally abused or neglected children. Although recognition of sexual abuse as a social problem postdated the Kempe et al. (1962) description of physical abuse by about 20 years (Finkelhor, 1984), states have reached roughly the same level of definitional consensus concerning sexual abuse as they have for physical abuse. As an added feature of specificity, many states explicitly rely upon criminal codes for definitions of sexual abuse. There is greater correspondence between criminal codes and child protective service statutes and regulations in definitions of sexual abuse than for other types of maltreatment (Oberlander, 1998).

Physical Abuse

Definitions of physical abuse include a reference to physical harm or risk of physical harm, but some definitions (e.g., in Florida and Nevada) also include mental harm or the likelihood of mental harm. Definitions tend to focus on the seriousness or severity of harm in order to avoid the burden of state intervention in the lives of families whose children are not in grave danger. Most standards require that the harm or danger of harm must be the result of intentional or non-accidental infliction of physical injury by a caretaker or other person responsible for the child. In most definitions, harm must be serious or severe (including such injuries as broken bones, burns, internal injuries, loss of hearing or sight). Bruises might not be included unless the child was treated in a way that indicates more serious injury is likely in the future. The Missouri definition specifically makes a distinction between physical abuse and corporal punishment. It explicitly excludes discipline, including spanking that is administered in a reasonable manner. In some definitions, the risk of harm must be imminent (Kalichman, 2000; Melton et al., 1997).

The Juvenile Justice Standards (Wald, 1977) were written as model legislation for state statutes in order to curb the tendency in some definitions toward too much breadth or too low a threshold for state intervention. Recognizing that corporal punishment remains a somewhat widely used form of discipline, the standards were written to neither endorse corporal punishment nor include it as part of the definition of serious or severe physical abuse. The Juvenile Justice Standards defined physical abuse as "a child has suffered, or there is substantial risk that a child will imminently suffer, a physical harm, inflicted non-accidentally upon him or her by his or her parents, which causes, or creates a substantial risk of causing disfigurement, impairment of bodily functioning, or other serious physical injury" (see p. 58). The *Guidelines for Psychological Evaluations in Child Protection Matters* (1998) (hereafter in this chapter referred to as *Guidelines*) define physical abuse "as the suffering by a child, or substantial risk that a child will imminently suffer, a physical harm, inflicted non-accidentally upon him or her by his or her parents or caretaker" (see p. 11). It does not include the reference to serious physical consequences contained in the Juvenile Justice Standards (or as contained in the *Guidelines'* definition of physical neglect described below).

Some state definitions are less conservative than the Juvenile Justice standards in making reference to specific types of physical consequences. For example the Wisconsin definition of physical abuse is, "Physical injury inflicted on a child by other than accidental means." The West Virginia definition is similar to Wisconsin's definition. On the other hand, some states go even further than the Juvenile Justice Standards, describing what is meant by physical consequences and including death as a specifically-named consequence of physical abuse (see, for example, the Florida, Massachusetts, and Wyoming definitions). Some states include severe malnutrition or non-organic failure to thrive in definitions of physical abuse (see, for example, the California definition); whereas, other states include it in physical neglect definitions. For examples of definitions from all 50 states, see Kalichman (2000).

Physical Neglect

Every state has some provision for state intervention if there is neglect of a child. Sometimes neglect is defined solely as physical neglect (as opposed to emotional neglect which is described below). The variation among definitions is greater than it is for physical abuse (Melton et al., 1997). As with physical abuse, the Juvenile Justice Standards include the term *harm* and describe types of serious or severe harm. The Juvenile Justice Standards define physical neglect as follows: "...a child has suffered, or...there is a substantial risk that the child will imminently suffer, physical harm causing disfigurement, impairment of bodily functioning, or other serious physical injury as a result of conditions created by his or her parents or by the failure of the parents to adequately supervise or protect him or her" (see p. 59). The *Guidelines* (1998) mirror the Juvenile Justice Standards, defining physical neglect as "a child suffering, or at substantial risk of imminently suffering, physical harm, causing disfigurement, impairment of bodily functioning, or other serious physical injury as a result of conditions created by a parent or other person legally responsible for the child's welfare, or by the failure of a parent or person legally responsible for the child's welfare to adequately supervise or protect him or her" (see p. 12).

In contrast with the definition of physical abuse, there is no use of the term *non-accidental* in the Juvenile Justice Standards definition of physical neglect. Some states include terminology that explicitly states or that implies that there must be intent. Other statutes contain terms such as *negligence* or *inability* to supervise or protect a child. The Massachusetts statute states that the failure by the caretaker must take place "either deliberately or through negligence or inability ... provided, however, that such inability is not due solely to inadequate economic resources or solely to the existence of a handicapping condition." Some definitions, such as Indiana's, include specific references to the failure of a caretaker to provide the child with food, clothing, shelter, medical care, and education.

Emotional Abuse and Emotional Neglect

It is easy to imagine conditions that nearly everyone might consider emotionally abusive (such as locking a child in a freezer as a form of punishment or forcing a child to leave school at a young age in order to work as a migrant laborer). Consensus over definitions that *solely* encompass emotional abuse or neglect is difficult to reach. Circumstances, rather than signs or symptoms, of deprivation and failure to provide necessary care and supervision tend to be contained in definitions of emotional abuse or emotional neglect. Kalichman (2000) described the overlap between behaviors that constitute neglect and those that constitute physical abuse or sexual abuse. He illustrated variations in state definitions of emotional abuse and emotional neglect that fall within the band of the overlap. Similarly, Melton et al. (1997) suggest the category of emotional abuse/emotional neglect might be nearly superfluous. They contend that in most circumstances where there is consensus that emotional abuse has occurred, there are other grounds for invocation of jurisdiction. Complaints of emotional abuse or neglect seldom are the sole grounds for a petition to assume custody or to terminate parental rights (Nurcombe & Parlett, 1994). They usually are added to a broader complaint of maltreatment. States are less interested in assuming jurisdiction over children who might be psychologically unhealthy because of aloof or indifferent parenting practices than it is in parental behaviors (or absence of proactive behaviors) that results in serious or severe harm. Documenting the harmful effects of emotional abuse and neglect is a difficult endeavor. There are far more articles and books on the topic of the impact of child physical abuse and sexual abuse than on the impact of neglect of any kind (Dubowitz, 1999).

The difficulty of defining emotional abuse and emotional neglect, compared to the difficulty of defining other forms of abuse, is seen in the variety of approaches to it. For example, even though there is little available literature on the specific impact of neglect (and virtually no pathognomonic signs of neglect) (Belsky, 1993a; Harrington, Dubowitz, Black, & Binder, 1995), the Juvenile Justice Standards make reference to impact and parental willingness to provide treatment in their definition. They define emotional abuse and neglect in the present tense, "a child is suffering serious emotional damage [not necessarily as a result of parental actions], evidenced by severe anxiety, depression, or withdrawal, or untoward aggressive behavior toward self or others, and the child's parents are not willing to provide treatment for him or her" (see p. 59). The *Guidelines* (1998) define emotional neglect as "the passive or passive-aggressive inattention to a child's emotional needs, nurturing or emotional well-being; also referred to a psychological unavailability to a child" (see p. 12). The *Guidelines* (1998) state that emotional abuse also is referred to as psychological maltreatment. They defined it as "a repeated pattern of behavior that conveys to children that they are worthless, unwanted or only of value in meeting another's needs; may include serious threats of physical or psychological violence" (see p. 12). Nurcombe and Parlett (1994) describe emotional abuse as "the infliction of psychological harm on a dependent child by a parent or caretaker who, by overt attitude, word, and deed, persistently exhibits severe rejection, contempt, or dislike" (see p. 135).

Some state definitions are noticeably vague. The New Mexico statute simply requires that a child was emotionally or psychologically abused by his parent. Other state definitions of emotional abuse or neglect mirror the Juvenile Justice Standards' focus on impact. For example, both the Massachusetts and Wyoming definitions include an observable or substantial reduction or impairment in the child's ability to function (Wyoming adds "with due regard to culture"). Louisiana makes reference to specific types of emotional abuse or neglect in their inclusion of "the *exploitation* or *overwork* of a child to such an extent that his health, moral or emotional well-being is endangered" (emphasis added). In some states, sexual exploitation is considered emotional abuse and in other states, it falls under the rubric of sexual abuse.

Sexual Abuse

As described above, states frequently directly refer to criminal codes when defining sexual abuse. Many statutes directly incorporate definitions codified in criminal law. For example, the Massachusetts statute defines sexual abuse as non-accidental behavior by a caretaker that "constitutes a sexual offense under the laws of the Commonwealth" (Massachusetts 110 CMR, s. 2.00). The tendency to defer to penal codes is related to two phenomena. Unlike the relationship between signs or symptoms of physical abuse and penal codes, it is common for all acts associated with sexual abuse to be codified in criminal statutes (Kalichman, 2000). The mechanism for initiating a criminal investigation is therefore more readily available for acts of sexual abuse than it is for many types of physical abuse. The tendency also follows in part from the model legislation of the Juvenile Justice Standards. Sexual abuse is not defined or described in the Juvenile Justice Standards in the same manner as other abuse. The standards instead encourage use of definitions of sexual abuse found in a state's penal code. The Juvenile Justice Standards nonetheless include a reference to *serious harm* resulting from the sexual abuse.

Although the Juvenile Justice Standards' inclusion of serious harm from sexual abuse is synonymous with the definition or description of physical abuse, examples of serious harm from sexual abuse are not provided in the standards (as they are with physical abuse). Specific signs and symptoms of physical abuse are commonly manifestly encompassed in legal definitions as examples of serious injury. When narrowly defined, there is less ambiguity over what type of behavior merits a required report of child maltreatment. The weakness of narrow definitions is their failure to represent the universe of physical abuse that might be of concern to state authorities. On the other hand, broad definitions result in higher rates of reporting of unfounded cases or cases that do not rise to the level of concern for state authorities. The complexity of defining sexual abuse (either broadly or narrowly) or providing examples of it is illustrated by attempts to differentiate between serious harm and less serious harm resulting from it. Physical signs and symptoms rarely form the basis for legal definitions of sexual maltreatment (Kalichman, 2000). Definitions of sexual abuse are more likely to rely on circumstances, situations or behaviors. Clinical sequelae of sexual abuse that might constitute *serious harm* is more difficult to define for sexual abuse than for physical abuse (Finkelhor, 1984; Kuehnle, 1996). As many as 75 percent of cases of sexual abuse present with no specific physical signs of injury or abuse (Kalichman, 2000).

The *Guidelines* (1998), in contrast to the Juvenile Justice Standards, define sexual abuse as "contacts between a child and an adult or other person significantly older or in a position of power or control over the child, where the child is being used for sexual stimulation of the adult or other person" (see p. 11). Georgia provides an example of a definition that does not refer to penal codes, defining sexual abuse or exploitation as acts, performed in the presence of a child, that are "immoral, obscene, or indecent influences . . . likely to degrade the child's moral character." It specifies acts that entice a child for "indecent purposes," incest, and the involvement of the child in sexually explicit materials (Kalichman, 2000). Some statutes specify that a parental act of sexual abuse is grounds for termination, as is a parent's failure to protect a child from sexual abuse, if there is opportunity to do so (for example, see Michigan 712A, 19b). There must be an accompanying reasonable likelihood that the child will suffer injury or abuse in the foreseeable future if returned to the caretaker's custody.

THE PSYCHOLEGAL NEXUS: LEGAL AND CLINICAL DEFINITIONS OF MALTREATMENT

Historically, mental health professionals were asked to conduct evaluations after the child protective service investigation into maltreatment was completed (Melton et al., 1997). In recent years, especially with the increasing demand for sexual abuse evaluations, evaluators have been retained earlier in the process (Bulkley, 1987; 1988; Kuehnle, 1996). Child protective service workers have a legal mandate to answer two questions: whether child maltreatment occurred as defined in criminal and/or family codes, and how grave or imminent the risk is for further maltreatment. The latter question is relevant to the need to determine the appropriate disposition, that is, whether to petition for an emergency (immediate) or eventual (post-investigation) removal of the child from the caretaker's custody (Melton et al., 1997). The second question usually follows from the first, but the second question sometimes is asked in absence of a substantiated complaint of maltreatment. The two questions tend to be treated as one inquiry, but more recently states have moved to differentiate between the two questions so that each phase is given adequate attention. Many child protective services regulations and procedures draw a distinction between the investigation phase and the assessment phase (Kalichman, 2000).

The investigation phase arguably lies solely in the province of child protective service investigators and law enforcement officers (if applicable). The question of "What happened?" usually is regarded as a legal inquiry embedded in penal codes and child protective service regulations and statutes, not a mental health inquiry or referral question. Moreover, case law (although inconsistent) frequently explicitly rejects the notion that an expert may testify to whether an accused individual fits or does not fit the profile of a sex offender (*Hadden v. State*, 1997) and whether a child does or does not display symptoms that may or may not be associated with sexual abuse (*Flanagan v. State*, 1993). Such referral questions raise ethical problems because the legal determination of whether abuse or neglect occurred is "outside the specialized knowledge of mental health professionals" (Melton et al., 1997, p. 455). The *Guidelines* (1998) discourage questions of what happened, who perpetrated abuse, and whether a particular child was abused. Others take a less rigorous view, arguing that there is a clinical foundation for some types inquiry into whether a child was abused or neglected and by whom (Bulkley, 1987, 1988; Myers et al., 1989; Walker, 1990). Although no definitional guidance or specific diagnostic criteria are provided, "Physical Abuse of Child," "Sexual Abuse of Child" and "Neglect of Child" have been included as diagnostic entities in the *Diagnostic and Statistical Manual* since the publication of the fourth edition (American Psychiatric Association, 1994).

Sources of clinical definitions are found in empirical studies, diagnostic manuals, and guidelines for clinical practice (examples include American Psychological Association, 1998; Belsky, 1993a; Milner, 1986; Strand & Wahler, 1996). Legal definitions are found in penal codes, family law codes, and juvenile justice codes (where some states hear maltreatment matters). Child protective services regulatory definitions emanate from administrative law. They sometimes accompany statutory definitions, but they are not meant to supersede them. The nexus of those definitions constitutes the psycholegal scope of inquiry into child maltreatment and its impact. Courts often recognize a dual clinical and legal foundation for inquiries into child maltreatment. They recognize the role of an evaluator is different from that of an investigator and from that of a treating clinician. They rely on the legal process to determine the relevance of clinical data to evidentiary rules and eventual findings of fact. But they value the clinical data that an evaluator might gather to supplement evidence gathered in the course of a criminal or child protective services investigation (Bulkley, 1987, 1988). (However, some studies have found that clinical data and expert opinions have little impact on judicial determinations, see Melton et al., 1997). Judges often allow evaluators latitude in asking clinical interview questions concerning whether child maltreatment occurred and by whom. Rarely do judges solely rely upon expert opinions in making a judicial funding of child maltreatment, but many judges routinely seek those opinions (Bulkley, 1987, 1988).

LIMITATIONS IN THE LAW'S CAPACITY TO MONITOR FAMILY RELATIONSHIPS

The foregoing review has illustrated that definitions of child maltreatment have varying degrees of clarity and cogency. Definitions have the potential to raise or lower thresholds for state jurisdiction. Child protection policies and regulations rest on a complex set of empirical data, political climates, and constitutional protections for the rights of parents and children. Policies sometimes are changed after careful consideration of research relevant to child maltreatment. For example, the Kempe et al. (1962) and Goldstein et al. (1979) studies had an impact on child protective services policies by highlighting and describing the problem of child abuse, and by introducing developmental features and psychological constructs. Goldstein and colleagues (1979) cited empirical studies to support their recommendations that child protective service placement decisions should safeguard the child's need for continuity of relationships, and placement decisions should reflect the child's sense of the passage of time (not the adult's). Those recommendations are reflected in many current state statutes. In other instances, policies have been shaped by public outcry over egregious maltreatment cases that failed to draw the attention of state authorities or insignificant cases to which state authorities overreacted. Policies are also shaped by case law when cases successfully challenge the abridgment of rights.

Goldstein and colleagues (1979), in their seminal work on child protective service policy recommendations, described the law as a crude instrument for establishing or supervising family relationships. Although it may separate individuals and ultimately estrange or destroy relationships, it has less force in compelling relationships to develop or change in some way. The state rarely has the necessary resources to monitor the day-to-day lives of children and families, nor is that capability desired by most citizens. Because the law "will not act in the child's interests but merely adds to the uncertainties" (Goldstein et al., 1979, p. 51), they recommend that the state should confine itself to the prevention of harm (not to the promotion of best interests). They argue that the state should consider the least detrimental alternative rather than the best available alternative in placing children with substitute caregivers.

To illustrate a contrasting view, Dwyer (1997) has argued that children should have autonomous legal rights in connection with their upbringing. He asserts that the right to parenting should be viewed as an entitlement to a much higher standard of parenting that the law currently provides. He makes an equal protection argument that the state has an obligation to set higher parenting standards than it presently does. He endorses public funding support for parents that would be sufficient to ensure that parents might acquire the skills, knowledge, and resources necessary to be good parents. He suggests clear parenting standards should be drafted and supported by child welfare agencies and that energy and resources should be directed toward giving children equal moral standing to other individuals or classes in society. Onheiber (1997) describes a similar view, arguing that greater emphasis should be given to the value of children in society, with relatively less emphasis on the parental rights. He advocates for the enunciation of basic parental standards through parental licensure and national economic policies favoring parental commitment to children. He states that prevention measures aimed at enhancing the capabilities of parents should be the primary mechanism for reducing child maltreatment.

Melton et al. (1997) provide a critique of the child protective service system's emphasis on investigation at the expense of service provision. Relying on the work of the United States Advisory Board on Child Abuse and Neglect (ABCAN, 1990, 1995), they describe the impact of mandated reporting requirements and the investigation process on the current focus and allocation of financial resources of child protective service systems. They use the observation of the law's incapacity to effectively supervise family relationships to support the view that child protective policies should be altered drastically to establish a system (and supporting resources) within which parents and other caretakers can request and receive help before child maltreatment occurs. Their argument essentially is one of priority for primary prevention (and tertiary services) rather than a reporting system with punitive connotations (Melton, 1987; Melton et al., 1997).

MINIMAL PARENTING COMPETENCE AND "GOOD ENOUGH" PARENTS

Case law repeatedly has upheld the *minimal competence* notion. The minimal competence standard (either manifestly or implied in state statutes) specifies that caretakers who come to the attention of the child protective service system must demonstrate only minimal parenting competence in order to regain custody of their children. Termination cases exemplify the state's attention to minimal parenting competence in balancing the triad of *parens patriae* doctrine, the *best interest* doctrine, and the rights of parents. In cases that typify those that go to termination proceedings, the state must prove, by clear and convincing evidence, extreme maltreatment and (except in the most egregious cases) the likelihood of serious harm in the foreseeable future. Furthermore, the state must demonstrate parental incapacity (specific deficits in parenting behavior, skills, or functioning that are associated with the breach of parenting responsibility). The state must demonstrate failure to remedy the behavior or conditions that led to the breach of parenting responsibility, and an irretrievable breakdown in the parent-child relationship (Nurcombe & Parlett, 1994). The relative emphasis on each of these factors varies from case to case (Dyer, 1999). According to state statutes, not all of these conditions are explicitly necessary for termination. However, an examination of case law reveals that most successful termination cases involve more than one condition of statutorily defined unfitness. Successful cases that rely on one or a small number of factors are rare and usually involve some egregious or idiosyncratic features (Nurcombe & Parlett, 1994).

Parens patriae doctrine empowers the state to protect the interests of the mentally handicapped, the mentally ill and minors. In *Prince v. Massachusetts* (1944) the U. S. Supreme Court formally recognized and upheld the doctrine of *parens patriae* (which theretofore was policy driven rather than constitutionally driven), when it upheld the right of the Commonwealth to prevent children from distributing religious newspapers in violation of state child labor laws, even though the child labor laws infringed on the religious liberty and freedom of the children's parents (who were members of the Jehovah's Witnesses). As described earlier, the doctrine known as the *best interests of the child* arose in the 19th century in the context of child custody disputes. The doctrine holds that when the interests of parents, children, and the state collide, the court's decisions should be guided by what would be in the child's immediate and ultimate benefit (Melton et al., 1997; Nurcombe & Parlett, 1994).

In child protection matters, *parens patriae* doctrine, the *best interest* doctrine, and the rights of parents coexist. Although fast track legislation has shortened the duration of the pendency of child protective services involvement leading to a termination petition, states still must meet evidentiary requirements after the petition is filed. Cases continue beyond the statutorily specified time frames not because of legislative barriers to filing a petition for termination but because of the high evidentiary and statutory threshold required for a judicial finding of termination and because of the high personal stakes for parents who are unwilling to risk losing their children by moving for a hearing on the issue of termination. At various junctures of child protection matters, the following legal dispositional options are available to the court (Nurcombe & Parlett, 1994): to dismiss the case and return the child to the family, to return the child home but to keep the case open for the provision of further services; to retain custody of the child with the provision of relevant services to the child and the caretaker with the ultimate goal of reunification; to retain custody of the child with the ultimate goal of permanent guardianship (which may or may not involve further provision of services to the caregiver given that the goal might again be revised), and to terminate parental rights.

When their children are in placement (that is, when the state assumes physical custody), parents may retain some residual rights in some states. Most parents retain the right to visit their child unless the court makes a finding that visitation is unsafe for the child (Nurcombe & Parlett, 1994). Although the fast track to adoption has influenced the length of time parents have to comply with and respond to services, it has had little impact on the rights of parents to visit their children while their children are in placement.

RECENT DEVELOPMENTS IN CHILD PROTECTIVE SERVICE REGULATIONS

FAST TRACK LEGISLATION

As evaluators work with children and families in child protection matters, it is important to monitor shifts in policies and regulations that occur below the threshold of major moves for legislative and statutory changes. Paradigms that prioritize child safety and fast track legislation for waiver of parental permission for adoption are relatively new philosophies in child protective service systems. With the passage of the Adoption and Safe Families Act in 1997 and legislative emphasis on permanency planning on the federal and state level, it is likely the frequency of cases involving a petition for termination of parental rights will increase. By mandating more stringent time limits in the adoption process, it will move children out of foster care into permanent families more quickly. It should be noted, however, that time limits alone probably are insufficient for termination of parental rights. The constitutionality of time limits, or fast track legislation has been challenged successfully after being described as arbitrary. The Illinois statute gave the state the power to seek termination of parental rights if the child was in foster care for 15 months during a 22-month period. Once the state invoked the 15-month ruled, the burden shifted to the parent to prove that the child's best interest was to be returned home within the next six months. In Chicago, a Kane County judge ruled unconstitutional the statute that allowed for termination of parental rights for no other reason than a child has been in foster care or 15 months. An emergency appeal was filed in Illinois Supreme Court, but the child eventually was placed in the permanent custody of the state due to other factors (the mother's drug abuse relapse). This possible aberration has not slowed the impact of the Adoption and Safe Families Act of 1997, but it leaves the statute open to further Constitutional challenges.

THE CONTRAST BETWEEN FAST TRACK LEGISLATION AND FAMILY REUNIFICATION LEGISLATION

Traditionally, policies and regulations have emphasized family preservation policies, recognizing the need for children (even those who are maltreated) to maintain their attachment to original caretakers (see Omnibus

Budget Reconciliation Act of 1993). Similarly, policies and regulations that emphasize parental amenability to treatment and other interventions tend to accompany family preservation policies (Blanch et al., 1994). *Family reunification* is the primary goal under such policies. Concern over children languishing in foster care (and being moved through multiple placements, also known as *foster care drift*) at the expense of finding a permanent placement led to the shift in policy toward child safety and what became known as *permanency planning* (Klee, Kronstadt, & Zlotnick, 1997). Nationally, 340,000 children are in foster care, with 39 percent remaining in temporary placements for two years or more (Nurcombe & Parlett, 1994).

PERMANENCY PLANNING

Child safety and permanency planning policies emphasize the child's safety needs over reunification. Although the child's appraisal of attachment and safety in foster care and other substitute arrangements is given some attention, greater emphasis is placed on continuity and stability of caregivers (with the goal of establishing a permanent home for the child). Children are moved from temporary foster placements to potential pre-adoptive placements as soon as possible (Klee et al., 1997). Placing children in pre-adoptive placements creates another set of social service system and substitute caretaker/child dynamics, reviewed more fully in later chapters (U.S. General Accounting Office, 1991, 1993, 1995).

Child protective service policies and regulations that emphasize permanency planning may adhere to sentiment expressed in statutory fast track provisions by mirroring emphasis on the child's perception of the passage of time, and its developmental variations. Accompanying policies and regulations may manifestly prohibit multiple placements in order to prevent foster care drift. Children under those policies or provisions might be moved to a residential placement more quickly in order to prevent the likelihood of multiple foster care placements due to safety concerns (for example aggression or sexual acting out in a child) across foster placements or foster caregiver burnout when a child's behavior proves difficult to manage or supervise.

SUMMARY

1. Care and protection matters raise fundamental individual and societal concerns about the nature of family life and the appropriate bounds of state intervention. The dynamics of individual and group process in care and protection matters reflects those fundamental concerns.

2. The emphasis in the law on minimal parenting competence is central to child maltreatment definitional challenges, to discordance between advocates for children's rights and advocates for privacy rights, and to discordance between legal goals for children and families and research or treatment endeavors for victims and perpetrators of maltreatment.

3. Prototypical child protective service system statutes and regulations reflect historical emphasis on encouraging and strengthening family life within a context of mandated reporting, with the breadth of reporting criteria and categories of reporters increasing over the decades. The *best interest* standard prevails. Recent federal legislation (the Adoption and Safe Families Act of 1997) promotes state efforts to introduce and support "fast track" legislation in parental rights termination statutes.

4. It is too early in the legislative change process to determine whether such legislation has achieved the goals of swifter parental adherence to service plans, fewer transfers of children in placement, shorter out-of-home placements, swifter moves toward termination of parental rights when indicated, or post-termination adoption of victims of child maltreatment.

3

Framing Referral Questions

Requests for parenting evaluations come from several sources. One source is a court order, usually making explicit or implying prior agreement of all involved parties that the appointed evaluator will conduct an evaluation. Other sources include an agreement between the attorneys of both parents to retain one evaluator, but without disclosure to child protective services or other parties; an *ex parte* motion for an evaluation and associated funding by the attorney of one party (e.g., the attorney for one parent, the attorney for the child); a representative or attorney for child protective services; or via contracted services with a local or regional office of a child protective service agency. Occasionally a parent will seek his or her own evaluation with indirect assistance from counsel (or without any assistance if they are proceeding *pro se*), but it is advisable to consider possible legal and ethical complications that might arise prior to accepting such a referral. The evaluation methodology that follows from the referral question should be the same regardless of the referral source (Borgida, Gresham, Swim, Bull, & Gray, 1989).

This chapter provides suggestions for framing referral questions in a manner that enhances the potential utility of the evaluation results. The first task of any evaluation is to make sure all involved parties have a shared understanding of the reason(s) for the evaluation (Beckerman, 1998;

Oberlander, 1995a). When there are multiple parties with multiple legal representatives, the referral question should be mutually understood by everyone before scheduling the first evaluation appointment. At the outset of the evaluation, the referral question should be explained carefully to the parties being evaluated. For comprehensive evaluations requiring more than one evaluation session, it is useful to re-explain the purpose of the evaluation prior to each meeting. For strategic reasons, attorneys may request that evaluation questions be addressed in a stepwise fashion (for example, assessing parental mental health functioning, then risk of harm, and then the parent-child relationship in three distinct steps or reports). The evaluator should make sure that any agreement to accommodate the preferred strategy of a referring attorney does not compromise the integrity of the evaluation process.

There are common referral questions that are asked by the court or by referring attorneys. (Unfortunately, just because a question is common does not mean it lies within the scope of practice for a forensic evaluation.) Some examples of common and acceptable questions are contained in the *Guidelines for Psychological Evaluations in Child Protection Matters* (1998). Challenges in framing referral questions usually center on the role of the expert in relation to the role of the fact finder, or on the role of the expert in relation to child protective service investigators or police investigators. A prevalent issue that emerges in clarifying the referral question is differentiating forensic evaluation questions from language or questions in regulations, statutes, and hearings (Rogers & Ewing, 1989; Melton et al., 1997). Although statutes might contain language that sounds clinical, the definitions of terms in statutes are legal, not clinical. In parenting evaluations, there is a common recurring tendency for referring parties to ask "Who did it?" or "What happened?" questions (Oberlander, 1995b). In those circumstances, the evaluator might wish to have an initial discussion with the referring attorney, exploring each person's view of the difference between (a) a criminal investigation of legally defined child maltreatment, (b) a child protective services investigation of maltreatment allegations, (c) a forensic assessment of the capacity of children to speak on their own behalf, (d) an assessment of the impact or consequences of child maltreatment, (e) a risk assessment and (f) other permutations of potential referral questions (Heiman, 1992; Oberlander, 1998).

Mutually defining the referral question is necessary in order to address the scope of behavioral correlates deemed relevant to the portion of the statute or legal standard in question. In some cases, knowledge of case law is necessary to properly frame evaluation questions. Precedents established in case law might change the focus of a statutory provision, might deem certain referral questions unacceptable or moot, might clarify the desired content of referral questions, or might bar expert testimony on certain data such as profile data or novel evaluation practices. Establishing a mutual understanding of the referral question also provides an opportunity for dialogue about the expected level of confidentiality (that emanates from attorney-client privilege) of the results should an attorney wish to exercise the option of quashing unfavorable results. Discussion about the referral question provides an opportunity for the evaluator to emphasize to the referral source(s) that the evaluation will be objective and the conclusions might or might not be favorable to the referring party.

ESTABLISHING A MUTUAL UNDERSTANDING OF REFERRAL QUESTIONS

THE SOURCES AND IMPETUS FOR EVALUATION QUESTIONS

Care and Protection Procedural Influences

After the initial adjudication hearing in which the threshold for legal proof of maltreatment necessitating state jurisdiction is reached, there might be a request for an evaluation to assist the child protective services system in determining the intervention needs of the caregivers and children. Interventions usually are specified on a service plan that is developed by representatives of the child protective services system. Evaluation results sometimes are used by child protective services to develop a service plan. Some jurisdictions include an initial evaluation as standard fare. Others request it on a case-by-case basis. Attorneys for the caretakers or for the child might request an independent second opinion evaluation if there is dispute about the need for a particular intervention or placement on the service plan.

As the case proceeds, the goal of the attorneys for the parents might be to demonstrate that their clients have responded sufficiently to services to the degree that their parenting has improved and their risk of child maltreatment has attenuated. In phrasing the referral question, the evaluator might wish to describe the strengths and weaknesses of such an approach, describing how parenting improvements might be supported by data and how risk factors are measured. Whether the client's progress was sufficient, however, lies in the judicial realm of decision-making (Grisso, 1986). If child protective service workers have ongoing concerns about the case, the goal of the child protective services attorney might be to request an evaluation to gather data that would help them understand the client's treatment response and risk, reasons that might explain a good or a poor treatment response, reasons that might explain differences of opinion about the caretaker's treatment response, and remaining issues to be addressed prior to case resolution. Child protective service attorneys sometimes seek consultation when cases are seen as borderline in terms of whether the agency's goal should be reunification or termination. In each of the above scenarios, a report potentially might contain rich descriptive data that would be sufficient to address the referral question. In some circumstances, direct opinions actually mask the richness of the data because they focus the reader's attention on the decision rather than the decision matrix (Oberlander, 1998).

Evaluation Data and Evidentiary Concerns

Attorneys sometimes tend to focus on evidentiary issues in their requests for evaluations. If the attorney's goal is to gather data that would satisfy evidentiary standards, the evaluator needs to make sure that there are reasonable clinical means to achieve that goal. The referring attorney and the evaluator need to consider factors that might deem report data inadmissible (Levine & Battistoni, 1991). They should consider the impact of evidentiary issues and admissibility on the nature and scope of the referral question. In framing the referral question, an attorney might wish to discuss issues such as hearsay rules, what constitutes circumstantial evidence (such as the legal relevance of prior bad acts or uncharged misconduct), rules governing expert testimony, the expected content of expert testimony, and/or legal issues relevant to "syndrome" testimony (or legal reasons to avoid "syndrome" testimony) (Kinscherff & Ayoub, 2000; Oberlander, 1995b).

Referral Questions that Anticipate Ultimate Issue Testimony

Referral questions that closely approximate the ultimate issue before the court sometimes result in opinions that are frowned upon by the court. Ultimate issue testimony is not forbidden *per se*. Federal Rule of Evidence 704(a) states: "testimony in the form of an opinion or inference otherwise admissible is not objectionable because it embraces an ultimate issue to be decided by the trier of fact." Although many state judges have permitted ultimate issue testimony, there are cases in which it specifically has been excluded. Courts may limit or exclude ultimate issue testimony if there is danger of jury confusion or unfair prejudice (Myers et al., 1989).

In re K.L.M. (1986) involved a social worker's testimony that a child was abused because the minor showed anxiety, the minor answered negatively when asked if the minor's father had committed other improper acts, and the minor had knowledge of the appearance of semen during an improper act. The social worker rendered an opinion that the minor was a victim of sexual abuse. Although the court viewed the error as "harmless," the court's view of the inappropriateness of ultimate issue testimony in this case centered on several concerns: the expert witness purported to have information about the accuracy and truthfulness of the testimony of the minor, the minor was not a trial witness (and therefore the state had the burden of demonstrating the minor could not speak on her own behalf because of infancy or some disability), and the state had a burden of showing the expert's statements bore an *indicia of reliability*. The court ruled that expert's testimony *per se* was not improper because it was relevant to the reliability of the minor's statements. The court objected to the breadth of the opinion. In delivering the opinion of the court, Justice Green (pp. 1267–68) stated:

> We are concerned with the opinion because it covered the ultimate issue of the entire case. We are aware that opinions are no longer precluded merely because they cover an ultimate issue. Here, the question of the accuracy of the minor's statement was the most important question in the case. As we have indicated, expert testimony was helpful to the trier of fact in regard to how a 4-year-old would be likely to react under the circumstances. Beyond that, no need existed for further expert testimony. An opinion that a party should win is not a permissible expert opinion. This is so even though expert opinion is permissible upon some of the ultimate issues involved in determining who should win.

In general, courts have held that an expert may not vouch for a witness by testifying that a particular child was capable of telling the truth or actually did tell the truth (Goldstein, 1999). See *People v. Roscoe* (1985); *Davis v. State* (1988). The analysis of the impact of case law on referral questions below provides a further description of the court's rejection of such testimony. Referral questions nonetheless sometimes might involve a direct request for substantive proof that a child was abused or neglected (Kuehnle, 1996). In such cases, it is helpful to seek specificity about what is actually meant by the question. Avoiding ultimate issue referral questions sometimes is as simple as asking the referring party for clarity.

Accessing Privileged Data or Communications

If the referral question suggests a need for the evaluator to contact particular collateral sources, the attorney might need to make preliminary steps to gain access to witnesses. Many states have privilege statutes (statutory provisions for the protection of confidentiality) that apply to certain professional or personal relationships. For example, most jurisdictions recognize some form of psychotherapist-patient privilege (but they vary as to who qualifies as a psychotherapist). In maltreatment cases, this privilege often is abrogated by the court (Goldstein, 1999). The attorney might need to request the assistance of a limited purpose guardian *ad litem* to aid the court in determining the appropriateness of abrogating psychotherapy-child patient privilege (in particular, a limited purpose guardian *ad litem* might make recommendation to the court, who ultimately controls privilege for child patients), spousal privileges, parent-child privileges, clergy-penitent privileges, or the confidentiality of state records (such as official reports of maltreatment by mandated reporters). The attorney might need to make an official request for redacted records of child protective service reports (usually records are redacted to shield the identity of the mandated reporter). When criminal codes are relevant (when a parallel case is heard in criminal court), the state may allow only an *in camera* review of certain records (Goldstein, 1999). For example, in *Pennsylvania v. Ritchie* (1987), a defendant who was being prosecuted for sexual abuse sought discovery of child protective service investigation records. The defendant alleged the records contained exculpatory information. Citing the strong state interest in confidentiality of maltreatment investigation records, the Supreme Court held that the defendant's Sixth Amendment and due process rights required only a judicial *in camera* review of records to determine if they contained exculpatory information.

Spousal privilege applies to any communications between spouses during a marriage. The privilege permits one spouse to decline to testify against the other during their marriage. Spousal privilege sometimes is abrogated in civil and criminal cases involving child maltreatment (Goldstein, 1999). Common law preserves privilege for parent and child communications, but the vast majority of modern court rulings have rejected such privilege (Goldstein, 1999). Some states recognize a clergy-penitent privilege, but it does not extend to clergy members in the role of counselor.

DAUBERT AND OTHER ADMISSIBILITY STANDARDS

Depending on the nature of the case, attorneys making referrals may wish to have a preliminary discussion of rules governing expert testimony and the relevance of *Daubert v. Merrell Dow Pharmaceuticals, Inc.* (1993) or other prevailing standards for admitting scientific testimony. Rule 702 of the Federal Rules of Evidence establishes the basic principles that govern the admissibility of expert testimony. The trial judge determines whether testimony meets those requirements. The most important question is whether the testimony will assist the judge or jury (Myers et al., 1989). Federal Rule of Evidence 702 is exemplary of its state counterparts in evidence codes (Goldstein, 1999): "If scientific, technical or other specialized knowledge will assist the trier of fact to understand the evidence or to determine a fact in issue, a witness qualified as an expert by knowledge, skill, experience, training, or education, may testify thereto in the form of an opinion or otherwise."

In *Daubert* (1993), the U.S. Supreme Court held that Federal Rule of Evidence 702 established a standard for admitting scientific or expert testimony that seeks to assure that it is both *relevant* and *reliable* (p. 589). Most states have adopted the *Daubert* rules via case law, but some states still use the *Frye* test (1923) (which requires expert testimony to be based on general scientific *acceptance* in the relevant scientific community). In considering the admissibility of expert testimony, the *Daubert* rules require the court to consider "whether the reasoning or methodology underlying the testimony is scientifically valid and ... whether that reasoning or methodology property can be applied to the facts at issue" (pp. 592–593).

A typical *Daubert* (1993) inquiry involves consideration of some or all of the following issues (Goldstein, 1999): (a) whether the theory underlying the testimony can be or has been tested to determine whether hypotheses can be falsified; (b) whether the theory or technique has been subjected to peer review and publication; (c) the known or potential rate of false positive or false negative error; (d) the existence and maintenance of standards for the technique; (e) the extent of the theory or technique's acceptance in the relevant scientific community. Evidentiary battles over what kind of testimony on maltreatment satisfies the *Daubert* standard in some ways mimicked earlier cases applying the *Frye* test. For example, testimony on "syndrome" evidence that experts sometimes offer has been contested. Although syndrome testimony usually is barred, experts have been permitted to testify about symptoms and diagnoses that might be a function of child maltreatment. *Shahzade v. Gregory* (1996) was a case in which expert testimony was admitted concerning the existence of repressed memories. The testimony was admitted in part based on DSM-IVs recognition of dissociative amnesia. In *Isely v. Capuchin* (1995), expert testimony on PTSD and repressed memory was admitted.

The foregoing evidentiary concerns illustrate the importance of discussing the evidentiary and admissibility issues from the standpoint of the legal system and their relationship to methodological issues and the scientific reliability and validity of evaluation results. Not all initial discussions will include broad issues such as privilege statutes or *Daubert*, but it is important to be aware of their potential impact on referral questions and evaluation methodology. There also are pragmatic reasons for establishing a mutual understanding of the referral question. It is important to know how to plan the evaluation procedures and the scope of interview content. Establishing a mutually understood referral question sets the tone for smooth communication between evaluators and attorneys.

FUNDAMENTAL QUESTIONS IN PARENTING EVALUATIONS

Examples of common referral questions, phrased to avoid statutory or other legal language, appear in the *Guidelines for Psychological Evaluations in Child Protection Matters* (1998, p. 4):

1. How seriously has the child's psychological well-being been affected?
2. What therapeutic interventions would be recommended to assist the child?
3. Can the parent(s) be successfully treated to prevent harm to the child in the future? If so, how? If not, why?
4. What would be the psychological effect upon the child if returned to the parent(s)?
5. What would be the psychological effect upon the child if separated from the parents or if parental rights are terminated?

The *Guidelines* (1998) describe other points of consideration, such as whether the evaluator might wish to interview or observe the parties individually or together, and the relevance of topics such as family history, personality functioning, the developmental needs of the child, the nature and quality of the parent-child relationship, and evidence of trauma. Psychologists are encouraged to consider specific risk factors related to child maltreatment such as substance abuse or dependence, domestic violence, financial circumstances, and the health status of family members. The evaluator is encouraged to review information from other sources and to consider cultural, educational, religious, and community factors. Consultation is suggested for referral questions that contain factors outside of the range of mental health expertise (such as hearing problems, physical health concerns, or other issues).

Dyer (1999) elaborates on the referral question examples in the *Guidelines* (1998). The impact of maltreatment on the child's psychological functioning might include medical impact, self esteem, level of anxiety, vigilance, rumination, traumatic sexual (abuse reactive) behavior, intellectual deficits, social deficits, and emotional delay. Therapeutic interventions for the child might include an assessment of whether the child is capable of benefiting from treatment, whether a parent might be capable of supporting a child's involvement in treatment, and the willingness of a parentt to attend and meaningfully participate in sessions that require the parent's inclusion. Whether the parent can be successfully treated might include an assessment of substance abuse or dependence recovery, DSM-IV (or DMS-IV-TR) diagnoses and their relationship to rehabilitation potential, and prognosis. Prognosis might need to be embedded in statutorily relevant time frames for the case. Issues relevant to the fourth question in the *Guidelines* (1998) might involve an assessment of how the parent would react to a child who will suffer the loss of foster parents after their return home, the degree to which the parent is attuned to the child's needs and empathetic to those needs, the parent's readiness to appropriately manage behavior problems in the child, and the parent's ability to refrain from criticizing or making negative statements about the substitute caregiver in front of the child (Dyer, 1999). The fifth question in the *Guidelines* (1998) might involve an assessment of the child's reaction to parental visitation, reports or observations of the quality and consistency of parental interactions during visitation, reports of the reliability of parental visitation attendance, reports or observations of the child's reaction to separation at the end of visitation, and the child's attachment to a substitute caregiver (Oberlander, 1998).

Dyer (1999) provides examples of ways in which referral questions might be made specific. Examples include requests to assess the parent or child's current intellectual or personality functioning, whether a mental health disorder might interfere with parenting, the prognosis for a mental health disorder, whether intellectual limitations might prevent a parent from following directions to administer necessary medical interventions, or whether intellectual limitations or problems in judgment might limit a parent's ability to understand when and how to seek appropriate emergency medical attention. Specificity of referral questions yields a report that has both clinical (intervention planning) and legal utility (case status). Specificity narrows the scope to a brief assessment when the referral question has a limited focus (Oberlander, 1998).

THE LANGUAGE OF QUESTIONS AND THE LANGUAGE OF THE COURT

THE LANGUAGE OF LEGAL DEFINITIONS OF CHILD MALTREATMENT

As described earlier, some breaches of parental responsibility are concurrently investigated by child protective services and the criminal system. Sometimes definitions are uniform across both legal settings and sometimes they are different. Mental health professionals operating in evaluation and treatment venues usually use still another set of definitions that are based on clinic policies, theoretical constructs, and definitions that are subsumed by diagnostic entities. The goal of the legal system (both child protective services and the criminal system) is to prove that sexual abuse occurred and to prove that a particular individual perpetrated the abuse (Myers et al., 1989). Child sexual abuse usually occurs in a private setting with an overlay of secrecy. The secrecy sometimes is magnified by an added element of threats or other coercion to refrain from reporting the abuse. Even when a child reports abuse, there often are concerns about the child's capability to make a credible initial report and to later testify in an unfamiliar and formal setting (Kuehnle, 1996).

Three issues typically propel attorneys to seek expert testimony from mental health professionals: the possibility of ineffective testimony from the child, a lack of eyewitnesses, and what usually is a paucity of physical evidence (Myers et al., 1989). Testimony stems from an evaluation of the child or family. However, some forms of expert testimony do not require any knowledge of a particular child (such as when an expert describes behaviors commonly observed in sexually abused children). In evaluating the expert's ability to address legally relevant definitions of child maltreatment, the court might wish to evaluate the sources upon which the expert relied. Potentially inadmissible sources of information are written and verbal hearsay (Levine & Battistoni, 1991). Written hearsay includes information that might be found in clinical records, police records, child protective service records and the child's written statements. Verbal hearsay includes the child's statements and might also include nonverbal conduct (Myers et al., 1989). The court makes a judgment of what constitutes hearsay based on the type of information "reasonably relied upon by experts in the particular field in forming opinions or inferences upon the subject" (Federal Rule of Evidence 703). Most courts tend to be inclusive, allowing introduction of evidence. However, when the information is so unreliable that lacks probative value, it usually is excluded (Myers et al., 1989).

Courts qualify experts to render opinions about child maltreatment based on whether they possess sufficient "knowledge, skill, experience, training, or education" (see *State v. Moran*, 1986). In evaluating an individual's expertise, the court might consider educational attainment or degrees, specialization, extent of experience with the population of interest, familiarity with relevant behavioral sciences literature, membership in relevant professional organizations, publications of relevance, and whether the individual has been qualified as an expert in the past (Melton et al., 1997). An expert opinion must be based on a "reasonable degree of certainty" (sometimes phrased psychological, clinical, or medical certainty). Because absolute certainty is rare in cases of child sexual abuse, the court usually allows a degree of flexibility. Uncertainties in an expert's opinion can be described during direct and cross-examination or an expert may refrain from offering an opinion, describing observations and data instead of rendering an opinion (Myers et al., 1989).

Distinguishing between Questions of Law and Questions of Fact

In grappling with definitional issues and their relationship to ultimate issues, some scholars have made a distinction between questions of law and questions of fact. In child sexual abuse cases, ultimate *facts* include whether abuse occurred and who committed the abuse, whereas the ultimate question of law is whether the defendant is guilty (Myers et al., 1989). Others have made a distinction between rendering ultimate issue opinions (whether a child was abused; who the perpetrator was) and using legal language in rendering opinions (phrasing opinions that subsume statutory or regulatory language in describing of maltreatment or whether the perpetrator's act of abuse met statutory criminal codes or regulatory definitions) (Melton et al., 1997; Myers et al., 1989). In both instances, the issues admittedly are intertwined.

Using the Myers et al. (1989) distinction between questions of fact and questions of law, it is advisable to avoid referral questions that contain questions of law. For example, the referral question, "Should this parent's rights be terminated?" is a question of law. Similarly, a question that uses statutory language might be regarded as a question of law. Let us use the Michigan termination statute as an example. The referral question, "Did the parent cause physical injury or physical or sexual abuse such that there is a reasonable likelihood that the child will suffer from injury or abuse in the foreseeable future if placed in the parent's home?" probably would be regarded as a question of law because it uses language from the termination statute. The most common objection to such referral questions and resulting expert opinions is that it invades the province of the jury. Another common reason such testimony is excluded is because it is not "beyond the ken" of the jury (Melton et al., 1997; Myers et al., 1989).

Descriptive Reports and Testimony

Referral questions that approximate facts rather than questions of law might include a request to evaluate the parent's response to interventions designed to lessen their risk of maltreatment. Questions focused on the child might include whether a child is more behaviorally distressed than might be expected of a non-abused child, whether the child shows idiosyncratic features that would not be expected in a non-abused child, whether

the child shows a sexualized reaction such as sexual acting out or prostitution, and whether the child's distress can be distinguished from the
expected, and perhaps more serious, level of disturbance in a psychiatric
population of children (Myers et al., 1989).

Alternatives include descriptive reports and testimony. Examples
of descriptive data include the words the child used to depict age-
inappropriate sexual contact, whether a child's symptoms and behaviors
are consistent with a reaction to child sexual abuse, a summary of relevant empirical literature on children's reactions to sexual abuse, comparing a child's statements or behavior to developmental expectations such as
whether the child demonstrates age-inappropriate sexual knowledge, and
testimony that the absence of physical evidence does not preclude sexual
abuse (Kuehnle, 1996).

Statutory Language Governing Termination of Parental Rights

Legal System Approaches to the Use of Language

In framing referral questions, attorneys might encourage evaluators
to consider the statute and to subsume its language in the phrasing of
opinions. Some courts have allowed at least limited elements of such testimony. Furthermore, not all courts have viewed expert opinions on the
ultimate facts as impermissible. In *Townsend v. State* (1987), the Nevada
Supreme Court allowed expert testimony on whether abuse occurred. In
Glendening v. State (1988), the Florida Supreme Court allowed an expert to
testify as to whether a child was the victim of sexual abuse.

Objections and Counter-Arguments to the Use of Statutory Language in Questions and Reports

Whitcomb (1992) summarized what are sometimes described as ethical and moral objections to referral questions containing statutory language
and potentially leading to ultimate issue opinions. Objections are centered
on the following concerns. Child sexual abuse (the most common form of
abuse about which an expert might render an opinion in child protective
service cases) is a relatively new field of study. Empirical data are limited
and much remains unknown about manifestations of abuse reactions and
the overall impact of abuse. Whitcomb (1992) contended there is insufficient knowledge of forensic assessment principles among individuals who
conduct sexual abuse evaluations. Similarly, there is insufficient awareness

of role differences between clinicians who might act as advocates and evaluators whose goal should be objectivity. Note, however, that Borgida et al. (1989) found that experts who testify in child maltreatment cases tend to be well credentialed, specialized in both forensic assessment and child psychology, and well aware of the need to put any advocacy tendencies in abeyance. In their study, partisanship was not a statistically significant factor in reports of how experts form opinions. Other critics are less concerned about role confusion and partisanship than general misconceptions about base rate data. They contend that the use of group probability data (such as whether the defendant shares the characteristics of abusers or whether the victim shares the characteristics of abused children) tells the evaluator little about whether a particular child was abused and by whom (Grisso, 1986; Melton et al., 1997).

Bulkley (1988, 1992) summarized objections to such testimony from a legal perspective in her argument that most victim identification or victim impact testimony fails to meet basic evidentiary requirements for admissibility. However, she reached the opposite conclusion for rehabilitative testimony. Rehabilitative testimony explains confusing behaviors of the child victim after the defense has attacked the child's credibility. Rehabilitative expert testimony is designed to address misconceptions or a lack of knowledge that jurors might have about the behavior of child victims. It is offered to rebut and not to prove that the child was sexually abused. Bulkley recommends the jury should be instructed that the expert's rehabilitative testimony should not be used to determine the truthfulness of the victim's claim of sexual abuse.

Although no symptom or set of symptoms is pathognomonic of sexual abuse, some scholars believe an opinion that a child was sexually abused is justified when symptoms related to abuse are present in conjunction with a report that bears a reasonable degree of reliability, or more than circumstantial evidence (Myers et al., 1989). Fulero and Finkel (1991) conducted an empirical study comparing the effects of diagnostic testimony, testimony that uses statutory language related to the ultimate issue, and ultimate issue testimony in insanity trials. They found that level of testimony had no effect on the verdict pattern. Walker (1990) cautioned that expert testimony might have a differential impact depending upon the standard of proof used at trial. There are substantial differences between the impact of evidence that demonstrates it is more likely than not that an act occurred and evidence that it occurred by clear and convincing evidence or beyond a reasonable doubt. Although a plausible hypothesis, no empirical studies have investigated the differential impact, if any, of expert testimony based on the standard of proof in family court or criminal trials involving allegations of child maltreatment.

The Relevance of Case Law to Referral Questions

Myers and colleagues (1989) described the influence of case law on the breadth and limitations of referral questions. They examined cases that involved the use of an expert to diagnose child sexual abuse, to "prove" that abuse occurred, to vouch for a complainant's credibility, and to enhance the complainant's credibility. The courts tend to reject syndrome testimony more often than other forms of expert testimony. Courts seem evenly divided over whether a non-syndrome description or diagnosis of child sexual abuse is admissible or inadmissible. To illustrate, although Minnesota courts previously had rejected syndrome testimony, in *State v. Myers* (1984), the Minnesota Supreme Court allowed expert testimony that diagnosed a child as suffering from symptoms typical of sexually abused children and a subsequent diagnosis of "child sexual abuse." In *State v. Moran* (1986), the Arizona Supreme Court allowed expert testimony proffered to rehabilitate a child's testimony, but placed limits on the expert's testimony relevant to whether the child's behavior was consistent or inconsistent with sexual abuse. In *State v. Hudnall* (1987), the South Carolina Supreme Court rejected testimony designed to "prove" that abuse occurred. The court found the testimony irrelevant because it did not add probative value to the child's testimony nor was it offered to explain any inconsistency in the child's response to possible trauma.

In *Allison v. State* (1987), the court allowed rebuttal testimony describing behavioral characteristics that are common to sexually abused children, but did not allow an opinion that a particular child was abused. The court based its rejection on the view that the jury, having the benefit of extensive testimony on the subject, was fully capable of deciding whether the child was abused and by whom. Similarly, in *Russell v. State* (1986), the Arkansas Supreme Court rejected an expert's testimony that a child's statements were consistent with sexual abuse. The court held the expert's testimony did not aid the jury because the jury was capable of determining whether the history provided by the victim was consistent with sexual abuse.

By contrast, most courts have rejected expert testimony limited exclusively to syndrome testimony. In *Lantrip v. Commonwealth* (1986) and in *People v. Bowker* (1988), the Kentucky Supreme Court and the California Court of Appeals respectively rejected testimony on "child sexual abuse accommodation syndrome" because there was no showing that the syndrome had general scientific acceptability as a means of diagnosing or detective child sexual abuse. (Summit, 1983, did not intend for the syndrome to be used as a means for diagnosing or detecting abuse. His analysis assumed the abuse already had been substantiated or adjudicated.) In *Bussey v. Commonwealth* (1985), the court rejected child sexual abuse accommodation syndrome testimony and any other syndrome evidence. However, child sexual abuse accommodation syndrome testimony was permitted in several criminal court cases to describe the reactions of children as a class (*Keri v. State*, 1986; *People v. Gray*, 1986; *People v. Luna*, 1988).

In *State v. Haseltine* (1984), the Court of Appeals rejected an expert's testimony on "the pattern of behavior exhibited by incest victims" and the expert's opinion that there was "no doubt whatsoever" that the child was sexually abused. The Court of Appeals objected to the latter opinion as "too certain and unequivocal" thereby causing unfair prejudice to the defendant. The court objected because the strongly stated opinion that the child was abused was too similar to an opinion that the child told the truth. In a similar case (*State v. Jensen*, 1987, affirmed 1988), the court rejected expert testimony describing behavioral characteristics common in sexually abused children because the testimony was offered to prove that abuse occurred and therefore was equivalent to testimony that the child was telling the truth. In their analysis of these cases, Myers et al. (1989) suggest that both sets of testimony might have been deemed permissible if the testimony focused more on describing the child and less on concluding that the child was sexually abused. They illustrate that the legal distinction between ultimate facts and law might seem to be a matter of emphasis or nuance, but the court sometimes takes the distinction quite seriously. In a more perfunctory case (*People v. Roscoe*, 1985), the California Court of Appeals rejected expert testimony that equated the expert's opinion that the child was abused with an opinion that the child was telling the truth.

PROBLEM QUESTIONS

EXAMPLES OF POTENTIALLY UNANSWERABLE QUESTIONS

There have been many examinations of whether particular referral questions are unanswerable from the point of view of the legal system because of their potential inadmissibility (Ogloff, 1999). There might be a clinical answer or objective method of observing, describing and summarizing behavior without any corresponding legal merit in the probative value of the data. Sagatun (1991) provided an extensive list of questions that are of concern to the trier of fact. Oberlander (1995b) analyzed similar questions with respect to the level of inference required of the evaluator. When posed as referral questions, the questions might be considered problematic by the legal system depending upon the interpretation of the question, the methodology used to assess the question, the quality of supporting data, and the absolute versus flexible tone of the opinion that follows from such questions. As we have seen from the previous analysis of case law, no question is likely to be deemed inappropriate by the legal system in all circumstances. However, evaluators should be aware of the potential problems such questions pose. Sagatun's (1991) list includes the following questions:

1. What are the characteristics of abuse?
2. What are the behaviors commonly observed in sexually abused children?
3. Does the alleged victim have these characteristics and does the victim fit the profile of an abuse child?
4. Does the alleged offender fit an offender profile?
5. Is the child witness telling the truth?
6. Is the alleged perpetrator telling the truth?
7. Was the alleged victim actually abused or traumatized in some way?
8. Did the alleged offender commit the abuse?

It is apparent from the cases cited above that expert testimony on any of the above issues might or might not be deemed permissible. The court appears more divided on some issues (the admissibility of testimony that describes or makes diagnostic conclusions about symptoms and behaviors consistent with maltreatment) and heavily weighted in one direction on other issues (testimony that approximates or directly addresses whether a child witness is telling the truth). Even in cases in which courts seem heavily weighted in one direction, some testimony (e.g., the credibility of children's statements) of a more general nature might be permissible. A properly qualified expert may testify to the characteristics of child victims as a class. In most cases, such testimony may not be offered until a party to the case has challenged the assertion that the child was abused (Sagatun, 1991). Because of differences in the presence of physically observable data and diagnostic validity, case law on the admissibility of testimony (as a link to the occurrence of actual abuse of an individual child) relevant to child sexual abuse accommodation syndrome has not been as consistent as evidence of battered child syndrome (Myers et al., 1989; Sagatun, 1991).

Expert testimony presented by the prosecution on the typical characteristics of perpetrators of abuse or by the defense that the defendant does not fit that profile is more likely to be excluded (Myers et al., 1989; Oberlander, 1995b). The defendant, however, is usually allowed more latitude in demonstrating that he or she does not fit the profile of an abuser than the prosecution is allowed in demonstration he or she does fit the profile. Defendants sometimes are allowed to introduce evidence relevant to character and propensity to engage (or not engage) in sexually deviant behavior (Sagatun, 1991).

Provided that the evaluator has a meaningful discussion with the referring source to clarify the nature of the questions and the expectations of the referring party, none of the above questions are proscribed *per se*. However, in most circumstances both the clinical and legal utility of the evaluation will increase considerably if due attention is given to the potential probative value and admissibility of forensic mental health expertise (Ogloff, 1999). In initial discussions of referral questions, attention should be given to limiting the potential for capacious conclusions, limiting the potential for usurping the province of the trier of fact, or moving into the foray of irrelevance or unreliability of evaluation data. Most legal proscriptions of expert testimony in case law are based on testimony that adds little probative value, makes absolute conclusions, mimics statutory language or ultimate language too closely, or makes a judgment of the truthfulness of another witness.

Absolute proscriptions likely would erect an artificial barrier to relevant expert opinions and data (Bonnie & Slobogin, 1980). In child maltreatment cases, this might deprive the finder of fact of the most useful information that sometimes can be offered. The objections of scholars who believe mental health expertise is limited and that unrestricted testimony obscures the moral and social nature of questions of child maltreatment (see, e.g., Morse, 1978a, 1978b) usually can be circumvented with careful attention to specific referral questions designed to avoid the above concerns. Slobogin (1989) argues that the worth of expert testimony is largely a function of how it is presented, with opinions that are phrased as absolute or highly conclusive (such as an opinion of a defendant's guilt) being much more problematic than data-based and flexible conclusions that identify the strengths and weaknesses of the data that were relied upon.

Examples of Expansive Questions and Other Problems

Some scholars argue that no meaningful distinction can be made between descriptions and opinions, and that prioritizing one approach over the other unnecessarily broadens the field of inquiry. They contend that the sheer nature of legal proceedings involves grappling with extremely difficult judgments and decisions. The difficulty facing courts in applying an ultimate opinion rule is as complicated as trying to answer the question of "How many fish are needed to make a school?" and "At what moment does a sapling become a tree?" (Rogers & Ewing, 1989, p. 366). Evaluators must accept the likelihood that most questions of alleged child maltreatment will involve at least some degree of complexity. Framing a good referral question requires the evaluator and the referring party to strike a balance between the complexity of the legal goal of adjudicating questions of social and moral conduct and the clinical goal of providing meaningful and legally relevant clinical data.

Rogers and Ewing (1989) suggest that basic adherence to good ethical conduct is a suitable way to avoid expansive referral questions. Although they acknowledge that public perceptions of the magnitude of expert testimony problems and actual numbers of professionals engaging in misconduct are dissimilar, they point out that there is little empirical data on the actual number of professional who engage in misconduct. Examples of misconduct include: hired guns whose opinion and testimony is for sale, professional bias in attitudes toward the veracity of allegations of child maltreatment or perpetrators of maltreatment, and poor awareness of jurisdictional legal standards relevant to forensic assessment cases. They suggest that research on clinical judgment and decision-making might contribute to expansive questions if research is limited to linear models of assessing the accuracy of judgments. Such research obfuscates more credible analyses of the validity and reliability of the data and opinions of mental health professionals. They cite an example of the success of Endicott and Spitzer's (1974) use of specific criteria in forming professional judgments, as contrasted with studies that simply add variables to an equation to determine the most optimal false positive/false negative rates.

Another method of avoiding expansive evaluation questions is to view the evaluation as a consultation. Monahan and Walker (1988) suggested there are situations in which an attorney might wish to request the assistance of a mental health professional in preparing a written brief for the court rather than conducting an evaluation. This approach allows the introduction of what they termed *social authority*, or conclusions of empirical research, as contrasted with evaluation conclusions about case facts. The way that courts might evaluate empirical social sciences data would be similar to their evaluation of legal precedents. Social authority in briefs accepted by a higher court would have more weight than those accepted by a lower court, well-reasoned briefs would have more weight than poorly reasoned briefs. Briefs with empirical studies analogous to the facts of the present case, and social authority approved by other courts, would have more weight than those that have not yet met with approval.

One of the best strategies to avoid expansive, objectionable, disorganized or confused referral questions is to commit the referral questions and the evaluator's obligations to writing. Some evaluators include this information in their informed consent materials and others use specific service contracts that spell out the conditions of the referral; the referral questions; the expected behavior of the attorney, the evaluator, and the parties being evaluated; and the conditions under which the case is deemed completed or terminated (Kuehnle, 1996). In cases where the evaluator nonetheless feels under pressure to engage in evaluation procedures or testimony to which he or she did not agree at the outset, it is best to seek consultation from colleagues or from the evaluator's own attorney before proceeding further (Reynolds, Hays, & Ryan-Aredondo, 2001). Some strategic changes have no harmful effect on the integrity of the evaluation process. However, if the evaluator believes his or her conduct might be compromised in an ethically or legally inappropriate manner, seek consultation.

The Merits and Drawbacks of Stepwise Evaluation Questions

Stepwise evaluation questions involve conducting an assessment of one party in a bifurcated or trifurcated manner, addressing separate evaluation questions in a sequential manner. A typical case involves three brief evaluation reports that address separate issues that might otherwise be combined in a comprehensive assessment. The stepwise approach usually is undertaken for legally strategic reasons, although there sometimes might also be clinical reasons for addressing issues separately. The merits of a stepwise approach include extra time to carefully consider different facets of the case, ongoing consultation with planned feedback meetings between the referring attorney and the evaluator, sufficient initial information and time for an attorney to determine if he or she wants to open the evaluation process to discovery, and a lengthier rapport-building process prior to addressing difficult questions such as a parent's account of past abuse or description of their appraisal of parenting weaknesses.

Drawbacks to stepwise approaches include the possibility that an opinion might be committed to writing (e.g., in a first-step report that is limited to a diagnostic assessment of the parent) that might change if later responses to interview questions or new evaluation data (e.g., in a second-step phase that addresses risk of maltreatment) reveals new or different information relevant to the first step. Some evaluators find writing separate reports on the same party to be a cumbersome task. When opinions change, a report addendum adds clarity, but attachments sometimes are read hastily or misconstrued as opinion uncertainty. Where there is a lack of clarity or shared understanding of attorney/client privilege under such a strategy, the evaluation records and results might be successfully subpoenaed prior to completion of the stepwise process.

Avoiding an Expanded Role for the Expert

Experts sometimes are subjected to the potential misuse of data, reports, or testimony that were intended for a different clinical or forensic purpose (Oberlander, 1998). For example, evaluators in care and protection matters may be asked to provide, or to submit to cross examination of, information in parallel criminal proceedings. When evaluators work in the context of care and protection proceedings, it is important to take steps to avoid being drawn into a parallel criminal proceeding. Experts sometimes are expressly retained to render opinions relevant to allegations of child maltreatment in criminal matters. However, if the original referral took place in the context of a family court or child protective services matter, testimony in a parallel criminal proceeding usually ends up being both awkward and gratuitous.

Evaluators can seek protection from testifying in parallel criminal proceedings by requesting a court order in family or juvenile court that the evaluation results cannot be released for other purposes (Sattler, 1998). Such court orders should be requested prior to initiating the evaluation (some courts automatically provide such protection). Another way to avoid being drawn into criminal proceedings is to explain the clinical limitations of extrapolating from reports intended for other purposes to the party seeking to subpoena the evaluation report or the expert. Because criminal proceedings sometimes are placed on the docket more slowly than family or juvenile court matters, a third method is to make sure the party seeking to subpoena the evaluation report understands that some data become invalid with the passage of time (in legal lingo, this is known as a "cold" report).

Retaining the Integrity of Brief Evaluation Data and Conclusions

When an attorney and an evaluator agree to a brief evaluation approach, it is important to set limits on the expansion of the referral questions or the evaluation methodology (Azar, Lauretti, & Loding, 1998). Some evaluators form brief evaluation questions because of contractual limitations or obligations. For example, an agency might contract with child protective services to conduct specific evaluations that are highly focused on a particular and recurring evaluation question. An evaluator might work in a family or juvenile court clinic setting where the main goal is to settle the brief questions of the day rather than the overall questions of a case. Referral questions in such circumstances must be specific and focused.

It is important to have a mechanism for continually educating attorneys and the court about the benefits and limitations to brief evaluation approaches (Azar et al., 1998). When there is a mechanism for frequent and consistent interchange between referring and evaluating parties, brief evaluations, focused on limited facets of the case, can help move cases through the care and protection process and keep the court dockets moving. Without such a mechanism, there is potential for misuse of brief reports, misunderstanding of the goals of brief reports, and frustration with results that potentially address issues that are peripheral to the case. Brief evaluations that cease to be brief usually are too broad or too comprehensive to be useful in the limited time allotted to narrow petitions or less formal preliminary or procedural matters that are heard in family or juvenile court.

SUMMARY

1. Fundamental to the utility of care and protection evaluations and data interpretation is the process of forming an appropriate, legally and psychologically meaningful, manageable, and answerable referral question.
2. Because of the breadth of possible referral questions in care and protection matters, professional competence is needed across many domains: forensic assessment, child psychology, child development, parenting, the etiology of child maltreatment, the capacities of children to report maltreatment, the impact of maltreatment, psychological assessment, dissimulation and other influences on self report data, and amenability to treatment.
3. Admissibility standards are an important consideration in framing referral questions, choosing evaluation methodology, and interpreting data.
4. Jurisdictional differences in case law relevant to appropriate referral questions, admissibility standards, and discordance between statutory meanings and mental health meanings of particular terms of art have bearing on practice.
5. Problem referral questions typically can be reframed or rephrased to address the legal and practice standard concerns described in this chapter.
6. Fact finders appreciate a well reasoned but direct response to referral questions. However, appropriately derived inconclusive results or a response of, "I don't know," is not necessarily unhelpful to

the finder of fact. Cogency combined with a thoughtful response to the complexity of cases usually meets with a positive response from consumers of care and protection evaluation reports. In judging the utility of reports for fact finders, the logic used to arrive at a conclusion frequently carries more weight than the actual conclusion.

4

The Psychology of Parenting

Theory and supporting empirical research serve as an evaluation framework in care and protection matters. Although theory sometimes has only broad application to care and protection evaluations, it adds scientific integrity to the evaluation process. Theory facilitates the use of logic and reasoning that serve as a basis for interpretations and conclusions. Flaws in logic and reasoning are the subject of questions of clinical and forensic competence, challenges to the scientific integrity of the data and conclusions, and claims that the evaluation report is *void for vagueness*, a legal phrase for evidence or language that lacks meaningful substance or probative value. Theory serves as an organizing framework for explaining parental motivations and functioning, identifying factors associated with maltreatment, and determining whether factors associated with maltreatment can be modified with treatment or other interventions. Treatment outcome studies that are theoretically driven and empirically validated provide the basis for making judgments about prognosis.

THE FORENSIC RELEVANCE OF THEORY AND RESEARCH ON PARENTING

MACROSOCIAL AND MICROSOCIAL INFLUENCES OF THEORY

The child protective service system's ultimate focus in care and protection proceedings is to encourage the family to move toward a goal of reunification; or, when reunification is not feasible, to move toward a goal of adoption or some other form of permanent placement for the child. When the adoption goal is identified, it is usually because all other avenues have been exhausted or because maltreatment was so egregious that interventions did not seem justifiable. When the goal of adoption or permanent placement is formally identified, parents usually are presented with the option of voluntarily relinquishing their rights. Understandably, many parents decline such a request. Should they decline, the child protective service system then petitions the court to hold a termination proceeding. In order to move forward, there must be a sufficient evidentiary basis for holding a proceeding. The pre-termination phase is a point at which evaluation requests are popular because of evidentiary concerns. However, evaluation reports rarely stand alone as an evidentiary basis.

From an evidentiary view, the court is interested in issues of physical abuse, abandonment, physical and emotional neglect, sexual abuse, other forms of child maltreatment, current parental fitness, future fitness, sibling relationships, foster placements, guardianship plans, adoption plans, other placement decisions, visitation rights, and issues that interfere with parental fitness (criminal conduct, domestic violence, substance abuse and dependency, medical or physical disability, mental impairment or illness, or unavailability) (Kantrowitz & Limon, 2001). The role of biological, psychological, and social theories of parenting is not manifest in most legal proceedings, nor does theory have explicit bearing on rules for introducing evidence. At a macrosocial level, however, theories of parenting impel social policy, statutes and regulations relevant to child protective service systems. Theories drive policy in manifest and latent ways. For example, the impact of attachment theory on child protective services policies was seen in the 1950s and 1960s in the closing of large nurseries and orphanages as the first-choice solution for children whose parents could not care for them. Instead, there was increasing use of short- and long-term foster care (Rutter & O'Connor, 1999). From a theoretical and social perspective, one of the central tenets of child protective service system statutes and regulations is that parents have a profound influence of the development of their children. Parental influence on child development has been researched for decades (Lamb, 1999). The impact of child maltreatment is a somewhat more recent but heavily studied topic (Belsky, 1993a; Cassidy & Shaver, 1999).

At a microsocial level, theories of parenting behavior infuse specific care and protection cases. In some individual cases, there might be little manifest attention to theory and supporting empirical research. However, individual court actors (especially those serving in the capacity of expert witness) nonetheless tend to reach conclusions about cases based at least in part on social constructs of parenting behavior and theoretical notions of what constitutes a "good enough" parent. As we will see below, however, forensic reports in care and protection matters would benefit from a greater theoretical emphasis and less attention to societal assumptions about parenting (Lamb, 1999, Small, 1998). In some care and protection matters, theory and supporting research play a central role. Rarely, though, is theory the sole influence on a case outcome. Members of society hold deeply divergent beliefs about the nature of parenting, the role of families in society, the closed versus open nature of family life, methods of child rearing and discipline, and the very definition of what constitutes family life (Belsky, 1993a; Burchinal et al., 1996). Factors such as gender, religious affiliation, professional affiliation, political affiliation, socioeconomic status, age cohort, and culture influence views of family life (Zayas & Solari, 1994).

DEFINING FAMILY

Consensus on what constitutes family life is difficult to reach from a legal or theoretical perspective. The traditional norm of family life is illusory, existing primarily in social policies, theoretical models, and assumptions of legal scholars and social scientists about the societies, communities, or subcultures that are studied and observed (Cassidy & Shaver, 1999). Most legal and social science discussions traditionally have focused largely on the influence of middle-class nuclear family constellation on child development (Lamb, 1999). There have been many recent legal and social science challenges to notions of what constitutes a "traditional" or "nontraditional" family (Belsky, 1993b; Lamb, 1999). The belief in the nuclear family as an exemplar for raising psychologically healthy children reflect an incorrect assumption that modern family structures were historically common and preferable.

Although the nuclear family is not a historically stable phenomenon, the role of women as primary caretakers is remarkably stable. Social and anthropologic studies have illustrated that women have "always and everywhere" assumed primary responsibility for the care of very young children (Lamb, 1999). However, even historically stable family structures or factors can vary significantly under certain circumstances. This cultural and historical universal has not precluded the sometimes significant nurturing involvement of fathers and other caretakers, nor has it precluded a significant role for women in other activities such as subsistence provision (Lamb, 1999; Small, 1998).

Another cultural and historical universal is that family life traditionally has adapted to the changing face of ecological change (Lamb, 1999). Over time, human parenting behavior has been incredibly malleable. Adaptation occurs readily relative to other species. Even when biological predispositions are demonstrated in humans, they typically exist as tendencies that are highly subject to environmental influences (Small, 1998). In order to maintain objectivity in care and protection evaluations, it is essential to know prevailing theories, the cultural and historical constraints of theories, exceptions to theories, and deviations in special populations (Burchinal et al., 1996; Zayas & Solari, 1994).

Knowledge of theories of family life and diversity in family life helps the evaluator sift through the influence of individual and societal assumptions about family life across culture and across history. Attachment theory is prevalent because of its visibility and its empirically grounded conceptual framework. Attachment theory in the 21st century is similar in many ways to its original inception over 30 years ago (Bowlby, 1969; Cassidy & Shaver, 1999). As the theory has evolved, it has become more specific, it has extended in different directions, and it has encountered considerable criticism that ultimately promoted its further evolution (Cassidy, 1999). Today, attachment theory has an evolutionary or biologic component and a social interaction component, covering the span of broad bio-psycho-social theories. Other theories of parenting behavior, such as psychoanalytic and object relations theories, cognitive theory, behaviorism, and social interaction theory also are fairly robust and parsimonious (Bell et al., 1986; Geller & Johnston, 1995; Haskett et al., 1995; Peterson et al., 1997).

THE BIOLOGIC FEATURES OF PARENTING

Infants and children appear as they do for evolutionary reasons. Childhood is an evolved stage with a lengthy period of growth and development. The evolutionary mystery of the anatomy and behavior of children is full of puzzles such as why human babies cannot hold their heads up, why they cannot stand soon after birth, and why brain development persists after birth. Human babies share many characteristics of other primates such as head shape, primate teeth, color vision, good depth perception, flexible hands, and upper skeleton anatomy. The one distinct feature from other primates is the human pelvis, legs, and feet. They have been adapted to bipedalism (Martin, 1990; Small, 1998; Trevathan, 1987).

The parenting behavior of adults is evolutionarily driven by infant demands. Human babies are relatively helpless, focused primarily on food, sleep, eating, defecating, and seeking comfort. By contrast, fawns are *precocial* babies, characterized by several evolutionary features. They spend more time in the womb, they are more alert at birth with open eyes and the ability to control limbs and move about the environment, and their central nervous system is more advanced at birth relative to altricial infants (Dienske, 1986; Small, 1998). *Altricial* infants (such as mice) have small bodies at birth, small brains relative to body size and they are fast breeding, compared to the large bodies, big brains relative to body size, and slow breeding of precocial animals such as gorillas (Small, 1998; Tague & Lovejoy, 1986). They grow faster after birth. The size of the brain of a typical precocial baby is 4.5 times bigger than the typical altricial infant brain of the same body weight (Martin, 1990). Over the course of growth and development, the magnitude of brain to body size difference disappears. Outside the womb, the smaller brain grows almost three times as fast as the bigger brain of precocial animals. Both are alternative evolutionary paths to survival (Fleagle, 1988; Small, 1998).

Although classification schemes have some overlapping features, most primates are relatively precocial at birth (Muir, 2000). They cannot run from predators or feed themselves. They can explore with their eyes and hands and they are biologically predisposed to seek out their mothers' nipples and suckle soon after birth (Small, 1998). Humans are classified as *secondarily altricial* (Dienske, 1986). Human evolutionary ancestors were precocially adapted (large brains relative to body size) and then evolved some altricial traits because the brain, through selection, developed further than any other primate species (Muir, 2000). Because of the strong selection for increased brain tissues, which requires more calories to maintain than other types of tissue, human babies are born relatively earlier than other primate babies, with underdeveloped brains. Human infants are born without a mature central nervous system, lacking the neurological or central nervous system network to walk and talk (Small, 1998; Rutter & O'Connor, 1999). As a consequence, human infants are highly dependent and in constant need of care from their parents (Dienske, 1986; Small, 1998). Human gestation is a 21-month process, nine months in utero and twelve months post-natal (Martin, 1990). Because the placenta cannot do an adequate job of providing nutrition to the baby after the baby reaches a certain weight, human babies are evolutionarily impelled to birth after about a nine-month in utero gestation process (Muir, 2000; Small, 1998). Bipedalism also explains why human babies are born with underdeveloped brains. The architecture of the female human pelvis, as adapted to bipedalism, simply could not accommodate the size of a fully developed infant brain were childbirth to occur after a full period of brain gestation. The fontanels on the human infant brain are designed to mold the head as it moves through the pelvic passage (Small, 1998). Brain size in our evolutionary ancestors doubled several times over (Leutenegger, 1972; Small, 1998). The first member of the human genus, the *Homo habilis*, had an adult brain size of 750 cubic centimeters. About one million years later, the hominid brain doubled again, reaching its present average adult size of 1200 cubic centimeters (Small, 1998; Muir, 2000). Usually large-bodied animals have proportionally small infants and small-bodied animals have large-bodied infants. Human mammals are an exception, bearing rather large infants relative to maternal weight. Birth prior to full central nervous system development is an evolutionary accommodation to the necessary compromise between advanced brain tissue development and bipedalism (Leutenegger, 1972; Fleagle, 1988).

Human parenting is evolutionarily distinct from other mammals by its intensely social nature, its extended period, and the long-term affiliation between parents and offspring. Its duration and intensity is a major distinguishing mark of the human species relative to other primates (Rutter & O'Connor, 1999; Small, 1998). Natural selection demands mutual emotional and highly interactive needs between human parents and children. From an evolutionary standpoint, attachment between individuals who spend extensive amounts of time together makes sense. Humans, compared to other primates, recognize each other by sight and sound, touch, sit with, are preoccupied with, and follow each other about. The essence of attachment is the desire to be with one another, feeling comfortable with one another, and "falling in love." *Attachment* describes a mutual process (although the mutuality might not be symmetrical, see Ainsworth, 1989), whereas *bonding* is more specific to one person's reaction to another within a dyad. The bonding construct nonetheless characterizes an interactional and interdependent dyadic process (Sperling & Berman, 1994).

The term bonding describes behaviors that occur within a specific period of time (usually in the first month of infancy). Nature has selected for parent-infant bonding because of the necessity of selecting an evolutionary process that preserves the lives of dependent infants. Parents and infants are impelled by evolution to bond so that the parent will feed and protect the infant and so that the infant will seek proximity to the parent in order to be fed and protected (Small, 1998). The parent to child bond has been taken for granted by society to such a degree that, until recently, few members of society or scientific scholars questioned its nature or deviations from it (Bowlby, 1969, 1973, 1980; Bowlby et al., 1956; Sperling & Berman, 1994).

PRONATALIST BEHAVIOR

Imprinting and Bonding

The term *bond* or *bonding* was coined in the 1930s by a group of European ethologists in their research on how imprinting works across different avian species. *Imprinting* describes an evolutionary process whereby a newly hatched gosling or chick focuses on the first thing it sees after hatching and follows it around. The bond is established primarily by the infant as it seeks proximity during the critical imprinting period (Small, 1998; Trevathan, 1987). After the passing of the critical period, the newborn cannot be persuaded to attach to any other object. The bond typically is made with an adult animal that can provide food and protection (Lorenz, 1935), most often it is the mother. For altricial animals, who are more physically dependent, it is the mother or other adult who establishes the bond with the infant (Trevathan, 1987). Cellular and molecular studies have begun to reveal the mechanisms and regulations of neural pathways by which oxytocin and vasopressin influence complex social behaviors such as pair bonds and parental behavior (Insel, 1997).

Oxytocin and vasopressin are found exclusively in mammals and are implicated in prototypically mammalian functions. Oxytocin has an important role in uterine contraction during labor and milk production and ejection during nursing. Vasopressin has a more general influence on the maintenance of overall health, but in males it also has been implicated in the regulation of attachment behavior and post-mating aggression. Animal studies (prairie voles) have shown that they are important in promoting monogamous behavior, forming a partner preference, mating, reproduction, paternal aggression toward predators, maternal care, and recognition of offspring (Insel, 1997). In addition to hormonal influences, proximity over time is an important feature in animal studies (Insel, 1997). Mothers must be exposed to their newborns within minutes of birth in order for imprinting (which in this case consists of smells and appearances) to occur (Lorenz, 1935; Klopfer, 1971). Without the opportunity for post-birth contact, mothers will reject their newborns even if they are returned within hours (Klopfer, 1971). Evolutionary theory explains this process because of selection based on the threat of misidentification in large herds (Small, 1998).

Theories of Human Bonding

Early theories of human bonding postulated that hunger and relief from pain and discomfort were the mechanisms for attachment. The mother's response to the infant drives and behavior was explained by the experience of pleasure and the reinforcement of the maternal role of provider, nurturer, and protector (Freud, 1910, 1957; Trevathan, 1987). In the 1960s, a series of studies demonstrated that bonding was not solely the result of associations with feeding (Ainsworth, 1967; Harlow, 1962). Harlow showed that food and relief from physical discomfort had little to do with the development of the mother-infant bond. Harlow placed newborn rhesus monkeys in a cage with two artificial "mothers." Both artificial mothers were constructed of wire and wood with fake monkey faces. One was equipped with nipples that delivered milk and the other was covered in terry cloth. In a series of repeated tests, the newborn monkeys sporadically nursed from the milk-producing mother but spent the majority of their time clinging to the terry cloth mother. Harlow demonstrated the tendency of rhesus monkeys to seek comfort is profound in relation to the tendency to seek sustenance (Harlow, 1962; Harlow & Harlow, 1965). Moreover, when the motherless rhesus monkeys grew to adulthood, their capacity for mothering was socially inept and inadequate because they never bonded with their own mothers. Harlow and Harlow (1965) concluded that the parent-infant bond is a blueprint from which all other attachments develop and are modeled.

Bowlby (1969) hypothesized that attachment behavior grew out of the initial parent-child bond. He described it as the predictable outcome of frequent parent-child proximity. From an evolutionary standpoint, Bowlby (1969, 1973) postulated that humans lived in an environment favoring genetic selection of attachment because of the intertwined relationship between infant dependency and parent-child proximity. Proximity increased the likelihood of protection of the infant and therefore survival of the species. Attachment was a natural extension of dependency and proximity. The biological purpose of proximity-seeking behavior was the lowered probability that a predator would kill an infant located close to its mother. The socioemotional and interactional function of proximity-seeking behavior grew out of evolutionary adaptations that allowed constancy and stability of parent-infant relationships over time (Bowlby, 1980).

Attachment and Bonding

Evolutionary Sources of Attachment and Bonding

In explaining attachment, Bowlby (1969) borrowed the concepts of bonding and behavioral systems from ethology and broadened them into a social interaction realm. Moving away from drive theory toward a theory of inherent motivation, he illustrated that children became attached to parents whether or not the parents met their physiological needs (Bowlby, 1956). The *behavior system* that is encapsulated by the construct of attachment is not a specific set of constant or uniform behaviors. It is a variety of behaviors that might differ across specific populations and across the course of child development, but the behaviors have similar meaning and serve similar functions (Sroufe & Waters, 1977). Behavioral systems are defined by the following features: (a) a variety of behavior is coordinated to achieve a specific goal and adaptive function; (b) goal directed behaviors are activated and terminated by endogenous and environmental cues; (c) behaviors are goal corrected or modified in a nonrandom fashion, adapted to a wide range of environmental and developmental changes; (d) behaviors are guided biologically by a feedback system that monitors internal and environmental cues that stimulate activation and termination; (e) behaviors become integrated over time as they serve functions that achieve the goal; and (f) behaviors are organized and integrated by cognition or mental representations in humans (Bowlby, 1969; Hinde, 1982; George & Solomon, 1999). The behavior system perspective of proximity-seeking and attachment contributes to the flexibility of attachment theory across time and context. Infants and children achieve the same goals of seeking proximity and protection using different behaviors in different contexts and at different ages, usually preferring the most efficient and effective behaviors achieved at their developmental level in a specific context (Cassidy, 1999).

Attachment (also described as the attachment bond) as defined by Ainsworth (1989) is part of a larger class of affectional bonds. It is different from bonding in its persistence, its specificity, its emotional significance, the level of actual or desired proximity with the person, the level of distress at involuntary separation, the emotional discomfort that is felt even when separation is voluntary, and the tendency to seek security and comfort from that person. According to Bowlby (1969), seeking security or protection, the defining feature of attachment behavior, is central to the notion that attachment is principally a child-to-adult phenomenon. Bowlby (1969) postulated that infants seek security because it is a characteristically human socio-biological behavior. The parental response creates an interactional attachment process. Bowlby (1956) demonstrated that children become attached even to abusive parents.

Behavioral Indicators of Attachment

Infants show attachment by approaching, following, clinging, seeking contact, crying, smiling, and calling. Attachment begins in the first month of life. One-month-old infants show signs of distress, such as irregular sleeping or eating patterns, if a stranger cares for them. But for the most part, infants are quite flexible in the first six months, willing to let any attentive person hold or feed them. Attachment becomes more observable in 6- to 15-month-old infants, when they hold onto familiar people and cry when they leave. At 15 months it is even more apparent and then its observable effects begin to taper off. In the middle of the second year, infants are more likely to search for their mothers than to cry. At 24 months, children show relatively little distress when mothers leave, but they seem delighted when they return (Ainsworth & Bell, 1974).

Attachment is not exclusively embodied by observable behavior (Cassidy, 1999). The existence of attachment cannot be inferred solely from the presence or absence of a set of behaviors. Most characteristic attachment behaviors also serve other behavioral systems. Proximity-seeking behavior in a child does not always indicate attachment. Not every approach serves the goal of attachment, for example, it might reflect exploration or socialization (Ainsworth et al., 1978; Sroufe & Waters, 1977). It is possible for an infant to seek proximity to strangers; however, the "strange situation" (described below) reveals that comfort from strangers toward distressed babies is not as satisfying as that provided by a mother in secure infants (Ainsworth et al., 1978). Similarly, a child might direct proximity-seeking behavior toward a friend or relative in the absence of a parent, but the significance of the relationship with that individual might not reflect attachment. Loss of that individual does not have the devastating effects on the child as the loss of a strong attachment figure. Observation periods that contain no proximity-seeking behavior do not necessarily mean there is no attachment between the child and the adult. A contented child in comfortable surroundings might show few proximity-seeking behaviors. Freedom to explore away from the mother or other adult might reflect a healthy security in an attachment relationship. The strength or presence of attachment behaviors *per se* in a discrete period of observation is not tantamount to the strength of the attachment (Cassidy, 1999). The construct of *penetration* (Hinde, 1979) characterizes the centrality of one person to the child's life regardless of the context-dependent and time-dependent strength or intensity of attachment. Penetration explains the changing nature of attachment as a child grows older (Ainsworth, 1989).

The Capacity for Multiple Attachments

Infants have the capacity to form multiple attachments, with most forming more than one attachment (Bowlby, 1969; Ainsworth, 1967). In most instances, the mother's attachment figure role is clear. The father, especially when sensitively responsive, also tends to become an additional attachment figure early in the infant's life (Cox, Owen, Henderson, & Margant, 1992). Siblings (Stewart & Marvin, 1984; Teti & Ablard, 1989) and day care providers sometimes serve as attachment figures. There is a limit to the number of attachment figures that the infant can incorporate. Infants develop a small hierarchy of attachment figures, distinct from the larger group of individuals with whom the infant interacts (Weintraub, Brooks, & Lewis, 1977). The hierarchy of attachment figures and the distinction from other relationships is determined by the infant's distress response to separation and loss (Tracy, Lamb, & Ainsworth, 1976) and a selective preference, or *monotropy*, or a principle attachment figure for comfort and security (Bowlby, 1965).

Monotropy can be seen in infants when they are given an opportunity to select a special caregiver of their own (Burlingham & Freud, 1944). Monotropy and the hierarchy of attachment are seen in how much time the infant spends in each attachment figure's care, the quality of care provided, each adult's emotional investment in the child, and repeated presence across time of the attachment figures in the child's life. In an evolutionary context, the probability of infant survival is enhanced if one individual takes principle responsibility for the child. It ensures that care of the child is not overlooked. When faced with danger, the child does not have to assess or judge who might be most available, most responsive, or best suited to help (Cassidy, 1999).

The Origins of Sensitivity in Attachment Figures

Evolutionary theory would suggest that parents must shift perspective away from being protected and toward providing protection (George & Solomon, 1999). Evolutionary theory uses an ethological behavioral systems approach to explain the motivations underlying parenting, critical aspects of parenting, parental sensitivity, parent-child conflict, flexibility in parenting behavior, and cultural deviations in caregiving (Klopfer, 1971). Both sensitivity and conflict are inherent aspects of parent-child relationships because individual behavior is the product of the interaction among multiple behavioral systems. A parent, in addition to being a caregiver for a particular child, might be a caregiver to other children, a friend, a sexual partner, a worker, a relative, and a child to his or her own parents (George & Solomon, 1996, 1999). Parental behavior is constrained by environmental factors such as the availability of resources, cultural norms, and individual factors (Belsky, 1999). Flexibility within behavioral systems allows parents to adapt to the lessening demands of children as they develop from infancy through toddlerhood and into childhood and adolescence. Flexibility also contributes to the selection of behaviors that adapt to changes in environmental and cultural demands (Kermoian & Liederman, 1986).

The *assimilation model*, endorsed by most attachment theorists, suggests that caregiving is the developmental outcome of early attachment experiences (Bowlby, 1969; Bretherton, 1985). *Assimilation* is the process by which new experiences and information are integrated into existing mental representations of human behavior and behavioral systems. Empirical studies of the process of assimilation have focused on the strong correspondence between mothers' mental representations of attachment behavior systems and the quality of their infants' attachments to them (George & Solomon, 1999). The mechanism for intergenerational transmission of attachment and caregiving behavior systems is maternal *sensitivity*, but the construct of sensitivity may not be specific to mothers. Empirically, there has been little research on sensitivity in fathers and other caregivers and its relationship to the quality of caregiver-child relationship. Lamb (1997) demonstrated that fathers are capable of sensitivity (as defined in the assimilation model). Other research has demonstrated mother/father differences in the predictive impact of sensitivity on parent-child relationship quality (Belsky, 1993b). Much research on the construct of sensitivity, the assimilation model, and attachment theory has focused on mother-child relationships. Less is known about the fidelity of the theory as it applies to other caregiver-child relationships.

Ainsworth's Typology of Attachment

Although the construct of sensitivity traditionally has had a predominant place in assimilation models, a multidimensional approach would suggest the modest correlation between maternal sensitivity and quality of caregiver-child relationships is explained by its predominant but nonexclusive influence on the relationship. Classification schemes illustrate a variety of attachment outcomes, based on the quality of maternal sensitivity. Ainsworth developed a typology of attachment, classifying children as secure and insecure in their attachment to caregivers. Later research that expanded on her work added *resistant/avoidant*, *anxious/ambivalent*, and *controlling/disorganized* attachments to the typology (Ainsworth & Bell, 1974). Caregiver sensitivity is related to a child's development of secure relationships with attachment figures (Ainsworth & Bell, 1974), and it is especially important for temperamentally reactive or behaviorally inhibited infants in their development of secure attachments (Suomi, 1995). Ainsworth's typology of attachment in infants and toddlers focuses on observations of caregiver-child interactions and the quality of peer relationships later in childhood. The typology has been used as a classification scheme in studies of attachment outcomes (Belsky, 1996; Fagot & Pears, 1996; Souldice, & Stevenson-Hinde, 1992). *Secure* attachment develops when the child's security needs consistently are met with acceptance and warmth. The child learns to express needs fluently, confidently and calmly. The child develops the capacity to temporarily tolerate security distress. The *resistant* or *avoidant* pattern develops when security distress consistently is met with rejection from the attachment figure. The child learns to avoid expressing security needs. There is less positive reciprocity in the relationships of resistant or avoidant children. The *ambivalent* pattern develops when the attachment figure responds to security needs inconsistently. The child learns to over-express needs in order to increase the probability of a response. The *controlling/disorganized* pattern develops when the attachment figure is unable to exercise adequate parental control or is in some way frightened of or frightening to the child. Infants and toddlers classified as disorganized tend to become controlling in later peer relationships (Ainsworth & Bell, 1974).

Other Influences on Attachment

Sensitivity, although prominent, is but one aspect of multidimensional parenting behavior. Belsky (1999) emphasized other influences on the caregiver-child relationship, such as parental personality, child temperament, and contextual features such as the parents' marriage. Central to the ethological view, however, is the development of the caregiving system, a set of complex biological and experiential interactions. Behavioral systems begin with immature forms of behavior that are developed and integrated into organized, flexible, and mature behavior. Infant behavioral systems that are essential to survival (attachment and feeding) develop quickly. Behavioral systems important later in life to the survival of the species (sexuality and caregiving) develop and mature more slowly (George & Solomon, 1999). Precursors to mature behavioral systems can be observed before the system has reached maturity. They differ in quality, organization, integration, goal-directedness, and discrimination of stimuli activating caregiving (Bowlby, 1969). Children show "play-mothering" behavior in childhood, especially around infants, infant animals, other animals, and dolls. However, their behavior is fragmented and the behavioral sequences are incomplete. They are easily distracted in ways that might place an actual baby in jeopardy of survival. The behavior also is dependent on the child's experiences of maternal care. Play-mothering does not occur, for example, in rhesus monkeys who are isolated from their mothers in the first year of life (Pryce, 1995). In many cultures, mothers tutor older children in the care for younger ones. In some cultures, siblings take on major responsibility for the care of younger siblings. There have been no studies of whether early caregiving experience hastens the maturity of the caregiving behavioral system. The shift in adolescence to maturity of the caregiving system corresponds to biological changes associated with puberty. Hormonal influences on mammalian and primate mothering initiate the adolescent transition toward maturity of the caregiving system. Although cultural mores and taboos influence the average age of first pregnancy in girls and women, many older adolescent girls (ages 17 to 19) show remarkable interest in and thoughtfulness toward mothering (George & Solomon, 1999).

What Causes Parents to Provide Care and Make Personal Sacrifices for Their Children

The caregiving system undergoes relatively rapid developmental maturation during pregnancy through the months following birth. The qualitative shift for mothers is accompanied by intense hormonal and neurological changes. Hormones have an important but not exclusive role in producing sensory acuity, emotional calm, and emotional closeness to infants (Fleming et al., 1995). There is an upsurge of thoughts and worries about parenting that promote self reorganization. Hormonal changes during childbirth influence the reorganization in the promotion of contact-seeking behavior immediately following birth (Klaus, Kennell, & Klaus, 1995). Hormonal factors (Insel, 1997) interact with other variables to sustain the attachment. The opportunity for extended closeness enhances maternal sensitivity, especially for mothers at risk. It has a less robust relationship to later mother-child attachment. The experiences that a mother brings to her baby's birth, her representation of herself as a caregiver, her interpretation of the birth experience, and her experience of the birth itself interact to influence the caregiving system (Klaus et al., 1995).

The influence of the baby on the caregiving system is transactional (bidirectional and dynamic, or nonlinear), influenced by infant characteristics, parent characteristics and mental representations of attachment (George & Solomon, 1999). Infant characteristics such as physical attractiveness (Langlois, Ritter, Casey, & Sawin, 1995), distinctive emotional expressions (Suiomi, 1995), cries and other vocalizations (Leger, Thompson, Merritt, & Joseph, 1996), frequent opportunity for physical contact (Klaus et al., 1995), and infant temperament (Belsky & Rovine, 1987) influence caregiving behavior. *Temperament* is a construct describing the infant's emotional reactivity, degree and frequency of psychomotor arousal, and capacity for regulation (George & Solomon, 1999). It is related to caregiving behavior, but it only indirectly influences the type of attachment that develops (secure versus insecure) (Belsky & Rovine, 1987). The mother's perception of the infant and her perception of the mother-child relationship are prominent factors (Egeland & Farber, 1984; Pianta, Marvin, Britner, & Borowitz, 1996). Social and contextual variables can enhance or compete with caregiver-child relationships. The mother's partnership with the baby's father or another co-parent influences ability to provide care, but relationship satisfaction alone is not a strong predictor of mother-child attachment (Cobb, Davila, & Bradbury, 2001). High interparental conflict and low interparental communication is a more robust predictor of mother-child attachment. It is especially predictive of disorganized attachments (George & Solomon, 1999).

The caregiving behavioral system is guided by a set of cognitive or representational schemata related to providing care (George & Solomon, 1999). Behavioral systems are regulated in the mind by working mental representations or cognitive models that continually evaluate, emotionally appraise and organize (or reorganize) experiences (Bowlby, 1969). Attachment classification predicts parental mental representations of caregiving. Parents classified as having secure parent-child attachments tended to be flexible in their mental representations of caregiving, and realistic about potential threats to child security. They had the capacity to evaluate caregiving in relationship to a specific situation, the child's personality and developmental needs, personal child-rearing goals, and the needs of the parent. Parents classified as having an avoidant or ambivalent attachment to their children evaluated themselves or their children as unwilling or unworthy, emphasized the negative aspects of interactions, and dismissed or devalued their children's attachment needs. Parents classified as having ambivalent parent-child attachments tended to promote dependency, but they appeared insensitive to cues from their children. They had difficulty integrating the positive and negative, or desirable and undesirable aspects of situations. Uncertainty and confusion clouded the quality of their appraisal of situations. Although the mental representations differed across parent groups, three groups nonetheless provided "good enough" protection and care (George & Solomon, 1996; 1999). Mothers in secure mother-child relationship found a way to balance the child's needs with those of the mother. Mothers with a rejecting pattern of mental representations and behavior tended to prioritize their needs over the child's needs (for example enrolling the child in activities or putting someone else in charge so they could pursue their needs), but they were not oblivious to the child's needs. Mothers with an uncertain pattern of mental representations and behavior tended to prioritize the child's needs over their needs (for example, scheduling employment hours or errands to occur when the child was in school or asleep), but they did not completely sacrifice their needs. In summary, biologic theories of parenting behavior focus on attachment and caregiving behavioral systems (Brazelton, 1981; George & Solomon, 1996, 1999). The desire and ability to provide protection is the central organizing feature of the caregiving system. Sensitivity to a child's need for protection is a potent predictor of non-abusive parenting (George & Solomon, 1999).

THE PSYCHOLOGICAL FEATURES OF PARENTING

Psychoanalytic Theories of Parenting

Sigmund Freud described the process by which an individual becomes a conduit for cultural inheritance and reiterates or relives biological and historical phenomena (Freud, 1927/1961). Later psychoanalytic and ego analytic theoreticians described alienation between generations and its influence on parenting (Benedek, 1970). The family is viewed as a *psychological field* and development is viewed as a *transactional* process between parents and children (Coburn, 2000). Psychoanalytic theory shares this view of transactional process with evolutionary theorists, but it adds social (or triangulated) and individual (or personality) dimensions. The core of the psychological field of family is the mother and father, who bring their personalities and developmental histories to the relationship triangle with the infant (Offerman-Zuckerberg, 1992). The marital couple becomes a system, with each personality representing a subsystem (Benedek, 1970). The transactional system involves unconscious communication, reflected in processes such as affect attunement, emotional resonance, and empathy. Within the nonlinear dynamic system, transactional processes subsume both social and neurobiological aspects of parent-to-parent and parent-to-child interaction in the context of mutual and reciprocal influences (Beebe & Lachmann, 1994; Coburn, 2000).

Freud differentiated two kinds of object love between adults. *Anaclitic* love is modeled after a child's need for a parent who feeds, provides and protects. *Narcissistic* love is the search for the idealized self or the ego ideal.

Attraction between two individuals sets in motion a process of the search for need fulfillment and idealization (Freud, 1923/1961). Through cathexis and anticathexis (a mutual flowing back and forth of gratification and repetition of gratification, each object introjects the other, becoming a part of a mutual self-system of the other (Benedek, 1970; Freud, 1923/1961). An intersubjective third (or the "us" of a relationship) develops, blurring the intrapsychic distinction between anaclitic and narcissistic love (Freud, 1937/1981). Over the course of a successful relationship, mature love is described as the complex attainment of dynamic reorganization of the ego within the individual and the intersubjective experiences of the couple (Stolorow, Brandshaft, & Atwood, 1987). Common ambitions, desires, children, achievement of goals, and frustration of goals all serve to strengthen the identification between marital partners (whether the identification is positive or negative). The depth of identification is the product of the original intensity of needs that brought the couple together and that gives the relationship its exclusive significance even after sexual passions have declined. The sexual partnership might endure, but the relationship becomes desexualized as the mutual need fulfillment reaches greater depth and significance than the sexual drives that were part of the process that originated the relationship (Benedek, 1970).

Introjection and Identification

Love matures in the context of a transactional process. Two individuals in love begin with suspense and frustration accompanied by a decline of self esteem as they experience regression and fear of rejection of their needs. They recover through increasing and mutually gratifying love. The love matures through bidirectional, but uneven, need fulfillment as they gradually embrace the introjected images of the other (Benedek, 1970). The process of introjection includes the expression of needs, need fulfillment, frustration of some needs, and recapitulated memories (Ferenczi, 1993). Emotionally corrective experiences form and alter the introjected image of the other through bidirectional nonlinear dynamic system processes. The gradual desexualization of passionate love leads to identification between partners who share life situations, children and goals, and a deeper stratum of their personalities. The gradual "us" that emerges in the intersubjective third is a product of the fundamental processes of object relations—introjection and identification—and their influence on personality organization (Stolorow et al., 1987). Introjection and identification are primary processes by which the mental structures of personality develop (Ferenczi, 1993). Their structure and dynamic changes are supported by the memory traces of the confluence of biologic drive motivations and life experiences of need expression and fulfillment (and frustration). They are the bridges between biology and personality, and between personality and social functioning (Benedek, 1970).

To illustrate the process of introjection, consider the mother-infant relationship and the biologic drive of hunger. The relationship begins with an ambivalent core. The parent must resolve the drive to protect the infant with the fear of inadequacy of protection capabilities (related to intrapsychic memory traces of vulnerability and dependency in childhood). The hunger drive is a biological need, potentially satisfied by the search for the mother. The nursing infant satisfies the hunger drive by stimulating the breast of the mother, relieving tension from the accumulated milk and stimulating further production of milk. The mother provides food that leads to gratification or satiation of the need (Benedek, 1970; Klein, 1980). Other olfactory, tactile, auditory, and visual needs are submerged in the experience of hunger. The repetition of the feeding experience results in the introjected "pleasant feeding mother" image. Memory traces of discomfort and pain introject a painful, angry or "bad" mother image. If the mother does not satisfy the child's hunger needs, the child becomes frustrated (angry and crying). Those behaviors affect the mother's experience, which becomes one of a "frustrating and bad" mother. Through a series of reciprocal interactions, the baby develops object representations of a "good" or "bad" mother and self representations of a "good" or "bad" self (Fonagy, 1999). The behaviors are recapitulated, they merge with the self, and the object representations and self-representations become established in a relatively inseparable connection of reciprocal interactions, creating structural and dynamic personality changes in both participants. Over time the infant develops confidence, an intrapsychic experience that acts as an organizer of later object relations through a gradual differentiation between the infant and the mother. The process builds on itself in a symbiotic manner as a thriving infant symbolizes good mothering and good mothering stimulates the infant to thrive and develop confidence. As the infant develops confidence, the mother gains self confidence, resolving internal conflicts with her mother and conquering the fear of mothering (Benedek, 1970; Fonagy & Target, 1997).

Confidence and the *ambivalent core* are primary structures that interact throughout the development of the child's personality, continually modified by the emotional symbiosis between parent and child (Klein, 1980; Sandler & Sandler, 1998). The process is triangulated by concurrent transactional processes between father and mother, mother and child, and father and child. The triangulated transactional processes lead to many reciprocal processes, inducing intrapsychic or personality changes in each of the participants according to their level of maturity, their drive-motivated needs, the closeness of the drive to its physiologic source, the complexity of the drive as it relates to memory traces of earlier drives and need frustration or fulfillment, and the function of needs in a particular interaction (Benedek, 1970). Parenting is a parallel confluence of unconscious drives and conscious attempts to work through past intrapsychic and intrafamilial conflicts (Offerman-Zuckerberg, 1992).

Depending on the school of thought, the primacy of the processes of introjection, identification, confidence and the ambivalent core may have more or less importance as fundamental processes by which parenting and other behaviors are influenced, shaped, reorganized or thwarted (Winnicott, 1971). Most psychoanalytic theories agree, however, that most individuals attempt to undo and redo, and to reenact and recreate the parenting experiences that the individual wished for or the child that the individual wishes to have. Children provide the opportunity for parents to work through pain, deprivations and limitations of past experiences (Fonagy, 1999).

Need Fulfillment

The goal of providing for and protecting children is embedded in need fulfillment and instinctual behavior (Freud (1923/1961). The need to reenact or recreate the parenting experience is what drives parental behavior (Fonagy, 1999). Parenthood provides the opportunity to turn wishes into a reality that shapes a child's life (Offerman-Zuckerberg, 1992). The instinctive aspect of parental behavior is energized by procreative influences and hormonal stimulation during and after pregnancy (Sandler, Holder, Dare, & Dreher, 1997). Gradually, hormonal and emotional symbiosis between parent and child evolve into a less physically dependent and more interactional process. The energy that propels ongoing communication between parent and child is that of empathy. Empathy is a specific human quality that enables the individual to sublimate biological processes. *Sublimination* is the translation of instinctual desires to higher aims. *Empathy* is an energy charge from within the unconscious that directs the ego's attention and facilitates perceptions, mental representations and behavior toward a further integration of needs, wishes, and biological and emotional symbiosis (Benedek, 1970). Intrapsychic conflicts are worked through when the intrapsychic energy of empathy finds synergy and exerts control over ego functions whose aim is to provide for and protect the child. Synergy manifests itself in appropriate boundaries between adult and child, whereas unresolved conflict often is reflected in inappropriate boundaries (physical and emotional closeness or distance that is painful at an emotional and intrapsychic level) (Stolorow et al. 1987).

The intrapsychic flow of empathy is best described in relative terms in its degree of conscious versus unconscious process (Offerman-Zuckerberg, 1992). Nearly every parent has the startling experience of hearing the words of their own mother or father when speaking to their child. Parents vary in the degree to which they acknowledge such remembrances. Recapitulations or repetitions are a familiar and ubiquitous aspect of parenting (Slade & Cohen, 1996). When the concurrent symbiotic biologic and emotional processes produce relatively accurate empathic thoughts, perceptions, and emotions, the protective responses of the parents fulfill the safety needs of the child and the sublimated need for emotionally corrected parent-child experiences for the adult (Stolorow et al., 1987). Within the child, and with each child in a different way, the parents unconsciously (and sometimes purposefully) relive aspects of their developmental histories. The child gratifies significant aspirations by enlarging the scope of parental personalities and identities. The child's identity is shaped and formed. The triangle of father, mother, and child represents the psychological field that supports the individual development of each participant (Benedek, 1970).

Adult Development and Identity

The parents' investment in the child brings about reciprocal intrapsychic processes that promote developmental changes in the parents' personalities (Mahler & McDevitt, 1980). Transitions are reflected in the maturing of empathy, maintenance of boundaries, healthy or positive translations of introjected images into self representations, use of sublimation as a primary defenses, and symbiosis and identification that is followed at an appropriate time by *separation and individuation* (Mahler, Pine, & Bergman, 1975). The intrapsychic processes that promote development also appear as adult developmental outcomes. Although the capacity for empathy exists from infancy, mature or accurate empathy results from developmental transitions in adulthood. The symbiotic parent-child form of mature empathy molds the parent's identity and stimulates the internalization of self representations of parenting. From the mental wish to reenact or recreate the parenting experience and from the intrapsychic energy of empathy comes the ability to effectively understand the child through feeling, thinking, sensing and intuiting. The experience of accurate empathy comes without fearing a loss of boundaries or perceiving a threat to one's own identity (Stolorow et al., 1987). The experience of empathy, even in its healthiest manifestations, sometimes transforms into guilt when needs conflict. For example, parents sometimes experience internal conflicts over whether to prioritize the child's needs or their needs (Offerman-Zuckerberg, 1992). The accuracy of empathy (coupled with attachment, predictability and constancy) is a determining factor in the eventual emergence of a solid identity in the child (Mahler & McDevitt, 1980), but it also promotes the development of a positive self representation in the adult (Offerman-Zuckerberg, 1992).

Healthy transitions in adult development and identity are based in the negotiation of relationship boundaries (Stolorow et al., 1987). In addition to primary and permanent triangles or relationship triads, there are transient subtriads (formed between the child with relative primacy accorded to one or the other parent) and supertriads (that include outside members or extrafamilial forces). The persistence and significance of groupings is determined by the level of current problems within the family, developmental transitions within and across the members of the original triangle, transitions in the triangle as a whole, and the eventual need for separation and individuation of the child (Mahler et al., 1975). The whole system and the hierarchical ordering of its subsystems and supersystems evolve with time, development, conflicts and transitions. Tension usually recedes into the background, but the continuity of the triangle is disrupted if one member of the family departs in a significant way or dies (Benedek, 1970).

Chronic relationship tension may induce ego distortions that yield a less healthy system of defense against negative self representations (Winnicott, 1965). Ego distortions can have the same effect as unexpected separation or death, disrupting the child's development of an individual identity and tolerance of separation from attachment figures (Mahler et al., 1975). Disruptions to introjection, identification, accurate empathy, maintenance of appropriate boundaries, and/or sublimation alter caretaking behavior. They delay or alter expected changes and transitions in the adult's development and identity. Compromised caretaking behavior (most notably in provision and protection) accompanies the disruptions (Mahler et al., 1975). Research has shown that the quality of integration of parent-child memory traces affects the quality of caregiving (Slade & Cohen, 1996).

Stern (1994) expanded on the concepts of separation and individuation and the representational world. He described the construct of the *emerging moment*, a subjective integration of all aspects of lived experience, with input from emotions, behaviors, sensations, and schematic representations of the internal and external world. The infant organizes experience around the motives and goals of biology and object relations. Other influences in the moment include affective states, self esteem, safety, and gratification of physical needs. The caregiver responds in the context of multiple and simultaneous representations of the lived experience, basing behavior and responses on prototypes that are less affected by any single experience. The response is based on aggregated common patterns of lived experience. Modifications in lived experience are internally or externally generated (Stern 1985, 1994). Stern's conceptions mirror attachment theory constructs of mental representations, but the process is thought to be more idiosyncratic and thus not as empirically robust. However, some of Stern's work lends itself to empirical demonstration because of the careful integration of infant observations studies with constructs related to interpersonal development (Fonagy, 1999).

Internal Conflict Resolution

Negative behavior in the child forces the parent to confront what he or she dislikes within the self system (or in significant past or present object relations). Depending on the level of awareness and maturity of responses to interpersonal and intrapsychic conflict, the parent might react with a regressed or a mature pattern of behavior. If ego boundaries are weakened by the conflict and its associated memory traces, the angry parent might identify with the angry child, opposing rather than educating the child. If ego boundaries are strengthened by the conflict, the parent consciously enters the role of educator, responding in a productive way to repressed or remembered significant events of the parent's developmental history (Benedek, 1970). The relationship continuously evolves in a symbiotic manner, with the secure child anticipating a particular and consistent parental reaction to behavior and the mature parent responding to the child's developing and changing capacity for behavior control. Intrapsychic conflict might produce transient or chronic regressions. The degree of regression is related to the degree to which the protective aspects of parenting behavior are compromised (Balint, 1959).

Research Support for the Developmental Features of Parenting

Researchers studying analytic processes that disrupt attachment and cause relationship disturbances have focused on the failure of parents to acknowledge and integrate memories and affective sequelae of their own parents' behavior. They have illustrated that a parent's ability to hear and respond to a baby is influenced by memories of past interfering factors and by unacknowledged affect related to the experience (Slade & Cohen, 1996; Stern-Bruschweiler & Stern, 1989). Some studies have shown that the degree to which the mother is free to remember and reflect upon attachment experiences shapes the way she responds to her child's attachment behaviors and emotional displays (Benoit & Parker, 1994). Mothers who integrate positive and negative aspects of early attachment relationships tend to tolerate their children's expressions of feelings and needs without fearing loss of security, boundaries, or ego strength. Mothers who dismiss or who are detached from memory traces of early attachment relationships tend to have children who are classified as avoidant. Mothers who are preoccupied with memory traces of early attachment relationships tend to have dependent children who have difficulty with self soothing (Slade & Cohen, 1996).

Intergenerational transmission of past conflicts can be illustrated within classification schemes for affect regulation. Borrowing from attachment theorists, analytic theorists have studies rates and processes of intergenerational transmission using the Ainsworth Strange Situation (Ainsworth, Blehar, Waters, & Wall, 1978) and the Adult Attachment Interview (George, Kaplan, & Main, 1985; Slade & Cohen, 1996). The Strange Situation is used to measure and classify the child's tendency to seek maternal comfort upon reunion after an absence. The Adult Attachment Interview is used to measure the coherence, fluency, and emotional tone of maternal representations of early attachments. Researchers have found evidence for concurrent and predictive validity of the Adult Attachment Interview in relation to the Strange Situation (Main & Goldwyn, 1995; Main, Kaplan, & Cassidy, 1985; Ward & Carlson, 1995). Researchers have suggested that the major attachment classification categories (secure, insecure, avoidant, resistant, disorganized, and unresolved) reflect distinct modes of regulating affect and cognition (Cassidy, 1994; Slade & Cohen, 1996). The observations reflect symbiotic behavior between the parent and child. For example, a secure parent sees negative infant affect as facilitating communication and dialogue. An insecure parent views the same negative affect as destructive to the maintenance of security and so emit an excluding or exaggerating response to the negative affect (Cassidy, 1994).

Researchers have examined discordances and discontinuities in parent-child attachments. Security in mothers tends to be predictive of security in babies and maternal insecurity is predictive of infant insecurity. However, other classification categories are less predictive of infant outcomes (Slade & Cohen, 1996). Psychoanalytic understanding of the processes underlying identification with and internalization of a parental figure would support a more complex view of intergenerational transmission. It leaves open several possibilities. Representations of past attachment relationships might be based on distortions as well as reality. Disruptions in attachment relationships might be transient or relatively permanent (Winnicott, 1965). Disruptions to attachment might have a small or weighty impact depending on the nature, timing and meaning of the disruption. Parents may respond to distortions in attachment figures or disruptions in attachment by working through or resolving conflicts (Slade & Cohen, 1996). Parental caregiving is profoundly influenced by an individual's memory traces. But it is the integration of the positive and negative aspects of memory traces of past relationships and the emotional sequelae that promote an organized caregiving system. The organization of the caregiving system flows from the integration of early attachment relationships into current representations of self and others. The organization and quality of the caregiving system is dependent upon the degree of fluency in resolving intrapsychic and therefore interpersonal conflict. Individual attainment of security in the parent-child relationship and other attachment relationships propels parenting behavior from symbiosis and interdependency through the process of separation and individuation (Mahler et al., 1975; Slade & Cohen, 1996). Distortions or disruptions to the process arrest the fluency of resolving inevitable conflicts, compromising the quality of development and identity in the parenting role.

Psychoanalytic theories explain parenting as an adult developmental process. Although parenting is not inevitable, nor is it classified as a stage of adult development, analytic theorists view parenting behavior through a developmental lens. Other theories of parenting behavior place less attention on its developmental features. Greater emphasis is given to internal processes, cognition in interpersonal contexts, the influence of emotions on behavior, and social constructions of the role, significance and meaning of parenting. Socioemotional theories that arose from cognitive and social cognitive theories have examined emotional functioning in a developmental context, examining both the structure and function of emotions across the lifespan, in adult contexts and developmental phases, and in specific behavioral functions such as parenting. The next section review theories of parenting from those viewpoints.

Cognitive, Social Cognitive, and Socioemotional Theories of Parenting

Cognitive theories focus on individual cognitive constructions or schemata that form the basis for parenting. Social cognition theory examines the influence of cognitive-interactional processes such as problem solving behavior on parenting. Socioemotional theories embed the advances of cognitive theories of parenting in a larger theoretical framework of parenting with the suggestion that the interactional influence of cognitions and emotions orient, organize and motivate parenting behaviors, especially during critical periods of arousal. Cognitive schemata are formed and modified through developmental processes, but the general focus of cognitive theories and research is on the here and now. Cognitive theory was advanced in the 1970s, based in theories of psychotherapy for behavior change. Beck and colleagues developed cognitive and cognitive-behavioral approaches to psychotherapy (Beck, Rush, Shaw, & Emery, 1979). Ellis developed rational emotive therapy (Ellis, 1977). Broadly speaking, the focus of both psychotherapies is *cognitive* restructuring, or helping the individual logically analyze maladaptive thought patterns and replace them with reality-oriented adaptive patterns.

A *schema* is an organizational system of related thoughts, beliefs, or meanings that influence a set or subset of behaviors. Schemata vary in their development and complexity and they operate nearly automatically. People are relatively unaware of any specific implementation or influence of schemata on behavior (Fiske & Taylor, 1991). Cognitive theorists do not classify schemata as unconscious or subconscious. Schemata and other thought processes are available for examination (Beck et al., 1979; Ellis, 1977). The complexity and maladaptive nature of schemata might make some thought patterns less readily available than others, but there is no parallel notion that access might be unavailable or blocked by internal mental processes. Whereas analytic thought patterns are classified according to availability, schemata are classified according to type (Fiske & Taylor, 1991). Parental behavior and the parent-child relationship are outcomes of an organization of role schemata. Parental behavior follows from a broad schema, within which subsets influence specific aspects of parenting, such as how to respond to a child's behavior in a specific context. Subsets form the basis for assumptions or conclusions about the best way to intervene when the child needs to learn a new skill or has a particular behavior problem. Schemata act as a filter for other cognitive processes, including attributions for behavior. Cognitive theories use *attributions* or attributional style to explain influences on parenting behaviors. An attribution is an internally generated causal explanation for behavior. Researchers have focused on interactions between internal versus external attributions and stable versus unstable attributions (Dix & Reinhold, 1991).

Attributional Theory, Expectancy Theory and Social Cognitive Theory

Researchers studying the influence of causal attributions on parent-child relationships have focused on parents' attributions for their own behavior and for the behavior of their children. The internal versus external dimension and the stable versus unstable dimension have shown the most robust influence across studies. Other types of attributions, such as general versus specific, have shown less robust influences on quality of parenting behavior (Dix & Reinhold, 1991). Parents' attributions for their own behavior span a control versus helpless dimension. An internal locus of control is associated with personal autonomy. An external locus of control is associated with helplessness. Parental attributions for the behavior of children focuses on appraisals of the intent of the child.

Parents with an attributional style that presumes personal control and a relative lack of negative intent in the child tend to experience little arousal in encountering difficult behavior in a child. Parents with an attributional style that presumes little personal control and that interprets the child's behavior as threatening or involving negative intent tend to experience hyperarousal (Bugental, Mantyla, & Lewis, 1989). They are more likely to engage in coercive escalation that might in turn lead to an abusive incident. Parents who assign high importance to external and unstable events (such as luck) and low importance to internal and stable factors (such as ability) are particularly reactive to difficult behavior in the child (Bugental, Blue, & Lewis, 1990). Parents are more upset when they think that children understand, intend, and have control over difficult behavior (Dix & Reinhold, 1991). Parents experience stronger negative emotion with children if they conclude that they are incompetent as parents, unable to cope, or unable to control events (Bugental & Cortez, 1988).

Expectancy theory adds an emotional dimension to cognitive theory with even greater emphasis on arousal that accompanies attributions of negative intent. Mothers who tended to attribute negative intent to others in ambiguous situations were more likely to react negatively to the child's difficult behavior. They were more likely to start a coercive interaction and they were more likely to continue to behave aggressively regardless of whether the child's difficult behavior increased, remained the same, or decreased (MacKinnon-Lewis, Lamb, Arbuckle, Baradoran, & Volling, 1992). Parents who quickly turned to coercive interactions or behavior tended to be more physiologically and affectively aroused than those who use other methods of interaction and behavior control (Frodi & Lamb, 1980). Parental attributions and arousal/affect interact to influence the discipline practices of parents (Bugental & Cortez, 1988). Distressed parents experienced high negative emotion and low positive emotion when they selected unrealistic interaction goals (goals that their children were unable or unwilling to pursue). Distressed parents expected more mature behavior from children than comparison mothers (Vasta, 1982).

Theories of social cognition followed the research of early theories of the influence of problem solving on social and emotional adjustment (Jahoda, 1953, 1958). In theories of social cognition, emphasis is on adaptive thinking processes or *learning sets* that enable the individual to create or discover solutions to a variety of unfamiliar problems. The social feature of the theory lies in the emphasis on interpersonal competence. Social learning processes that are involved in response acquisition and problem solving are emphasized (Kendall & Urbain, 1982). Research has shown that problem solving quality has an influence on effective parent-child conflict resolution (Klein, Alexander, & Parson, 1977). Interpersonal cognitive problem solving abilities include *alternative thinking* or the ability to general multiple possible solutions to a given interpersonal problem or conflict, *consequential thinking* or the ability to foresee both immediate and long-term consequences of a particular alternative and to incorporate this assessment into decision making; and *means-end thinking* or the ability to think through a series of specific actions needed to reach a specific goal. Means-end thinking also involves the ability to recognize potential obstacles to specific actions and to plan a sequence of behaviors within a realistic time frame (Kendall & Urbain, 1982).

Theories of Affective Organization and Socioemotional Development

Research has supported several basic conclusions about the influence of emotions on parenting behavior. Strong emotion is a daily aspect of parenting. Raising children involves intense joy, affection, anger and worry. When conceptualized as a stable individual variable, parental emotion predicts the quality of the caregiving environment. Other factors related to parental emotion (occupation, marital relationship, other stresses and supports) influence the variety of emotions that parents experience toward their children. Emotional regulation is a key aspect of parenting. Theories of affective organization suggest that complex affective systems ensure that vital individual concerns are promoted. *Parenting concerns*, having cognitive and emotional features, contain the central emotions and thinking patterns that motivate parenting. Concerns activate a host of thoughts and emotions that orient and mobilize behavior designed to promote parental goals for children. Emotions are prominent in parent-child interactions because children are a primary concern, vital to a parent's daily behavior and life goals. Positive and empathic emotions promote attunement to children and facilitate parental responsiveness. They enable parents and children to coordinate mutually beneficial interactions (Dix, 1991).

Chronic and intense negative emotion in parents is related to family distress and dysfunction. It is a prominent feature of abusive parenting, but parent-child conflict is a frequent occurrence even in non-abusive dyads (Dix, 1991). Emotions are activated in response to a parental appraisal of the child's behavior as either contrary to or enhancing their concerns. Difficulty resolving conflict is the outcome of a parent's perception that the child's behavior is inconsistent with parenting goals or expectations (Maccoby & Martin, 1983). Negative emotions are a barometer for problems in the parent-child relationship. Distressed parents perceive that they are poorly skilled or incompetent. Their concerns for their children are undermined by competing concerns (Dix, 1991).

Emotion induces changes in social perception and cognition, influencing attention to stimuli (Derryberry & Rothbart, 1984). It influences encoding, storage and retrieval of information relevant to a specific interaction (Izard, 1984). Emotion influences allocation of processing time and processing capacity (Derryberry & Rothbart, 1984) and the meaning attributed to information (Izard, 1984). Emotion influences the decisions rules or strategies that people to solve problems (Isen, Means, Patrick, & Nowicki, 1982). Emotions are seen in expressive behavior such as gestures, facial expressions and tone of voice. Affective communications, both verbal and nonverbal, are important regulators of the organization and intensity of parent-child interactions (Sroufe, 1979). Displays of positive affect elicit from children enthusiastic and positive emotional responses that increase the probability of child compliance with adult requests and directives (Lay, Waters, & Park, 1989). Displays of negative affect elicit irritation, disappointment, anger, and other negative emotions (Bugental et al., 1989).

Parental emotions and their influence on intentional behaviors and motivations for parenting are not well understood. Biological constraints are believed to define the underlying structure and organization of emotions (Thompson, 1993). Developmental influences also are an important catalyst for emotional regulation and expression. Parental awareness and understanding of emotions is critical to regulation of their intentional use in effective parenting (Dix, 1991). Parents must assess what the emotion is and determine why it is occurring. They must appraise the effect the emotions might have on parent-child interaction if they are expressed (Masters & Carlson, 1984). Parents must develop cognitive, affective, and behavioral routines that control when and how emotion is experienced and expressed in the context of parent-child interactions. Controlling negative emotions and cognitive distortions lessens the frequency of child abuse (Patterson, 1982). Although less is known about the specific mechanisms or processes of emotional regulation (or dysregulation) that promote or inhibit other parenting behaviors (Dix, 1991), research has shown that the vast number of parental emotional displays toward children are positive (Weiss & Schwarz, 1996).

Functionalist Theories

In the 1980s, research on emotion moved away from an emphasis on the disorganizing character of emotional arousal, or portrayals of emotion as a function of cognition or social interaction (Thompson, 1993). The impetus for the structural view of emotion was interest in its ontogenesis. Emotion was portrayed as a discrete and coherent constellation of physiological activity, individual subjectivity, and behavioral expression.

Research focused on the differentiation of basic emotions and the developmental catalysts for their emergence, recognition, expression, and elicitation (Izard, 1991; Thompson, 1993). Research began to focus on emotion as a central feature or main effect of organized and competent behavioral systems. Functionalist theorists suggest the quality and intensity of emotional experiences are defined less by biologically constrained constellations of expression and arousal and more by the individual's ongoing transactions with the environment (Barrett & Campos, 1987; Campos, Campos, & Barrett, 1989).

Emotions are central to individual goals and their attainment. Emotions are characterized as patterns of expressions, united by individual-environment relations and action tendencies (Barrett & Campos, 1987). Internal and situational contexts influence action tendencies that are regulated by a dynamic and self organizing system of emotional reactions. Emotions have a regulatory and a motivational quality. The management of emotions promotes the attainment of goals. There is a bidirectional relationship between the appraisal process and emotional arousal (Thompson, 1993). As with other affective organization theories, functionalist theory has not fully explained the mechanisms whereby emotions become a central influence on behavior (Barrett & Campos, 1987). The theory has explained that emotions are not just biologically adaptive. They are flexible and dynamic, they tend to enhance performance, and they change quickly and efficiently in response to changing conditions (Thompson, 1993). Functionalist theorists have just begun to address the overall span of parenting behaviors (Garber & Dodge, 1991). Theorists have not explained how general parenting behavior is organized by emotional experiences, how parenting concerns and parenting goals are acquired, and how goal attainment is promoted by biology, context or experience as a central feature that motivates the organization and regulation of emotions (Thompson, 1993).

Socioemotional and functionalist theories broadened in the mid-1980s into an emotional theory embedded in many larger theoretical frameworks, including attachment theory. Of particular interest is the prominence of security as a defining entity of the quality of parent-child attachment. Also important is the emotional construct of parental sensitivity, another defining aspect of secure parent-child attachments (especially important to secure attachments between parents and infants). Both security and sensitivity are central to socioemotional and functionalist explorations of the persistence and depth of emotional experiences in parent-child relationships (Thompson, 1993). These advances have promoted the study of internal representations of attachment across the lifespan (Bretherton & Watson, 1990).

Behavioral and Social Learning Theories of Parenting

Behavioral and social learning theories view behavior as the product of learning experiences. In behavioral theory, primary focus is given to operant principles or external contingencies (reinforcement, punishment and extinction) as processes that shape human behavior. Greater attention is given to environmental factors than internal factors. The major difference between the behavioral approach and the social learning approach is one of emphasis rather than theoretical principles (Moore, 1982). In social learning theory, primary focus is given to learning experiences that occur through reciprocal social interactions. Environmental or situational determinants are important, but interactions are thought to be the conduit for internalization of social and nonsocial cues for behavior (Bandura, 1965). The earliest consistent use of the phrase "social learning" is found in the work of Bandura and colleagues (Bandura, 1965; Bandura, Ross, & Ross, 1961, 1962; Bandura & Walters, 1963). Their research investigated the effects of social interaction on learning and development, but it added a dimension of vicarious learning.

Bandura and colleagues investigated the effects of modeling and imitation on the behavior of young children. They postulated that modeling and imitation are the primary interaction processes through which behavioral repertoires are acquired. They did not abandon operant principles such as reinforcement and punishment, but they suggested those processes were of secondary importance in developing new behavior. They postulated that reinforcement and punishment contributed to the stability and generalization of behavioral repertoires that were acquired through modeling and imitation. They demonstrated that children exposed to aggressive models showed increased aggressive behavior (Bandura, 1977; Bandura et al., 1961, 1962). The focus on modeling, imitation and vicarious learning resulted in an emphasis on internal mediators or cognition. The cognitive emphasis was not primary, but social learning theorists focused attention on self reinforcement and other internal processes that would explain how children learn from viewing social interactions even when they do not participate in them (Moore, 1982).

Social learning theory emphasizes the socializing influence of the family. Researchers have studied childrearing practices, comparing families with and without problems to examine behavior differences the home environment (Moore, 1982). They concluded the mechanisms responsible for problem behavior in children are reflected in dysfunctional interactions between family members (Delfini, Berna, & Rosen, 1976; Forehand, King, Peed, & Yoder, 1975). Patterson and colleagues (Patterson, Littman & Bricker, 1967; Patterson & Ried, 1970) developed coercion theory, based on

principles of social learning theory, to explain how dysfunctional family interactions develop. They demonstrated that children's behavior problems
result from inappropriate or inconsistent contingencies applied by parents (Moore, 1982). Coercion theory postulates that a desired outcome is
achieved through either subtle or forceful aversive conditioning of another
individual. Unskilled parents permit aversive behaviors (crying, demanding, or tantruming) to persist beyond the acceptable age range of around
three or four years of age. When they intervene, they do so erratically or inconsistently. The child persists with aversive behaviors because they yield
desired outcomes (Cairns & Paris, 1971; Warren & Cairns, 1972).

Physiological Arousal, Hyperarousal and Socially Reinforced Appraisals

Behavioral researchers have investigated personal characteristics of
parents, examining the differences between abusive and non-abusive parenting (Belsky, 1993a). Behavioral studies have focused on physiological
reactivity of parents to tape-recorded sounds of children. In studies of
baby cries, researchers found that parents who experienced greater physiological reactivity experienced less sympathy and greater irritation and
annoyance in response to the crying (Frodi & Lamb, 1980). Other studies have shown that parents classified as abusive are highly physiologically reactive to videotapes of both stressful and non-stressful parent-child
interactions or child behavior (Disbrow, Doerr, & Caulfield, 1977; Wolfe,
1985). Behavioral researchers have theorized that experiences of abuse in
childhood could lead to high reactivity to stimuli in adulthood, but research
has not yet demonstrated a robust longitudinal link between victimization
in childhood and high reactivity in adulthood (Belsky, 1993a). Studies have
shown that physiological reactivity alone is not sufficient to turn an aversive or coercive parent-child interaction into an abusive episode (Bugental
et al., 1989; Bugental et al., 1990).

Characteristics of maltreating parents include a tendency to give a
negative appraisal to social or parent-child interactions. In social learning theory, appraisals are linked to social and self reinforcement of
thoughts. Thoughts are viewed as discrete internal behaviors that are reinforced through social experience and self dialogue (in vicarious learning)
rather than the internal processes described by cognitive theorists. Based
on their appraisal of the child, interactions of neglectful parents include
unresponsiveness, infrequent initiation of interaction, little responsiveness to the child's initiation of interaction, little prosocial behavior, and
more negative interactions than abusive parents (Bousha & Twentyman,
1984; Disbrow et al., 1977). Interactions of abusive parents include negative interactions, little supportiveness, and few positive behaviors such

as instruction, joining play, talking to the child, and praising the child) (Bousha & Twentyman, 1984; Trickett & Susman, 1988). They include little positive affection toward the child (Lahey, Conger, Atkeson, & Treiber, 1984) and controlling, interfering, or hostile interactions (Bousha & Twentyman, 1984; Crittenden, 1981; 1985). Disciplinary practices differ from comparison groups. Abusive parents are more likely to rely on physical punishment and negative control strategies such as hitting, grabbing, or pushing (Lahey et al., 1984). Comparison groups are more likely to rely on reasoning and inductive strategies (Trickett & Kuczynski, 1986; Trickett & Susman, 1988).

Parenting Style and the Influence of Personality on Parenting Behavior

Social learning theorists have classified parents according to their parenting style (Peterson, Smirles, & Wentworth, 1997; Weiss & Schwarz, 1996). Three major parenting styles were identified: *authoritarian, authoritative, and permissive* (Baumrind, 1971). Authoritarianism was first identified as a personality construct (Adorno, Frenkel-Brunswik, Levinson, & Sanford, 1950) by researchers interested in the relationship between undesirable characteristics of the self that are channeled in the form of aggression and unconscious images of authority figures (Peterson et al., 1997). The construct took on a different definition when it was placed in the context of developmental theories (Erikson, 1963). It was contrasted with *generativity* in hypotheses of developmental influences on personality functioning, with authoritarian parents described as negative, prejudiced or rigid in thinking, uninterested in political issues, and assuming a more punitive stance to parenting and other interactions. Generativity was associated with openness to experience, interest in political issues, and authoritative parenting (Peterson et al., 1997).

The crisis of generativity versus stagnation occurs in young adulthood after an individual forms an intimate relationship with another person. Intimacy serves as a foundation for considering broad issues of caring for society and subsequent generations (Erikson, 1963). It relies on fundamental institutions such as the family that promote intergenerational continuity in traditions and behavior patterns (Peterson et al., 1997). Authoritarianism is a counterpoint to generativity, emerging from poor negotiation of generativity versus stagnation and leading to *rejectivity* or a ruthless and cruel stance toward interactions with more vulnerable individuals (Erikson, 1982). Although they share the common thread of respect for tradition, generative individuals carefully consider the needs of the next generation whereas authoritarian individuals are concerned with passing on a specific set of beliefs and values. Generative individuals have beliefs that might span a wide sociopolitical range and they have a high level of tolerance during interactions with vulnerable individuals. Flexibility is inversely related to authoritarian views. The concern is to maintain the status quo (Peterson et al., 1997). Kotre (1984) suggested there is a bright side to authoritarianism and a dark side to generativity. The orthogonal spatial relationship between the two constructs, reliably seen across different empirical studies, illustrates that extremely high levels of either generativity or authoritarianism might lead to violent behavior toward individuals who are excluded from the protective scheme of either approach. Nonetheless, in most studies of parenting style, authoritarianism has been linked to aggressive or inappropriate parenting behaviors (Peterson et al., 1997).

Erikson (1963) and others (Peterson & Stewart, 1993) hypothesized that parenting is an expressive mode for generativity. Generativity is associated with high quality parenting behavior. Authoritarianism is associated with punitive parenting. Considerable debate exists concerning longitudinal effects of the relationship between authoritarianism and low quality parenting (Altemeyer, 1988; Hopf, 1993; Peterson et al., 1997). However, studies have illustrated different parenting behaviors across groups of parents described as permissive, authoritative, or authoritarian. Permissive parents make few demands on their children and they use minimal interventions and punishments. Authoritative parents provide firm and clear guidelines for children's behavior, using reasoning, flexibility and warmth in their interactions. Authoritarian parents use intrusive and directive interactions and they use physical and psychological punishment for misbehavior (Baumrind, 1971; Peterson et al., 1997). Although longitudinal data are unavailable, young adult parents who score high on measures of authoritarian parenting also have parents who score similarly (Peterson et al., 1997).

In a series of longitudinal studies on the influence of parenting style on child and adolescent adjustment, Baumrind (1968, 1971, 1989, 1991a, 1991b) expanded her classification system to seven parenting types: *authoritative, democratic, nondirective, authoritarian-directive, nonauthoritarian-directive, unengaged,* and *good enough.* She found that good adjustment in adolescent children was associated with *authoritative* parenting (use of firm and consistent discipline by warm and supportive parents). *Democratic* parenting (supportive and conventional but nondirective) produced adolescents with substantially higher drug use than children from homes with authoritative parents (their adjustment was otherwise similar). *Nondirective* parenting (supportive, unconventional and lax parents, previously described in the classification scheme as permissive) produced adolescents who were less competent, less achievement oriented, and less self regulated than those whose parents were *authoritative* or *democratic.* *Directive* parents (controlling, firm, rejecting, and traditional) produced adolescents who lacked social responsibility, were conforming, and opposed drug use. *Authoritarian-directive* parents (highly intrusive parents who were otherwise similar to directive parents), produced adolescents with slightly worse outcomes than non-intrusive but directive parents. The *unengaged* parenting style (rejecting and neglecting parents) produced adolescents with the lowest achievement and adjustment scores. *Good enough* parents produced moderately competent adolescents.

Attempts to replicate Baumrind's findings (Dornbusch, Ritter, Leiderman, Roberts, & Fraleigh, 1987; Lamborn, Mounts, Steinberg, & Dornbusch, 1991; Steinberg, Lamborn, Darling, Mounts, & Dornbusch, 1994; Steinberg, Mounts, Lamborn, & Dornbusch, 1991) have added to the growing base of empirical evidence that the authoritative parenting style is associated with children who exhibit few internalizing or externalizing behavior problems, and are prosocial. Consistent effects have been found across gender, ethnicity, socioeconomic status, family structure, and time (Weiss & Schwarz, 1996). In contrast to the Baumrind studies (which used direct observation), the supporting studies have been criticized for their single-informant design (mainly using student reports to assess parental behavior and family adjustment). Weiss and Schwartz (1996) addressed this problem by including reports of the student, the mother, the father, one sibling, and the student's roommate. Ratings were averaged for analysis. They found that Baumrind's typology was stable (but they could not comment on the *good enough* typology because they did not include it in their study). However, significant effects were due primarily to poor adjustment scores, poor academic achievement scores, and poor substance use scores from children with unengaged or authoritarian-directive parents. There was a stronger effect for children from homes with unengaged parents than for children from homes with authoritarian-directive parents. Children from authoritative homes received the first or second most favorable scores in the majority of instances, but the magnitude of significance was smaller than those seen in the Baumrind studies. Some of the magnitude differences were attributable to sample size differences, but Weiss and Schwarz (1996) concluded that the data supported a less robust relationship between *authoritative* parenting style and good adolescent adjustment.

Skill Development and Role Mastery

Abidin (1986) developed a social learning model that integrated a range of variables believed to be central to the role of parenting, hypothesizing that parenting stress is a central mediator of parent-child interaction. Factors related to parenting stress included the relationship with the spouse, social support (including quality and breadth of social network), occupational variables, the parent's attachment history, parental health, restrictions on the role of parent (related to time demands and other factors), and personality variables (including competence versus depression or other pathological states) (Abidin, 1986; 1992). Stress has a robust relationship to dysfunctional parenting. The relationship is not a simple linear relationship. It is mediated by the degree of parent-child engagement, parent characteristics, child characteristics, environmental characteristics, daily hassles, and life events (Abidin, 1992).

The manifestation of stress in parenting behavior is inhibited (by an absence of) or augmented by parental resources or skills. Those skills include forming a social support network, developing a parenting alliance with the spouse or other significant caretaking individuals, mastery of basic parenting skills and competencies, access to relevant material resources, and cognitive coping capacities. The parenting role is subjectively defined and it includes a set of beliefs or self expectations that serve as a moderator or buffer of the influences on the stress experience (Abidin, 1992). Parents are hypothesized to have an internal working model of the self as parent. From this theoretical view, the internal working model blends socially reinforced beliefs about the parenting role (Abidin, 1992), and individual goals or expectations for the self and others (Crittenden, 1989). Parenting stress is viewed as a motivational variable that activates the utilization of personal resources in order to behave in a manner consistent with the "self as parent" parenting role (Abidin, 1992).

In order for parenting stress to serve as a motivating influence on adaptive parenting, the factors that contribute to stress must be manageable rather than chronically overwhelming, the cost-benefit analysis of specific parenting actions must include a repertoire of actions that are consistent with beliefs encapsulated by the parenting role, beliefs or self expectations that constitute the parenting role must promote health parent-child engagement, and the repertoire of personal skills and resources must be designed to address the range of ordinary to overwhelming levels of stress (Abidin, 1992). In behavioral and social learning theories, skill development and role mastery take on a high level of significance in the development of adaptive parenting behaviors (Abidin, 1992; Moore, 1982).

THE SOCIAL FEATURES OF PARENTING

Social psychological and sociological theories of parenting have examined microsocial and macrosocial factors that influence parenting behavior patterns. Theorists have studied the relationship between parenting and variables such as socioeconomic status, parental age and maturity, cultural influences, definitions of families, and community influences (Belsky, 1993a; Fox, Platz, & Bentley, 1995). Some of the factors are historical (societal attitudes toward nontraditional family units), some are contemporaneous (relative levels of poverty), and some are sociopolitical (policies concerning family violence). In the foregoing sections, we have seen how some theories are adept at explaining both adaptive and maladaptive parenting practices. Others are weighted in the direction of explaining maltreatment with less attention to other parenting behavior. Social psychological and sociological theories explain a broad spectrum of sociopolitical philosophies that underlie adaptive and maladaptive parenting behaviors and practices. Some scholars have demonstrated that microsocial and macrosocial theories have clinical utility in their application to case conceptualizations, treatment interventions, and evaluation methodology (Belsky, 1993a; Peterson et al., 1997). Others have analyzed their applicability to social welfare policies and child protection policies (Belsky, 1993a; Klee et al., 1997; Melton, 1994). What follows is a review of microsocial and macrosocial theories on factors that motivate parenting behavior.

Socioeconomic Status and Parenting

There are many pathways through which poverty influences parenting practices and child development. Poverty affects health and nutrition, parental mental health, parent-child interactions, the home environment, and neighborhood conditions (Brooks-Gunn, Britto, & Brady, 1999). Compared to non-poor children, impoverished children have increased rates of low birth weight and growth stunting, conditions that are associated with reduced intellectual functioning, learning disabilities, grade retention, and school dropout (Brooks-Gunn & Duncan, 1977). Impoverished parents are less likely than non-poor parents to be emotionally and physically healthy (Adler, Boyce, Chesney, Folkman, & Syme, 1994). Stressful conditions associated with poverty, such as inadequate housing, insufficient amounts of money, and unsafe neighborhoods influence levels of psychological distress (Brooks-Gunn et al., 1999). Impoverishment has a negative effect on adult marital relationships (Ray & McLoyd, 1986) that can in turn affect parenting behavior (Elder, 1974). Chronic job loss and unemployment have a greater impact than transient unemployment, but both have a negative influence on parenting (McAdoo, 1986; McLoyd, 1989, 1990). Physical aspects of the home, variations and brightness of rooms, structural integrity, absence of danger, and enriching aspects in the home influence children's cognitive development. Impoverished parents have fewer choices of neighborhoods and schools. Low income is related to residence in neighborhoods characterized by social disorganization, low cohesion, and few resources (Sampson & Morenoff, 1997; Wilson, 1987).

Census figures revealed that about 14 million, or one in five children were living in families whose incomes fell below the poverty threshold. In 1996, the poverty threshold was $12,516 for a family of three and $16,036 for a family of four. Although children under age 18 comprise 27 percent of the total population, they represent 40 percent of the poverty population (U.S. Bureau of the Census, 1996a). The largest percentage of impoverished families is female-headed household (unmarried or divorced mothers) with unemployment, underemployment and ineffective child support enforcement (Brooks-Gunn et al., 1999; Cherlin, 1992; Edin & Lein, 1997). Family poverty might be transient, occasional, recurrent, or persistent (Ashworth, Hill, & Walker, 1994). About 15 percent of impoverished families with children remain in persistent poverty for more than 10 years (Duncan & Rogers, 1988).

The impact of impoverishment on child development is substantial. Impoverishment affects health, emotional development and behavior. The actual effect size for most developmental outcomes is uncertain because of collinearity. Many studies do not control for other family characteristics that might account for variance in associations between family income and developmental outcomes (Brook-Gunn et al., 1999). In an analysis of large multi-site developmental studies, controlling for mother's education, family structure and other developmental variables, researchers calculated the effect of family income (Brooks-Gunn & Duncan, 1997). They found the family income had large effects on children's ability and achievement (for example, verbal ability, reading scores, and math scores), with a greater impact seen in early childhood compared to adolescence. Family income had less effect on children's motor development, social development, mental health, physical health and behavior (Duncan & Brooks-Gunn, 1997; McLeod & Shanahan, 1993).

Effects on physical health, though not substantial, are seen in indicators such as low birth weight, infant mortality, and number of hospitalizations. Adverse birth outcomes are more prevalent for impoverished women, unmarried women, women with low levels of education, and Black women (Brook-Gunn & Duncan, 1997; Brooks-Gunn, Klebanov, & Duncan, 1996). Group differences on variables related to nutritional status (growth stunting, low height) show smaller effect sizes, most likely because of the availability of food stamps (Currie, 1997). Lead exposure rates (lead blood levels) are negatively correlated with family income (Brooks-Gunn et al., 1999).

Effects on cognitive abilities and school achievement are reflected by children's verbal ability scores on standardized tests. The effect of income on verbal ability is seen as early as age two. The effect is amplified for children in persistent or deep poverty (Brooks-Gunn et al., 1999). Impoverished children between ages 7 and 8 show lower IQ scores, lower verbal IQ scores, lower math and reading achievement scores, and more frequent grade retention than their peers (Smith, Brooks-Gunn, & Klebanov, 1997). Impoverishment has a modest effect on school performance and grade point average (Hanson, McLanahan, & Thomson, 1997), and on school completion (Haveman & Wolf, 1995). The effects of income on school completion are more pronounced for children who are impoverished in early childhood and for those in persistent or deep poverty (Duncan, Yeung, Brooks-Gunn, & Smith, 1998).

Although effect sizes are not strong for behavioral outcomes, persistent poverty shows a relationship to "internalizing" problems in children such as depression, anxiety and moodiness (McLeod & Shanahan, 1993). Teenage pregnancy rates for impoverished teenagers is three times the rate for non-poor teenagers, but significant results often are accounted for by demographic factors other than impoverishment (Brooks-Gunn & Duncan, 1997). In general, poverty affects academic achievement more than emotional functioning and behavior, and the strength of the effects of poverty weaken during the adolescent years, probably because other variables (school influences, neighborhood, peer influences) strengthen during adolescence (Brooks-Gunn & Duncan, 1997). A comparison of the effects of income compared to family structure (such as parent absence) suggests that family structure influences emotional and behavioral outcomes more than poverty (McLanahan & Sandefur, 1994).

Poverty often occurs concurrently with many other risk factors for poor developmental outcomes. Cumulative risk studies suggest that the accumulation of multiple risk factors rather than individual risk factors, account for many developmental delays in children (Sameroff, Seifer, Baldwin, & Baldwin, 1993; Sameroff, Seifer, Barocas, Zax, & Greenspan, 1987). Variability and effect sizes are not even across populations. Non-poor children who were exposed to multiple cumulative risk showed similar IQ scores to poor children with multiple cumulative risk. But poor children with no risk factors still had IQ scores lower than non-poor children with no risk factors (Liaw & Brook-Gunn, 1999).

The finding that poverty and low income are related to child abuse and neglect has been replicated many times (Burgdoff, 1980; Pelton, 1978; Zuravin, 1989a). Based on income level in the early 1980s, one study (Spearly & Lauderdale, 1983) found lower rates of neglect in families that earned more than $15,000 (compared to their counterparts who earned less) and lower rates of abuse in families who were not receiving welfare benefits (compared to their counterparts who received AFDC welfare benefits).

The length of time on welfare and the length of time a family was classified as impoverished increased the risk of neglect and abuse (Dubowitz, Hampton, Bithoney, & Newberger, 1987; Zuravin & Grief, 1989). In a national stratified survey conducted in 1980, families earning more than $20,000 per year were half as prone to child maltreatment as those who earned less than $6,000 (Straus, Gelles, & Steinmetz, 1980).

Limited parental education and employment have been linked to maltreatment (Zuravin & Grief, 1989). Both contemporaneous and longitudinal studies have demonstrated the effects of underemployment and unemployment on rates of child maltreatment, suggesting a causal, not merely correlational, link (Bycer, Breed, Fluke, & Costello, 1984; Lichtenstein, 1983). Family size contributes to abuse and neglect (Connelly & Straus, 1992; Polansky, Chalmers, Buttenweiser, & Williams, 1981; Zuravin, 1991b). Amount of time between births contributes to abuse and neglect (Altemeier, O'Connor, Vietze, Sandler, & Sherrod, 1982).

Parental Age and Maturity

Research has demonstrated an inverse relationship between maternal age and child maltreatment (Connelly & Straus, 1992; Zuravin, 1988). In large measure, it is attributable to higher rates of maltreatment among teenage parents (Bolton & Laner, 1981; Herrenkohl & Herrenkohl, 1979; Leventhal, 1981). Youthful parenting is intertwined with other factors. For example, less positive parental nurturing and discipline were seen in mothers who were younger, who had more than one child living at home, who were single, who had a lower income level, and who had a lower level of educational attainment (Fox, Platz, & Bentley, 1995). Teenage mothers were less likely than girls who delayed childbearing to complete high school or seek vocational training, and they were more likely to be single parents than girls who delayed childbearing (McLanahan & Teitler, 1999). Studies of the association between youthful parenting and parental aggression may simply reflect the general inverse association between age and aggression (Belsky, 1993a). However, parental maturity, regardless of parental age, may play a role in child maltreatment. Although its relationship to parental maturity is unclear, unplanned pregnancy (regardless of parental age) is related to abuse and neglect (Altemeir et al., 1982).

Social Networks and Community Factors

Social support has been linked with physical and psychological health (Mitchell, Billings, & Moos, 1982). It has been conceptualized as a psychological resource for counteracting the negative effects of stress (Brownell & Shumaker, 1984). Social support is stronger in cohesive communities than in transient communities. In neighborhoods matched for social class, families with lower rates of maltreatment have more extensive social networks (Garbarino & Kostelny, 1992). Although results are inconsistent, researchers have shown that parents with lower rates of child maltreatment have larger peer networks (Starr, 1982), have more contact with family members (Zuravin & Grief, 1989), receive more help from extended relatives (Polansky et al., 1981), feel less lonely and socially isolated (Milner & Wimberley, 1980), and have access to a telephone (Dubowitz et al., 1987). Parents with periodic help from others are least likely to be harsh or rejecting in their parenting style (Korbin, 1991). The buffering quality of social networks is strengthened when families remain in their neighborhood and communities for a relatively long length of time (Spearly & Lauderdale, 1983). Families are less prone to maltreatment when they use available resources and when they involve themselves in community activities (Polansky et al., 1985).

Although community cohesion contributes to the strength of social support, individual qualities also play a role. Parents with lower rates of child maltreatment interpret the quality of neighborhood friendliness and helpfulness in more positive terms than neglectful parents (Polansky et al., 1985). In a comparison of neighborhoods matched for social class, community climate had a strong relationship to rates of maltreatment. In cohesive neighborhoods, people were eager to discuss their neighborhood, describing it as a poor but decent place to live, as having strong leadership, and as having available resources and services. In contrast, less cohesive neighborhoods were described in negative terms, with poor leadership, high crime, and few open and light spaces available for community events (Garbarino & Kostelny, 1992).

SOCIOCULTURAL INFLUENCES ON PARENTING

Family Typology

Cultural views of what constitutes a "traditional" family are shaped by social and economic influences. The human species has a remarkable capacity for social adaptability. Family structure is linked to that adaptability in predictable ways. The modern view of what constitutes a traditional family, a two-parent family in which the male has primary responsibility for subsistence and the female has primary responsibility for nurturing and caring for children, is based to some degree on assumptions that family typology is an enduring phenomenon. In actuality, shared responsibility for economic provision and, at least to some degree, shared responsibility for child care is more common historically than a division of responsibility

(Lamb, 1999). The nuclear family with divided male and female parental role responsibilities emerged as a social biproduct of the industrial revolution. Rather than working in shops or fields near their home, men traveled to factories or mines located some distance from their homes. Rather than perfecting skills to pass on to the next generation, men found work as unskilled laborers. Monetary wages became more common than subsistence and bartering. Women's contributions to the household income decreased. Nonetheless, most women entered the paid labor force and remained employed except for maternity and childrearing leave. Around the turn of the 20th century, the general increase in wages allowed some families to opt for a single earner family typology (Lamb, 1999). The cultural mythology that accompanied the dual parent, single earner family typology took on a high level of significance in popular culture.

Even in stages of history in which the traditional nuclear family was less common, women assumed primarily responsibility for early child care. As their children grew older, parents tended to share responsibility for rearing children. However, child development was less well understood and child care was accorded little attention by either mothers or fathers (Aries, 1962; Kessen, 1965). Parents generally spent less time nurturing and attending to the needs of children (Lamb, 1999). Children were employed at very young ages (Aries, 1962; Kessen, 1965). In modern generations, families have evolved into a variety of typologies. Single parent households, though never uncommon in history, have become more prevalent because of high divorce rates and one-parent household or "illegitimate" births (McLanahan & Teitler, 1999). Blended families of biological and step-parent families with half siblings and step-siblings are common (Hetherington & Stanley-Hagan, 1999). Many noncustodial parents are assuming a more active and involved relationship with their children (Thompson & Laible, 1999), some adoptive families are accepting children that historically might not have been placed in an adoptive home (Grotevant & Kohler, 1999), some families are headed by lesbian and gay parents (Patterson & Chan, 1996), and multiracial families are more common than they were in the past (Rosenblatt, 1999). Family units with extended family members in the household remain relatively common in some cultural groups (McAdoo, 1986).

Family Typology and Single Parenthood in One-Parent and Divorced Families

SINGLE PARENTHOOD. Historically, the number of illegitimate children born to unwed mothers was considerable, especially in the medieval era. The stigma attached to illegitimacy and divorce developed in the

Victorian era (Lamb, 1999). Today, nearly one third of children are born to unmarried parents. The vast majority of those parents never lived together. Another one-third are born to married parents who later divorce before the child reaches age 18 (McLanahan & Teitler, 1999). Single parent households have caused considerable concern among policy makers over the causes of father absence, the impact of the demanding nature of single parenthood on child development, and the relationship (if any) between social problems and single parenthood. Single parenthood (most notably single motherhood) has been championed by some policy analysts as the primary cause of many social problems such as poverty, high school dropout rates, teenage pregnancy, and juvenile delinquency (Blankenhorn, 1995; Popenoe, 1988). However, it is arguable that single parent households simply are more vulnerable to the already existing problems of poverty and economic uncertainty (McLanahan & Teitler, 1999). Children's behavior problems in single parent households might not be linked to single parenthood *per se*, but instead might be the byproduct of previous problems associated with family disruption such as marital discord and post-divorce acrimony (Skolnick, 1991).

Longitudinal data on three major outcomes in young adulthood (educational achievement and attainment, teenage and out of wedlock childbearing, and early labor force engagement and earning) were reviewed (McLanahan & Sandefur, 1994; McLanahan & Teitler, 1999). The reviews suggested that growing up in a one-parent household doubles the risk of high school dropout from approximately 15 percent in two-parent households to about 30 percent in one-parent households (the differences are retained after controlling for parental race, parental educational level, family size, and place of residence) (Furstenberg & Teitler, 1994; McLanahan & Sandefur, 1994; Wojtkiewicz, 1993). Compared to one-parent families, youth in two-parent families had a slightly higher grade point average, somewhat higher standardized test scores, better school attendance records, and a more favorable attitude toward college attendance (Anstone & McLanahan, 1991). Youth in one-parent households were less likely than those from two-parent families to attend college or to graduate from college (McLanahan & Sandefur, 1994). Adolescent girls in father-absent households were more likely than girls in two-parent households to become a teenage parent (McLanahan & Teitler, 1999). Premarital childbearing was more common in women who were raised in father-absent households compared to two-parent households, especially in groups of Caucasian and Hispanic women (Cherlin, Kiernan, & Chase-Lansdale, 1995; Wu, 1996; Wu & Martinson, 1993).

Youth in two-parent households were more likely than those from one-parent households to make a successful transition from school to work

(McLanahan & Teitler, 1999). Young men from one-parent households were about 1.5 times more likely to be without work than those from two-parent households (Haveman & Wolfe, 1994; McLanahan & Sandefur, 1994). The effects subsided only by one-fifth when differences in ability (earlier test scores) were taken into account (McLanahan & Sandefur, 1994). The effects on earnings were inconsistent (McLanahan & Teitler, 1999), with one study finding reduced earnings in children from one-parent households compared to step-parent households (Peters & Mullis, 1997) and another study finding reduced earnings in children from divorced households and step-parent households but not in widowed parent households (Hauser & Sweeney, 1997).

DIVORCE.   The rise in the rate of divorce has had a tremendous impact on family structure (Heller, 1996). In the early 1960s, nearly 90 percent of all children were raised by both of their biological parents through the age of 18. Today, less than 50 percent of children reside with both parents (McLanahan & Teitler, 1999). Post-divorce family typologies and family blends appear in many forms. Family structure and the relative degree of non-custodial parental involvement are influenced by statutes and judicial decisions about custody. Some post-divorce households retain a high degree of involvement from both parents and others take on a structure and function more synonymous with a single-parent household. Some of them include the involvement of one or two step-parents and still others evolve over time to incorporate and then exclude a series of cohabiting or step-parenting figures (McLanahan & Teitler, 1999).

Until the mid-1800s, children customarily were placed in their father's custody in post-divorce proceedings. Post-divorce custody contests were rare. Under common law, children were deemed their fathers' possessions (Lamb, 1999; Melton et al., 1997). The traditional belief that custody should be awarded to fathers was challenged in the 1830s (Lamb, 1999). In the late 19th century, after *Chapsky v. Wood* (1881), the determining factor in a child's custody became the child's own best interests. With *Chapsky* came a change in perspective that became known as the *tender years doctrine*. The tender years doctrine quickly took hold as the predominating factor in custody determinations. Unless the tender years presumption could be rebutted by a showing of maternal unfitness (usually more focused on adultery than any real concern with the mother-child relationship), the mother was presumed to be better suited for assuming the caretaking role (Derdeyn, 1976; Melton et al., 1997).

The best interest standard later evolved into an indeterminate approach, with broad judicial discretion to determine the factors relevant to a particular custody decision (Mnookin, 1975). Maternal preference weakened in the mid- to late-20th century with emerging social and legal concern for equality in custody determinations. Although maternal custody has remained the norm in many jurisdictions, the general trend is toward determining the child's best interests based on newly developed statutory directives that usually include an examination of the child's relationship with both parents (Melton et al., 1997). Some courts have adopted the *primary caretaker rule*, requesting evidence as to which parent has been primarily responsible for caregiving. Other courts adopted the *joint custody rule*, giving parents shared legal custody or authority to make decisions on behalf of the children unless such an arrangement would be harmful to the children (Melton et al., 1997). The initial proponents of joint custody arrangements intended for physical custody to be shared, but logistical difficulties made such arrangements less common over time. Some courts also use a *friendly parent rule*, granting sole custody to the parent most likely to facilitate the child's relationship with the other parent (Derdeyn & Scott, 1984).

Even though custody standards evolve and change, the large majority of post-divorce families are headed by women (Lamb, Sternberg, & Thompson, 1999). The functioning of the family unit changes with post-divorce changes in residence, economic resources, and amount of time devoted to caregiving. During the period immediately following the divorce, crisis of some type is inevitable (Thompson, 1983). Women sometimes experience a steep decline in their standard of living after divorce. Although most children of divorced parents receive child support from the non-residential parent, only half of non-residential parents pay the full amount awarded by the court (Lamb et al., 1999). Many divorced mothers face the added stress of obtaining or updating vocational skills, completing educational goals, and finding economically and personally rewarding work. Each parent must forge a new type of involvement in their children's everyday lives and routines (Lamb et al., 1999). Children continue to show behavioral sequelae of stress responses to divorce one year following divorce. Stabilization usually follows the post-divorce anniversary period, with children showing better outcomes when parents report personal stability and happiness. Children's long-term adjustment is a function of early success at coping and stress management and the stability and support of the post-divorce home environment (Thompson, 1983).

Adoptive Parent/Child Relationships

More than one million children live in adoptive families in the United States (Center for Adoption Research and Policy, 1997). Adoption affects family structure in many ways. The technical meaning is a legal transfer of responsibility for parenting a specific child from one adult or couple to another adult or couple (Grotevant & Kohler, 1999). A step-parent might legally adopt a child of his or her spouse, a non-parent relative might adopt a child in the family system, or an adopted child might be unrelated to adopting parents. Adoptions sometimes result in multiracial and multicultural family systems. Some transracial adoptions are local (within the United States) and some are international adoptions (Brodzinsky, 1987). Other alternative family systems include adoptions into gay and lesbian two-parent families. Some children are adopted alone and others are adopted as a sibling group or other type of group (Grotevant & Kohler, 1999). Children vary in age at time of adoption from infants to adolescents. Some children have spent time in foster care prior to adoptive placement and others have not. In 1995, it was estimated that nearly 494,000 children were in some form of foster-care or out-of-home placement, with 15 percent placed with a goal of adoption (Spar, 1997). Some foster children with a permanency planning goal are adopted by foster parents or other unrelated adoptive parents. Increasing numbers of foster children have been or will be adopted by extended family members in the biological family of origin (Grotevant & Kohler, 1999). The practice of adoption of foster care children by biological relatives is supported by policy in many states and by statute in some states (Oppenheim & Bussiere, 1996).

Some adopted children enjoy good physical and mental health at the time of adoption and others have identified disabilities or risk factors for the development of physical or mental disabilities (Grotevant & Kohler, 1999). Research on post-adoption satisfaction in parents has shown mixed findings. Some studies have shown that adoptions of children with developmental disabilities result in higher rates of adoption disruption compared to adoptions of children without disabilities (Barth & Berry, 1988). Other studies have found that most parents derive considerable satisfaction from adoptions of children with developmental disabilities and most of those adoptions are successful (Rosenthal & Groze, 1992; Glidden, 1991).

Adoptive family structure and parenting practices are embedded in a large framework of adoptive parents and their extended family members, and birth parents and their extended family members (Brodzinsky, 1987). The child, adoptive parents, and birth parents have been referred to as the *adoption triad* or as a *yoked family* (Reiss, 1992). Six processes are particularly salient in adoptive families: acknowledgement of difference (balancing the need to acknowledge differences without placing too much emphasis on them), compatibility, control (dealing with the loss of control felt by parents who were infertile and adopted children who could not choose whether or not to be adopted), identity (integrating adoption dynamics into the ongoing process of identity development), entitlement (claiming the parent's emotional right to be the child's full parent and the child's right to be the parent's full child), and coping with loss (parents mourning the loss of birth fantasies and children mourning the loss of biological parents) (Grotevant & Kohler, 1999). The degree of secrecy versus open communication in adoptive families has an impact on adoptive parenting practices (Grotevant & McRoy, 1997, 1998). Studies on the effects of adoption (and aspects of adoption such as secrecy versus openness) have shown mixed results, but most longitudinal data have supported positive outcomes in families that develop a comfortable degree of communication about the adoption (Brodzinsky, 1987; Grotevant & Kohler, 1999). Research is emerging on the strengths of adoptive family members and parenting practices (Grotevant & Kohler, 1999).

SUMMARY

1. Reports based in theory and supporting research add scientific integrity to the evaluation process.
2. Knowledge of theory and supporting empirical research maximizes clarity in referral questions, clarity and cogency in reports, and the choice of central or relevant measures and methods. It provides a framework for the application of logic and reasoning in the integration of assessment data.
3. Theory and empirical research must be viewed in light of constantly changing family structures, malleability of human behavior, the difference between tendencies and inevitabilities, and the difference between historical universals and sociocultural influences.
4. Theories of parenting behavior include biological, sociobiological, developmental, cognitive, social cognitive, socioemotional, behavioral, social learning, social, and sociocultural explanations of parenting. Although some theories are more robust than others, none has prominence in explaining motivations for parenting, parenting behaviors, explanations of child maltreatment, or the impact of maltreatment.
5. Whether a particular theory or an eclectic approach is used in an evaluation, the evaluator needs sufficient training to competently explain the strengths and limitations of the data in light of

theoretical backdrop. All data interpretation involves a theoretical backdrop, regardless of whether it is manifest or latent in a forensic assessment report.

6. Data integration and interpretation are strengthened when reasoning and logic are derived from theory and supporting empirical research. Weaknesses in logic usually become apparent in the over-inter-pretation, misinterpretation, minimization or neglect of relevant data.

5

Multicultural Issues and Nontraditional Families

Evaluations take place in the context of cultural, ethnic, regional, and system dynamics. Families live in varying stages of acculturation, assimilation and multiculturalism. Acculturation refers to living in broader society while retaining native language familiarity and usage, ethnic pride and identity, familiarity with cultural heritage, and generational proximity to members of the ethnic group. Assimilation refers to adaptation to broader society that involves a weakening of cultural ties and traditions. Multiculturalism refers to the coexistence of different cultural traditions. Family structure differences also influence family process and child development. The previous chapter reviewed parenting theories and research. This chapter expands on parenting practices, drawing from multicultural and nontraditional constructs of parenting and family life. It challenges the evaluator to consider diversity in parenting practices and child development, and to identify and understand the contextual features of evaluations that come from cultural, ethnic, and family structure differences across family groups. Interpretations of behavior that are based on knowledge of contextual features facilitate useful recommendations for the appropriate level or type of intervention necessary to address child maltreatment.

Although we have much to learn about the diversity in family structure, family process, and manifestations of maltreatment, there is a burgeoning base of literature on multicultural and nontraditional families. The term *multicultural* is used here to cover a broad spectrum of cultural, racial and ethnic diversity in parenting practices and in definitions or manifestations of child maltreatment. The term *nontraditional* is borrowed from the work of Michael Lamb and colleagues (1999) and it refers to diverse family structures such as stepfamilies, families with gay or lesbian parents, single employed or unemployed parents with little or no involvement from the other parent, fathers as primary parents, incarcerated parents or those with significant arrest histories, and families with significant extended family involvement.

This chapter examines the impact of different parenting styles on child development, definitions of child maltreatment, and the impact of child maltreatment. Several caveats are in order. Although emphasis in this chapter is placed on between-group differences, there usually is substantial heterogeneity within groups. Research studies of the similarities and differences in parenting or child maltreatment across groups usually contain small sample sizes and different definitions of maltreatment across studies. Emphasis was placed on family problems in early studies of diversity and nontraditional family structure. Minority or nontraditional groups were compared to other groups and to "control" groups representative of larger society (control groups usually were European-Americans and/or nuclear families). In some cases, research translated the values, beliefs, and practices of larger society into norms for parenting practices and child development (Garcia Coll, Meyer, & Brillon, 1995). Minority and nontraditional groups sometimes were viewed as having deficient parenting practices and child development standards (Slaughter & McWorter, 1985). More recent research has focused on strengths, weakness, and descriptions of family processes across and within groups. Child maltreatment is a problem in all cultures, races, ethnic groups, and family structures. Cultural identification, race, ethnicity, or family structure is not predictive in any meaningful way of child maltreatment as a global set of behaviors. Idiosyncratic manifestations of child maltreatment might have a relationship to culture, race, ethnicity or family structure. Parenting practices are influenced by cultural values, heritage and a relatively common history that reflects the practices considered important to the survival and success of children (Forehand & Kotchick, 1996; Harkness & Super, 1995).

PARENTING DIVERSITY ACROSS CULTURAL, RACIAL, AND ETHNIC GROUPS

DEFINING CULTURE, RACE, AND ETHNICITY

The United States is becoming increasingly diverse in race and ethnicity (Forehand & Kotchick, 1996). According to recent census data, roughly 25 percent of the United States population identifies itself with one of four major ethnic minority groups (U.S. Bureau of Census, 1992). Roughly 12 percent of the United States population is identified as Black, 9 percent are Hispanic or Latino, 3 percent are Asian and Pacific Islander, and 1 percent is Native American (U.S. Bureau of Census, 1992). If current legal and illegal immigration rates and rates of domestic population growth continue, Hispanic or Latino families will overtake Black or African American families as the second largest group by early in the 21st century (U.S. Bureau of Census, 1993). The terms *culture, race,* and *ethnicity* have varying meanings. None of these terms are specific scientific concepts or words with definitions having fidelity across dictionaries or other sources of word meanings.

Use of the any of these terms carries an inevitable risk of being drawn into oppressive systems in which the terms are central (Rosenblatt, 1999). The terms invite discussion about human differences. Although it is difficult to discuss differences in the absence of stereotypes or prejudices, differences and identifying terms for groups cannot be ignored (Forehand & Kotchick, 1996; Rosenblatt, 1999). Terminology inevitably contains some element of stereotyping. Many labels used to identify culture, race or ethnicity have their roots in thoughtless and sometimes malicious patterns of prejudice and discrimination. Attempts to identify politically correct or modern labels come with their own set of problems with respect to the degree to which they encapsulate the identity of a group without marginalizing or stereotyping. For example, *African American* became a term of art in the late 20th century, but the result was a misidentification of individuals who identified with the term *Black* but who had no African heritage or lineage. *Hispanic* might capture the essence of some groups with Spanish heritage or lineage, but the term ignores individuals of Portuguese descent (although some definitions of the term Hispanic include people of Portuguese descent, most do not). Some individuals who identify with the term *Latino* might not mind an interchangeable use of the terms *Hispanic* and *Latino* and others might feel misidentified. Latino tends to refer to Spanish-speaking individuals. Latino, a term of choice by many groups, refers to the root of the language or Latin. But in a broader sense, the term Latino captures non-Spanish-speaking groups as well. It can have broad applicability, inclusive of Brazilian, Portuguese and sometimes Italian descent, among others. Similarly, not all *Caucasian* individuals are of European-American descent even though the popular stereotypic response is to assume so. In U.S. census definitions, for example, Caucasian includes people of Semitic descent. The term Caucasian has as much vagueness as terms used to describe other ethnic groups.

Social race is a constructed reality that has little relationship to the biological bases of race. To illustrate the social influence on categories of culture, race, or ethnicity, it is useful to examine categories that have evolved over time in the U.S. Census Bureau. The U.S. Census Bureau has included a question regarding race in each census since 1790 (Office of Management and Budget, 1977). Categories of race have changed over the years. In 1790, four categories were in use: Free White Males, Free White Females, All Other Free Persons, and Slaves. So it is not surprising that even official attempts to classify the U.S. population according to race have been controversial. By 1970, nine categories were used, and by 1990, 15 categories were used (White, Black, Indian [American], Eskimo, Aleut, Chinese, Japanese, Filipino, Korean, Vietnamese, Asian Indian, Samoan, Guamanian, Other Asian or Pacific Islander, and Other Race). Even when efforts to identify race are well intended (to create a method of tracking population demographics and needs of minority communities), personal responses to the identification or "labeling" of race highlight the controversial features of labels. This chapter adheres to the identifying terms that were used in the research studies cited in this chapter. Features of populations and subgroups are described as they were in the cited studies. Because of lack of specificity in some studies, it is likely this chapter contains some nonspecific uses of terms used to describe culture, race and ethnicity.

How Parenting Practices Influence Child Development in a Context of Diversity

A person's understanding of the world and the self is shaped in part by cultural heritage, which is tied to economic subsistence patterns. Those understandings or cultural beliefs influence and direct parenting practices that in turn influence child development (Harkness & Super, 1995). Ogbu (1981) developed a cultural-ecological view of child development to explain how culture influences child development. He theorized that culture determines definitions of competencies that are important to survival and success. Definitions of competencies are drawn from economic subsistence patterns and they also are threaded through folk theories of childrearing. Cultural anthropologists have studied the meanings and behavioral lessons that groups glean from literature (Davis, 1984; Davis & Joakimsen, 1997). Anthropological and ethnographic research has illustrated the relationship between patterns of economic subsistence and patterns of childrearing (Harkness & Super, 1995; Whiting, 1981). For example, groups that existed on daily hunting and gathering of food valued initiative, imagination, and self-reliance as goals of child development. Children were socialized to value independence, motivation, and achievement. Groups that existed in pastoral or agricultural settings socialized their children to be responsible, obedient, conservative and respectful of authority. The economic and sociopolitical influences that developed around subsistence patterns determined the adaptations and competencies that parents infused in their children (Whiting, 1981). Socioeconomic influences intermingle with cultural influences. Socialization of children to value compliance, emotional detachment, and self-reliance is characteristic of groups that commonly experience economic hardship and uncertainty. More economically stable groups socialize children to value independence and assertiveness (Harkness & Super, 1995).

Cultural Values, Parenting Practices, and Child Development

Theories of parenting that consider cultural diversity began to appear in the late 19th and early 20th centuries (DuBois, 1899; Thomas & Znaniecki, 1918), with a description of parenting from diverse cultural perspectives. In the 1960s and 1970s, attention was given to educational and social problems in minority communities and families (Blassingame, 1972; Gutman, 1976). It was only in the 1990s that research began to emerge that explained general parenting processes in minority communities (Gadsden, 1999; Leyendecker & Lamb, 1999). Although there remained an emphasis on comparisons to European-American parents, the phenomenological and relational heterogeneity and homogeneity within and across cultural groups began to take a positive and explanatory theoretical form (in contrast to earlier emphasis on parenting problems and social problems in minority communities). The strengths of parenting practices in culturally diverse forms began to emerge (Gadsden, 1999; Leyendecker & Lamb, 1999). Forehand and Kotchick (1996) applied behavioral theory to cultural diversity in parenting practices and child development. They described "attitudinal and behavioral styles" of parents from different ethnic backgrounds.

BLACK FAMILIES. Forehand and Kotchick (1996) described African American parents as dually influenced by generational transmission of

African culture and the experience of slavery in America. Traditional African values and beliefs include childrearing as a communal task shared by adult members of a community and extended family networks, including neighbors, relatives and church members. Slavery contributed to informal substitute caretakers and informal adoption practices within communities because children often were separated from biological parents (Greene, 1995). Educating children about the impact of racism is a central feature of African American parenting that grew out of slavery and persisted in modern discriminatory environments (Garcia Coll et al., 1995).

Research on Black families traditionally focused on comparative studies of Black families in larger society, especially Black families living in poverty and one-parent homes. Declines in marriage rates in Black families were contrasted with those of larger society. Studies that included any data on racial differences in family structure or function were applied to discussions of Black families (Gadsden, 1999). Research on Black families in the 1990s focused more heavily on Black female-headed households with research on Black fathers emerging more slowly (McLanahan & Sandefur, 1994). The emphasis remained on differences between Black and Caucasian families and the persistence across time of a gap between the two groups in educational attainment, income, and marriage rates. Declining marriage rates were associated with increases in female-headed households. For example, in 1970, 68 percent of Blacks were married, 28 percent of Black one-parent households were headed by women and 4 percent of Black one-parent households were headed by men. By 1994, 47 percent of Blacks were married, 48 percent of Black one-parent households were headed by women and 6 percent of Black one-parent households were headed by men. Because of the pervasiveness of unemployment among young Black men, the presence of the father in the home may not substantially change the level of poverty that Black children experience (Gadsden, 1999). Research on Black families has been constrained by an emphasis on why families fail. There has been far less attention to the ways in which Black families achieve success, and the basic function, beliefs, structures, and relationships within Black families (Taylor, Chatters, Tucker, & Lewis, 1990). Recent research has shifted the focus away from achievement and economic success to the ways in which families think about their lives. It has focused on how constructions of life events shape and are shaped by experiences, expectations, and images of and within Black families (Gladsden, 1999).

The form of the extended family distinguishes Black and Caucasian families. The term *extended* describes families that diverge from the nuclear family typology. In Caucasian extended families, non-nuclear members usually include elderly parents of the conjugal parents. Black extended families often comprise several households in which children are not viewed as belonging to a single or private family (Shimkin, Shimkin, & Frate, 1978). Extended families serve a variety of purposes within Black family life. They offer a range of childhood and early adulthood support to young men and women. Among impoverished one-parent households, 50 percent (usually females) are embedded in an extended-family household with access to family community for monetary assistance, childcare and childrearing assistance, and emotional support (Gadsden, 1999; Shimkin, Shimkin, & Frate, 1978). Black families historically became extended in a range of other ways, particularly through informal foster care arrangements or informally placing dependent children in homes other than those headed by the biological parents (Miller, 1993). Black people, both married and unmarried, assume responsibilities for the care and upbringing of Black children in a way that differs from most Caucasians. Black families, regardless of socioeconomic status and number of parents heading the household, identify more readily than Caucasians with kin networks. Kin networks are a central feature of Black families that influence child development across the life course (Gadsden, 1999).

African American children are socialized to value familial strength, positive self image, perseverance in the face of adversity, positive racial identity, learning from elders, and the capacity for dual identification with African American and larger American society. Religion is an important facet of socialization in African American culture, with parents relying upon the structure of religious beliefs and religious communities to provide role models, guidance, support, and oversight of children and parenting practices (McAdoo, 1991). For example, religious beliefs in African American parents are predictive of parenting practices in low income families (Kelley, Power, & Wimbush, 1992). In an exploratory study of parenting competence, African American parents said they obtained considerable comfort and guidance from participation in religious activities (Hurd, Moore, & Rogers, 1995).

ASIAN AMERICAN FAMILIES.   In their analysis of Asian American parenting practices, Forehand and Kotchick (1996) emphasized the common elements between folk theories of parenting and a prevalent emphasis on the principles of Confucianism across Asian American groups (including Chinese, Japanese, Korean, Vietnamese, Cambodian, Thai, Filipino, Laotian, Lao-Hmong, Burmese, Samoan, and Guamanian). They also concluded there is a paucity of comparative studies of cultural variations among Asian American groups. To illustrate the similarities, analyses have emphasized generational transmission of the values of parental control, obedience, discipline, respect for elders, familial obligations, reverence for tradition, maintenance of harmony, negotiation of conflict and the importance of formal education (Forehand & Kotchick, 1996; Lin & Fu, 1990). The goals of child development include proper development of character (Ho, 1989), emotional maturity, self control, and social courtesy (Garcia Coll et al., 1995). Internal goals, self direction, human malleability, effort, self improvement and the viability of self change are values influencing the goals (Lin & Fu, 1990).

Using the same theme of the influence of Confucianism on socialization of children, other researchers have examined whether immigrant Chinese parents maintain socialization practices tied to their culture of origin or whether they accommodate to the socialization practices representative of larger United States society. Studies have shown that Chinese children are taught mutual dependence, group identification, self discipline, good manners and the importance of education (Ho, 1989). Chinese mothers have been described as controlling, restrictive, and protective (Bond & Wang, 1983), showing little overt affection toward children (Roback, Sanders, Lorentz, & Koestenblatt, 1980). External punishments and frequent scolding are used to achieve compliance (Wu, 1985). However, very young children are treated leniently, with warmth and affection, and with more strict approaches after children reach the age of understanding (Ho, 1989). Immigrant Chinese mothers (in Norfolk, Virginia) quickly showed similar childrearing goals when compared to Caucasian American mothers, but they tended to rely more heavily on physical control and harsh scolding. Both groups emphasized obedience and reported considerable use of reasoning in response to common parenting concerns (Kelly & Tseng, 1992). The study did not control for maternal age or education, recency of immigration or level of distress in adapting from China to United States residence. The immigrant Chinese mothers had been living in the United States between one and fifteen years.

LATINO FAMILIES.   Research on Latino or HispanicAmerican families has mirrored research on Black families in its emphasis on comparative studies of Latino families in larger society. Much of this research illustrated remarkable heterogeneity within and across Hispanic groups originating from Central American, South America and Europe among other places. Research on Latino families is complicated by quickly changing United States population demographics. The majority of Latino families have immigrated within the last two generations (Buriel & De Ment, 1997). The immigration experience has shaped family and social networks, socioeconomic status, and acculturation (Rogler, 1994). *Familism*, or a deeply ingrained sense of belongingness, orientation, and obligation to family, is a core feature of Latino family life (Leyendecker & Lamb, 1999). Family cohesion is viewed as a protective force (Buriel & De Ment, 1997). Latino families tend to have sociocentric rather than individualistic cultural values. Like Black families, they rely upon the extended family as a primary source of social contact and support. For example, Cuban teenage mothers receive extensive support from family members (Field, Widmayer, Adler, & De Cubas, 1990) and many Latinos are willing to sacrifice individual needs for family needs (Triandis, Marin, Betancourt, Lisansky, & Chang, 1982). Parenting attitudes emphasize interdependence and reciprocity over independence. However, because immigration sometimes has cut families off from older generations, Latino families are more likely to have young children and less likely to have grandparents living in the United States. Many immigrants from Latin countries support family members in the United States as well as those still living abroad. Some of those families live with the stress of knowing other families were left behind in economically troubled, politically dangerous or war-torn countries (Leyedecker & Lamb, 1999).

In most immigrant families, the process of acculturation proceeds more rapidly for children than for parents (Vega, 1995). The generation gap faced by most families is magnified by a cultural gap between parents and children (Suarez-Orozco & Suarez-Orozco, 1994). However, there are common threads in Latino families. Studies of lower- and middle-class mothers in Puerto Rico, lower-class Puerto Rican mothers in the United States, recent mother immigrants from Central America, and European-American mothers have shown that Latino mothers work to instill social qualities and integration into the family and community, whereas European-American mothers work to instill independence, self confidence and achievement in children (Harwood, Scholmerich, Ventura-Cook, Schulze, & Wilson, 1996). Multiple significant attachments are fostered within the extended family regardless of where the extended family unit lives. Urban Latino families are more likely than urban European-American families to rely on relatives for emotional support and child care (Spence, 1985). Child care is provided more often by friends and relatives than paid child care workers. Infants and young children in Latino families are more likely to engage in multiple interactions on a day-to-day basis than the dyadic experiences more common to European-American children (Leyendecker, Lamb, Scholmerich, & Fracasso, 1995). Latino parents show less preference for time-structured lifestyles. However, Latino parents do not differ from European-American parents in the amount of time spent with infants, amount of time engaged in feeding, amount of time spent in social or object play, or attentiveness and responsiveness to the infants' needs and signals (Leyendecker, Lamb, & Scholmerich, 1997).

Forehand and Kotchick (1996) described the term Latino as inclusive of Central and South Americans, and people of Hispanic origin from the

Caribbean, for example, Puerto Rico and Cuba. They described parenting practices that emphasized familism, family loyalty, reliance on extended family and social support networks, interpersonal relatedness, mutual respect, inner importance, personal dignity, and self respect. Parenting was shared by parents, older siblings and extended family members. A permissive and placating style predominated, with relatively less emphasis on individual identity and achievement orientation or strict discipline (Garcia Coll et al., 1995). Specific maternal teaching behaviors included preferences for modeling, visual cues and directives compared to other methods such as verbal inquiry or praise (Laosa, 1980).

NATIVE AMERICAN FAMILIES. Native American culture is comprised of at least 400 distinct tribal groups and villages with diverse cultural heritages. There are 511 federally recognized native groups and 365 state-recognized tribes with more than 200 distinct languages (not dialects) (LaFramboise, 1988). Sixty percent of Native Americans are of mixed ethnic and racial heritage (Trimble, 1990). Within Native American tribal groups, family patterns differ based on the degree of acculturation. Red Horse and colleagues (1978) described three family lifestyle patterns in the urban Chippewas of Minnesota. *Traditional* families were those that adhered to tribal customs such as home use of their Native American language and practice of traditional religious beliefs. *Bicultural* families were those who adopted many customs of the larger society but still related well to traditional Native American families and customs. *Pantraditional* families were those struggling to recapture Native American customs and traditions. The extended family network was common to all three lifestyles (Red Horse et al., 1978). The family structure of Native American families is somewhat distinct in terms of family size and prevalence of the extended family (Seideman et al., 1994). European-American tradition defines family networks in a three-generation pattern. Native American families are described in both vertical and horizontal lines, containing upward of 200 relatives (Red Horse, Lewis, Feit, & Decker, 1978). Relational terms that are familiar to popular culture have a different meaning when describing the ways in which Native American individuals are related.

The thread of similarities in parenting beliefs includes harmony with nature, mythology, humility, respect for elders, respect for traditions and customs, sharing wealth and resources, and the centrality of family and tribal life. Childrearing responsibilities are shared and communal, with value placed on collective, cooperative and noncompetitive ways of living. Because of an emphasis on the inviolability of the individual, it is uncommon for Native Americans to speak on behalf of or control the actions of others, including children. Child development is shaped by tactics of persuasion, fear induction, embarrassment and shame (Garcia Coll, 1995).

Parenting practices of Native American families differ from larger society on a variety of dimensions, although the degree of difference is muted in some instances by the process of acculturation. Native American mothers rarely yell at their children, they exert little pressure on children to return to a task they abandoned, and they use many positive nonverbal expressions and gestures to communicate with their children. Native American parents rely on visual modes of teaching, showing a preference for observation over intervention when the behavior of children deviates from what was instructed or expected (Seideman et al., 1994). The role of grandparents is strong and authoritative in many Native American families. Grandparents assume both official and symbolic leadership of family communities. Where proximity is not possible, the grandparent role of monitoring of parental behavior and the behavior of grandchildren is assumed by another older community member. Some Native American communities lost that tradition during the time frame in which children were reared in government boarding schools (other traditions also were lost in that time period; Red Horse et al., 1978; Seideman et al., 1994).

Collinear Factors and Heterogeneity

Heterogeneity within groups is influenced by social, economic, and psychological influences (Harrison, Wilson, Pine, Chan, & Buriel, 1990). Research on ethnic minority and economically disadvantaged families sometimes implies that groups are homogeneous. Although groups that are chronically and significantly impoverished show less within-group heterogeneity than other groups, the impact of group differences related to ethnicity often weaken when variables such as socioeconomic status and level of assimilation are controlled. More robust group differences are sometimes seen for occupation rather than ethnicity or socioeconomic status. Kohn (1969) demonstrated that parents' strategies for socialization of children are closely linked to their occupations. Working class parents in routinized and closely supervised jobs tended to stress conformity, obedience, cleanliness and courtesy. Parents whose jobs required independent decision making and self supervision emphasized autonomy, curiosity and self reliance (Kohn, 1969; Wauchope & Strauss, 1990).

Even within groups of homeless families, heterogeneity is evident. Most homeless families are headed by single mothers, about half of whom have children under age six. In many urban areas, African Americans are over-represented among the homeless, comprising more than 70 percent of the homeless populations in cities such as Chicago, Philadelphia, Cleveland, and Washington, D.C. (Koblinsky, Morgan, & Anderson, 1997; U. S. Conference of Mayors, 1993). Parenting practices might differ for parents of boys and parents of girls. Less language stimulation was provided by mothers of boys regardless of housing status (Koblinsky, Morgan, & Anderson, 1997). In a study that examined gender differences, economically disadvantaged employed African American mothers (from a southern Ohio city) with higher levels of depression had more negative perceptions of children. There was a greater amount of negative perceptions of boys than girls in the depressed sample. Higher educational attainment mitigated the effect of depression on perceptions of children, regardless of the child's gender (Jackson, 1994). Depending upon housing and economic conditions, permissive, authoritative, or authoritarian parenting styles might influence child development in different ways, with one style producing better outcomes in one context and another producing better outcomes in a different context (Baumrind, 1971; Dornbusch et al., 1987).

Diversity in Definitions of and the Perceived Helpfulness of Social Support

The quality of social support networks is a mild to moderate buffer for parental stress (Belsky & Vondra, 1989). The limited information available on ethnic and racial diversity in the utilization of social support suggests there are differences in the nature of social networks and the use of social support as a buffer of stress (Azar & Benjet, 1994). Some groups are more likely to rely upon extrafamilial support networks and others are more likely to rely on family networks. Some groups have broadly defined friendship networks and others tend to rely on a few close and intimate friends. Social support is not a uniform stress buffer across or within cultures. For example, a study of Chinese nationals suggested social support is a buffer for individuals with an internal locus of control, but it has a negative effect for those with an external locus of control (Liang & Bogat, 1992). Hispanic individuals tend to forego the use of friendship networks to buffer stress, relying instead on relatives or non-relatives accepted as family (Herrerias, 1988). Emphasis on family solidarity and family obligation helps protect the family's continuity and preserve its cultural heritage (Zayas & Solari, 1994). Cultural patterns of communication influence how the helpfulness of supportive family members is characterized. For example, among Koreans, it is unusual to describe the self or family members in a positive light. To do so violates the rules of social etiquette (Kim, McLeod, & Shantzis, 1992).

For some groups living in dangerous neighborhoods, social isolation might be adaptive (Greene, 1990). Social isolation is not always linked to maladaptive stress responses. Among minority individuals with low socioeconomic status, multiple moves to find work and adequate housing may account for social isolation more than parental patterns of adaptations to stress (Azar & Benjet, 1994). Low socioeconomic status is not always predictive of the quality and helpfulness of social support as a moderator of parenting stress. Even in some low-income groups, social support serves as a significant moderator. For example, in a southern metropolitan sample of single and economically disadvantaged African American adolescent mothers, social support emerged as a significant predictor of resilience in mothers (Mulsow & Murry, 1996).

Family support has been described as an important facet of effective parenting in economically disadvantaged African American families (Unger & Wandersman, 1985). Its influence on parenting behavior is multifaceted. For example, one study revealed four factors in the quality of mother-grandmother relationships and its effect on the parenting of mothers. The factors were described as emotional closeness, positive affect, grandmother directness (demanding behavior and clarity) and individuation (a balance of autonomy and mutuality). Individuation had the strongest influence on parenting behavior. Mothers whose relationships with their own mothers were characterized as open, flexible and autonomous interacted in a similar fashion with their own children. The effects of the mother-grandmother relationship on the parenting of mothers varied with age and co-residence of the grandmother (Wakschlag, Chase-Lansdale, & Brooks-Gunn, 1996). The quality and nature of family support may have contextual differences. In a study of Black grandparents (in several urban northwestern communities) who assumed a surrogate parenting role of young children with drug-addicted parents, grandparents did not receive consistent or reliable familial social support (Burton, 1992).

Other studies suggest that extrafamilial support is more robust than family support in economically disadvantaged African American families. In a study of the relative influence of social support and family structure, social support was a better moderator than family structure on maternal responsiveness and child outcomes (Burchinal, Follmer, & Bryant, 1996). Some studies have shown that family structure (co-residence of father or grandmother) moderates stress and influences child outcomes (Tolson & Wilson, 1990), but others (Chase-Lansdale, Brooks-Gunn, & Zamasky, 1994) have failed to corroborate those findings. In a longitudinal study of cognitive and social outcomes in African American children (in North Carolina), Burchinal and colleagues (1996) examined the mother's social network, the family structure, and the quality and stimulation of the home environment. Mother-child interaction variables were analyzed and the study showed that social support, not family structure, was consistently related to quality of maternal parenting. Similarly, a study of economically disadvantaged

African American families (in a large northeastern city) demonstrated that when the effects of maternal well being and parenting practices were controlled, kinship support had a non-significant impact on the adjustment of adolescent children. When mothers and female guardians reported higher levels of self esteem and self acceptance, their adolescent children showed better adjustment (Taylor & Roberts, 1995).

Aspects of social support for African Americans, such as network size, network density (the number of individuals within the network who knew one another), network composition, and type of support, are highly correlated. Mothers with larger social networks generally had more parenting assistance, more frequent social interactions each day, and more dense networks. Mothers with larger support networks provided more stimulating home environments across infancy and early childhood than those with smaller networks. They showed more developmentally appropriate parenting. They were more responsive, accepting and involved, and less directive and controlling (Burchinal et al., 1996). In an exploratory study of self-defined strengths in African American families (in North Carolina), parents across all socioeconomic strata reported receiving considerable support from other adults. Based on self-report data from parents, social support enhanced parenting competence and child adjustment (Hurd et al., 1995).

Diversity in Discipline Techniques

In Miami, a group of researchers examined differences in parental preference for discipline techniques (Reyes, Routh, Jean-Gilles, Sanfilippo, & Fawcett, 1991). Based on a demographic analysis of the four most prominent ethnic groups in Miami (Haitian, Hispanic, Black American and White American), they administered the Child Development Questionnaire to mothers who brought their child to the pediatrician for an injection. They used three different language forms of the questionnaire: English, Haitian Creole, and Spanish. They scored the questionnaire according to the frequency with which the mothers reported using five different categories of discipline: modeling and reassurance, positive reinforcement, reinforcement of dependency, punishment, and use of force (hands-on discipline). Controlling for the influences of maternal education and age, they found a significant effect for use of force, with Haitian mothers reporting more use of force than the other groups. The Haitian and Hispanic group difference was confounded by maternal age. Haitian mothers reported relatively infrequent use of modeling and reassurance compared to the other groups. The researchers did not have sufficient group sizes to control for the effects of first-generational status or socioeconomic status. The authors noted that

Haiti is the poorest country in the Western hemisphere (Wilentz, 1989), with a 50 to 60 percent rate of unemployment and an 80 percent rate of illiteracy. They noted Haiti is ruled by totalitarian regimes that rely upon use of force to gain compliance.

Discipline styles of African American parents have been characterized as strict and harsh; however, economically disadvantaged families of achievement-oriented children have been described as warm and supportive of their children. African American mothers (in an urban northeast sample) who reported using tactics such as scolding, nagging, or threatening also described poorer outcomes in the behavior of their adolescents than parents who granted autonomy and independence to adolescents (Taylor & Robert, 1995). Black and White mothers (from eight medical center sites across the United States) who scored higher on the Warmth and Supportive Presence scales of the Home Observation for Measurement of the Environment (HOME) (Caldwell & Bradley, 1984) were better able to produce good outcomes in their children on measures of cognitive stimulation (as measured by the HOME Learning and Quality of Assistance scales). Although results remained significant, less variance was accounted for in the Black families than the White families in the sample (Berlin, Brooks-Gunn, Spiker, & Zaslow, 1995). The authors examined subtle variations in scores, interpretations of parents in their view of their children's behavior problems, possible between-group differences in parental interpretations of children's behavior, the interactive nature of parenting practices and behavior problems in children, and the confounds of race and class. Their careful interpretation of the data illustrated the importance of refraining from classifying parental discipline style as "strict" versus "warm" based on the results of a limited number of studies. To the extent that conclusions can be made based, the above studies suggest strictness might not be pervasive in African American or Black families. Strict discipline practices or restrictiveness may result from a belief that the normal range of child conduct is less tolerated in African American children, who must outperform other children to be viewed as competent or well behaved children (Greene, 1990). Harsh discipline in the form of emotional withdrawal and physical punishment has been viewed as common in African American families. More recent research suggests socioeconomic status is a better predictor of harsh discipline practices than ethnicity (Dodge, Petit, & Bates, 1994; McLoyd, 1990).

The discipline practices of Native Americans have been characterized as nonverbal, with few attempts by mothers to structure and intervene in the activities of young (three months to three year old) children (Seideman et al., 1994). On the HOME scale and the Nursing Child Assessment Teaching Scale, urban-dwelling Native American mothers from Oklahoma City and Tulsa deviated from norms in their responses to social and emotional cues (listening carefully to children, refraining from interrupting children, refraining from negative or uncomplimentary remarks), the clarity of their cues to children, the clarity of their speech, refraining from shouting, refraining from overt expressions of annoyance or hostility, and refraining from slaps or spanks. Many positive nonverbal responses to the behavior of children were observed.

In a study of the differences in the discipline of young children (ages three to six) between Caucasian mothers in the United States (Houston, Texas) and Japanese mothers (Hyogo, Japan), it was found that United States mothers gave their children more input but they also expected them to follow more rules than did Japanese mothers. They began socialization to rules when children were at an early age. United States mothers used material and social consequences as discipline more frequently than Japanese mothers. Japanese mothers were more likely to report using reasoning and scolding with their children. They were more likely to report using physical punishment in specific situations, but they made fewer overall demands and were less focused on rules. They believed young children should be tolerated and indulged. They reserved more forceful discipline for situations involving a child's confrontation of authority. The results were based on the use of the Parenting Dimensions Inventory that assesses eight dimensions of parenting: nurturance, responsiveness to child input, non-restrictive approaches, amount of control, type of control, maturity demands, consistency, and organization (Power, Kobayashi-Winata, & Kelley, 1992).

Cultural Views of Relatedness

In a study of cross-cultural differences in attachment, Rothbaum and colleagues concluded that three of the core hypotheses of attachment theory result primarily from the cultural relativity of the theory. They questioned the broad applicability of attachment theory (Rothbaum, Weisz, Pott, Miyako, & Morelli, 2000). They described the influence of Western theories of relatedness on attachment theory, suggesting that other cultures view sensitivity, competence and a secure base differently than United States parents. They emphasized that other predominant theories have been criticized as culture bound or embedded in Western European influences and American individualism. For example, psychoanalysis emphasizes separation and individuation, family systems theory emphasizes differentiation of family members, and many theories of child development emphasize mastery and independence in infants and children

(Cushman, 1991). Because heavy emphasis is placed on the evolutionary roots of attachment theory, little attention has been given to cross-cultural research or theory (Rothbaum et al., 2000).

In a study of attachment classifications in economically disadvantaged Hispanic mother-infant dyads and the relationship to patterns of maternal parenting, researchers examined the applicability of the Ainsworth Strange Situation to an Hispanic sample that included the two largest Hispanic groups living in the Bronx, those originating from Puerto Rico and those from the Dominican Republic. The researchers (Fracasso, Busch-Rossnagel, & Fisher, 1994) found that the pattern of attachment classifications differed from those reported in Euro-American populations. The results produced an equal number of securely and insecurely attached infants. Gender differences were apparent in the attachment patterns, with two-thirds of boys securely attached and two-thirds of girls insecurely attached. Maternal sensitivity differed from common definitions of maternal sensitivity in larger society. Degree of acculturation did not seem to have an impact on the results. In their discussion of the results, the researchers examined socioeconomic status and cultural determinism. They concluded it was difficult to assess whether insecurely attached infants would follow a culturally determined trajectory of development that might differ from larger society but result in reasonable adolescent and adult adjustment, or whether the results reflected a risk factor for possible developmental problems (Fracasso et al., 1994). In another study comparing Anglo-American mothers and Puerto Rican mothers, both groups of mothers preferred securely attached children to insecurely attached children, but they differed in the reasons for their preferences. Anglo-American mothers focused on children's self confidence and independence. Puerto Rican mothers focused on the children's demeanor, obedience, and quality of relatedness (Harwood & Miller, 1991). Across groups, higher proportions of infants have been classified as insecurely attached in minority cultures compared to middle-class American culture (Lamb, Thompson, Gardner, & Charnov, 1985). The modal classification in all countries examined (by meta-analysis of attachment studies) however, remains "secure" (van Ijzendoorn & Kroonenberg, 1988).

Multiracial Families and Child Development

Multiracial families are the product of mixed race unions or adoption of a child of another race (Rosenblatt, 1999). Census data collection techniques often do not capture the reality of race and ethnicity. To the degree that census data is accurate, it suggests there has been an increase in multiracial marital unions in the United States since 1967. In 1995, 1,392,000 married couples in the United States were composed of partners of different races (U.S. Bureau of the Census, 1996b). They are less frequent than expected based on population demographics, and they tend to be distributed in urban coastal areas. Different race constellations are found in different parts of the United States (Rosenblatt, 1999). With respect to interracial adoptions, in 1990, it was estimated that 8 percent of all adoptions were interracial (Simon, Alstein, & Melli, 1994).

There is little quantitative literature on the experiences, dynamics and traditions of multiracial families (Rosenblatt, 1999). Research is difficult because the issues in one multiracial constellation might be quite different from those in another multiracial constellation. Based on their qualitative study of interracial (Black and White) couples living in the Minneapolis-St. Paul communities, researchers identified common issues across couples and situations. Most of the couples viewed themselves and their lives to be ordinary, differing little from other couples. Couples differed markedly in how much racism or discrimination they experienced, but they all reported some experiences of racism or discrimination (problems in renting or purchasing a home, problems securing a mortgage, government and university forms that presumed a small number of discrete racial categories, some difficulty with acceptance in religious establishments, being stopped by police officers, and difficulty being accepted by certain people in the neighborhood) (Rosenblatt, Karis, & Powell, 1995).

The study described other qualitative issues. Identity issues were common and they were more predominant in children of multiracial couples. The children did not face competing loyalties. They were troubled by the need of larger society to define them. School peer groups put pressure on multiracial children to choose one identity or the other. It was important to African American parents of multiracial children that the child be knowledgeable about African American heritage and the challenges of racism in society. Families sometimes faced opposition from some of the members of their families of origin, but the opposition tended to dissipate over time. White women who married Black men faced opposition (at least as characterized in the popular press) by Black women (Rosenblatt et al., 1995).

Transracial adoptions were relatively rare in the United States until after World War II, when a large number of American soldiers and their families adopted Asian children. Nearly 3,000 Japanese children and 840 Chinese children were adopted into American (mostly White American) families between 1948 and 1962. The Korean War and then the Vietnam conflict created additional phases of interracial adoptions of Asian children

(Silverman & Fiegelman, 1990). Many Native American children experienced transracial adoptions as the result of the Indian Adoption Project in the Bureau of Indian Affairs and the Child Welfare League of America. Close to 700 children were placed until the project was abandoned due to Native American opposition. The overall number of adoptions slowed in the 1960s. From the early 1960s to the early 1970s, citizen advocacy groups promoted the adoption of Black children into White homes (Simon & Alstein, 1977). They saw transracial adoption as an answer to the problems of persisting foster care and institutionalization. But as the number of children in transracial adoption placements rose, workers began to question whether sufficient efforts were made to place Black children with Black families and whether transracial adoptions compromised the integrity of the Black community. Currently, there are only about 1,000 to 2,000 Black-White placements per year, mostly involving older children, physically or emotionally disabled children, or sibling groups (Silverman & Fiegelman, 1990).

Although the absolute number of adoptions has fallen, the constellation of transracial adoptions has shifted, with a slow and steady increase of adoptions of children from Central and South America into White American families (Silverman & Fiegelman, 1990). Current statistics on the frequency and rate of transracial adoptions are difficult to find because of the demise of the National Center for Social Statistics, traditionally charged with the task of collecting adoption statistics. Immigration data on the numbers of immigrant orphans suggests there are between 3,000 and 5,000 international adoptions per year, primarily of Korean, Indian and Hispanic children (Silverman & Fiegelman, 1990).

Research on the adjustment of children in transracial adoptions is limited because of the tendency to rely upon parental reports. Existing research suggests most transracial adoptions are successful, parents tend to honor the culture of the adopted child, children identify with their culture of origin, children identify with their race and the race of their parents, children show good overall adjustment, and adoptees who reached adolescence and adulthood seemed firmly committed to their adopted parents (Fanshel, 1975 Simon & Alstein, 1977). In families that isolated Black transracially adopted children from the Black community, the children accepted some negative stereotypes about Black people in American society (Simon & Alstein, 1981). White parents of Black children encountered more racial hostility than other groups of transracially adopting parents (Fiegelman & Silverman, 1983). Although aggregate results suggest good outcomes, at least a small portion of each the above studies reported adjustment problems in some transracially adopted children. No studies are available on whether the base rate of poor adjustment outcomes in transracial adoptees is similar to that seen in other family structures, nor is research available on factors predictive of poor adjustment.

DIVERSITY OF FAMILY STRUCTURE

FAMILY STRUCTURE AND CHILD DEVELOPMENT

To illustrate the impact of family structure on child development, researchers have examined child development trajectories and outcomes in families that are considered nontraditional. Different family structures are quite common but the term nontraditional suggests they are a deviation from the norm. In reality, it is quite normal and even traditional for families to contain a variety of member constellations (Lamb, 1999).

HEAD OF HOUSEHOLD

Families with Single Parents (Absent Fathers)

Most research on families headed by single parents has focused on single motherhood. In the United States today, less than half of children grow up in dual-parent households. Nearly one-third of children are born to single parents (the vast majority of whom remain single). Another third are born to parents who divorce before the children reach adulthood. Research has shown that developmental outcomes in children living in single parent households differ by gender, race, and parental education and occupational attainment (McLanahan & Teitler, 1999).

In single parent families, gender differences in children's adjustment are believed to be related to two issues: the need of boys for an adult male role model and the somewhat greater tendency for girls to reject the introduction of a new man into the household (Thorton & Camburn, 1987). Gender roles may affect patterns of acting out as a way of protesting parental departure or the introduction of a stepparent (McLanahan & Teitler, 1999). Race differences are seen in children's adjustment to single parent households in post-divorce situations. The higher rate of divorce and single parenthood in Black families leads to more community social support, but when the impact of divorce is accompanied by low socioeconomic status, the impact on Black children may be greater than other groups (Stack, 1974). Father absence doubles the risk of school withdrawal regardless of race, but it doubles the risk of teenage pregnancy among White and Hispanic teens compared to a 25 percent increase in risk in

Black teens (but Blacks have a higher base rate of risk) (Wu & Martinson, 1993).

Families with Fathers as Primary Caregivers

In one study of United States families, 23 percent of employed married mothers with a child under age five reported the father was the primary caretaker during the mother's working hours (Pleck, 1997). Fathers as primary caregivers, however, have not received much attention in the behavioral sciences literature (Russell, 1999). The few research studies that exist are restricted by small sample sizes (Russell & Radojevic, 1992). Based on preliminary studies, there are two types of families in which fathers act as primary caregivers: those in which only the mother is employed (Grbich, 1992; Pruett, 1987) and those in which both parents are employed and the father tends to have daytime parenting responsibilities during the mother's work hours (Geiger, 1996). Most studies of fathers as primary caregivers describe the father as highly participatory, but few studies describe the details of that participation (Russell, 1999). Studies focused on fathers who spend relatively more time with children than mothers, but there was a broad range of hours per week and duration of time (e.g., number of months) that fathers acted as primary caregivers (Russell, 1999). Variables of interest have included overall amount of father involvement in direct child care, amount of father involvement in the socialization of children, amount of father involvement in physical care of children, involvement in decision making about the children, the availability of fathers to children (Radin, 1982; Sagi, 1982), division of household labor and repair, and responsibility for family finances (Russell, 1989).

Four types of explanations have been identified as antecedents for fathers as primary caregivers: paternal inability to find employment, an increase in family employment (because of both parents were employed or because of greater maternal earning power), career interests (with mothers more interested and fathers relatively less interested in their careers), and egalitarian beliefs about parenting and gender roles (Geiger, 1996; Grbich, 1992; Radin, 1994). Fathers were likely to report active parenting involvement in families with fewer children. Age of the child did not seem to be related to father involvement (Russell, 1999). The success of families with fathers as primary caregivers was dependent a mutual capacity for spousal role support (Radin, 1994). Over time, families tended to revert to traditional roles (Grbich, 1992), usually because of social disapproval experienced by fathers caring for very young children and infants, and because of social isolation due to relative lack of day-to-day extrafamilial social support. Families also reverted to more traditional roles for financial reasons. Change to less traditional roles tended to be mediated by gender role orientation and egalitarian beliefs (Russell, 1999).

With respect to the impact on child development, the influence on children is not particularly strong (Russell, 1999). Self-report data from fathers supported the view that the quality of father-child relationships improved when fathers were primary caregivers. However, observational data provided only weak support for improvements in the quality of relationships (Lamb, Frodi, Hwang, Frodi, & Steinberg, 1982). Support was stronger when variables such as affection, attunement, and preferred parent were included in the analysis (Geiger, 1996). Longitudinal studies found no support for less traditional gender role attitudes in children, but children did tend to report approval of nontraditional employment patterns and childrearing patterns (Williams, Radin, & Allegro, 1992). Social competence (empathy and locus of control) was correlated with father participation, especially when fathers were perceived as supportive, nurturant, sensitive and warm (Radin, 1982; Sagi, 1982). Degree of father involvement was correlated with verbal intelligence scores for both boys and girls, with a more pronounced effect for boys. It is unclear whether fathers' parenting values were more achievement oriented or whether the increase was due to increased stimulation from both parents (Radin, 1982).

Stepfamilies

According to the 1992 census, the stepfamily is the fastest growing family structure in the United States (U.S. Bureau of the Census, 1992), with about 17 percent of all families headed by a married couple with children falling into that category (Glick, 1989). Stepfamilies form after the death of a spouse or partner, termination of a former cohabitation or marriage, and parents who never married. Family structures might include both residential and non-residential children from previous relationships. Half-siblings might be born into the family (Hetherington & Stanley-Hagan, 1999). Children of divorce who are younger than age five have a 59 percent chance of entering a stepfamily before age 18, children between five and nine have a 35 percent chance, and children older than nine have a 14 percent chance (Bumpass & Sweet, 1989).

Research on the impact of divorce and remarriage on child development began with a focus on divorce, with a later focus on stepfamily functioning. Early research focused on problems and deficits in stepfamilies (Ganong & Coleman, 1994; Orleans, Palisi, & Caddell, 1989). Later research focused on diverse experiences and processes contributing to individual differences in family adjustment (Hetherington, 1993). Research on stabilization of family units led to estimates that disequilibrium and eventual stabilization takes anywhere from two to three years to as long as five to seven years (Cherlin & Furstenberg, 1994). Pathways for stabilization are linked to antecedents and family history. Children from high-conflict pre-divorce families show better adjustment during stabilization. Children from families with little overt acrimony show increased problems during stabilization (Amato, Loomis, & Booth, 1995). Children benefit from improved financial circumstances in stepfamilies (Zill, 1994), but they may resent the stepparent if they had a close relationship in a single-parent household or an involved non-custodial parent (Hetherington & Jodl, 1994).

The risk of maladjustment in children during and after stabilization in a stepfamily is related to multiple risk and protective factors that interact in multifaceted ways. Factors of importance include the quality of family relationships, the stability of family relationships, changes in financial stability, changes in residence and school, individual characteristics of the parents, individual characteristics of the children, and correspondence with normative developmental changes such as puberty. As the number of concurrent or sequential changes increases, so does the risk of an adverse outcome. However, stabilization also might produce positive changes, increased resources, and new opportunities for gratifying family relationships (Hetherington & Stanley-Hagan, 1999). Because single custodial mothers tend to remarry more often than fathers, most research has focused on stepfather families. A few have examined stepmother families. Very few studies have focused on blended or complex stepfamilies (with both partners bringing custodial children, non-custodial children or the birth of new half siblings) (Hetherington & Stanley-Hagan, 1999).

The younger the child is at the time of entering a stepfamily, the more likely the child will develop an attachment to the new stepparent (Hetherington, 1993). Young children also are more likely to face multiple family transitions (Thomson, 1994). Divorce occurs more rapidly and frequently in remarriages, with one-fourth of them disrupted within five years (Martin & Bumpass, 1989). One in ten children faces two divorces of their residential parents before age 16 (Furstenberg, 1988). It is unclear what percentage of children face multiple adjustment to cohabiting partners of their residential parents. Older children have a more difficult time adjusting to stepfamilies than younger children. Compared to younger children, they report more sustained internalizing and externalizing problems and deficits (in social and academic spheres) (Hetherington et al., 1992). About one-third of adolescent boys and one-fourth of adolescent girls disengage from their families by spending little time in family activities, spending little time at home, and leaving home early (Cherlin & Furstenberg, 1994).

Some of them form a close relationship with another adult (such as the parent of a friend) and others become involved with antisocial peers or receive no alternative adult supervision (Hetherington & Stanley-Hagan, 1999).

There are some gender differences in children's adjustment to step-parents, but differences tend to weaken as children enter adolescence (Hetherington & Stanley-Hagan, 1999). The presence of a stepfather improves boys' adjustment but it has no effect or a negative effect on girls' adjustment (Amato & Keith, 1991). Boys tend to adjust more quickly to a stepparent than girls (Brand, Clingempeel, & Bowen-Woodward, 1988). Preadolescent girls who show a poor adjustment to a stepparent are at increased for poor social and academic competence in adolescence (regardless of the stepparent's gender) (Lee, Burkham, Zimiles, & Ladewski, 1994). Sometimes adjustment problems remit after stabilization (Amato & Keith, 1991). The vast majority of children in stepfamilies do not experience significant problems; however, the rate of problems such as school dropout, academic problems, unemployment, conduct disorder, teenage pregnancy, and other behavior problems increases twofold from about 10 percent in first-marriage families to about 20 to 25 percent in children of divorced and remarried families (Mekos, Hetherington, & Reiss, 1996).

Families with Gay or Lesbian Parents

It was not until the last decade of the 20th century that researchers began to study gay and lesbian individuals as couples and as parents (Patterson & Chan, 1999). Lesbian parents have received greater attention in the literature, especially those who gave birth in a heterosexual relationship and then later adopted a lesbian lifestyle (Kirkpatrick, 1996). However, increasing numbers of lesbian women have chosen to have children in the context of a lesbian identity or relationship (Patterson & Chan, 1999). A similar research trend was seen with fathers, first focusing on gay fathers who had children in a heterosexual relationship followed by the assumption of a gay identity, and later focusing on gay men who had children in the context of a gay identity or relationship (Patterson & Chan, 1996). Families with gay and lesbian parents have many antecedents and structures, including those who start out in heterosexual relationships, those with one (or both) homosexual partners who decide not to divorce after assuming the homosexual identity, those who are single or have same-sex partners, those whose same-sex partners assume a step-parenting role and those who do not, and blended stepsibling families after a gay or lesbian union. Gay and lesbian couples are bearing children through donor insemination, with known and unknown donors, or through surrogacy. Known donors may assume parental, avuncular, anonymous, or other roles (Patterson & Chan, 1999; Pies, 1990). Gay and lesbian couples also become parents through foster care and adoption (Patterson, 1995; Ricketts, 1991). An important issue in lesbian and gay families is the extent to which biological relatedness affects experiences and definitions of kinship (Weston, 1991).

Research on developmental outcomes in children of gay and lesbian parents generally has included only White, well-educated, middle-class, largely professional families in and around urban areas (Patterson & Chan, 1999). Therefore, generalization to other groups is limited. Much of the impetus for research on children with gay or lesbian parents has come from judicial concerns about developmental outcomes (Falk, 1989). Research has focused on three main areas: psychosexual development, other aspects of personal development, and social relationships (Patterson & Chan, 1999).

Research on gender identity (Kirkpatrick, Smith, & Roy, 1981) and gender role behavior (Hoeffer, 1981; Gottman, 1990) revealed no differences in children's development as a function of parental sexual orientation (Kirkpatrik, Smith, & Roy, 1981). The number of children who developed a lesbian, gay, or bisexual identity did not exceed presumed population base rates as a function of parental sexual orientation (Bozett, 1989; Gottman, 1990). Studies of patterns of child sexual abuse showed that gay parents were no more likely than heterosexual parents to perpetrate child sexual abuse (Jenny, Roesler, & Poyer, 1994). Studies of other developmental features, including psychiatric and behavior problems (Tasker & Golombok, 1995, 1997), personality (Gottman, 1990), self concept (Huggins, 1989), locus of control, and moral judgment (Rees, 1979) revealed no differences between children of lesbian mothers and those of heterosexual mothers. Longitudinal data revealed no differences in levels of anxiety, depression, need for mental health consultation, or occupational history in adult children of gay and lesbian parents (Tasker & Golombok, 1997).

Studies of children's social relationships have revealed anecdotal concern about children's worries of being stigmatized because of their parents' sexual orientation (Rafkin, 1990), but group data have revealed no evidence for compromised peer relationships, and no differences in the extent or duration of peer teasing during childhood. However, adult children of lesbian mothers who recalled being teased were more likely to say it concerned sexual orientation (Tasker & Golombok, 1995). Adult children were more likely to remember being teased and to report low self esteem if their father expressed negative emotions about the mother's lesbian identity (Huggins, 1989). Children showed better adjustment if they learned of their parent's sexual orientation early in childhood compared to early to middle adolescence (Paul, 1986). Children of divorced lesbian mothers typically reported regular contact with their fathers (Hare & Richards, 1993).

PARENTAL INCARCERATION

About 1.5 million children have an incarcerated parent (Seymour, 1998). Consistent with literature on impoverished families, the effect sizes in studies of incarcerated parents are difficult to determine because of problems of collinearity. Research has shown that children of incarcerated parents are at increased risk of criminal behavior, poor school outcomes, substance abuse, behavior disorders, antisocial behavior, anxiety, and depression (Genty, 1998). Children report their adjustment problems are related to three factors: separation from their parent, social stigma, and deception about the parent's whereabouts or the reason for the incarceration (Gabel, 1992). Studies have shown that incarcerated parents express interest in information about childrearing, better visitation for their children, and help with trust and communication with their children. Both fathers and mothers seem to value their parental identity and family commitments (Kazura, 2001). Studies of the impact of parenting interventions with incarcerated parents have shown mixed results, and most studies suffer from a lack of follow-up on the stability of intervention impact (Landreth & Lobaugh, 1998). Parenting interventions seem to have a greater impact on parenting behavior than on children's self concepts (Harrison, 1997).

Studies of incarcerated fathers have shown that correctional policies and child welfare practice have a significant influence on shaping parenting opportunities, abilities and relationships with children (Hairston, 1998). Not all prisons provide parenting interventions. Among those that provide interventions, there is little consistency in the duration, content or breadth of intervention (Clement, 1993). Factors such as distant prison locations, the nature of proximal versus distal physical interaction allowed during visits, and inconvenient visiting schedules affected reunification efforts by child protective service systems. These factors play a role in the capacity of incarcerated mothers to maintain a bond with their children (Block & Potthast, 1998). Time-driven models of permanency planning usually do not accommodate for the length of incarceration sentences, impediments to parental participation in service plans, or impediments to parent-child visitation (Beckerman, 1998; Genty, 1998).

SUMMARY

1. Socioeconomic and cultural influences determine the adaptations and competencies that parents infuse in their children.

2. Cultural patterns influence family structure, definitions of kin, and family dynamics with diverse manifestations of the nature and perceived helpfulness of social support selection of discipline techniques, and patterns of relatedness. Based on national statistics on families entering the child services system, minority families are over-represented in care and protection samples.
3. Diversity of family structure and its influence on child development trajectories and outcomes is a relatively new branch of research. "Nontraditional" family constellations make up a substantial proportion of American families, and those constellations are reflected in care and protection samples.
4. Incarcerated parents represent an under-researched population of parents. Developmental outcomes in children of incarcerated parents are difficult to characterize in the aggregate because of small effect sizes and problems of collinearity with variables such as impoverishment.
5. It is useful to be informed about unique manifestations of family processes and dynamics based on group membership. Knowledge of empirical data relevant group characteristics lessens the likelihood that misunderstandings might affect data interpretation or recommendations. However, aggregate data should not be over-interpreted. Within-group heterogeneity limits generalizations that can be made.

6

The Etiology and Impact of Child Maltreatment

Concern about the etiology and impact of child maltreatment is a product of 20th century thought. As described earlier, the Battered Child Syndrome was first identified in 1962 by Kempe and colleagues. Most of what is known about the sequelae of child sexual abuse and other abuse was generated by clinical observations and research in the 1980s (Finkelhor, 1990; Green, 1993). Research on the impact of child neglect is a relatively recent development. The previous chapters of this book focused on theories of parenting behavior and the relevance of theory to the forensic assessment of children and families involved with the child protective service system. This chapter focuses on empirical research on child maltreatment for which the foregoing chapters provided a theoretical basis. The empirical research is embedded in the theoretical framework from which it is drawn.

This chapter describes types of maltreatment and the impact of maltreatment. It examines definitional issues in a broader framework of nosology. Types of maltreatment are drawn from legal and regulatory definitions of child maltreatment and from theoretically derived formulations of child maltreatment. Expanded information and recent developments in case law are provided to clarify the basis of the legal typologies of child maltreatment and to contrast them with typologies or operational definitions of child maltreatment used by empirical researchers. The middle portion of this chapter describes aggregate empirical research and survey reports on the individual impact of child maltreatment. Child maltreatment has a different impact at different developmental levels. The impact varies with factors such as age of onset, chronicity, severity, nature of the relationship with the perpetrator, and other factors. The differential impact is reviewed where empirical research is available to support outcome differences. However, heterogeneity of impact within developmental stages is seen because of individual factors (such as the resilience of some children) and social factors (such as varying degrees of rapidity and quality of individual and social responses to child maltreatment).

TYPES OF CHILD MALTREATMENT

MEASUREMENT ISSUES

The state of research practice on measuring the incidence and prevalence of child maltreatment is moving forward, but it is not particularly advanced. Noticeable improvements have been made in the last several decades, but research has remained hampered by basic measurement issues. Research on each type of maltreatment has been carried out by different groups of investigators using different definitions for the same general category of maltreatment, use of definitions in one category of maltreatment that overlap with other categories, and incomplete screening of population samples for the presence of maltreatment types other than those under study. Despite its greater prevalence, neglect has received much less definitional or research attention than other forms of child maltreatment. Definitional problems impede the ability of researchers, clinicians and legal scholars to integrate findings across studies, to determine whether specific types of child maltreatment (or combinations of types) result from predictable cumulative risk patterns in perpetrators, or to identify predictable or distinct sequelae in victims. Treatment outcome research is equally difficult for similar reasons (Zuravin, 1991a).

There is variation among legal scholars and empirical researchers in the number of categories (and subcategories) and the spectrum of behaviors subsumed by their nosologies. Two prototypical examples (Besharov, 1985; Zuravin, 1991a) are offered. Although many similarities are seen in the two approaches, the examples illustrate the contrast between nosologies that are valuable to policymakers and those that prove valid and reliable for researchers. For the purposes of conducting meaningful research, the development of classification systems or typologies begins with the grouping of relevant variables into categories based on core similarities (Zuravin, 1991a). Variables must be sufficiently distinct from those in other categories, so that overlap does not result in a high degree of classification error, or false positive and false negative classifications. Developing categories of child maltreatment poses a challenge because symptoms and behaviors that correlate with abuse reactions also tend to correlate with a generalized stress response (Finkelhor, 1990). Even "core" or basic behaviors associated with child maltreatment vary in frequency and in their correlation with other behaviors that might differ in degree or intent (such as the use of physical discipline). For example, physical abuse involves physical aggression toward a child. Physical neglect involves omissions in care. But the behaviors of concern are diverse, requiring the formulation of subcategories to maintain classification integrity (Zuravin, 1991a).

Although physical abuse involves an act of commission, behaviors falling under the rubric of acts of "commission" differ in chronicity, frequency, severity, and in their social acceptability (in mild forms) as physical discipline. Some types of aggressive behavior, such as spanking, slapping, shaking, and striking a child with an object, are more likely to be viewed by some people as acceptable forms of physical discipline (although attention usually is given to refraining from abuse even among those who use or advocate the use of such methods). By contrast, behaviors such as scalding, biting, choking, or attacking a child with a weapon are viewed by most people as unacceptable forms of physical discipline. Such behaviors tend to occur with less overall frequency than those that are regarded as types of physical discipline (Zuravin, 1991a). Although there is controversy about the acceptability of physical discipline, it remains a somewhat common form of discipline (Belsky, 1993a). Similarly, although behaviors that fall under the rubric of neglect have "omission" in common as a core similarity, one type of omission might be quite diverse from another type. A failure to provide adequate supervision, for example, is qualitatively different from a failure to meet physical needs (such as feeding, medical care or mental health care) (Zuravin, 1991a). The frequency, chronicity, and severity of child maltreatment are operational problems that affect classification integrity. Parental culpability sometimes is used as a qualifier in some types of neglect (to distinguish them from cases where parents have insufficient financial resource to meet basic physical and safety needs) (Belsky, 1993a; Zuravin, 1991a). Neglect cannot be ruled out, though, simply on the basis of impoverishment because some impoverished families manage resources better than others. Poor management of resources, even when they are scarce, can result in a higher degree of neglect relative to families who are comparably poor (Zuravin, 1991a).

Despite a proliferation of research on child sexual abuse in the 1970s and 1980s, fundamental definitional issues remain unresolved. There is little consensus among researchers, lawmakers and clinicians about the meaning of any of the terms describing *child sexual abuse*, and there is little agreement about what acts (other than the most apparent or most cross-culturally taboo acts) fall under the rubric or subcategories of child sexual abuse. Some behaviors are considered sexual by almost everyone (such as intercourse or genital fondling) and other behaviors are regarded as ambiguous in their sexuality (such as a parent appearing nude in front of a child) (Haugaard, 2000). Early research used broad definitions of child sexual abuse (Finkelhor, 1979), resulting in some of the high prevalence rate estimates for child sexual abuse (Haugaard, 2000).

The use of broad definitions of child sexual abuse made it problematic to consider abuse severity as a factor in forming laws, policies, and treatment approaches to child sexual abuse. Severity usually is judged by factors such as the frequency and duration of abuse, the presence of physical pain, the use of physical force by the perpetrator, and the type of sexual activity (Haugaard, 2000). Broad definitions make it difficult to study the short- and long-term impact of sexual abuse or to formulate useful interventions. Studies of undergraduates suggest that those who are affected by severe or repeated abuse represent only a small proportion of samples that are captured by broad definitions (Fromuth, 1986; Haugaard & Emery, 1989). Researchers and policymakers have just begun to organize efforts to systematically study child sexual abuse by creating a classification and definition system for all forms of child maltreatment. The National Institute for Child Health and Human Development (NICHD), in collaboration with the Children's Bureau of the Administration for Children and Families (ACF), developed an initiative to encourage the development of a reliable classification system for child sexual abuse and other forms of maltreatment (Haugaard, 2000). Responsible for major legislation such as the 1997 Adoption and Safe Families Act, the Children's Bureau of the ACF, is the focal point of organized federal responses to child maltreatment (Golden, 2000).

THE CONTRAST BETWEEN RESEARCH DEFINITIONS AND POLICY-DRIVEN DEFINITIONS

Research Definitions

Zuravin's (1991a) research nosology attempts to clarify definitional issues in a way that would help researchers gather data in a consistent and reliable manner across studies. Zuravin specifies categories and subtypes, helping researchers to isolate populations of interest in order to enhance the fidelity of research designs, treatment approaches and outcome assessments. Zuravin encourages researchers to consider the following concepts in the development of a nosology of child maltreatment. The *consequences of behavior* or endangerment of the child's health and welfare is one criterion for child maltreatment. Endangerment (rather than the legal focus on demonstrable harm to the child) is operationally defined according to specific caretaker behaviors. The *type of behavior* is described and divided into subtypes. For example, Zuravin recommends two subtypes of abuse (discipline behaviors and infrequent behaviors as described above), and 14 distinct and non-overlapping subtypes of neglect. She recommends that categories within the framework of abuse should not overlap with each other or with behaviors subsumed under definitions of emotional maltreatment.

Zuravin (1991a) examines definitions in their characterization of who is a perpetrator. She recommends that *perpetrators* of abuse should be defined broadly to include permanent caretakers, temporary caretakers, persons living in the same household as the child, and professions with roles of responsibility and who hold the child's trust. Perpetrators of neglect should be defined narrowly to include only permanent caretakers and those to whom the caretaker delegates responsibility for the child. Zuravin recommends that some of the subcategories of neglect (e.g., supervision, personal hygiene, education, failure to provide a permanent home) should require a pattern of *chronicity* in order to meet the threshold for falling within the subcategory. For subcategories of abuse, less assaultive behaviors such as grabbing, shaking or spanking would require chronicity to meet the threshold for falling within the subcategory unless they result in injury (regardless of severity). Highly assaultive behaviors would be regarded as abusive even if they occurred only one time. Zuravin (1991a) discourages any inclusion of *perpetrator intent to harm or culpability for harm* as a definitional criterion. She discourages the inclusion of any aspect of child provocation, and any analysis of the *age of the child* as a factor in defining child maltreatment, except for two subtypes of neglect: supervision and custody-related neglect.

Policy Definitions

Legal definitions of maltreatment tend to focus on seriously harmful parental behaviors. Even though legal definitions focus on serious harm, room is usually left for judicial discretion in the interpretation of definitions. Legal definitions, therefore, sometimes are purposefully vague for some terms and descriptions. Legal definitions assume what parents did once in the past, they might do again unless the presumption of continued harmful behavior is rebutted (Goldstein, 1999). Legal approaches to classification give attention to the issue of "minimal competence," recognized manifestly and latently by laws governing the threshold for state involvement in care and protection cases and especially in termination cases.

In a summary of definitions of serious harm, Besharov (1985, 1990) recommended restricted definitions falling in distinct categories of serious parental harm to children. Harm that could be demonstrated from a legal standpoint was the underlying principal within each of the categories. The categories are similar in their emphasis on serious harm to many of those reviewed earlier in this book in the introduction to definitional issues. Besharov's nosology contains restricted definitions that typify those found in legal codes. It recognizes the legal system's embrace of discretion and the tendency to define child maltreatment with a low degree of specificity. There is a pragmatic element in its focus on harm for which state intervention might have a realistic and reasonably meaningful impact. It emphasizes the type of harm for which coercive intervention by the state would do more good than harm. It differs from research approaches in the range of continua within each category, the focus on legally demonstrable serious harm (or potential for serious harm), and in the tendency to subsume legal realism in the law's historic allowance for significant parental autonomy.

Besharov's nosology (1985, 1990) consists of 11 categories of child maltreatment. *Physical battering* includes physical assaults (striking, kicking, biting, throwing, burning) that caused or could have caused serious physical injury to the child. *Physical endangerment* includes reckless behavior (leaving a young child alone, placing a child in a hazardous situation) that caused or could have caused serious physical injury to the child. *Physical neglect* includes failure to provide food or clothing, and attention to hygiene or other needed care that caused or could have caused serious physical injury, illness or disability. *Medical neglect* includes failure to provide medical, dental or mental health care needed to prevent or treat serious physical or mental impairment, illness or disability. *Sexual abuse* includes vaginal, anal or oral intercourse; vaginal or anal penetration; or other forms of inappropriate sexual contact that caused or could have caused serious emotional injury. *Sexual exploitation* includes use of a child in pornography, prostitution or other sexual exploitation that caused or could have caused serious emotional injury. *Emotional abuse* includes either emotional or physical assaults such as torture or close confinement that caused or could have caused serious emotional injury. *Developmental neglect* includes failure to provide necessary emotional nurturing and cognitive or physical stimulation that caused or could have caused serious developmental problems. *Improper ethical supervision* includes parental conduct that contributes to child delinquency. *Educational neglect* includes failure to send a child to school in accordance with the state's educational laws. *Abandonment* includes leaving a child alone or in the care of another under circumstances that demonstrate an intentional abdication of parental responsibilities.

Although there have been moves to establish a uniform nosology for child maltreatment (Besharov, 1985, 1990; Zuravin, 1991a; Cicchetti & Barnett, 1991), there is no overall nosology to guide the reader, policymakers, legal scholars, or behavioral sciences researchers. Studies and case law that are reviewed in the next sections were selected based on relevance to care and protection matters and to the legal construct of *minimal parenting competence*. Examples in the law do not always have a parallel research base. Limiting this chapter to a review of care and protection samples in research would result in a scant data base because of the measurement issues described above, and because of ethical concerns that prevent controlled studies on the population of interest. Although seminal risk studies suggest cautious generalization is reasonable, it is good practice to look for converging external validity among studies (Dubowitz 1999; Slovic, Monahan, & MacGregor, 2000). As a general guideline for digesting the clinical and legal meaningfulness of particular research studies to individual cases that are typical of the child protective service system, the reader may wish to refer to the proposed typologies of Besharov (1985) and Zuravin (1991a) described above (or to watch for developments in the literature, including those described above by Haugaard, 2000). Besharov (1985, 1990) and Zuravin (1991a) are offered as prototypes of legal and research-based nosologies, but there are other proposed structures in the literature. Because most research does not follow the categories and subcategories described by the above typologies, the information below is based on aggregate data within broad categories of child maltreatment.

THE IMPACT OF MALTREATMENT

Estimates of the Scope of Child Maltreatment

Data on Care and Protection Cases

Data on children and families involved with child protective service systems is collected by the U.S. Department of Health and Human Services (DHHS). DHHS amended the system of data collection in 1996 and the most recently published data are presented here. According to the DHHS (National Child Abuse and Neglect Reporting System, 1999), there were approximately 903,000 victims of child maltreatment in 1998 and approximately 826,000 victims in 1999. A child may have been counted each time he or she was found to be a victim of maltreatment. Based on responses from the 50 states to the 1999 National Child Abuse and Neglect Reporting System (National Child Abuse and Neglect Reporting System, 1999), of the estimated 2,974,000 referrals received by child protective services agencies, 60.4 percent were "screened in" or referred for further investigation and 39.6 percent were "screened out." More than half of reports (54.7 percent) were received from professionals. The remaining percent of reports were received from nonprofessionals (family members or community members). Slightly less than one-third of investigations (29.2 percent) led to a supported or substantiated disposition. The report defined substantiated as "an investigation disposition that concludes that the allegation of maltreatment or risk of maltreatment was supported or founded by state law or state policy." Victims of child maltreatment were defined as those children found to have experienced "supported" or "substantiated" maltreatment (or who were found to be at risk of experiencing it).

According to the report (National Child Abuse and Neglect Reporting System, 1999), almost three-fifths of all victims (58.4 percent) suffered neglect, one fifth (21.3 percent) suffered physical abuse and a smaller percentage (11.3 percent) suffered sexual abuse. More than one third (35.9 percent) were victims of other maltreatment, including abandonment, threats of harm to the child and congenital drug addiction. The lowest reported incidence was for psychological maltreatment, which had a rate of 0.9 victims per 1,000 children. The percentages total more than 100 because more than one-third of victims were victims of more than one category of child maltreatment. The highest victimization rates were found in the newborn-to-three age range (13.9 maltreatments per 1,000 children in this age range in the population). Rates declined as age increased. Rates of most forms of maltreatment showed no gender differences. The sexual abuse rate for female children (1.6 female children per 1,000 in the population) was higher than the rate for males (0.4 per 1,000 in the population).

Victimization rates by ethnicity ranged from a low of 4.4 per 1,000 in Asian/Pacific Islanders to 25.2 per 1,000 in African Americans (National Child Abuse and Neglect Reporting System, 1999). Other rates were 10.6 (White), 12.8 (Hispanic) and 20.1 (American Indian). Children victimized prior to 1999 were almost three times more likely to be re-victimized in the six month period following the first victimization than children with no prior history of victimization. Fifteen states provided sufficient data to analyze risk factors that might influence recurrence. In comparison to children who suffered physical abuse, those who were neglected were 44 percent more likely to experience recurrence. Children who suffered more than one form of maltreatment were 27 percent more likely to experience recurrence when compared with those who suffered physical abuse. The youngest children (newborn to age three) were most likely to experience recurrence. Rates dropped as children grew older. Compared to White non-Hispanic children, African American children were 17 percent less likely to experience recurrence and Asian/Pacific Islander children were 28 percent less likely to experience recurrence. Children whose victimization was reported to child protective services by law enforcement officers were less likely than other children to experience recurrence. In 1999 (National Child Abuse and Neglect Reporting System, 1999), 171,000 children were placed by child protective services into foster care. An additional 49,000 children whose parents sought voluntary services were placed in foster care. Court actions were initiated for about 26.1 percent of child maltreatment victims. Four-fifths of victims (79.3 percent) were provided with court-appointed representatives.

Data on Perpetrators of Child Maltreatment

The 1999 National Child Abuse and Neglect Reporting System (National Child Abuse and Neglect Reporting System, 1999) provided data child maltreatment perpetrators (defined as "a person who has maltreated a child while in a caretaking relationship to that child"). Three fifths (61.8 percent) of perpetrators were female and female perpetrators typically were younger than male counterparts (41.5 percent of female perpetrators were younger than 30, 31.2 percent of male perpetrators were younger than 30). The most common pattern of perpetration was a female parent acting alone. Nine-tenths of all victims were maltreated by at least one parent. Female parents perpetrated neglect and physical abuse for the highest percentage of victims. Male parents perpetrated sexual abuse for the highest percentage of victims.

Fatalities

An estimated 1,100 children die of child maltreatment, a rate of approximately 1.62 deaths per 100,000 children in the population. Data across five years (1995 to 1999) showed that the rate of maltreatment fatalities has been fairly stable, fluctuating between 1.62 and 1.68 (National Child Abuse and Neglect Reporting System, 1999). Of the available data, children younger than age one account for 42.6 percent of fatalities and 86.1 percent were younger than six. The rate declined consistently through age eight. Maltreatment deaths were more often associated with neglect (38.2 percent of cases) than with other forms of maltreatment (26.1 percent resulted from physical abuse alone, 22.7 percent resulted from physical abuse and neglect, 5.1 percent resulted from physical abuse and other, 2.7 percent resulted from neglect and other, 1.6 percent resulted from neither physical abuse nor neglect, and 3.5 percent had no causal category reported). More than one-tenth (12.5 percent) of the families of child fatalities had received child protective services in the five years prior to the death.

THE LINK BETWEEN MALTREATMENT AND CHILD PSYCHOPATHOLOGY

The impact of maltreatment historically has been viewed as uniformly negative and disruptive (Wekerle & Wolfe, 1996). In the 1980s, the impact of maltreatment was investigated with increasing specificity. Researchers recognized that child maltreatment affects victims differently, with some victims remaining asymptomatic, and with little consistency in clinical presentation among symptomatic victims in specific patterns of sequelae (Cicchetti & Rizley, 1981). Researchers recognized the difficulty of attributing a child's symptoms to trauma reactions relative to other factors such as disorganized and chaotic family environments or generalized stress (Finkelhor, 1990). Diverse outcomes were seen, especially in studies that included an analysis of mediators of positive adjustment and outcomes (Wolfe, 1987). Variability was seen in the duration of child psychopathology, with some cases remitting fairly rapidly and others persisting into adult forms of psychopathology (Wekerle & Wolfe, 1996). Developmental differences were observed in children's reactions to trauma, with modifications seen as children reappraised traumatic events at different developmental stages (Finkelhor, 1990). There is considerable individual and developmental variability in the manifestation and severity of symptoms in reaction to abuse (Green, 1993). Nonetheless, there is an emerging base of prospective empirical studies that support a link between child maltreatment and child psychopathology, with moderate consistency of impact across principle domains of functioning (physical, cognitive, socioemotional) (Famularo, Kinscherff, & Fenton, 1990; Heiman, 1992; Helfer et al., 1997; Finkelhor, 1990; Wekerle & Wolfe, 1996).

CONCEPTUAL AND DIAGNOSTIC CLASSIFICATION SCHEMES

Posttraumatic Stress Disorder

A common model for understanding the impact of child maltreatment is the diagnostic framework of posttraumatic stress disorder or PTSD. Although there are other diagnostic conceptualizations that encapsulate the impact of child maltreatment, posttraumatic stress disorder has received the most attention. As defined by *DSM-IV* and *DSM-IV-TR* (American Psychiatric Association, 1994, 2000), diagnostic criteria for PTSD include the precursor of a traumatic event in which the person experienced, witnessed or was confronted with actual or threatened death or serious injury, or a threat to the physical integrity of the self or others. The event must be followed by a specified number of symptoms. The duration of time between the event and the onset of symptoms covers a range of time, from within the first three months of the trauma to a delay of months or even years. The person's response to the traumatic event must involve horror, helplessness or intense fear; or in children, behavioral expressions of disorganization or agitation. Symptoms include persistent re-experiencing of the event in one or more forms, persistent avoidance of reminders and numbing of responsiveness in three or more ways, and persistent hyperarousal in two or more ways. Symptom duration must persist for more than one month and the symptoms must cause distress or impairment in social, occupational or other important spheres of functioning. Young children usually do not relive or re-experience the trauma as vividly as adults. Their distressing dreams or nightmares might consist of monsters, rescuing others, or threats to self or others. Reenactments might be seen in repetitive play.

For victims of child maltreatment, PTSD might arise from direct victimization, witnessing maltreatment, learning about maltreatment of a sibling, or domestic violence against a parent. The response is classified as acute for symptoms of less than three month's duration, chronic for symptoms of more than three month's duration, and delayed onset if the individual becomes symptomatic six or more months after the traumatic event (American Psychiatric Association, 1994, 2000). Although they are not part of the formal diagnostic criteria, associated features that might be seen in victims of childhood sexual or physical abuse (among other forms of trauma) include impaired affect modulation; self-destructive and impulsive behavior; symptoms of dissociation; somatic complaints; and feelings of ineffectiveness, shame, despair, hopelessness, or hostility; feeling permanently damaged; loss of previously sustained beliefs: social withdrawal; feeling constantly threatened; impaired relationships; or change from individual's previous personality. It is unclear how frequently the associated features accompany the disorder. Lifetime prevalence estimates for PTSD range from 1 percent to 14 percent. Estimates in at-risk populations (combat veterans, victims of volcanic eruptions and victims of criminal violence) range from 3 percent to 58 percent (American Psychiatric Association, 1994, 2000).

Complete recovery is seen in about half of PTSD patients within three months. Many others have persistent symptoms for longer than 12 months after the trauma. The severity, duration, and proximity to the traumatic event are important factors affecting the development of PTSD. PTSD is not the only expected outcome of trauma. Other disorders that might follow trauma include reactive attachment disorder, panic disorder, agoraphobia, obsessive-compulsive disorder, social phobia, specific phobia, major depressive disorder, somatization disorder, and substance related disorders (American Psychiatric Association, 1994, 2000).

Proposed Sub-typologies of Child Posttraumatic Stress Disorder

Some researchers and theorists are not satisfied with the framework of PTSD as a broad diagnostic entity meant for victims of different forms of trauma (Wekerle & Wolfe, 1996). In her research on childhood trauma, Terr (1991) identified Type I and Type II PTSD, with Type I occurring in victims of a single traumatic event and Type II occurring in victims of multiple or chronic traumata. A mixed Type I and Type II response might be seen in victims of sudden or shocking deaths or accidents. Type I is more common and less disruptive to daily functioning. Type II results in more severe psychopathology and may be accompanied by personality disturbances. Some of Terr's observations of reactions or symptoms are similar to descriptions of children's reactions in the DSM-IV, but Terr described a broader range of children's symptoms. Several studies have supported this formulation of PTSD in children (Famularo et al., 1990; Kiser, Heston, Millsap, & Pruitt, 1991).

In Type I PTSD, children's symptoms fall into three categories: a full and detailed or "etched-in" memory of the event, retrospective reworking or reappraisal of the trauma, and misperceptions of responsibility and blame. In Type I PTSD, children retain active memory of the traumatic event. Mis-sequencing of events is commonly seen in children regardless of how active their memory of the trauma might be. In Type II PTSD, children's symptoms fall into four categories: denial and emotional numbing, self hypnosis and dissociation, rage, and persistent sadness. Children with Type II PTSD are less awareness of their symptoms, they might have functional memory impairment for aspects of the trauma or aspects of their childhood histories, they show indifference to pain, they are viewed as lacking empathy, and they feel invisible. They commonly avoid intimacy and they have difficulty with awareness of feelings or labeling feelings. The anaesthetized or emotionally numbed pattern of Type II PTSD might be cyclical with feelings or expressions of rage. In some cases, aggressive behavior might become an habitual pattern. In other cases it might fluctuate with extreme passivity because of the child's fear of the anger (Terr, 1991; Wekerle & Wolfe, 1996).

PHYSICAL ABUSE

The Psychological Impact of Physical Abuse

Prevalence estimates for physical abuse in child protective service system populations are reported above. According to FBI statistics, 20 percent of murders occur between family members (Garbarino, Guttman, & Seeley, 1986; Helfer & Kempe, 1987). Mortalities from physical abuse result from beating or other blunt trauma (multiple or single episode), burns, firearm injuries, stab wounds, asphyxia (smothering, choking, strangulation, drowning, gas poisoning, hanging, chest compression, excluding oxygen), and poisoning or force feeding of noxious substances (Helfer et al., 1997). Some behaviors associated with Factitious Disorder by Proxy (injecting a noxious substance into a child to gain sympathy for being the parent of an ill child) can result in death (Robins & Sesan, 1991).

Researchers have described the impact of physical abuse in terms of symptoms and behavioral sequelae. The experience of being a victim of physical abuse might or might not be the principal etiological factor for psychopathology in a particular child (Wekerle & Wolfe, 1996). Although researchers have found consistent patterns, there is no uniform or isomorphic relationship between the experience of abuse and the expression of symptoms. Factors associated with the psychological impact of physical abuse are as follows (Crittenden & DeLalla, 1988; Helfer & Kempe, 1987; Helfer et al., 1997; Hoffman-Plotkin & Twentyman, 1984; Wekerle & Wolfe, 1996):

- *Developmental delay*: Slow weight gain. Slow physical growth. Delayed moral development.
- *Impaired cognitive development and academic progress*: Slow language development. Grade retention. Lower IQ than comparison samples of non-abused children.
- *Distorted social response*: Anxious attachment to parents. Attempts to get near the parent but withdraws when parent tries to get closer; avoidance of eye contact with parent, asks to be picked up then kicks the parent. More responsive to other adults than the parents. Negative emotional response to all people. Troubled peer relationships. Impaired social cognition. Reduced reciprocity in interactions. Inflexible patterns of behavior. Avoidant behavior toward maltreating parent. Lack of concern when others are distressed.
- *Withdrawal or apathy*: Avoidance of the parents. Apathetic solitariness, shyness. Low degree of communication, avoidance of socialization.
- *Hyperarousal*: Crying or irritability. Refusal to calm down. Nervous habits. Nightmares. Compulsive compliance.

- *Depression and self-destructive behavior*: Infliction of pain to self. Suicidal thoughts. Overeating or other somatic disturbances in adolescence.
- *Low self esteem*: Feel unloved, unwanted, inferior, inadequate. Feel disconnected from any social system. Distrustful of people. Feel deserving of maltreatment.
- *Aggression or other conduct problems*: Ready to hit back. Overactive and noncompliant. Provocative behavior. Truancy or runaway behavior in adolescence. Member of an antisocial group in adolescence. Power struggles. Counteracting peer aggression with aggression.
- *Substance Abuse.*

Cases involving Physical Abuse

Child protective service definitions sometimes correspond to criminal codes defining physical abuse. Criminal codes regulating the physical abuse of children fall into three categories: common law crimes of murder, manslaughter and mayhem; common law crimes of assault and battery; and statutory crimes of child maltreatment (aggravated abuse, unreasonable corporal punishment, child endangerment). Prosecuting the perpetrator of the death of a child is complicated by the fact that there often are multiple caretakers in a household, making it difficult to prove causation and perpetrator identity. Historically, judges and juries sometimes have been reluctant to render a finding of requisite intent or to convict the perpetrator of the most serious charges. Because the parental privilege to discipline often is a key element in the alleged perpetrator's defense, legal scholars view the distinction between legally permissible use of physical discipline and child abuse as an important one (Goldstein, 1999).

For example, in *State v. Thorpe* (1981), a father charged with the murder of his four-month-old daughter was convicted of assault and battery and sentenced to one year imprisonment and a $500 fine. Three issues influenced the case outcome: proving causation, finding malicious intent, and reluctance to render a verdict on a serious charge. In his defense, the father said the infant died an accidental death inflicted by the child's mother. The father admitted he spanked the infant shortly before her death, but he "did not realize how hard I hit her" because he was "very high strung" from lifting weights. Similarly, a common defense in shaken baby syndrome is to plead ignorance of the consequences of shaking an infant, that a reasonable person would not have known that such shaking recklessly endangers an infant's life (Goldstein, 1991). Courts differ as to whether felony child abuse resulting in death is synonymous with felony murder.

People v. Caffero (1989) ruled that felony child abuse is not a dangerous act within the meaning of the felony murder rule. By contrast, *Fagara v. State* (1987) and *Hendrick v. State* (1987) ruled otherwise.

Case law in criminal and civil matters involving physical abuse has addressed the distinction between physical abuse and physical discipline. For example, in *State v. Jones* (1986), a man cohabiting with a mother punished the mother's 16-year-old daughter, "frequently whipping her without any cause," "giving her about 25 blows with a switch...with such force as to raise welts upon her back," "choked her, and threw her violently to the ground," "one witness saw her tongue hanging out of her mouth while being choked." The appeals court reversed the criminal finding of assault and battery on the grounds that the test of criminal responsibility is the infliction of permanent injury. Similarly, in *State v. Kaimimoku* (1992), a daughter used profanity in response to a father's yelling and use of profanity toward the mother. The father responded by yelling and using profanity toward the daughter, he hit her with an open fist on the right side of her face and he punched her more than one time on her shoulders with a closed fist, causing her to sustain bruises. The father was arrested for the offense of abuse of a family or household member. He was found guilty at a bench trial, but the appeals court reversed the ruling on the grounds that the state did not show evidence that the father struck the daughter for any purpose other than punishment. In *Kama v. State* (1987), a mother summoned the police because the father was spanking his son with a belt and the spanking was "just a little bit out of hand." The son had pulled a knife on a younger child and then lied to both parents about it. The mother had spanked the child prior to the father's spanking. The son testified that the father spanked him, hit him in the face with his fist, hit him with a belt, kicked him in the stomach, and picked him up off the floor by his ears. The appeals court upheld a conviction of aggravated child abuse on the grounds that the trial court did not err in its refusal to instruct the jury on lesser offenses of misdemeanor child abuse and simple battery. The court made a distinction between punishment motivated by malice and punishment for the purpose of "education," stating the father's conduct was excessive, cruel, and merciless.

South Carolina Department of Social Services v. the Father and Mother; In the Interest of the Child (1988) was a case in which a father used a belt to spank a 13-year-old girl who lied about where she had been. The father and mother were found to have abused and neglected the child because the spanking caused bruises and because the mother did not intervene or report the incident. The parents challenged the state's statute concerning physical abuse, arguing they were exercising freedom of religion in their use of physical discipline. They argued that the statute denied them their right to religious liberty. The court ruled that the law cannot regulate what people believe, but it can regulate how people act even if they act on their religious beliefs. The court noted that the trial judge's remedy was minimal, not requiring removal of the child from the home, but merely requiring the parents to seek counseling monitored by the Department of Social Services and the guardian *ad litem*. The court found the statute constitutional.

The court found corporal punishment to be excessive in the case of *In re Rodney C., A Child Found to be Neglected, In re M. Children, Children Found to be Neglected* (1977) in the case of a mother who testified that she punished the children by having them bend over and hold their ankles, while keeping their knees locked. She required them to hold the position for up to half an hour. She said her children screamed and vomited when she used this method of punishment. In *Hooper v. Rockwell* (1999), evidence supported termination of a mother's parental rights on the grounds that she engaged in severe and repetitive abuse. Law enforcement officers found one child frightened, dripping wet, and bruised. An officer testified that the mother confessed to dunking the child in icy bath water as a form of punishment. Three clinical psychologists, one psychiatrist, and one counselor testified the children were physically abused, they did not want to return home, and they were extremely anxious, frightened and angry when the mother visited them.

In *Richland County Department of Social Services v. Earles* (1998), evidence supported a family court's termination of a mother's parental rights on the grounds that the mother's home could not be made safe within 12 months. Evidence showed she was the sole caretaker, that one child was severely malnourished, that the child was starved while forced to watch her brother eat, that she had been beaten and burned, and that both children had been repeatedly sexually abused. Evidence also showed that prior rehabilitation efforts had been unsuccessful. In *South Carolina Department of Social Services v. Brown* (1995), the court ruled that termination of the father's rights was in the best interest of a surviving child, after the death of one child under the father's care while the mother was at work. The child was diagnosed with battered child syndrome and died from multiple rib fractures that were medically determined to have been inflicted within three hours of the child's death.

In rendering judicial decisions, courts have considered factors such as the child's age, the proportionality of the punishment, the necessity of using force during punishment, the child's best interest (force sometimes is viewed as a parental privilege if used to further the best interests of the child), reasonableness, the means of punishment, whether the punishment falls within the bands of "usual punishment," the child's gender and custodial status, and the chronicity of the abuse. The privilege to discipline in some states is a parental privilege that may not apply to other residents of a home even if common law would regard them as *in loco parentis*. With respect to the means of punishment, some methods may not always be *per se* abusive in the eyes of the court, but if they are implemented with sufficient force to break bones, rupture spleens and liver or cause neurological damage, then they are regarded as unreasonable and excessive. Other means, such as biting, kicking, using weapons and burning, frequently are presumed *per se* unreasonable. For the most part, courts have been unsympathetic to a caregiver's defense based on claims of religious, ethnic, cultural or class differences (Goldstein, 1999).

SEXUAL ABUSE

The Psychological Impact of Sexual Abuse

In sexual abuse cases, mortality is likely to be linked with physical trauma or contraction of a fatal sexually transmitted disease (Berkowitz, 1991). Prevalence estimates for sexual abuse in child protective service system populations are reported above. In 1999, the estimate was 11.3 percent of cases. There were no fatality cases falling within the specific category of sexual abuse (National Child Abuse and Neglect Reporting System, 1999). Overall prevalence estimates for sexual abuse vary widely, from 3 to 31 percent of males and from 6 to 62 percent of females (Kuehnle, 1996).

Researchers have described the impact of sexual abuse in terms of symptoms and behavioral sequelae. In addition to the symptoms and behaviors described below, other conditions are hypothesized to be associated with the aftermath of sexual abuse, including substance abuse, borderline personality disorder, dissociative identity disorder, and sexual dysfunction disorders (Green, 1993). Researchers have made an effort to draw a connection between the impact of sexual abuse and disorders such as posttraumatic stress disorder (Terr, 1991); however, as described above, diagnostic conceptualizations of the impact of sexual abuse usually are too narrow, they sometimes have a misplaced emphasis, some victims have other symptoms falling outside of specific diagnostic entities (or within other diagnostic entities), and much of sexual abuse does not occur under conditions of "danger, threat and violence," usually required as a precursor to a diagnosis of posttraumatic stress disorder (Finkelhor, 1990).

The diagnostic criteria for posttraumatic stress disorder do not sufficiently take into account developmental factors, especially the ways in which younger children react to or show the effects of trauma (Saywitz, Mannarino, Berliner, & Cohen, 2000). It is challenging to assess the differential impact of one type of trauma relative to other traumata in the child's life, and almost every study of the impact of sexual abuse has found that some victims show little or no symptoms (Finkelhor, 1990; Kuehnle, 1996). Although children are victimized at different rates based on age, there are surprisingly few gender differences in the response of boys and girls to sexual abuse (Finkelhor, 1990). Factors associated with the psychological impact of sexual abuse are as follows (Berkowitz, 1991; Finkelhor, 1990; Green, 1993; Heiman, 1992; Kuehnle, 1996):

- *Regressive behavior*: Clinging. Bedwetting. Encopresis. Enuresis. Excessive crying. Tantrums.
- *Hyperarousal*: Sleep disturbance. Insomnia. Nightmares. Exaggerated fears. Intrusive recollections of abuse. Intensification of symptoms when exposed to reminders of the abuse.
- *Anxiety*: Fearfulness and anxiety. Phobic avoidance. Chronic tension. Anxiety attacks.
- *Avoidance and Dissociation*: Dissociation and hysterical symptoms. Emotional numbness. Out-of-body experiences.
- *Depression, cognitive distortions, and low self esteem*: Depression. Feelings of alienation, isolation, and stigmatization. A negative self image. Feelings of being damaged or different. Impaired sense of self. Overestimation of the amount of danger or adversity in the world. Sense of betrayal. Sense of shame, guilt, or fear. Chronic feelings of helplessness.
- *Disturbances in sexual behavior*: Sexual hyperarousal. Sexually aggressive behavior. Repetitions and re-enactments of the sexual victimization. Compulsive masturbation and other sexually related problems. Promiscuity and prostitution. Inappropriate or precocious sexual behavior. Indiscriminate sexual behavior. Difficulty differentiating affection from sexual relationships. A high level of sexual play. Impaired sexual impulse control. Sexual inhibitions or phobic reactions.
- *Tension reducing activities*: Bingeing and purging. Self-mutilation. Runaway behavior.
- *Somatic complaints*: Complaints of headaches, nausea, vomiting, etc., with no known physical cause.
- *Aggressive behavior*: Hitting. Oppositional and Defiant Behavior.
- *Substance abuse*.

Cases involving Sexual Abuse

Most civil abuse statutes (reporting and jurisdictional provisions), define sexual abuse merely by adopting the applicable criminal codes

(Goldstein, 1999). The crimes of rape, statutory rape and incest involve penetration as an element, whereas other sexual crimes do not (such as lewd and lascivious acts, exhibitionism and exploitation). Some scholars argue that penetration should not be a significant factor in defining sexual abuse and its harms (Goldstein, 1999; Goldstein et al., 1996). From the standpoint of interviewing children about their victimization by sexual abuse, a young child might not make a reasonable distinction between penetration and other forms of touching (Walker, 1999). The focus on penetration in the law raises the likelihood that interviews and interview tools (such as anatomically detailed dolls) might place central focus on penetration at the expense of gathering other clinically or legally important information relevant to the sexual abuse (Oberlander, 1995b). Criminal codes in many states have retained some archaic factors that fail to recognize modern research on child sexual abuse. For example, some statutes focus on the behavior of males toward females, they retain gender specific language, they make distinctions among orifices of penetration, and they define some sex crimes according to the degree of force or the degree of accompanying physical harm or risk of sexually transmitted diseases or pregnancy (Goldstein, 1999).

Powe v. State (1991) offers an example of a case that overturned a conviction of first degree rape because the state failed to offer sufficient evidence to prove the element of "forcible compulsion." The victim, age 11 at the time of the alleged incident, testified that Powe was her natural father and he sexually assaulted her. She testified that he told her to lay on his bed, he told her he was cold, he told her to get on top of him, he lifted her on top of him and unbuttoned and unzipped her pants, he put his hand inside her pants and touched her pubic hair and then pulled down his pants and put his penis in her vagina. The relevant statute defined forcible compulsion as "physical force that overcomes earnest resistance or a threat, express or implied, that places a person in fear of immediate death or serious physical injury to himself or another person." The state argued that the evidence, taken as a whole was sufficient to show an implied threat of such nature as to support a conviction for first degree rape. The state relied on precedent, citing cases in which children were sexually abused without use of physical force or coercion by the perpetrator. The court, in making its ruling, made an unusual distinction between a child's assumption that the conduct was acceptable because it was initiated by the parent and fear of threats or bodily harm. In a dissenting opinion, one justice opined that the evidence "clearly would support a finding that Powe is guilty of first degree rape... this is purely a case of a defective indictment... under the wrong subsection of the rape statute... Now, to correct the prosecutor's mistake, this Court has changed the meaning of "forcible compulsion."

Similarly, some courts have been found to be too lenient at the dispositional phase of sexual abuse or sexual exploitation cases. In *Alaska v. Jackson* (1989), the appellate court found the lower court's probationary sentence was "clearly mistaken" because it gave "insufficient attention to the seriousness of Jackson's criminal misconduct" and because it failed to "make adequate provision for the sentencing goal of community condemnation." Jackson was a 27-year-old gymnastics instructor and coach for private organizations and public schools. He became romantically and sexually involved with a 13-year-old girl, one of his students, having sexual intercourse with her six or seven times (after the girl turned 14). After the relationship ended, the girl reported it, with Jackson's encouragement. The lower court found that Jackson's conduct "had resulted from genuine and reciprocal affection" and that Jackson was "sincerely remorseful and contrite." The court found no evidence of similar conduct toward other minors. The court found that no incarceration was necessary and ruled that any remaining problems could be addressed by outpatient treatment as a condition of probation. The appellate court "disapproved" the sentence and recommended at least 90 days of incarceration.

In re Pardee (1991) was a case involving a mother, a father and two daughters. The father was incarcerated after pleading guilty to fourth degree criminal sexual conduct involving his older daughter. He later pleaded no contest to a petition for the family court to assume jurisdiction over the two daughters. A supplemental petition was filed seeking termination of his and his ex-wife's parental rights to both daughters. It included an amendment alleging that he also had sexually abused the younger daughter. The father voluntarily released his parental rights to the older daughter, but the court concluded that termination of the mother's rights was not warranted and that the child protective service department had failed to demonstrate clear and convincing evidence to terminate the father's rights to the younger daughter. The petition for termination was dismissed and a second petition was filed to terminate the rights of both parents. The court terminated the father's rights to the younger daughter. The father appealed on the grounds that dismissal of the prior termination proceeding barred a subsequent proceeding. The court found for the state on the grounds that a subsequent hearing is not barred if the facts change or new facts develop. The second hearing was based on different facts. There had been a subsequent determination that the younger daughter had been sexually abused and that she had shown emotional deterioration.

Except for the classic incest taboo, there has been an erosion of prohibitions of taboos on sexual behavior within families. Sanctions that protected members of a common household (regardless of any blood relationship) are not as rigid as they were in the past. The absence of cultural or legal prohibitions on sexual conduct between household members has made it difficult for courts to interpret statutes relevant to lewd and lascivious behavior or non-penetrative sex crimes (including touching offenses and non-touching offenses). The distinction between sexual acts and those that depend upon proof of perpetrator intent is important in the context of family relationships. Families share physical intimacies that could be interpreted as "sexual" if engaged in by non-family members. The breadth of some definitions of lewd and lascivious grants courts much discretion to intervene in family life. Although that broad discretion might be a protective benefit to children who suffer from sexual abuse that does not fall within the boundaries of other criminal definitions of sexual aggression (such as rape, statutory rape or incest), it also gives license to zealous individuals who might misinterpret nonsexual physical and emotional intimacies between children and caregivers (Goldstein, 1999).

NEGLECT AND ABANDONMENT

The Psychological Impact of Neglect and Abandonment

The most prevalent form of child maltreatment in the United States is neglect (Dubowitz, 1999). According to the National Child Abuse and Neglect Reporting System statistics (2001), in 1999 almost three-fifths of all victims in reports to child protective services (58.4 percent) suffered neglect. Neglect is defined in the child protective services reporting system as omission of care that harms or poses significant risk of harm to a child. The threshold for threatened harm is high, usually involving child abandonment or children left alone overnight. The three main subcategories of neglect (Dubowitz, 1999) are physical neglect (such as inadequate attention to food, clothing and health care needs), emotional neglect (such as inadequate affection or attention to developmental and emotional needs), and educational (such as inadequate attention to a child's education as defined by state law, failure to intervene when children are chronically truant, refusing special interventions for children with learning problems). Half the estimated annual child maltreatment fatalities result from neglect. Most fatalities result from either drowning or perishing in fires due to a lack of adult supervision. Fatalities also result from starvation, exposure to dangerous environments, and neglect of or failure to provide necessary medical care (Weise & Daro, 1995).

Despite the high prevalence of neglect relative to other forms of maltreatment, there has been relatively little empirical research on the impact of neglect. The dearth of research on the impact of neglect is especially problematic in light of studies that suggest most cases facing termination of parental rights are based on abandonment or neglect rather than physical or sexual abuse (Schetky, Angell, Morrison, & Sack, 1979). Research samples have been fairly small, and generalization has been a problem for other reasons. For example, many studies have used research samples of families referred to child protective services. Research outcomes are prone to biases in who gets identified, reported, investigated and offered services (Dubowitz, 1999). Vague definitions of neglect have caused external validity problems in comparing the results of different studies. Poverty has a high correlation with neglect, as does unemployment (American Humane Association, 1988), housing instability or frequent moves (Gaudin, Polansky, Kilpatrick, & Shilton, 1993), residence in high-risk neighborhoods (Zuravin, 1989a), and household crowding (Zuravin, 1986).

Researchers have described the impact of neglect primarily in behavioral terms. As with the impact of other forms of maltreatment, there is no common behavioral outcome. Factors associated with the psychological impact of neglect are as follows (Bousha & Twentyman, 1984; Crittenden & Ainsworth, 1989; Crouch & Milner, 1993; Dubowitz, Zuckerman, Bithoney, & Newberger, 1989; Eckenrode, Laird, & Doris, 1993; Egeland, Sroufe, & Erickson, 1993; Erickson, Egeland, & Pianta, 1989; Fox, Long, & Langlois, 1991; Herrenkohl & Herrenkohl, 1989;):

- *Impaired attachment between parent and child*: Increased dependency. Reactive Attachment Disorder.
- *Impaired cognitive development and academic progress*: Low levels of enthusiasm and persistence, low levels of creativity in problem solving. Receptive language problems compared to samples of children who suffered other forms of maltreatment. Impaired cognitive development and academic achievement. Low educational curiosity. Lower scores compared to non-abused children on measures of language ability and intelligence.
- *Impaired social development*: Passive and withdrawn compared to samples of children in other maltreatment categories. Anger and resistance in toddlerhood. Insecure attachment to caregivers.
- *Low self esteem.*
- *Psychological distress secondary to physical and medical problems*: Poor self image related to poor growth, fatigue and irritability secondary to poor diet and nutrition.
- *Aggressive behavior*: Higher levels of anger in children compared to samples of children who suffered other forms of maltreatment.
- *Risk of arrest for status offenses, delinquency and violent crimes*: Delinquent activities, gang involvement, risk taking behavior, truancy.
- *Substance abuse.*

Cases involving Neglect and Abandonment

Legal cases on child neglect have focused on the duty of the caretaker to provide food, medical care, safety, sanitary shelter and subsistence. Cases also have focused on failure to protect from abusers, failure to protect from dangerous environments, failure to discipline and failure to supervise (Goldstein, 1999). Courts have found that parents have a duty to provide adequate nutrition. In *People v. Pointer* (1984), the conviction of a mother was affirmed for child endangerment. The mother placed her two- and four-year-old children on a strict macrobiotic diet against the advice of the children's pediatrician. The mother was on the diet as she was breast-feeding one of the children. The child's growth was retarded and the child suffered neurological damage. In medical neglect cases, courts sometimes have held parents to a higher minimum standard when they have failed to provide for the special needs of their children (*In re D.K.*, 1976; *In re Jeffrey E.*, 1989).

In a case involving failure to provide medical care (*State v. Evans*, 1992), an unmarried and non-cohabiting father, who found their five children home alone at the mother's house (the children ranged in age from infancy to age seven), went seeking the mother because he thought the infant looked very ill. He observed the infant was not moving. He left the children alone and inquired in the neighborhood about the mother's whereabouts. When he found her, he asked her to come home immediately and then went to her home and waited for her. When she did not return home right away, he called her a second time and he asked her to come home right away. He went outside her residence and saw her coming home. He asked if he should call an ambulance. She said no because she made arrangements for a friend to take her and the child to the hospital. The father left the children in the care of the mother and her friend and did not follow up. One child died and the autopsy revealed the death was due to malnutrition and dehydration. The second child was diagnosed as suffering from malnourishment. Hospital staff members observed he was weak, dirty and emaciated. The father stipulated to facts concerning criminal neglect of two of the five children. The defendant was found guilty because he did not take independent action to assure the deceased child received the care he needed, and because he "knew or reasonably should have known" that the mother could not be trusted to provide the child with timely medical care.

In a case involving safety and sanitary shelter (*State v. Hollingsworth*, 1991), a mother was found guilty of seriously endangering her children's physical health and of failing to provide life necessities to the children. Two months after moving into a clean and freshly painted two-bedroom apartment, the landlord found it in "total disrepair" and called the police and child protective services. The apartment was found to have a terrible stench and it was swarming with flies, feces covered the toilet bowl, clothing was piled in a corner, and a fan without a protective shield was in operation. The child protective services worker observed one of the children urinate against the wall. The children were lethargic. The refrigerator was poorly stocked. In a case involving severe mental illness sufficient to compromise a mother's parental competence, a mother with chronic schizophrenia was described as "indifferent" to her daughter since the child's birth. The state also offered evidence that the mother required periodic hospitalization (*South Carolina Department of Social Services v. Broome*, 1992). In a case involving mental retardation sufficient to compromise a mother's parental competence, a mother with mental retardation was described as "unable to readily take care of herself or manage her own finances, nor could she follow simple instructions" (*Orangeburg County Department of Social Services v. Harley*, 1990).

Courts have found parents have breached the duty to protect their children in cases in which a parent failed to protect a child from an abuser. *In re Glenn G.* (1992) was a case in which the court found a mother neglectful even though the court also accepted her battered spouse defense (to a charge that she committed abuse by "allowing" the father to sexually abuse the children). The court opined that neglect was "a matter of strict liability." In *Phelps v. State* (1983), a mother was convicted of child abuse after the stepfather killed her child. In *Boone v. State* (1984), a mother was convicted of second degree murder after her boyfriend killed her child. In *People v. Pulido* (1986), a father was convicted for attempted manslaughter and child beating after the court found that he willfully failed to prevent the mother from beating their daughter. Courts have found parents neglectful when a mother has failed to infer the sexual abuse of her child from "objective" evidence such as vaginal irritation or changes in behavior (*In re Scott G*, 1986; *In re Jose Y.* 1991).

Abandonment includes cases of leaving vulnerable (by reason of young age or special needs) children home alone after school or during the nighttime for significant periods of time (*In re M.R., W.D., & C.J.*, 1983; *In re Linda*, 1986). Incarceration sometimes is deemed voluntary abandonment because of the disregard of parental obligations (Genty, 1998). The 1997 Adoption and Safe Families Act places pressure on state agencies to swiftly terminate the parental rights of some incarcerated parents. In determining whether parental rights should be terminated, the court usually considers more than the incarceration. Other factors include the parent-child relationship before and after the conviction and incarceration, the nature of the crime and what it says about the parent, the length of confinement, the extent of dislocation for the children, the merits for the children of retaining a relationship with the parent, and the trauma inflicted on a child who witnessed the crime or who lost a parent because of the crime (Beckerman, 1998).

Psychological Maltreatment

Cases that have come before the court concerning psychological maltreatment have involved caretakers who terrorized children, kept them in close confinement, engaged in severe degradation and humiliation, or engaged in severe psychological rejection (Goldstein, 1999). Those cases probably do not fall under the rubric of "neglect" *per se*, because they involve acts of commission rather than omission. Cases involving acts of omission that are categorized as psychological maltreatment (as a subcategory of neglect) include caretaker failure to prevent mental harm, failure to treat mental conditions, and severe ignoring or deprivation of love and contact. Failure to thrive cases sometimes are categorized as psychological maltreatment and other times as medical neglect. In cases involving children who witness domestic violence, the child must be in "imminent danger" in order for the court to find psychological maltreatment or risk thereof. Research has shown that children who witness inter-parental violence suffer effects such as depression, anxiety, cognitive problems, delinquency and proneness to violence (Somer & Braunstein, 1999). Some courts value expert testimony concerning mental or emotional impairment from witnessing domestic violence (cf *In the Matter of Bryan L.*, 1991).

Subsumed under the duty to provide medical care, some courts have found a duty to provide psychological treatment for mental illness. For example, *Keith R.* (1984) involved the refusal of a mother to seek psychiatric treatment, as recommended by two psychiatrists, for her five-year-old son who "wants to be a killer when he grows up," and who emitted "disturbed behavior" and "preoccupation with sexual matters." *In re J.M.P.* (1984) affirmed a finding of maternal neglect for refusal to seek residential treatment for a "seriously disturbed" child (even though the mother followed through on other less intrusive treatment). *In re Wachlin* (1976) involved a mother who refused to provide speech therapy or to follow a treatment plan for her child's delayed language development. Courts have been reluctant to find psychological maltreatment or neglect when there is disagreement between parents and child protective service workers on the choice of one recommended and reasonable treatment over another.

ETIOLOGICAL FACTORS

Child maltreatment is widely recognized to be multiply determined by a variety of causal agents (Cicchetti & Toth, 1995). The relative weight of factors is transactional, heightened by risk or potentiating factors and buffered by support and compensatory factors (Belsky, 1993a, Cicchetti & Carlson, 1989). It is difficult to isolate the potency of single risk factors in empirical studies (and the implications for treatment and prevention) because of the comorbidity of types of maltreatment (Belsky, 1993a), because of definitional and sampling problems (Pianta, Egeland, & Erickson, 1989), and because much research on maltreatment focuses primarily on parent-referred outpatient children (Belsky, 1993a) or self-referred parents seeking treatment (Helfer, 1987). With a few notable exceptions, most research studies on child maltreatment are cross sectional rather than prospective, making it difficult to determine causality or to examine the development of determinants and mediators of child maltreatment in family systems.

THEORIES OF CHILD MALTREATMENT

Sociobiology

Comparative psychology researchers have investigated the mistreatment of progeny across nonhuman species. Violence against offspring is so widespread that it would seem as "natural" as nurturant and sensitive parental behavior (Belsky, 1993a; Helfer et al., 1997). Although some researchers caution against broad interpretations of comparative studies (Umberson, 1986), sociobiological explanations of abuse describe many examples of violent behavior between parents and offspring in nonhuman species (Belsky, 1993a). Fundamental to evolutionary explanations of child maltreatment is the premise that the interests of parents and offspring are not always synonymous (Burgess, 1994; Daly & Wilson, 1981). Evolutionary theory emphasizes survival of the species, or the reproductive interests of individuals. When the provision of sensitive and nurturing care contributes nothing to or even undermines reproductive fitness, conflict is created that engenders abuse and neglect (Daly & Wilson, 1981). Central to this perspective is the notion that behavior serves a primarily reproductive goal. Child maltreatment in some circumstances actually enhances reproductive fitness; therefore, child maltreatment is most likely in contextual conditions that accentuate a biological conflict of interest between parent and child (Burgess & Draper, 1989). Those conditions include scarce resources, and instability or unpredictability of resources (Belsky, 1993a). Consistent with evolutionary theory, findings have been replicated supporting the hypothesis that competition for resources, that is, poverty and low income, are correlated with child maltreatment (Drake & Pandey, 1996; Zuravin & Grief, 1989). Poverty status and the duration of poverty are associated with increased risk of all forms of child maltreatment (Zuravin & Grief, 1989) and some extremely poor areas have higher rates of infant deaths (Jason & Andereck, 1983). Similarly, unemployment rates, a reflection of impoverishment, are correlated with rates of physical abuse (Krugman, Lenherr, Betz, & Fryer, 1986).

Consistent with the idea of biological conflict of interest as a central tenet in child maltreatment, evolutionary theory would predict that risk of child maltreatment increases as parental emotional investment in children is taxed by either unwanted pregnancy or large family size (Belsky, 1993a). Resources and emotional support are divided into increasingly smaller parcels and there is a decreased probability that other adults will be available to assist with caretaking (Zuravin, 1988). Unplanned pregnancies are related to physical abuse and neglect (Zuravin, 1991b; Zuravin & Grief, 1987), as is large family size (Polansky et al., 1981) and closely spaced births (Altmeier et al., 1982; Zuravin, 1988). The relationship between fertility and maltreatment remains significant even when socioeconomic status is statistically controlled (Zuravin, 1988). Sociobiological theory would predict that older parents, especially older mothers, are less likely to engage in maltreatment of children than younger parents by virtue of decreasing chances of producing additional children. There is an inverse relationship between maternal age and child maltreatment (Zuravin, 1988). Some child advocates worry that biological explanations for child maltreatment imply that child maltreatment is inevitable. Sociobiological theorists would suggest that awareness of the conditions that amplify biological conflicts of interest between parents and offspring is accompanied by awareness of conditions that reduce such conflict, thereby enhancing efforts to prevent maltreatment (Belsky, Steinberg, & Draper, 1991).

Attachment Theory

Researchers have used attachment theory to explain mediating processes in child maltreatment. No single attachment classification subtype or category is used as a determinant of child maltreatment. But there does seem to be a correlation between paternal attachment problems and child psychopathology representing of "externalizing" problems, and between maternal attachment problems and child psychopathology representing "internalizing" problems in children. Theorists have used aspects of attachment theory as the primary explanation for the intergenerational transmission of abuse and other propensities for child maltreatment (Green, 1998;

Page, 1999), with specific emphasis on altered attachments and internal representations in infancy and toddlerhood (Schmidt & Eldridge, 1986) that continue into adulthood (Morton & Browne, 1998; Weinfield, Sroufe, & Egeland, 2000). Maltreated children show classic signs of attachment problems when rated for proximity, contact seeking, contact maintaining, resistance, avoidance, search, and distance interaction. Compared to samples of children maltreated by adults other than parents, maltreatment by mothers is associated with a marked increase in the number of insecure, particularly insecure-avoidant behaviors (in observations of biological mother-child dyads) (Lamb, Gaensbauer, Malkin, & Schultz, 1985). Children who are maltreated develop less secure attachments to their maltreating parents, the early parent-infant relationship is internalized by the child and it later forms a prototype for future relationships (Morton & Browne, 1998). Attachment problems persist throughout development, although there also is evidence for "lawful discontinuity" or the capacity of some individuals to transition to more healthy attachments with other adults and with their children (Weinfield et al., 2000).

Attachment problems often covary with heightened risk of developing mental illness, and in some cases attachment problems are characterized as mediators or predictors of mental illnesses. Both problems interact to heighten the risk of child maltreatment. As measured by the Adult Attachment Interview and the Strange Situation procedure, there is a high rate of insecure attachments among children of anxious mothers (Manassis, Bradley, Goldberg, Hood & Swinson, 1994). Children of depressed caregivers also show higher rates of insecure attachment than children in the general population (Jacobson & Frye, 1991). There is a correlation between measures of child abuse risk potential and measures of insecure adult attachment (Moncher, 1996), but the predictive validity of insecure attachment in adulthood is unknown. In a seven-year study of substantiated reports to child protective service agencies, Zuravin and colleagues found that poor attachment relationships in childhood (based on retrospective self report data) was predictive of intergenerational transmission of abuse (Zuravin, McMillen, DePanfilis, & Risley-Curtiss, 1996).

Individual Theories of Child Maltreatment

Psychologists have studied common characteristics of maltreating parents. Psychoanalytic theories of factors associated with child maltreatment describe intrapsychic factors as the most necessary and the most basic aspect of abusive behavior. Although other factors (such as social and economic factors) are important, the central feature of psychoanalytic theories of maltreatment is the question of why some parents respond with child maltreatment while other parents in similar circumstances do not (Steele, 1987). Other individual theories emphasize personality styles associated with maltreatment, the association between mental health problems and child maltreatment, and social interaction patterns between maltreating parents and children.

Early attempts to characterize parents who engaged in maltreatment relied upon traditional understandings of the impact of mental health problems on parental functioning (Steele & Pollack, 1968). Researchers quickly found that some caretakers who harmed children showed characteristic symptoms of mental health problems, but others did not. Similarly, many abusing parents showed behaviors associated with character disorders (narcissistic personality disorder, antisocial personality disorder or borderline personality disorder), but child maltreatment was not necessarily associated with any of these conditions (Strand & Wahler, 1996; Steele, 1987).

Researchers have examined multiple perpetrator factors such as history of abuse in early life, lack of empathy for the child, excessively high expectations of the child, impaired parent-child attachment, perceptions that the child is in some way unsatisfactory, low self esteem, self neglect, poor coping resources, shallow and exploitative approaches to relationships, self-centered behavior, difficulty experiencing guilt or remorse, and poorly integrated sense of identity (Steele, 1987). Some individual characteristics that have been identified across several empirical studies indicate that maltreating parents have difficulty with inhibition of impulses, low self esteem, and impaired capacity for empathy (Friederich & Wheeler, 1982). Low self esteem, however, has not been linked consistently to child maltreatment (Lawson & Hays, 1989). Emotional stability was a powerful predictor of good caretaking in a prospective study of at-risk mothers rearing babies from birth onward (Pianta et al., 1989).

There is a greater tendency to focus on perpetrator factors (such as the presence of sexual attraction toward children and the absence of blocking inhibitions against sexual contact with children) in etiological studies of sexual abuse compared to other forms of child maltreatment (Finkelhor, 1984, 1990; Hartman & Burgess, 1989). Studies of personality variables in sexual offenders of children have shown that they are quite heterogeneous. Some sex offenders are described as timid and unassertive and others are described as controlling and domineering (Hall, 1992). A recruitment and engagement process is common, suggesting personality variables consistent with seduction and intimidation might be relevant (Sgroi, 1982). Finkelhor (1986) proposed that the perpetrator must be motivated to abuse and must be uninhibited about it, finding ways to overcome external inhibitors and the child's resistance.

MENTAL ILLNESS AND CHILD MALTREATMENT. There appears to be a link between mental illness and child maltreatment, but mental illness is not a necessary condition for child maltreatment. Many perpetrators of child maltreatment have no mental illness and many parents with mental illness do not engage in child maltreatment. The link between mental illness and child maltreatment is modest. Although many admitted perpetrators of child maltreatment report that they have a diagnosable mental illness, they also report other risk factors associated with child maltreatment. The relative weight of mental illness in comparison to other risk factors is unknown (Jacobsen, Miller & Kirkwood, 1997). In a study of 9,841 respondents identified through a household sampling procedure for the National Institute of Mental Health Epidemiological Catchment Area study, 147 adults stated they had abused children and 140 adults stated they had neglected children. Of those who reported abuse, 58.5 percent said they had a diagnosis of a mental disorder. Of those who reported neglect, 69.3 percent said they had a diagnosis of a mental disorder (Egami, Ford, Greenfield, & Crum, 1996).

Although many studies continue to link depression (Famularo, Stone, Barnum, & Wharton, 1986; Lahey, et al., 1984) and anxiety (Benjamin, Benjamin, & Rind, 1996) to child maltreatment, the literature has shown an inconsistent relationship between negative emotional experiences and child maltreatment (Frankel & Harmon, 1996). Newer studies have shown a more consistent link between negative emotional experiences (measured as states and traits) and child maltreatment in the form of intrusive care, hostile attitudes toward children, rejecting attitudes, detachment, and unresponsive parenting (Bishop & Leadbeater, 1999;). In a study of continuity and discontinuity of intergenerational transmission of child maltreatment, maternal depression served as a variable that was linked to continuity (Weinfield et al., 2000).

Research studies have attempted to isolate the symptoms or behavioral features of mentally ill parents that have a negative impact on their parenting behavior. Depressed mothers are less contingent, less emotionally positive, less energetic and they show less effort than comparison mothers (Downey & Coyne, 1990; Field, 1995). They speak more slowly and less often than comparison mothers (Breznitz & Sherman, 1987). In an epidemiological study of 673 mothers of children between ages eight and eleven, researchers found that maternal history of substance use disorder, anxiety disorder, or major depression was linked to low levels of maternal supervision and monitoring (Chilcoat, Breslau, & Anthony, 1996). Mothers with moderate levels of depression, compared to those with mild or severe depression, are at greater risk of physical abuse (Zuravin, 1989b). Compared to mothers without trauma histories, mothers with trauma histories report difficulty with inter-parental cooperation and partnership in shared responsibilities and discipline strategies, open communication with family members, self assurance, and enthusiasm in parenting (Cohen, 1995). They had less support from relatives, they reported that dissociative symptoms interfered with their parenting, their discipline was less supportive (more physical), they showed less affection toward their children, they were less able to express emotions, they had more cognitive distortions about their children and they felt less comfortable in the role of mother than a comparison sample (Benjamin et al., 1996).

NEGATIVE AFFECT AND NEGATIVE INTERACTIONS. Some studies have examined the obverse of negative affect to determine how affective experiences translate into positive or supportive exchanges between parents and children. Studies of maltreating parents have shown that maltreating parents have a higher rate of negative interactions with their children than non-maltreating parents. Compared to non-maltreating parents, physically abusive parents show fewer positive approaches to children, such as supportiveness, instruction, joining play, talking to the child, praising the child, responding to initiations by the child, and expressing positive affection toward the child (Bousha & Twentyman, 1984; Trickett & Susman, 1988; Lahey et al., 1984). They are more likely to be controlling, interfering or hostile (either covertly or overtly) (Crittenden, 1981, 1985).

Some researchers studying negative parent-child interactions have attempted to distinguish between abusive and neglectful parents. Studies of neglectful parents indicate the frequency and level of negative responses to children may be higher in neglectful parents compared to abusive parents (Burgess & Conger, 1978). In studies of neglectful mothers of infants (Crittenden, 1981, 1985), neglectful mothers were "unresponsive," they infrequently initiated interaction with or responded to their infants. With older children, neglectful parents showed low rates of social interaction (Burgess & Conger, 1978).

NEGATIVE INTERACTIONS, PHYSICAL DISCIPLINE AND CHILD MALTREATMENT. There is a link between parent characteristics that promote negative interactions with children and the use of physical discipline. Parents in families identified as "troubled" tried to control toddlers more often, were less likely to rely upon a combination of control and guidance strategies, had children who defied them more frequently, and experienced more escalation of negative affect on control encounters (Belsky, Woodworth, & Crnic, 1996). Similarly, there is a link between the use of physical discipline and physical abuse (Belsky, 1993a). The link is of concern in light of the pervasive use of physical discipline. Surveys of parents show that 90 percent of parents have used some form of physical punishment on their children (Straus, 1983; Wauchope & Straus, 1990).

Even with greater awareness of modern forms of discipline and childrearing, many schools continue to use physical punishment (Hyman, 1990).

The link between negative emotions, negative interactions and physical abuse is explained in theory (Graziano, 1994; Vasta, 1982) as a confluence of enduring traits (hyper-reactivity, negative affect) interacting with aggressive tendencies that become irritable and uncontrolled. The aggressive tendencies might be learned or they might be derived from the aforementioned personality traits, escalating in situations that the parent interprets as threatening or adversarial. An act of physical discipline with a functional goal of influencing child behavior turns into an intense, severe and repetitive act (Belsky, 1993a).

Researchers have shown that physically abusive parents are more likely to rely upon physical discipline and negative physical acts (pushing, hitting, grabbing, pinching) compared to non-abusive parents (Lahey et al., 1984). They tend to use power assertion tactics (such as threats and disapproval) more than reasoning and discussion (Trickett & Kuczynski, 1986; Trickett & Susman, 1988). They are less likely to use flexible discipline approaches, varying their discipline strategy or relying on non-physical forms of discipline in response to different types of child misbehavior (Webster-Stratton, 1985). Punitiveness is heightened by stress, regardless of whether the stress is related to child misbehavior or independent of it (Passman & Mulhern, 1977).

ATTRIBUTIONAL STYLE. Much of child maltreatment occurs in the course of routine parent-child interactions. Researchers focusing on the cognitive and emotional characteristics of maltreating parents have emphasized the importance of negative reactivity and attributional style (Belsky, 1993a). Based on the theory that maltreating parents are particularly reactive to aversive events, both in terms of their emotional arousal and their interpretations of those events, researchers in the past two decades focused on demonstrating the hyper-reactivity of maltreating parents (Belsky, 1996; Bugental et al., 1990). Maltreating parents are more physiologically reactive than non-maltreating parents to the tape-recorded sound of a crying child. They report less sympathy and greater irritation and annoyance in response to the crying (Frodi & Lamb, 1980). They show greater physiological reactivity to videotapes of both stressful and non-stressful mother-child interactions (Wolfe, 1985; Wolfe, McMahon, & Peters, 1997. Hyper-reactivity to aversive stimuli is explained by early learning and developmental processes in parents who were abused in childhood. Researchers have linked it to depression (Watson & Clark, 1992) and compromised or limited coping resources (Hillson & Kupier, 1994). Researchers have yet to demonstrate the relative contribution of developmental history in explaining hyper-reactivity as a trait compared to the significance of the linkage to mental illness (Belsky, 1993a).

Negative reactivity or hyper-reactivity to aversive stimuli may be necessary but not sufficient to turn a conflicted parent-child interaction into an abusive one. Making attributions of external causality is correlated with difficulty parenting children aged 15 and 21 months (Belsky et al., 1996). According to attributional theorists, maltreatment is most likely to occur when parents with a predominant attributional style of little personal control encounter misbehavior in their children (Bugental et al., 1989). Parental beliefs that a child's misbehavior is within the child's control are linked to parental anger and to the belief that the behaviors ought to be corrected (Geller & Johnston, 1995). The child's behavior is interpreted as threatening, so the parent experiences an accompanying physiological hyperarousal and negative emotions (MacKinnon-Lewis, Lamb, Arbuckle, Baradoran, & Volling, 1992). Parents who rely on external and unstable causal attributions such as luck (compared to internal factors such as ability) to explain parenting successes are particularly reactive to misbehavior in children (Bugental et al., 1990).

PREMEDITATED AND INTENTIONAL CHILD MALTREATMENT. Premeditated and intentional child abuse is a little studied phenomenon because of understandable difficulty identifying and recruiting appropriate research subjects. Premeditated and intentional child abuse usually is determined after-the-fact, based on medical observations of injuries such as multiple fractures of different ages, deliberate burns or scalds, pinch or human bite marks, and the induction of illness in the child (Southall, Plunkett, Banks, Faldov, & Samuels, 1997). Based on collaboration with child protective service workers and police child protection teams, a group of British researchers and clinicians (Southall et al., 1997) developed a covert video surveillance (CVS) technique to document what they termed "apparent life-threatening events" or ALTE (the United Kingdom has different privacy laws than the United States and the CVS was deemed legal by a child protection committee and by the United Kingdom court system prior to the outset of the study).

ALTE involves infants and young children presenting with recurrent apneic or cyanotic episodes (breathing problems and loss of oxygen). Many cases initially present as needing CPR. Between June 1986 and December 1994, 39 patients underwent CVS (36 for ALTE, 1 for suspected strangulation, 1 for fabricated epilepsy, and 1 for severe failure to thrive and suspicion of poisoning). Cases were authorized by child protective service teams with statutory responsibility for child protection in the United Kingdom. Parents were informed their child would undergo multichannel physiologic recordings until an event occurred. Parents were not told about the CVS. They were encouraged to care for their child as if at home. Leads were attached to the child, keeping him or her within camera range while nurses observed the families. The median duration of CVS was 29 hours (range

15 minutes to 15 days). In 30 cases, parents intentionally suffocated their child. In one case, a mother broke the arm (radius and ulna) of her three-month-old child. No criminal evidence was gathered in one case involving a parent of a five-month-old child whose three siblings had died from sudden infant death syndrome (SIDS) at ages 4.5, 0.6, and 1.4 months. Nonetheless, a subsequent court case established that the mother had suffocated and killed her previous three babies. One case involved a 20-month-old child with seven fractures of different ages and three episodes of probable strangulation. The suspected perpetrator was the father. CVS revealed no evidence of abuse. The mother was in the room with the child much of the time, and she showed a loving and caring attitude toward the child. The child ultimately was cared for by the mother alone. One CVS case revealed a mother attempting to poison her 43-month-old child with disinfectant and attempting to force a toothbrush down the child's throat. The mother was later convicted of killing the child's older siblings by salt poisoning. In one case, the mother admitted to fabricating near-death events and falsely alleging that a previous sibling had died of sudden infant death syndrome (SIDS). She had fraudulently obtained a death certificate on this nonexistent child. Other examples of ALTEs identified during CVS were provided in the article, which revealed quite disturbing behavior among severely abusive parents (Southall et al., 1997).

Southall et al. (1997) challenged conceptualizations of SIDS. The study gave credence to disorders that fall under the rubric of factitious disorder by proxy (also known as Münchausen syndrome by proxy). Southall et al. prefer to avoid the phrase factitious disorder by proxy because it inadequately describes the range of abuse that occurs. They observed that abuse often was inflicted without provocation and with premeditation. The parents in many cases provided plausible lies to explain the consequences of their actions. For example, one mother said she suffocated her son because of stress due to his crying and continually waking her from sleep. Under surveillance, she was observed, with premeditated planning, in an attempt to suffocate her infant when he was in a deep sleep. In some cases, abuse was inflicted frequently and nearly continuously. Southall et al. hypothesized that the premeditated and intentional abuse is sadistic in nature, but the etiology is poorly understood. None of the parents in the research sample had a psychotic mental disorder, 25 had a factitious (fabricated or induced) disorder, and 23 were diagnosed with personality disorders.

Southall et al. (1997) described other characteristics of their sample. In addition to the psychiatric diagnoses described above, 17 of the parents alleged sexual abuse or rape (five were false allegations and 12 were "unknown"). Fifteen of them deliberately harmed themselves with drug overdose and self mutilation, 15 inflicted abuse on the siblings of the patients undergoing CVS, and 12 made allegations of physical abuse (one false allegation and 11 "unknown"). Nine of the families had a history of child death due to SIDS, 9 were investigated for criminal behavior in at least one parent, five cases involved sibling ingestion of drugs or toxic substances, 19 of the parents were married and 20 were single or divorced (some single parents were cohabiting). Twenty-nine of the parents were less than age 20 at the time of the study. Many of the mothers reported major problems in their relationships with their partners. Some partners were described as passive and uninvolved and others were described as abusive to the mother. The authors concluded that the presence of bleeding from the nose or mouth and a family history of SIDS should prompt a high degree of suspicion of ALTE.

The practicality, legality, and ethics of covert video surveillance as a means of obtaining direct evidence of parental criminal maltreatment have been questioned (Kinscherff & Ayoub, 2000; Zitelli, Seltman, & Shannon, 1988). The forensic evaluator's conduct is subject to informed consent for covert video surveillance or medical diagnostic procedures, and compliance with mandated reporting of child abuse (Kinscherff & Ayoub, 2000). Others support the CVS procedure, citing compelling clinical examples similar to those described above (Epstein et al., 1987), and citing case law providing emergency exceptions to warrantless searches in order to provide immediate protection to a child (*State v. Hunt*, 1965).

FACTITIOUS DISORDER BY PROXY. The disorder described as Münchausen syndrome by proxy or factitious disorder by proxy is controversial. Factitious disorder by proxy has been described as a form of child abuse in which a parent feigns or creates illness in a child for the purpose of subjecting the child to unnecessary diagnostic tests and treatments. In a 1991 United States survey of 316 pediatric neurologists and gastroenterologists, Schreier and Libow (1993) identified 372 confirmed and 192 suspected cases of factitious disorder by proxy. Behavioral variations range from reports of fevers and allergies to life-threatening abuse of the type described in the above study. The disorder was named after the Baron von Münchausen, a soldier, politician, and fantastic storyteller in 1700s Germany. The Münchausen name first appeared in a medical article in 1951 to describe patients who seemed "addicted to hospitals," inducing illness in themselves to earn admission (Asher, 1951). The "by proxy" version of the problem first was articulate in 1977 in an article by Meadow, a British pediatrician (Kahan & Crofts Yorker, 1991).

A variety of illnesses are falsified or induced in children. Falsified histories or symptoms often include seizures, allergies, hematuria (blood in urine), fevers, hematemesis (vomiting blood), bloody stools, glycosuria (sugar in urine), fecal urine, autoerythrocyte sensitization, fecal vomiting, cystic fibrosis, thyroid disease, heart disease, and acute renal failure. Active inductions of illnesses include hypoglycemia, diarrhea, drowsiness and coma, sepsis, apnea, hypernatremia (high sodium count in blood), bleeding tendencies, metabolic instability, anemia, hemorrhagic otitis, poor weight gain, dermatitis and SIDS. Many methods have been used to induce illness, including deliberate poisonings, injection of insulin to induce hypoglycemia or coma, and injection of feces to produce infection (Kahan & Crofts Yorker, 1991; White, Voter, & Perry, 1985). The mortality rate in known cases is at least 10 percent (many cases include deceased siblings) (Kahan & Crofts Yorker, 1991).

Secondary gain of attention from medical practitioners (in the form of sympathy for the parent) usually is cited as the motivational factor underlying the behavior. Some theoreticians have also described the underlying motivation as the parent's desire to present himself or herself as an exceptional parent (Ayoub, Deutsch, & Kinscherff, 2000). Parents who present with factitious disorder by proxy usually also carry a diagnosis of hysteria, sociopathy, and narcissistic or borderline personality disorder (Kahan & Crofts Yorker, 1991). Nadelson (1979) views factitious disorder by proxy as a subgroup of borderline personality disorder. He described the disorder as a spectrum disorder, existing on a continuum of behavior from occasional falsification of illness that might be stress related to repetitive presentations of exaggerated or false symptoms, including the conscious production of signs that distinguish it from malingering. He described malingering as the production of false disease for the purpose of obtaining material gain such as money, lodging, food, or drugs. Analytic interpretations suggest some individuals with severe personality disorders use disease simulation as a primary mechanism for the primitive expression of rage, and to obtain attention, emotional support and nurturance. Factitious disorder by proxy is distinct from hypochondriasis, in which the patient believes he or she truly is or will become ill (Robins & Sesan, 1991).

Warning signs of factitious disorder by proxy include persistent or recurrent illness with no clear etiology; discrepancies among history, clinical observations, and the child's general health; symptom report discrepancies between parents or between parent and child; idiosyncratic medical findings; repeated failure of or poorly tolerated routine treatments; parental over-concern or under-concern; eagerness for invasive testing; considerable medical knowledge in the parent; a high level of concern for other patients; repeated hospitalizations or illnesses without diagnoses in the parent; unexplained symptoms in the parent similar to those of the child; and symptomatic presentation only in the presence of the parents (Kahan & Crofts Yorker, 1991). There may be sociocultural features because of the greater vulnerability in women compared to men for developing it (Robins & Sesan, 1991). From a family process perspective, the patient's partner may be an "enabler," and sometimes siblings, extended family members, and the index child are involved in the deception (Ayoub, Deutsch, & Kinscherff, 2000). Psychiatric cases usually involve false allegations by the parent of child sexual abuse or other forms of maltreatment by another individual. The motivation is sympathy from medical and mental health professionals (Kinscherff & Ayoub, 2000; Schreier, 2000).

Evidence relied upon in legal proceedings against parents suspected of factitious disorder by proxy include direct eyewitness accounts of parental engagement in the behavior, circumstantial evidence of the child's illness only in the parent's presence, urinalysis showing toxic drug levels, tiny holes found in a child's intravenous tubing, and syringes found in the mother's pocketbook (*People v. Phillips*, 1981). Clinicians who are concerned about the disorder believe it is under-diagnosed or that most diagnoses are delayed (Zitelli, Seltman, & Shannon, 1987). They express concern about morbidity and mortality of children affected by the disorder (McGuire & Feldman, 1989). Critics note that it is not a diagnostic entity that appears in the *DSM-IV* and *DSM-IV-TR* (except as research criteria) (American Psychiatric Association, 1994, 2000) or other widely accepted diagnostic manuals. The research criteria are useful in alerting treatment providers to possible cases, but the criteria currently are underdeveloped (von Hahn et al., 2001), especially for individuals who falsify psychiatric symptoms in their children (Schreier, 2001). Some theoreticians believe it is over-diagnosed because of base rate problems, difficulty with accuracy in diagnosis and the high probability of false positives (related to the low base rate) (Mart, 1999). Rand and Feldman (1999) described 11 cases of misdiagnosed factitious disorder and the ramifications for the family members (not the least of which was removal of the child from the home by child protective services). Allison and Roberts (1998) describe it as a syndrome lacking coherent diagnostic criteria and characterizing chronically and disagreeably ill patients with nothing in common but a tendency to confuse and antagonize treatment providers. They believe the relevant patient sample represents a heterogeneous population of disadvantaged parents, usually mothers, and chronically ill children.

Intergenerational Transmission

Theories about intergenerational transmission of child maltreatment developed in the 1970s (Fontana, 1973; Steele, 1976), spawning at least a decade of research on the link between perpetration of maltreatment and childhood histories of victimization by maltreatment (Dubowitz et al., 1987; Egeland, Jacobvitz, & Papatola, 1987; Helfer, 1987; Herrenkohl, Herrenkohl, & Toedtler, 1983; Steele, 1987). Despite persistent findings of an intergenerational link, most researchers expressed caution about the inherent limitations of sampling and methodology in studies illustrating the link (Belsky, 1980, 1993a; Cicchetti & Rizley, 1981; Widom, 1989b). Most studies relied on retrospective reports, small clinical samples with inadequate control groups, samples of parents already labeled as maltreaters, and data collection by researchers who were not blind to the parents' status as maltreaters (Belsky, 1993a). Stronger studies began to emerge, with standardized self-report measures and reasonable comparison groups. Those studies (Gil, 1973; Kaufman & Zigler, 1987; West, Williams, & Siegel, 2000) estimated the rate of intergenerational transmission to be 30 percent (plus or minus 5 percent), with a range of rates between 7 percent and 70 percent (Belsky, 1993a). Intergenerational transmission of child maltreatment is expected but it is not inevitable (Belsky & Pensky, 1988; Main & Goldwyn, 1984; Steele, 1987).

Maltreatment behavior is learned in childhood and expressed in adulthood in parenting roles (Wahler & Dumas, 1986; Strand & Wahler, 1996). Mediating processes for intergenerational transmission of maltreatment include modeling, direct reinforcement, coercion training, and inconsistency training. Coercion training and inconsistency training explain why behavior that is not pleasurable nonetheless becomes part of a behavioral repertoire because of its predictability in the context of an otherwise random dispensation of rewards and punishment (Wahler & Dumas, 1986; Wiche, 1992). Maltreatment behaviors probably interact with hostile personalities that emerge in maltreated children who have problems in adulthood with emotional regulation, aggression and empathy (Trickett & Kuczynski, 1986).

Learning may account for discontinuities in the intergenerational transmission of child maltreatment. Parents with histories of maltreatment who did not maltreat their own children (at least during the pendency of two prospective research projects) had more extensive social support networks, had experienced a non-abusive and supportive close relationship with one caretaker while growing up, were more openly angry at the child maltreatment, were better able to give a detailed coherent account of their histories of victimization by maltreatment, and developed a supportive relationship with a significant other or had a positive experience in therapy (Egeland et al., 1987).

Social Isolation and Social Support

There is an abundance of research linking social isolation and limited social support networks with elevated risk of child maltreatment (Belsky, 1996; Wilson, 1987). Mothers with limited support networks exhibit a lower level of activity with their infants (Burchinal, Follmer, & Bryant, 1996). When matched for social class, families in cohesive neighborhoods show less maltreatment than those in neighborhoods with less extensive social networks (Garbarino & Kostelny, 1992). Isolation also is related to individual characteristics. Among families living in the same neighborhoods, neglectful parents described the neighborhood as unfriendly and the neighbors as unhelpful. Non-maltreating neighbors described the neighborhood and neighbors in more positive terms (Polansky et al., 1985). Some neighborhoods have elements that heighten the probability of social isolation among the inhabitants. In Chicago neighborhoods where the maltreatment rates were higher than expected, people had difficulty thinking of anything positive to say about the neighborhood. In those neighborhoods, the physical spaces were dark and depressed, criminal activity was rampant and easily spotted. In neighborhoods matched for socioeconomic status where rates of maltreatment were lower than expected, people were eager to talk about the neighborhood and the community. The neighborhoods offered more services and had stronger political leadership (Garbarino & Kostelny, 1992).

Maltreating families tend to be more transient, moving more frequently than other families (Seagull, 1987; Zuravin, 1989a) and they use fewer community resources (Trickett & Susman, 1988). Although the result is not consistently found (Crittenden, 1985), some studies have shown that maltreating parents have smaller peer networks (Disbrow et al., 1977; Starr, 1982). They have less contact with and receive less help from immediate family members and other relatives (Polansky et al., 1981; Zuravin & Grief, 1989). Self report data reveals that maltreating parents report more loneliness and social isolation than comparison parents (Milner & Wimberley, 1980). They are less likely to have a telephone (Dubowitz et al., 1987). Adolescent parents become isolated from their peer group because of the lifestyle differences they face in comparison to their childless peers (Nitz, Ketterlinus, & Brandt, 1995).

Substance Abuse and Child Maltreatment

Substance abuse is a serious social problem for many reasons. Although there are biological and psychological variables associated with substance abuse, it is viewed as a social problem because of its impact on family life, community life, school and job performance, child care and household responsibilities, the legal system (arrests for intoxication or for driving under the influence), and because of the creation of physically hazardous circumstances (such as driving an automobile or operating machinery under the influence of alcohol or drugs). Patterns of drug use changed rapidly in the 1980s and 1990s, with a substantial increase in use among women of childbearing age (Chavkin & Kandall, 1990; Ryan, Ehrlich, & Finnegan, 1987). In the 1990s, the National Institute on Drug Abuse estimated that six million women of childbearing age used illegal drugs with one million using cocaine (Office of Inspector General, 1990). Children of substance-abusing parents are at increased risk for child abuse and neglect (Chasnoff, 1988; Famularo et al., 1989; Massachusetts Department of Social Services, 1989; Murphy et al., 1991). It is estimated that 675,000 children are seriously mistreated annually by a substance-abusing caretaker (National Committee for Prevention of Child Abuse, 1989). It is difficult to estimate how many children in the child protective service system are affected by parental substance abuse. State child protective agency reporting records indicate that substance abuse is a factor in 20 percent to 90 percent of all reported cases (National Committee for Prevention of Child Abuse, 1989). Other studies have estimated that 10 percent to 67 percent of child protective service cases involve parental substance abuse (Famularo et al., 1992; Kelley, 1992; Miller, 1990; Murphy et al., 1991).

The impact of substance abuse on child maltreatment begins early, usually in the prenatal period. Mothers who use drugs delay seeking prenatal care compared to those who do not, they speak less to their newborn children, they appear uncomfortable holding their babies, and they appear unsure of how to play with them (Black, Schuler, & Nair, 1993). Families headed by at least one parent who abuses alcohol have been described as lacking cohesion, attachment, emotional expression and shared activities (Berlin & Davis, 1989). In an observational study of standardized play tasks, parents with alcohol problems were judged to be less able to engage their children in play than control group parents (raters were blind to group status). They were less able to keep children on task, and they were less able to read and respond to cues from their children (Whipple, Fitzgerald, & Zucker, 1995).

Parenting styles of drug-using parents tend to be either authoritarian or overly permissive (Baumrind, 1985; Bernardi, Jones, & Tennant, 1989). Parental substance abuse is correlated with less effective parental discipline (Tarter, Blackson, Martin, Loeber, & Moss, 1993). In a study of 48 subjects (24 mothers of drug-exposed children and a comparison group matched in age, race, gender, and SES), a strong association was found between maternal drug use and child maltreatment resulting in removal of the children by child protective services. Over 40 percent of the drug-exposed children were in foster care, most often with maternal grandmothers (Kelley, 1992). Mothers who used drugs during pregnancy reported higher levels of parenting stress than comparison mothers.

Researchers have shown that other negative patterns of behavior are associated with substance abuse, even after the parent has been clean or sober for a period of time. In a study of mothers who were polysubstance abusers during pregnancy (with cocaine being the drug of preference), mothers made more negative statements and showed more negative affect than comparison adults matched for SES (Heller, Sobel, & Tanaka-Matsumi, 1996). Although they had some interactions that were categorized as "positive-compliant," they made more coercive and negative verbal exchanges with their children. They had difficulty terminating negative exchanges. Rather than trying to change the negative pattern to a positive pattern, they engaged in further coercive behaviors. They began with mildly aversive requests with negative affect and escalated to strong demands with increased negative affect. In another study of mothers who abused cocaine, mothers who were offered support showed less intense emotional reactions to parenting stress, but the effect was more robust among drug-free mothers than those who still used drugs (Black et al., 1993). Women in the drug-using group had more difficulty accessing formal resources than women in the comparison group.

Youthful Parenting and Child Maltreatment

About 500,000 children are born each year to adolescent mothers (Furstenberg, Brooks-Gunn, & Levine, 1990). Compared to children of older parents, children of adolescent parents are at risk for developmental delay (Brooks-Gunn & Furstenberg, 1986; Moore & Snyder, 1990), and they are at disproportionate risk for high rates of infant mortality and morbidity, cognitive impairment, delay in emotional development, child abuse, neglect, and early and pervasive school failure (Furstenberg & Brooks-Gunn, 1987; Shapiro & Mangelsdorf, 1994). Factors associated with developmental delay in children substantially decrease, but remain significant when factors such as socioeconomic status, maternal education and marital status are statistically controlled (Edelman, 1987). Zuravin and DiBlasio (1996) found six correlates of neglect (that correctly classified 85 percent of mothers) and four correlates of abuse (that correctly classified 79 percent of mothers) in a sample of 119 mothers who gave birth prior to their 18th birthday. Neglect was most strongly correlated with a maternal history of sexual abuse, being a runaway, trouble with the law, and residence with different caretakers. Abuse was most strongly correlated with a maternal history of emotional problems, preference for being alone in childhood, family of origin's receipt of government assistance, and the low likelihood of a positive attachment between the youthful parent and her mother.

As with mothers of all age groups, there are wide variations in parenting abilities among young mothers. The risk of adolescent parenthood for developmental delay in an individual child is difficult to predict. Based on self-report data, support from the child's father enhances maternal self esteem and efficacy, but it also adds to life stress. Support from immediate family members does not have much impact on risk, perhaps because adolescents are still in the process of individuation and seeking independent living. However, when differences between younger and older adolescent mothers were examined, results showed that younger mothers gleaned benefit from the support of immediate family members (Shapiro & Mangelsdorf, 1994).

SUMMARY

1. Definitional problems limit the correspondence between legal and mental health definitions of child maltreatment, and also limit the applicability of empirical research to specific case analyses of the etiology and impact of child maltreatment.
2. Definitions of physical abuse have greater behavioral specificity than other definitions of child maltreatment. Definitions of sexual abuse often reference criminal codes, making prosecution more readily available, but limiting the ability of investigators to make judgments about severity of impact and harm to child victims. Despite its greater prevalence, definitions of neglect are less consistent across jurisdictions.
3. Despite definitional problems in early studies, there is an emerging base of prospective empirical studies that support a link between child maltreatment and child psychopathology.
4. Theories of etiological factors related to child maltreatment are based in sociobiology, attachment theory, theories of the impact of mental illness and character problems, negative affect and negative interactions, the relationship between physical discipline and child maltreatment, attributional style, hyperarousal, intergenerational transmission, coercion training, social isolation, substance abuse, youthful parenting, and immaturity.
5. Although much is known about factors that are predictive of child maltreatment, the relative weight of individual factors is less well known. Care and protection matters frequently involve parents with multiple risk factors. Cumulative risk, chronicity of risk, and their impact are two relevant but under-researched phenomena.

7

Developmental Perspectives on Children in Need of Care and Protection

This chapter focuses on child development, with emphasis on the parenting needs of children at different levels of development, and aspects of children's development that influence their proficiencies in accurately recalling, reporting, understanding, and appreciating the impact of childhood trauma. Identifying children's parenting needs at different developmental levels, while also considering the relevance of the care and protection context, might seem a somewhat capacious endeavor. Theories of parenting provide a general framework for considering children's needs. In examining children's proficiencies as reporters of childhood trauma, this chapter isolates features of child development that are most common in forensic evaluations of children and families in care and protection proceedings. Special attention is given to children's perceptions of continuity and stability of residence and relationships, children's language development as it affects reporting capacity, and the integrity of memory in childhood and adolescence. This chapter reviews research relevant to the accuracy of the recollections of child victims, along with theoretical constructs of children's perceptions of shame, lies, family allegiance, secrets and the process of disclosure of abuse or neglect. Juxtaposed with the common problem of children's propensity to be loath to report family problems, the opposite problem of the suggestibility and magnification or embellishment of children's recollections is reviewed. Where it is possible to do so based on existing research, this chapter describes developmental differences in children's reporting capacity and susceptibility to suggestions or other influences.

Because children's idiosyncratic responses to abuse and neglect are neither consistent nor reliably predictable, evaluating children's reports of child maltreatment and the clinical, familial and contextual aftermath is a complex venture. This chapter uses the empirical studies on children's language development, recollections, and constructs of family concealment as a basis for introducing applied methods of detecting and minimizing the effects of suggestibility, malingering, embellishment, minimization, and dissimulation or denial of true events. The process of using techniques to heighten the possibility of detecting the presence or effect of these processes should not be mistaken for a methodology meant to find the truthfulness or falsity of children's statements. Nor should it be mistaken for a methodology to analyze of the credibility of children's statements. Discerning truth and falsehood lies in the realm of the factfinder.

Although it is reasonable for evaluators to describe data that might be relevant to the credibility of children's statements, findings that go to the issue of witness credibility also fall in the realm of the factfinder (see *People v. McNichols*, 1986, *State v.* Michael, 1994, and *State v. R.W.*, 1986 for judicial commentary on the preference of the court for data on children's competence, but not on their credibility). Case law is somewhat inconsistent, but the court frequently rules, either directly or indirectly, that investigation is not a proper role for forensic evaluations (see *Hadden v. State*, 1997 and *Flanagan v. State*, 1993). This chapter focuses on data that usually are relevant to children's competence as reporters of child maltreatment, and on the application of theory and empirical research to care and protection evaluations. Although this chapter focuses on techniques designed to enhance the candor of and central details in children's reports, those techniques are meant to supplement, as indicated, an evaluation process that examines the child's current functioning, changes in the child's functioning across time and settings, and relationships to caregivers and substitute caregivers.

CHILDREN'S PARENTING NEEDS

THE SKILLS AND DEMANDS OF PARENTING

Parenting encompasses an extensive set of behaviors that satisfy the needs of children at different developmental levels. Parents must first come to terms with the demanding nature of parenting (Bowlby, 1988). Looking after a baby or toddler requires a high degree of vigilance and energy. It is a constant set of responsibilities, with temporary relief only when other adults help out or when the child is in trusted day care or other child care. Although the demands on a parent lift to some degree as children grow older, children still require a great deal of time and attention, even as older adolescents. Healthy, happy and self-reliant children are the product of stable home environments in which highly invested adults devote significant time and attention to the child, and in which the caretakers are consistent in their routine, structure and discipline of the child (Bowlby, 1988; Goldstein et al., 1979). Although not all families look alike in their composition, fundamental aspects of parenting involve sensitivity, consistency, and emotional and physical availability (Ainsworth, 1989; Thompson, 1993).

Parenting behavior is not exclusively instinctive, nor is it exclusively the product of learning (Bowlby, 1988). It has strong biological roots, accounting for strong emotions associated with it, but historical experiences in childhood, adolescence, and before and during key adult partnerships also strongly influence parenting behaviors (Pryce, 1995). Much of the parenting role is a waiting and responsive one (Bowlby, 1988). Children rely upon a secure base for physical nourishment, emotional nourishment, comfort, reassurance, guidance to ensure the safety of the child's explorations, and confidence. Although the base widens as children grow more confidence, secure, and independent, older children and adolescents continue to rely upon the base for emotional equilibrium, cues for imitation and emulation, identification, and stability (Ainsworth, 1989; Offerman-Zukerberg, 1992).

Although much attention is given to concepts of dependence and children's striving for independence and autonomy as they grow older, a more apt construct for understanding parent-child relationships across the span of childhood and adolescence is "interdependence" (Mahler et al., 1975). A secure base is established through a bidirectional attachment relationship (Ainsworth & Bell, 1974; Ainsworth et al., 1978). Regardless of theoretical orientation, the parent-child relationship is in many ways viewed as mutually gratifying in circumstances in which the adult caregivers are responsive to the child's needs (Egeland & Farber, 1984;). The relationship is the essence, but it is not the whole of parenting. Parenting moves beyond the relationship realm to a set of characteristics and skills that promote positive development. They include sensitivity, physical proximity and contact appropriate to the child's level of development, physical and emotional nourishment, the capacity to provide comfort (Bowlby, 1988; Pruett, 1982), attunement to the child's actions and signals (Offerman-Zuckerberg, 1992), awareness of the impact of separation anxiety (Bowlby, 1988), and appropriate expectations for the child (Abidin, 1992). Single parenting is most effective with the availability of at least one other strongly supportive and available adult (McLanahan & Sandefur, 1994; Popenoe, 1988). Other elements of effective parenting include emotional support from family and/or friends (Pianta et al. 1989), effective stress management and stress reduction strategies (Mitchell et al., 1982; Nitz et al., 1995), the capacity to choose age-appropriate activities and stimulating environments for the child (Saferoff, 1993), and knowledge of how to implement effective and age-appropriate reinforcement and discipline strategies (Kelley et al., 1992). Parents need knowledge of how to negotiate conflict with the child (Milner & Wimberley, 1980), self-awareness sufficient to recognize and modify "close calls" of maltreatment (Milner & Wimberley, 1980), knowledge of how to choose qualified child care providers (Lamb, 1999), the capacity to establish a daily routine, knowledge of how to access community resources for the parent and child (Jackson, 1994; Jacobson & Frye, 1991), a source or sources for seeking parenting advice and support (Haveman & Wolfe, 1994), and awareness of dangers in the child's neighborhood and surroundings (Sagi, 1982).

Parents develop and modify specific skills and they make specific choices as their children grow and develop. Skill limitations are not necessarily highly predictive of child maltreatment, but the absence of a sufficient number of necessary skills is linked to maltreatment, especially neglect. Even though insufficient skills rarely stand alone as the link to maltreatment, many parenting training courses focus almost exclusively on skill development at the expense of variables that are more strongly predictive of maltreatment (Forehand & Kotchick, 1996; Harrison 1997). Some skills have ethnic or cultural origins, but fundamental parenting skills exist in some form across all groups. Effective parenting involves a broad repertoire of skills.

PARENTING SKILLS AND LEVELS OF CHILD DEVELOPMENT

In preparation for and in the first year of a child's life, the parent must perform specific tasks such as becoming familiar with the child's temperament, tracking milestones of the first year, smiling and cooing, avoiding adversarial views of the child's sleeping and eating patterns, choosing between breastfeeding and bottle feeding (and making the transition between the two), choosing a bottle and a brand of diapers that are right for the baby's physical characteristics, tolerating crying and discerning the meaning of different types of cries, and responding appropriately to colic, if necessary. The parent of an infant must purchase toys and establish play routines appropriate for an infant, choose a pediatrician, attend frequent well-baby pediatric appointments, do frequent loads of laundry, and respond to small (and sometimes not so small) ails such as baby allergies, teething, and ear infections (Brazelton, 1981). Parents in older housing units must be wary of possible dangers such as lead poisoning (Hauser & Sweeney, 1997). Parenting skills and tasks are highly demanding of time and attention, but they must be integrated into other activities and responsibilities of the parent.

Specific tasks in toddlerhood include encouraging speech and language development, eating habits, responding to crying behavior, encouraging motor development, helping the toddler deal with shyness and anxiety, being mindful of the importance of transitional objects and other substitute attachment objects, responding appropriately to negative behavior and tantrums, helping the toddler cope with frustration, and helping the toddler refrain from hitting and biting. Other tasks include encouragement of positive play, toy selection, providing socializing experiences, promoting curiosity, setting appropriate limits, helping the toddler learn to sleep in a bed rather than a crib, balancing work and time with the toddler, finding a way to take brief breaks from parenting while addressing the toddler's concerns about separation, and seeing the pediatrician (Brazelton, 1981; Greenspan & Greenspan, 1991).

As children enter the preschool years, parents need skills to assist with toilet training, tolerate a multitude of "why" questions, understand the child's world of fantasy and imaginary friends, comprehend the difference between child and adult understanding of what constitutes a "lie," and help the child negotiate fears and shyness. They need skills to prepare the child for school readiness, help the child channel aggression, and continue to promote eating and sleeping routines. Other skills include understanding the developing conscience and transmitting values at a level appropriate to the child's capacity for moral sensibilities and reasoning. Parents must continue to use appropriate reinforcement and discipline strategies (modifying them when necessary), and encourage responsibility and friendships for the child (Brazelton, 1981; Greenspan & Greenspan, 1991).

Skills necessary to parent children in the elementary school years include addressing the range and patterns of intelligence in children, dealing with problems such as swearing and lying, maintaining firm but flexible discipline and consequences, assigning appropriate chores to the child, promoting self control, helping children with self doubt, encouraging further responsibility and independence, teaching the value of money, promoting good deeds and community services, promoting good manners, and promoting sensitivity to diversity. Other skills include encouraging friendships, teaching children about privacy and modesty, encouraging sharing and role modeling, helping children not to grow up too fast, helping children cope with their desire for acceptance among peers, choosing extracurricular activities of interest to the child, understanding how quickly children's interests might change, finding ways to keep children active in summer months, and setting limits on the range of appropriate activities. Other tasks include working with schools and addressing problems children might have in school, and working with other organizations the parent finds important for the child's development (Brazelton, 1981; Greenspan & Greenspan, 1991).

CHILDREN'S PERCEPTIONS OF FOSTER CARE

How Children Characterize Their Experiences in Foster Care

Care and protection evaluations usually require the evaluator to consider the positive and negative intervening influences of foster care or other out-of-home placement on the child's functioning and the family dynamics. Children report a range of subjective experiences in their removal from their original caretakers. In many cases, foster placement is a crisis or form of trauma in and of itself (Crenshaw & Barnum, 2001; Kenrick, 2001). Although it is difficult to control for the variety of influences on children in foster care, studies of children's adjustment after foster care placement have shown that children report a more positive self image and more positive social relationships when they are placed with relatives, compared to children placed with non-relatives. The effect is especially pronounced for girls (Mosek & Adler, 2001). Although there are exceptions when siblings mimic the maltreatment behavior of their caretakers, siblings placed in the same foster home show better adjustment than separated siblings (Hindle, 2000; Klee, Kronstadt, & Zlotnick, 1997). Kinship care does not always protect against negative effects. It does not reduce the risk of multiple placements for highly disturbed children. In some cases it puts children at risk of premature or unsupervised contact with caretakers from whom they were removed (Gibbs & Mueller, 2000).

Children report a variety of frightening experiences in their actual removal from their parents, especially when the removal involves little forewarning or explanation, inaccurate or confusing explanations, riding in a police car, no opportunity to say goodbye to parents or neighborhood friends, or no opportunity to retrieve valued toys or other objects. Sometimes even well intended efforts by professionals (such as a stop for food or a snack by police officers) and foster parents (an overly warm greeting or comforting words of safety) are confusing to young children. For example, a child might not comprehend he or she is now safe if he or she lacked abstraction abilities to recognize what constitutes parental maltreatment or to equate it with danger or a lack of safety. Children often form strong attachments even to maltreating parents (Bowlby, 1988). Sometimes when a child engages in behavior that appears to "sabotage" a foster placement, they simply desire what is familiar (McIntyre & Keesler, 1986).

THE IMPACT OF PLACEMENT

Research has shown that foster care placement sometimes helps children show recovery from developmental delay and psychiatric disorders, especially for drug-exposed infants and children (Daly & Dowd, 1992; McNichol & Tash, 2001). However, many children do not fare well in foster care, especially when they face barriers to factors that would promote adjustment. Barriers to adjustment include lack of Medicaid coverage, untrained or inexperienced foster parents, and inadequate or uncoordinated mental health and support services (Klee et al., 1997). In a study of adult outcomes after foster care placement, there were significant differences between adults placed in foster care as children and those of similar backgrounds who were never in foster care. Participants in the retrospective study were age 19 or older. Those who had been in foster care obtained higher scores on measures of depression, lower scores on measures of marital happiness, and higher scores on measures of social isolation (Cook-Fong, 2000). It should be noted that the retrospective study understandably could not control for maltreatment experiences that led to the foster care placement.

Positive foster care outcomes depend on effective matching between children and foster families. Unfortunately, there is a dearth of empirical data to guide decisions based on goodness of fit between children and foster parents (Redding, Fried, & Britner, 2000). Foster care is a haven from further maltreatment, but the child sometimes brings to the foster care relationship the sequelae of maltreatment (Erickson & Egeland, 1987). Studies of foster care placement impact are complicated by pre-existing conditions and behavior concerns. A prevalence study of foster children in New York City showed 18 percent had psychiatric disorders, 13 percent had medical conditions such as vision or speech problems, 2 percent had neurological disorders, and 20 percent were mildly to profoundly mentally retarded

(Sibbison & McGowan, 1978). Other prevalence studies of emotional, behavioral developmental problems and medical conditions have shown a high rate of conditions compared to matched samples of children who are not in foster placement (Frank, 1980; Klee et al., 1997). Compared to a sample of never-removed children on welfare, 50 percent more children in a foster care sample fell in the moderately to severely psychiatrically impaired range (Swire & Kavaler, 1978). Foster children are at risk of developing conduct problems and other exacerbations of the sequelae of maltreatment if effective services are not offered to address the problems of concern in the family of origin and to buffer the effect of removal from caretakers (Fisher & Chamberlain, 2000).

The Impact of Multiple Placements

Research concerning foster care failures and multiple placements has shown that for children with emotional and behavior disturbances, quality of service delivery and quality of casework are important in maintaining permanence of placements (Redding et al., 2000). Child variables such as age and severity of behavioral and emotional problems are related to changes in placements. Younger children and children with higher levels of initial emotional and behavioral disturbance tend to undergo more placement changes than those who show healthier functioning at the outset of foster care placement (Redding et al., 2000; Widom, 1989a). Funding for services for foster children, also related to placement stability and success, usually comes from state agencies. Federal funding covers only the cost of food and housing (U.S. GAO, 1995).

Therapists have attempted to make sense of children's reactions to multiple placements on a case-by-case basis (Kenrick, 2001) and to give children a forum to describe their foster care experiences (Whiting, 2000). Much of what clinicians know about the impact of multiple placements is based on rationally derived extrapolations from attachment theory. There is little empirical research on the impact of multiple foster placements in children's capacity for satisfying relationships with substitute caretakers and others (Stovall & Dozier, 2000). Because of difficulty statistically controlling for the impact of prior events in the child's life, and for number and length of placements, empirical research on this topic is a difficult undertaking. Careful clinical attempts to match children with foster families minimizes the possibility of multiple placements (Laan et al., 2001), but there is a dearth of information about how to make appropriate matches (Lindsey, 2001; Redding et al., 2000). Under the reasonable assumption that it enhances the probability of successful placements, policy-makers encourage screening, careful selection and training of foster parents, placement monitoring, and troubleshooting after placements are made (Lindsey, 2001). Sadly, there nonetheless are many reported cases of maltreatment of children in foster and residential placements (Hobbs, Hobbs, & Wynne, 1999).

Experienced foster parents are less at risk of a failed placement than inexperienced foster parents (Guerney, 1982). Unfortunately, there often is a shortage of foster parents because of the poor image of foster care, poor compensation for the expenses incurred, and inadequate support for the concerns of foster parents (U.S. GAO, 1995). Although child protective services usually maintain privacy of foster resident addresses, foster parents sometimes face threats and harassment from the caregivers from whom the children were removed. Even when placements are stable, adjustment issues sometimes are difficult. Although statutes have been crafted to limit the amount of time that children are in placement before they are freed for adoption, foster placements often remain lengthy. The lengthy separation itself compromises parent-child relationships. It places greater strain on foster parents and foster children who must adapt to losses when children finally leave the placement (Klee et al. 1997).

Foster Parenting and Parental Alienation

Foster parents typically serve as a relatively objective source of information on the current functioning of children, children's reactions to visits with parents, and children's behavior after visits with parents. They often serve as useful collateral sources in care and protection evaluations. Foster parents have an opportunity to observe biological parent-child interactions that are more spontaneous relative to visits that might be supervised by child protective service workers or other professionals. Many foster parent training programs teach methods for encouraging contact between children and their biological parents (Sanchirico & Jablonka, 2000). Maternal visiting is, in fact, the strongest predictor of eventual reunification (Davis, Landsverk, Newton, & Ganger, 1996). Unfortunately, the frequency of parental visiting during children's placements in foster care tends to be low (Cantos, Gries, & Slis, 1997). Factors such as court orders, child protective service administrative policies and procedures encouraging visitation, and distinct case goals promote better visitation (Hess, 1988). Many agencies, however, have vague policies or no policies promoting or providing mechanisms that enhance the probability of parental visitation (Proch & Hess, 1987).

With appropriate training, pre-adoption parents are fairly resilient, showing the capacity to provide objective observations of children and their interactions with biological parents, and promoting a relationship and visitation between the child and the biological parents, even at the risk of losing a potentially adoptive child to reunification (Murray, 1984). Although foster parents often provide useful observational data about visitation transitions, including children's reactions before and after visits, sometimes their observations might be tainted (either unintentionally or intentionally) by their own wishes for the child. Some foster parents will candidly alert evaluators to possible blind spots in their appraisals and collateral reports, attributing it to their genuine affection for the child. In other cases they might be less aware or forthcoming. There might be differences in the emotional investment of foster parents, based on their status as pre-adoptive parents. In a comparison of pre-adoptive foster parents and non-adoptive foster parents, pre-adoptive parents reported a more positive attitude toward parenting and less interest in the financial incentives of foster care, but they also reported greater motivation to "rescue" children (Gillis-Arnold, Crase, Stockdale, & Shelley, 1998).

Well meaning foster and pre-adoptive parents might sometimes lose their objectivity because of emotional investment in foster children (Heineman, 2001). Foster parents sometimes lose objectivity because they feel exploited by the child protective service system or by biological parents (Roberts, 1993). As with all collateral data, it is essential to seek corroboration of data to buffer any possible tainting of reports. It is important to be wary of unusual cases in which an adult might encourage false or embellished reports from children of their visitation or pre-placement experiences with their parents. On the other side of the coin, foster parents sometimes are uniquely attuned to foster children, anticipating better than others any possible post-foster-care placement problems between biological parents and children. Even children with secure attachments to substitute caregivers sometimes continue to show the sequelae of maltreatment long after foster care placement. Others show a smoother adaptation to and better emotional recovery in and after foster care placement (Howes & Segal, 1993).

THE FORENSIC RELEVANCE OF THEORIES OF CHILD DEVELOPMENT

CHILD WITNESSES

There is a relationship between linguistic development and child-witness competence and credibility. At the nexus of the behavior sciences and law is a bidirectional influence of legal and psychological inquiry into the capacities of children (Melton & Wilcox, 2001). Although not all investigations of child maltreatment require reports from child victims, this section emphasizes cases in which the child's voice, perceptions, and experiences are important. Children's reports sometimes are credible. At other times, they might be tainted by the tripartite influences of suggestibility or false allegations, linguistic capacity, and childrens' notions (whether reality-based or not) of the child protective service system and by extension, the criminal justice system. There are a variety of developmental concerns that might influence competence and credibility. Cases have addressed children's language development (*Griffin v. State*, 1988; *People v. District Court In and For Summit County*, 1990), their spontaneous utterances or fresh complaints of child maltreatment (*Commonwealth v. Caracino*, 1993; *Commonwealth v. Snow*, 1991) children's memory capacity (*Commonwealth v. Corbett*, 1989; *State v. Hudnall*, 1987), children's understanding and appreciation of the difference between the truth and a lie (*Griffin v. State*, 1988), and the suggestibility of children (*People v. Brown*, 1994; *State v. Michaels*, 1994; *Tome v. United States*, 1995).

Children's language development is central to cases involving child witnesses. There are significant differences in the way children and adults use and comprehend language and encode and retrieve information held in memory. The mechanics of conversation sometimes have a vast impact on the responses children give to questions in a clinical interview, in a social services investigation, in a police investigation, or on a witness stand in a legal proceeding. Adding to the complexity of the mechanics of conversation is the multicultural quality of the population demographics of the United States (Walker, 1999). Nonetheless, children as young as ages two and three have the ability to recall and report past experiences accurately (Hewitt, 1999; Peterson, 1990). Children as young as age three have been deemed competent and credible testimonial witnesses in court (*Macias v. State*, 1989; *People v. Draper*, 1986; *State v. Brovold*, 1991; *State v. Hussey*, 1987; *State v. R. W.*, 1986; *State v. Ward*, 1992; *Strickland v. State*, 1988). Cases involving the competence of child witnesses date back to *Wheeler v. United States* (1895). The *Wheeler* court stated, "There is no precise age which determines the question of competency. This depends on the capacity and intelligence of the child, his appreciation of the difference between truth and falsehood, as well as his duty to tell the former."

Many states have reduced or eliminated rules that disqualify children as witnesses unless their competence is established. Instead, most states follow the federal rules establishing a presumption of competence "except as otherwise provided in these rules" (Federal Rule of Evidence 601). Judges may exclude the testimony of children who do not meet minimum credibility standards or who do not understand the requirement of an oath or affirmation (Federal Rules of Evidence 603; Goldstein, 1999).

In the tradition of *Wheeler v. United States* (1895) Federal Rule of Evidence 603 often is invoked to justify a preliminary inquiry into a child's capacity to understand the obligation to tell the truth. However, some courts have disallowed specific inquiry into the child's comprehension of an oath (*State v. Superior Court*, 1986) except in extreme cases. In some jurisdictions, child victims in sex abuse cases are qualified by statute, whether or not they would satisfy the requirements of testimonial competence in other kinds of cases (*Moates v.* State, 1989; *State v. Crossland*, 1991). Special jury instructions may be given when a child testifies (Goldstein, 1999).

There are many case examples of children who have been disqualified on the bases of lacking witness competence or the capacity to understand an oath. In *Idaho v. Wright* (1990), the trial court found that a child who was two and one half years old at the time of alleged sexual abuse was not competent to testify in court, though her hearsay statements were admissible. *State v. Hudnall* (1987) rejected the testimony of a three year old and *Commonwealth v. Corbett* (1989) rejected the testimony of a four and one half year old. *State v. Feltrop* (1991) rejected the testimony of a six-year-old nonvictim witness. Some cases have allowed children to proceed as competent witnesses, reserving credibility judgments (distinct from competence) for the trier of fact (*People v. McNichols*, 1986; *State v. Superior Court*, 1986).

Taint Hearings

A child's testimony may be excluded in a preliminary taint hearing if the court determines that the state tainted the child's memory through suggestive or otherwise impermissible investigation practices such as pressure or coercion (*Commonwealth v. Allen*, 1996; *Commonwealth v. Callahan*, 1998; *Fischback v. State*, 1996; *People v. Michael M.*, 1994; *State v. Michaels*, 1994). The law makes a distinction between children's credibility (their ability to know what is the truth and what is a falsehood) and the reliability of children's testimony (whether they are responding to suggestive interviews, pressure, or coercion). Taint hearings address the issues of reliability. The New Jersey Supreme Court initiated pretrial taint hearings to challenge potentially unreliable testimony. In *State v. Michaels*, the New Jersey Court of Appeals overturned the conviction of Margaret Kelly Michaels, noting that the questioning of the child witnesses was "suggestive and coercive," thereby tainting or successfully challenging the testimonial competence of the child witnesses. Other states (Delaware, Massachusetts, New York, and Ohio) followed suit in allowing taint hearings. In order for a taint hearing to be held, the defendant must produce evidence that the expected testimony of a child witness might be the product of suggestive or coercive interview tactics. Some scholars view taint hearings as a welcome safeguard for defendants and a remedy for improper interviews. Others view the process as flawed because it perpetuates unwarranted skepticism about the competence of child witnesses (Myers, 1995a).

The Confrontation Clause

Another aspect of children's capacities relevant to child maltreatment proceedings is the potential trauma that children might experience during face-to-face confrontation in court. In *Coy v. Iowa* (1988), the Supreme Court ruled that the Sixth Amendment's Confrontation Clause guaranteed the defendant a face-to-face meeting with witnesses appearing at trial. In *Coy*, the trial court used a screen to shield the witness from the defendant during testimony. The Supreme Court was not persuaded of the constitutionality of the Iowa statute, just passed in 1985, objecting to the absence of an individualized finding that the child witnesses in *Coy* needed special protection. Statutes protecting child witnesses from confrontation were not unique to Iowa. As of December 31, 1999, 37 states had developed and passed statutes governing the use of closed-circuit television testimony in criminal child abuse cases (NDAA, 1999).

In *Maryland v. Craig* (1990), the state sought to invoke a Maryland statutory procedure permitting the judge to receive, by one-way closed circuit television, the testimony of a child witness and alleged victim of child abuse. Maryland had an individualized procedure, requiring the court to determine that testimony by the child witness would result in serious emotional distress and impair the child's communication during testimony. The U.S. Supreme Court found it compelling that the Maryland statute preserved all other elements of the Confrontation Clause (competence to testify, testimony under oath, the ability to view the witness during testimony albeit by closed-circuit television). The court concluded the state's interest in the physical and psychological well being of child abuse victims outweighed, at least in some cases, the defendant's right to face-to-face confrontation. It concluded the Confrontation Clause did not prohibit the use of Maryland's procedure, despite the absence of face-to-face confrontation.

In the wake of *Maryland v. Craig* (1990), some cases have clarified the meaning of state statutes relevant to the Confrontation Clause, limiting the use of closed-circuit television and other courtroom modifications to cases in which it would prevent the child from reasonably communicating (*State v. Vincent*, 1989), requiring a showing that the child witness would be intimidated and inhibited to the extent that the trustworthiness of the testimony would be called into question (*State v. Jarzbek*, 1987), and requiring that any trauma to the child by virtue of testifying must be more than mere nervousness or reluctance (*State v. Crandall*, 1990). Courts have allowed other modifications that do not interfere with the defendant's opportunity to confront the witness. For example, the architecture of some courtrooms have been altered or rearranged to make the setting less formal. Children sometimes are allowed a child-sized table and chair, to bring toys, or to have a parent sit nearby. Objections sometimes are quietly made into a microphone with an immediate ruling by the judge. Some children have been allowed to sit in the lap of a support person during testimony (the adult is prohibited from any prompting). Some courts have allowed recesses and postponements, although they sometimes come at the cost of allowing children a rapid trial schedule with few continuances. Attempts have been made to reduce the number of individuals in the courtroom, although the Fifth and Sixth Amendments' right to a public trial usually precludes exclusion of the press. The basis for most challenges lie in the concern by defense counsel that accommodations elicit sympathy for the child witness or create the appearance that the child's testimony is especially weighty (Goldstein, 1999).

Hearsay Exceptions

In care and protection cases, the hearsay exception often is an issue of relevance. Not all states have adopted hearsay exceptions. When adopted, the hearsay exceptions that are most frequently used to admit children's out-of-court statements include: excited utterances, fresh complaints, statements made for the purpose of medical diagnosis or treatment, statements of bodily or sense impressions, the residual hearsay exception, and prior consistent statements (if the child testifies) (Goldstein, 1999). Landmark cases concerning hearsay include *Idaho v. Wright* (1990) (hearsay and reliability), *White v. Illinois* (1992) (hearsay and unavailability of testimony from the child, who was called to testify but who left the courtroom twice, in fear, without testifying), *People v. McNichols* (1986) (spontaneous declaration exception), *State v. Vosika* (1987) (medical diagnosis exception) and *In re K.L.M.* (1986) (a case similar to *Idaho v. Wright*, 1990, in its conclusion that cross examination of a young defendant would be of little value). In excited utterance cases, the duration of time ranges from admitting statements made several hours after an event to several months, from requiring excitement to permitting calm statements, and from requiring spontaneity to admitting statements made in response to questions. Fresh complaint hearsay testimony is testimony to corroborate the admission of a complaint of sexual misconduct in cases in which the victim falls mute or accommodates to the alleged perpetrator's reappraisal or denial of the event after the offense (Goldstein, 1999).

LANGUAGE DEVELOPMENT

Attorneys, judges and child protective service system representatives request assistance from evaluators in understanding the capacity of children to report trauma from maltreatment or to testify competently on that topic. There typically is concern about young children, but sometimes the capacities of older children and adolescents are questioned, especially if there are communication problems related to cognitive, psychiatric, or neurological impairment. Both developmental status and the interfering effects of impairments affect the linguistic capacities of children and adolescents. Much has been written about linguistic development in children and its applicability to forensic assessment (Berliner & Barbieri, 1984; Davies & Seymour, 1997; Fivush, 1993; Hewitt, 1999; Poole & Lamb, 1998; Saywitz, Jaenicke, & Camparo, 1990).

Walker (Walker, 1999; Walker & Warren, 1995) described basic developmental features affecting children's linguistic capacity. Although the following information is offered as guidance for interviewers, the historical and cultural context should be considered in individual cases. Children learn language through experience. Not all families and not all ethnic groups place the same value on or use the same meanings for words (Harkness & Super, 1995; Saywitz, 1989). Conversational habits within families affect the degree of descriptive information and elaboration that children use (Reese & Fivush, 1993). Language acquisition continues beyond preschool and elementary school. Children for whom English is a second language may struggle with English linguistic abilities compared to children who learned it as their first language (Walker, 1999). There are cultural variations in the nonverbal aspects of conversation (Harkness & Super, 1995; Kelley & Tseng, 1992). Terms used to describe the kinship of extended family members have different meanings in different ethnic groups (LaFramboise, 1988; Red Horse et al., 1987). Some skills, such as the capacity to comprehend abstractions and to provide a narrative, might not develop until middle to late adolescence (Haugaard, Reppucci, Laird, & Nauful, 1991; Laumann & Elliot, 1992).

Walker's (1999) linguistic research has stood the test of researchers interested in children's comprehension of the language of lawyers, and, by extension, the language of evaluators and investigators (Perry, McAuliff, Tam, & Claycomb, 1995; Saywitz & Camparo, 1998). The following points summarize Walker's (1999) linguistic research, her integration of the research of others, and her research on the applicability to the legal system:

Preschoolers:

- Are literal in their use and interpretation of language (e.g., "Can you afford a lawyer?" might yield a reply such as, "My mom drives a Ford.").
- Often do not understand or share adult meanings of words or phrases that might seem common to adults, but that fall outside a child's frame of reference or speech patterns (e.g., "abuse," "neglect," "sexual abuse," "domestic violence," "court," "judge," "in the past," "how many times," and "when did it happen," might be too complex).
- Sometimes can demonstrate abstractions, but only rarely can they meaningfully discuss them (e.g., would have difficulty describing why something is preferred, but could choose a favorite activity, food, or color).
- Have difficulty with categories and conceptual groupings (e.g., a child might insist that *Cheerios* are not cereal).
- Use some words prior to comprehension of their meaning, including words to describe kinship, size, and time (e.g., "one day" and "one month" might have the same meaning to a preschooler).
- Overgeneralize the meaning of words (e.g., after learning that a basket is a basket, might also refer to a box and a plastic tub as a basket).
- Use idiosyncratic words that have been encouraged by caretakers because of "cuteness," but that might be nonsensical to other adults (e.g., referring to a bottle as a "bobby").
- Rely upon simple action-oriented verbs and phrases to describe other individuals (e.g., "Donna takes me to the park.").
- Misuse pronouns (e.g., substituting "he" for "she").
- Might comprehend names and places better than pronouns (e.g., "Was Jane in the bedroom?" would increase comprehension compared to, "Was she in there?").
- Might be able to count, but might not understand quantity; that is, might count to five, but not know that five objects placed in front of him or her represents the quantity of five (e.g., a child might demonstrate that he can count to fifteen, but he might not give accurate replies to questions such as, "How many times did mummy hit you?").
- Are confused by simple negatives (e.g., "Didn't you go to school?" might be misinterpreted as, "You did not go to school, right?").

- Do not have competent use of words to convey past tense.
- Have not mastered vague action verbs such as "to do" (e.g., might say "Are you want some?" rather than "Do you want some?")
- Are more likely to use accurate words for familiar events compared to unfamiliar events.
- Use language in ways that appear inconsistent if compared to adult patterns of speech (e.g., if a child tells one adult about maltreatment, he or she might not see the need to repeat it to another adult or might alter the details fearing he or she was asked again because it was "wrong" the first time).
- Tend to respond to questions even if they do not know the answer.
- Response "yes" more than "no" when they do not know the answer to a question ("yes" is perceived as more socially desirable).
- Have better comprehension of simple sentences (with a subject, verb and object) than complex sentences.
- Comprehend questions better if they begin with the main idea (e.g., "Did Pat touch you when you were in the bedroom?" would be better understood than, "When you were in the bedroom, did Pat touch you?").
- Tend to focus on only one aspect of compound sentences or other complex sentences.
- Are confused by abrupt shifts in topic (e.g., might be confused by a conversation about lunch that segues into an interview about maltreatment).
- Tend not to contextualize their narratives (e.g., they leave out some or all aspects of intent, motive, emotion, descriptive features, chronology, or settings).
- Do not have insight when their comprehension is poor (therefore, asking "Do you understand?" often is fruitless).
- Believe that adults are truthful and sincere.
- Believe that adults would not try to trick them.

Elementary School Children:

- Continue to have problems discussing abstractions.
- Continue to poorly comprehend complex sentence structures.
- Might understand simple negatives, but likely would have difficulty with complex negatives or double negatives.
- Have difficulty comprehending passive speech.
- Continue to have some difficulty with accurate pronoun usage.
- Might repeatedly say, "I don't know" or fall mute rather than asserting, "I don't want to talk to you about that."

- Could provide a narrative, but might have difficulty with chronicity and organization.
- Have difficulty distinguishing between central and peripheral details when providing narratives.
- Misunderstand or fail to notice adult sarcasm, irony, double entendres, or other verbal and nonverbal complexities of adult speech.
- Probably still believe that adults are truthful and sincere.

Adolescents:

- Might or might not be at an adult level in their capacity to provide a narrative.
- Understand time and numbers in reference to the present more proficiently than in reference to history (e.g., "How many times did your mother hit you?" might yield a reply of "six," but clarification would be needed to determine if the youth's mother hit the adolescent across six episodes, hit the adolescent six times in the context of one episode of abuse, or if "six" is an arbitrary way of saying "more than one").
- Continue to have difficulty with complex negatives or double negatives (e.g., might miscomprehend "Isn't it true that you said you weren't hit by your father or you weren't struck by him?" or "You don't like not attending school, do you?").
- Continue to misunderstand or fail to notice linguistic ambiguity such as double entendres, metaphors, proverbs, idioms, and linguistically sophisticated jokes.
- Might not assertively request clarification if they fail to understand a question.
- Have difficulty sustaining attention to long or complex statements or questions.

CHILDREN'S CONSTRUCTIONS OF TRUTH AND FALSEHOOD

CHILD WITNESS COMPETENCE AND CREDIBILITY

The relationship between linguistic development and child-witness competence and credibility was described earlier. This section describes other developmental features that are related to child-witness competence and credibility.

Knowing the Difference between the Truth and a Lie

Criminal prosecution of child maltreatment has resulted in increasing reliance on children's testimony. Researchers took an interest in the testimonial capacities of children in the 1980s and 1990s (Haugaard et al., 1991), following an increase in the previous decades in criminal investigations of alleged perpetrators of maltreatment (especially sexual abuse). Increased attempts to identify perpetrators led to concern about false positive and false negative rates, the reliability of perpetrator identification methods, and the reliability of children's testimony. Most child maltreatment prosecutions do not involve direct testimony by children; however, children's statements are central to decisions concerning the arrest and prosecution of alleged perpetrators (Haugaard, 1993). In actuality, few adjudicated criminal cases of maltreatment (as low as 16.8 percent in three states examined) are resolved through trial proceedings (Lipovsky et al., 1992).

In order for a child to serve as a trial witness, most states require judges to make a determination that the child can discern the different between the truth and a lie (Bulkley, 1988, 1992). The law makes a distinction between testimonial competence and witness credibility. Competence standards are minimal, allowing for testimony of most witnesses. Trial judges are given broad discretion to determine the testimonial competence of a witness and to bar witnesses deemed not competent (*Commonwealth v. Corbett*, 1989; *Doran v. United States*, 1953). Witnesses who are deemed incompetent tend to be very young children or individuals suffering from mental disabilities (Haugaard et al., 1991). Evaluators often are concerned about children's truth-telling capabilities in order to determine the reliability of interview data relevant to children's reports of maltreatment. Children interviewed in the context of care and protection evaluations might later be called as trial witnesses. Sometimes the evaluator's referral question directly relates to the child's potential testimonial competence. Although nearly every state has held that a child must know the difference between the truth and a lie to testify competently, states differ in other criteria such as having the ability to recall past events and having the ability to tell the truth (some states view these factors as aspects of competence, but most states view them as aspects of credibility). Four states (Colorado, Connecticut, Missouri, and Utah) specify that alleged victims of child sexual abuse may testify without qualification (Goldstein, 1999; Haugaard et al., 1991).

Witness credibility, in contrast to competence, is determined by the willingness of a witness to offer truthful testimony or to accurately recall information. Credibility is determined by the trier of fact. In contrast to competence, the judge has no discretion to bar testimony that is deemed not credible or not persuasive (*Western Industries v. Newcor Canada Ltd*,

1984). The judge has pretrial discretion to determine whether a child has a shared or adult understanding of the truth, but credibility is relevant only after competence has been determined. Because of legal concern over the capacity of children to understand the truth and to tell the truth, most forensic evaluations and pretrial voir dire efforts by attorneys or judges include an initial assessment of the child's understanding of the truth. Six issues are of concern: the child's ability to distinguish between the truth and a lie, the child's understanding of the responsibility to speak the truth, the child's capacity at the time of the occurrence to perceive events accurately, the child's ability to retain an independent memory of the occurrence, and the child's capacity to translate memory into words, and the child's capacity to respond to questions about the occurrence (Haugaard et al., 1991; Weithorn, 1984).

Asking a child, "Do you know the difference between the truth and a lie?" is a fruitless endeavor because the question as little predictive value of a child's capacity to report an event accurately, and because neither a response or "yes" or "no" leads to a determination that the child can report events accurately (Goodman, Aman & Hirschman, 1987; Saywitz & Lyon, 1997). The question assumes the child comprehends the concept of "difference," can compare and contrast "truth" and "lie," has some degree of abstraction abilities, and has the linguistic capacity to articulate acceptable definitions of the relevant terms (Haugaard et al., 1991; Walker, 1999). Children up to seven years old have difficulty defining "truth" and "lie" or explaining the difference between the terms (Lyon & Saywitz, 1999).

Studies have demonstrated that children as young as 30 months old have a rudimentary understanding of what it means to lie (Chandler, Fritz, & Hala, 1989). By the age of four, children understand two components of lies (Walker, 1999): their nonfactual nature (Wimmer, Gruber, & Perner, 1984), and the potential consequence of punishment (Piaget, 1962). Children do not have a clear conception of lying relative to adult constructs (Kalish, Weissman, & Bernstein, 2000). In early childhood, they consider any statement regarded as "bad" by adults to be a lie. The anticipation of reward or punishment is central to children's understanding of what constitutes a lie (Siegler, 1986). Because they often yield the same negative consequences from adults as lies do, some children believe swearing is a lie and some children as old as 11 show confusion between lies and mistakes. For example, 90 percent of five-year-old children, 69 percent of eight-year-olds, and 48 percent of 11-year-olds said a child lied when inadvertently giving the wrong street directions to an adult (Peterson, Peterson, & Seeto, 1983). Four- to six-year-old children believe that a child is lying if he or she repeats a lie without knowledge that it is a lie. They believe a child is not lying if he or she repeats something the child believes to be a lie, even though it actually is true (Wimmer, Gruber, & Perner, 1984).

Children narrow their definition of lies between ages five and seven, dropping "swearing" or "naughty words" from their definitions of lies (Piaget, 1962). A child's definition of a truthful statement might center on whether or not it results in punishment, whereas adults might focus on the accuracy of the statement or the intentions of the individual making the statement (Haugaard, 1993). At around age seven, children begin to consider the intention of the speaker in their definition of what constitutes a lie (Burton & Strichartz, 1991).

Lyon and Saywitz (1999) conducted a study directly relevant to the capacity of children involved in care and protection proceedings to respond to witness competence questions. They demonstrated that children had difficulty providing definitions of "truth," and "lie." The children found it much easier to respond accurately to hypothetical questions such as, "If I tell you X, is it the truth or a lie?" Almost all of the five-year-old to seven-year-old children in the study demonstrated an understanding of truth and lies using the hypothetical questioning procedure. However, the four-year-old children in the study had difficulty making a distinction between the words "different" and "same." Although they did better than chance, they made numerous errors, especially in identifying lies. The four-year-old children also seemed reluctant to place "blame" on an adult (a researcher) who "lied" about something. They were more accurate in their identification of the truth or a lie when they were asked to point to pictures of "generic" children, identifying the child who made true or false statements about objects. In another study that assessed children's reasons for believing they should tell the truth in court, young children perceived truthful testimony as a way of avoiding punishment or disapproval. Older children were more concerned with upholding the laws and rules of society (Ruck, 1997). Most children who were reluctant to discuss the consequences of lying in response to questions about themselves were able to respond with reasonable accuracy to questions about the consequences of lying for "other children" (Lyon, Saywitz, Kaplan, & Dorado, 2001).

Most researchers studying children's understanding of the constructs of "truth" and "lie" have focused on the concern about unintentional false statements or false allegations by children. However, some researchers have examined children's conceptions of purposeful lying. Haugaard and colleagues (1991) examined childrens' perceptions of whether a child who was directed by her parent to make a false statement was lying. Children from three preschools, representing a cross section of social strata, saw one of two versions of a videotape. In the "self version," a man told a child standing near a pond to leave the pond otherwise he would summon the police. The man did not touch the girl by the pond. The girl went home. The police arrived and the girl admitted to being at the pond. She alleged that the man hit her twice before letting her return home. The police officer reminded her not to go near the pond and then he left. In the "mother version," the girl's mother told the girl she regarded the man as mean. She directed the girl to tell the police officer that the man hit her twice.

When children were interviewed in the Haugaard et al. (1991) study, five children were regarded as "confused" and eliminated from the sample. Those five children answered affirmatively to both questions, "Was it a lie?" and "Was it the truth?" They were unable to explain their responses. Of the remaining children, 29 percent stated incorrectly that the man hit the girl. Children watching the "self version" were more likely to incorrectly recall that the man hit the girl. Of the 71 percent of children who correctly stated the man did not hit the girl, 92 children said the girl lied to the police officer and six stated she told the truth (those six children had an IQ that was a half standard deviation lower than the group of 92 children). There was no statistically significant difference based on which version of the videotape the children viewed. In a comparison of the children to a sample of undergraduate adults, all of the adults correctly recalled that the man did not hit the girl. Haugaard and colleagues concluded that this critical aspect of children's definitions of lies did not automatically disqualify them as competent reporters of maltreatment, but the results raised concern about suggestibility in a small percentage of the children in the sample.

Haugaard (1993) examined whether children (preschool through third grade) had the ability to accurately identify whether a child's corroboration of an inaccurate statement by a parent constituted a lie or the truth. He asked children to view a videotape in which a boy falsely told a neighbor that the neighbor's daughter hit him. There were two versions of the videotape. In the first version, the boys' mother listened passively. In the second version, the boy's mother uttered the false statement and then the boy corroborated it. He found that only a small percent of preschool and kindergarten children misclassified the boy's or the mother's false statement as the truth. About 20 percent of the children in the sample (42 percent of preschoolers and 18 percent of kindergartners) inaccurately recalled that the neighbor's daughter hit the boy. All of the older children correctly classified the boy's and the mother's statements as lies.

Knowing the difference between the truth and a lie might be necessary for telling the truth, but it is not a sufficient condition for truth telling (Burton & Strichartz, 1991). In a review of studies that manipulated children's moral behavior, younger children were found to show uncompromising judgments of culpability and were unwilling to lie, even for someone who helped them gain a reward. Young adolescents made more flexible and situation-specific judgments of culpability, varying their truth-telling behavior according to the social context. Therefore, it is possible that young witnesses might be more honest than older child witnesses under some circumstances (Burton, 1984). Honesty as a personality variable also has been found to influence children's willingness to tell the truth (Burton, 1976). It has only mild influence as a developmental variable. Research specific to children's testimonial competence and credibility has found no pronounced developmental trends in honesty (Melton, 1981). Lying in older children and young adolescents is reduced by group discussions or lecture on the reasons why it is wrong (Fischer, 1970). Therefore, it may be helpful when children are reminded of their obligation to tell the truth and of reasons to tell the truth (Burton & Strichartz, 1991).

Motivational Influences for False Allegations

With the goal of developing a classification scheme for motivational influences on false allegations in maltreatment cases, Bernet (1993) reviewed the literature specific to false statements made by children or caregivers in the context of allegations of maltreatment. He drew from case examples described in the literature. Four general types of influence served as an organizational backdrop for Bernet's (1993) analysis: influences stemming from accusers, influences stemming from psychological disturbances; influences resulting from conscious manipulation, and influences stemming from iatrogenic effects. Influences identified in cases involving parental or other adult influences included: parental misinterpretation and suggestion, misinterpreted physical condition, parental delusion, parental indoctrination, interviewer suggestion, overstimulation, and group contagion. Influences identified in cases involving unconscious or non-purposeful mentation in the child included fantasy, delusion, misinterpretation, miscommunication, and confabulation. Influences identified in cases involving conscious or purposeful mentation in the child included pseudologia phantastica, innocent lying and deliberate lying. Influences that sometimes are regarded as purposeful and sometimes regarded as non-purposeful included confabulation and perpetrator substitution.

SHAME, FAMILY ALLEGIANCE, SECRETS, AND DISCLOSURE

The obverse of the problems of false allegations is difficulty mustering the courage to report true allegations. Although a child might have the capabilities needed to provide accurate information, the same child might not have the willingness to report information. There has been increased concern over the role of family, social and motivational influences on children's statements (Goodman, 1984). It is possible to reverse the typical age effects of younger and older children, contingent upon the force of familial, social, or motivational influences on the child's willingness to accurately report information. Although older children have the cognitive capabilities necessary to provide a complete and accurate account of an event, their cognitive abilities also increase their awareness of contextual features potentially influencing their willingness to divulge information (Pipe & Goodman, 1991). There are many contextual reasons why children make "omission errors," show reluctant to divulge information about maltreatment, or make outright denial of true events. Factors influencing a child's reluctance to provide information about true events include emotional discomfort, fear of reprisal, threats or bribery, and prolonged seductive approaches to abuse containing elements of victim blame (Bander, Fein, & Bishop, 1982). Researchers have begun to explore how and whether children of different ages keep secrets, when and to whom they are most likely to divulge secrets, and conditions that facilitate or inhibit disclosures (Pipe & Goodman, 1991).

Developmental researchers originally theorized that children under seven lack the capacity to keep secrets because they have no "theory of mind," they have difficulty taking the perspective of another, and they lack any sense of the separation between insiders and outsiders (Piaget, 1962). Recent studies have suggested children have many opportunities to learn about concealment through games and stories. Children's early experiences of concealment contribute to their developing awareness that the thoughts and knowledge of others might differ from their own (Vasek, 1986). The social contract between the teller of the secret and the child appears to be an important feature that distinguishes the difference between secrets and lies in the minds of children (Pipe & Goodman, 1991). Preliminary studies have shown that young children (ages five and six) readily conceal information when asked to do so by an unfamiliar adult. Even on 10-day and two-month follow up, 42 percent (at 10 days follow up) and then 25 percent (at two months follow up) of children denied knowledge of ink that the adult spilled on a pair of white gloves that the adult allowed the child to wear (Wilson & Pipe, 1989). Bussey (1990) added other conditions to a similar experiment involving a prized glass that the unfamiliar adult accidentally broke. Motivation for maintaining the secret was experimentally manipulated to include a control condition, asking not to tell to prevent the adult from getting into trouble, threat, bribery, or telling the child the accident was a "trick." Bussey found an age effect and a motivational effect. Among the five-year-old children, 45 percent concealed the accident, compared to 27 percent of the three-year-old children. Older children who were threatened or bribed were less likely to reveal the accident than children in the other conditions. For younger children, only the threat condition was significant.

In his classification of conditions that serve as motivating influences on false allegations, Bernet (1993) also described motivational influences for concealment: the secrecy that accompanies incest and other forms of child maltreatment, responses to pressure by family members to conceal maltreatment or to retract statements of maltreatment (Sgroi, 1982), and the "child sexual abuse accommodation syndrome" (Summit, 1983). Although child sexual abuse accommodation syndrome quickly fell out of evidentiary favor (that is, was deemed inadmissible) as a means of "proving" sexual abuse when children made accusations in an unconvincing fashion (Levy, 1989), it is generally accepted that at least some percentage of children who render true allegations tend to recant those allegations (Bernet, 1993; Summit, 1983). Many adult survivors of sexual abuse report never making a disclosure in childhood, keeping it a secret into adulthood (Blume, 1991). In order to better understand the relationship between nondisclosure as self protection, nondisclosure as a form of lying, lying to maintain nondisclosure, and the refusal of children to described the details of abuse even after it is discovered by other means, more specific research is needed that differentiates among types and processes of nondisclosure (Bussey, Lee, & Grimbeek, 1993).

THE RELIABILITY OF RECOLLECTIONS OF CHILD VICTIMS

Even when issues related to linguistic capacity and willingness to reveal or discuss maltreatment are surpassed in a child interview, questions sometimes are raised about the accuracy of children's memories and their abilities related to eyewitness identification. The accuracy of memory is directly related to the potential accuracy of children's testimony. Over the years, views about children's testimonial capacities have oscillated between two controversial poles: (a) children never lie about maltreatment, and (b) children's testimony carries a high risk of miscarriage of justice because of the potential for inaccuracy. Both of the poles neglect the complexity of factors related to children's memory and capacity for credible testimony (Melton et al., 1995). Memory development is a complicated process. Not everything gets encoded into memory. What gets into memory may vary in strength or salience. The status of information in memory becomes altered over time. Retrieval rarely is perfect or near perfect (Gordon, Schroeder, Ornstein, & Baker-Ward, 1995).

For children, as with adults, memory involves three processes: acquisition, storage, and retrieval. Acquisition or encoding involves the ability to perceive an event and to pay attention to it. Because acquisition sometimes involves the ability to understand order and to engage in interpretation of perceptions, it is a gradually acquired skill that is not comparable to adult memory functioning until children reach about age 12 (Collins, Wellman, Keniston, & Westby, 1978). Storage is an ability that does not increase with age. If an event is successfully encoded and stored in memory, young children have the ability to recall it as well as adults (Werner & Perlmutter, 1979). Retrieval involves the processes of recalling and reporting information (Herbert & Hayne, 2000). Children might store information reliably, but they might have difficulty communicating the contents of their memories. Children remember information in three ways: recognition, reconstruction, and recall.

Recognition memory, operating as early as infancy, is the simplest form of remembering (Bushnell, 2001). It involves the realization that an object or figure previously was experienced. It improves rapidly as children grow older. Face recognition memory, for examples, improves steadily through age 10, shows a surprising decline, and then improves again from age thirteen into adulthood (Carey & Williams, 2001; Goodman & Reed, 1986). Young children recognize simple figures as well as adults, but they do not recognize complex stimuli as well as adults. Reconstruction memory involves the capacity to describe the context within which an event occurred. Young children do well with simple reconstruction, especially when given reminders in recalling the context of an event (Hudson & Sheffield, 1999). They perform less well than adults on complex reconstruction tasks.

Free recall, the most complex process of remembering, requires the retrieval of previous events from storage with few or no prompts (Carver, Bauer, & Nelson, 2000). The recall skills of preschool children develop gradually, young elementary school children recall only one or two facts about events, and third to fourth graders recall about three. Junior high students recall about six and adults recall between seven and eight (Marin, Holms, Guth, & Kovac, 1979). Although young children recall fewer facts, what they do remember tends to be correct (Lepore, 1991; Goodman & Reed, 1986). Memory for central facts is stronger than it is for peripheral facts. When children recall aspects of a highly familiar environment (their own homes or their daily routines) their spontaneous recall is good but poorly sequenced (Johnson & Foley, 1984; McNichol, Shute, & Tucker, 1999).

DEVELOPMENTAL ISSUES

From a developmental standpoint, the accuracy of children's memory depends upon the type and complexity of information they report, and the interview context. Developmental factors influence each of these variables, so that children's memory is best conceptualized as an interaction between the child, the task, and the context. Memory is apparent in infancy, although such memories cannot be verbalized and might not be consciously accessible (Melton et al., 1995). Infants have rudimentary memory systems (Rovee-Collier & Hayne, 1987) and they remember some events (experienced repeatedly or even singly) over the course of several years (Myer, Clifton, & Clarkson, 1987). Infants' memory development is reflected in what they learn. For example, infants learn (by classical conditioning) to turn their heads in a particular direction when a tone sounds or when they hear familiar voices. Infants show a preference for familiarity and novelty during visual processing (Roder, Bushnell, & Sasseville, 2000). Even very young infants (aged 72 hours) show a preference for the mother's face compared to a stranger's face (Bushnell, 2001). The recognition memory of infants (remembering, when shown an object or figure, that the infant has seen the stimulus before) is stronger than recall memory (Rose, Feldman, & Jankowski, 2001).

Piaget (1954) theorized that recall memory was not possible in the first year of life. Schaffer (1971) theorized that recall memory is evident at about age six months, when the infant establishes an attachment to the parents. Attachment involves the ability to remember that the other person exists when he or she is absent. Some aspects of imitation are apparent in six-month-old infants (Meltzoff, 1990). Attention style (i.e., "short lookers" and "long lookers") has an impact on infants' abilities to retain information, with "short lookers" showing better retention over time (Courage & Howe, 2001). As time passes, infantile amnesia blocks many memories of early childhood (Rovee-Collier, Hartshortn, & DiRubbo, 1999). Even negative events such as early abuse can be forgotten (Gaensbauer, 1995). Purported narrative memories of events in infancy are not supported by empirical studies of memory in infants and toddlers (Carver, Bauer, & Nelson, 2000; Loftus, 1993).

Although recognition memory improves rapidly with age, age differences in recognition memory are far less pronounced than age differences for recall. For certain types of recognition tasks (nonverbal recall, responses to specific questions, and recognition of familiar drawings), the recognition memory of toddlers and preschoolers is quite accurate (Nurcombe, 1986; Kail, 1989). At ages two and three, children have the ability to accurately describe the core features of some events (Melton et al., 1995). Two-year-old children sometimes accurately recall specific events that occurred six months earlier (Fivush & Hammond, 1989). Recall appears to be stronger for negative events (Miller & Sperry, 1988; Goodman et al., 1990). Young children also show the ability to recall distinctive novel events and central features of repeated events (Nelson, 1986). But they are more likely than older children and adults to confuse similar events that they have experienced (McNichol et al., 1999).

Children's memory capacity to report child maltreatment is complicated by the delays that often occur in children's disclosures. Those delays typically are followed by further delays in the legal system's response to allegations (Melton et al., 1995). Little research is available on children's long-term retention of events, but existing data suggest that children's memory for novel or unusual events can be sustained for many years, especially when they are provided with reminders or repeatedly questions (Fivush & Hammond, 1989; Goodman, Hirschman, Hepps, & Rudy, 1991). Nonetheless, data also suggest that children's memory fades more quickly than adults (Brainerd, Reyna, Howe, & Kingma, 1990). Although negative memories can be forgotten (Gaensbauer, 1995), children are less likely to forget personally significant, embarrassing, emotional, or rehearsed information (especially actions) than less salient information (Davies, Tarrant, & Flin, 1989; Jones, Swift, & Johnson, 1988). Omission errors in children's memories may be more likely than commission errors. In a study of 72 girls, aged five to seven, randomly assigned to a genital or a scoliosis examination, 28 of 36 girls who received the genital examination failed to report genital touch. Only three of the 36 girls receiving a scoliosis examination mistakenly reported genital touch (Saywitz, Goodman, Nicholas, & Moan, 1991).

Although there is concern about the effects of stress on memory, research suggests that stress at the time of encoding is not a particularly powerful influence on the reliability of children's recollections (Goodman et al., 1987; Miller & Sperry, 1988). However, research on the effects of stress on memory has lacked uniformity in methodology and in the nature of the phenomena studied (Christianson, Goodman, & Loftus, 1992). Individual differences in memory for stressful events may explain the mixed results on this topic (Goodman, Quas, Batterman-Faunce, Riddlesberger, & Kohn, 1994). Some researchers have found that stress has a negative effect on memory encoding (Bugental, Blue, Cortez, Fleck & Rodriguez, 1992; Merritt, Ornstein, & Spicker, 1994).

THE INTERFERING EFFECTS OF LEARNING DISABILITIES, COGNITIVE IMPAIRMENT, AND MENTAL ILLNESS

Little is known about the memory and maltreatment reporting capacities of children with learning disabilities, cognitive impairment or mental illness (Milne & Bull, 1996). Although intelligence has a demonstrated relationship to children's capacity to describe possible sexual abuse (Fundudis, 1989), few studies have focused attention on how cognitive impairment impedes children's reporting capacities (Westcott & Jones, 1999). Some techniques, such as the cognitive interview technique (described below) help children with disabilities report more accurate information, but it does not reduce errors in children's responses to misleading information (Milne & Bull, 1996). Accurate estimates of the prevalence of parental maltreatment of children with mental, cognitive and learning disabilities are not available, but surveys suggest the problem merits attention (Verdugo, Bermejo, & Fuertes, 1995; Westcott & Jones, 1999). Some researchers have suggested that children and youth with intellectual disabilities may be more vulnerable to abuse than children without disabilities (Goldman, 1994; Valentine, 1990). Therapists have reported ways of managing the effects of learning disabilities, cognitive impairment, and attention deficit hyperactivity disorder on children's capacities to engage in psychotherapy for trauma victims (Sgroi, 1989; Smith & Nylund, 1997), but the relevance to forensic assessment is unknown.

SUGGESTIBILITY

The literature base concerning the suggestibility of children's recollections contains compelling but contradictory results (Ceci & Bruck, 1993). It is clear, however, that extreme views regarding children's suggestibility or lack thereof are unsupported by research data. Children are capable of high levels of reporting accuracy in the absence of influence by others. In the presence of influence, however, children have been described both as highly resistant to suggestion (Goodman et al., 1990; Jones & McGraw, 1987) and as susceptible to suggestion (Fehern, 1988; Schuman, 1986). Ceci and Bruck (1993) demonstrated that contradictory research results are linked to research design and data interpretation. They described the causal mechanisms underlying suggestibility, specifying under what conditions children are more likely and less likely to be suggestible.

What is Suggestibility?

Suggestibility, as defined by Ceci and Bruck (1993), concerns the extent to which children's encoding, storage, retrieval and reporting of information and events are influenced by a range of social and psychological factors. Ceci and Bruck (1993) define suggestibility as a situational and an interaction process, occurring either prior to or after an event, that might or might not alter actual memory of an event. That is, suggestibility might involve succumbing to social demands (acquiescence) or lying to please others, it might involve a more subtle process that indeed alters memory, and it can result from social as well as cognitive factors. Although personality variables are relevant, with some people showing greater vulnerability to suggestibility, it is viewed as a process that is social rather than intrapsychic (Ceci & Bruck, 1993). More traditional definitions characterize it as an individual or personality variable (Gudjonsson, 1992; Powers, Andriks, & Loftus, 1979). The narrower definition characterizes suggestibility as an unconscious process, a personality variable, and a post-event process (following rather than preceding an event) resulting in a distinctive alteration of memory. Individual variability in response to suggestibility is the central feature of the narrower definition (Gudjonsson, 1992; Oberlander, Goldstein, & Goldstein, 2001). The broader definition incorporates much of the intentional and unintentional behavior of concern in legal matters: subtle suggestions, seduction, leading questions, repeated questions, threats and other forms of inducement (Ceci & Bruck, 1993; Oberlander et al., 2001). Interested readers may turn to selected resources for a review of the history of suggestibility research (see Bruck, Ceci, & Hembrooke, 1998; Ceci and Bruck, 1993; Ceci, Toglia, & Ross, 1990; Wigmore, 1935).

SUGGESTIBILITY IN YOUNG CHILDREN

Developmental Differences in Susceptibility to Suggestion

Age has at least some relation to suggestibility. Nearly all relevant studies comparing three-year-old children to older children or adults have found an age effect (Goodman & Aman, 1990; Goodman, Hirschman, et al., 1991; Goodman & Reed, 1986; Leichtman & Ceci, 1995). Using nine-year-old, 12-year-old and college-aged participants, Cohen and Harnick (1980) tested recollection of the details of a 12-minute film of a petty theft. Participants were questioned immediately after viewing the film and one week later. In the first interview, 11 of the 22 interview questions contained misleading information. Young participants gave more inaccurate responses to both forms of questions compared to older participants. Upon follow up, the results were not reliably sustained. The researchers concluded that younger children were more likely to consciously submit to suggestions than older participants, but the suggestions did not affect the reliability of their memory upon follow up.

Using participants ages 6, 9, 11, and 16, King and Yuille (1987) seated participants in a room that was entered by a stranger to care for some plants. The stranger noted the time and said it was late. The children were asked to describe the stranger. Some of the interview questions were leading questions. The six-year-old children were significantly more suggestible than the older children and they also recalled fewer details about the stranger. Ceci and colleagues (1987) presented illustrated short stories to three-year-old and 12-year-old children. One day later, they gave half of the participants misleading information about aspects of the stories. Two days later, they asked children to select two pictures that appeared in the stories (from a series of four pictures). Age differences were obtained only for the sample of children provided with misleading information, with three-year-olds performing less well than the older children. No age differences were seen in the sample that received no misleading information. In a study of children's recollections of a filmed domestic scene in which a mother either was ambiguously caring or ambiguously abusive to her daughter, age-related differences were found in the participants' suggestibility, with a group of three- to four-year-old children showing greater vulnerability than a group of six- to seven-year-old children and a group of adults (Laumann & Elliot, 1992). The three age groups were interviewed with three modes of questioning: free recall, short answer cued recall, and leading questions that either were consistent or inconsistent with what was observed. When the leading questions that concerned the central theme of the film (whether the mother was or was not abusive) were analyzed separately, however, no significant age differences in vulnerability to suggestibility were found.

In an assessment of three- and six-year-old children's memories of a pediatric examination, Ornstein, Gordon and Larus (1992) asked misleading questions about the examination. They questioned half of the children immediately after the examination and one week later, and the other half immediately and three weeks later. In response to free recall and objective questions, older children provided more accurate information than younger children. Younger children gave fewer correct responses to misleading questions immediately and after one week. The age effect disappeared after three weeks (mostly because of decreased inaccuracy of older children's responses to misleading questions). In a study of the contrast in children's recollections of a blood test and innocuous touch (putting a loose cotton shirt over the child's clothes and then removing it), Oates and Shrimpton (1991) questioned four- to 12-year-old children. The children were questioned either four to ten days after the event, or three to six weeks after the event. There were no differences based on the blood versus shirt condition. Children were more accurate when questioned after the shorter duration of elapsed time compared to the longer duration. Children aged seven to 12 performed better than children aged four to six on free recall, direct questions, and resistance to some types of misleading questions. There were no age differences in resistance to misleading questions about the person who administered the blood test or who donned and doffed the shirt. The effect of delay was strong for misleading action questions, with a longer delay resulting in greater susceptibility to them.

Studies Showing Few Developmental Effects

In a study of participants' responses to a live staged argument (Marin et al., 1979), researchers asked four groups of participants (5, 8, 12, and college-aged) 20 objective questions and one misleading question. The impact of the misleading question was assessed after a delay of two weeks, when all 21 questions were asked in a non-leading fashion. Children did not differ from college students on immediate objective questions. The misleading question produced a significant effect on the accuracy of responses after a two-week delay, but the effect was similar across age groups. In this study, children were no more suggestible than adults. In another study of a live staged argument (Flin, Boon, Knix, & Bull, 1992), six-year-old children, ten-year-old children and a group of adults witnessed the argument during a nursing presentation on foot hygiene in a school auditorium. Half the participants were questioned about the argument after one day. The other half was questioned five months later. Three interview questions contained misleading information. In both sets of interviews, participants responded accurately across age groups. Only a few subjects of any age incorporated the misleading data into their responses.

Rudy and Goodman (1991) studied pairs of four- and seven-year-old children left in a trailer with an unfamiliar adult. One child was invited to play a game in which the adult dressed the child in a clown costume, lifted the child and photographed the child. The other child was invited to carefully watch what happened. Ten days later, the children were interviewed with suggestive and non-suggestive questions. Some questions containing actions potentially reflecting child abuse (such as the adult removing clothing from the child). Across each question type, there were few differences between the child involved in the actions and the child onlooker. Older children gave more accurate responses than younger children to non-suggestive questions regardless of whether the questions were abuse related. The same age effect was obtained on misleading questions, but only for the non-abuse questions. There was only one false claim of abuse by a four-year-old onlooker who said the adult spanked him and the other child.

In the study by Saywitz and colleagues (1991) (children aged five and seven receiving either a scoliosis or else a genital examination), children were asked suggestive and non-suggestive questions that were or were not abuse related. The older children's responses to suggestive non-abuse questions and to non-suggestive abuse questions were more accurate than the younger children's responses. There were no group differences in resistance to suggestive abuse questions. Both groups showed resilience in resisting suggestive abuse questions. Only three children in the sample of 215 five-year-old children raised false claims of abuse.

Resolving the Inconsistencies

Ceci and Bruck (1993) compared and contrasted some of the above studies, identifying many discrepancies in sample sizes, participants' ages, methodologies, the nature of the event to be recalled, whether the event was artificial or reasonably realistic, the timing of misleading information (before or during the memory assessment), the number or proportion of misleading questions, the linguistic complexity of the misleading questions, the duration of elapsed time prior to the interview, and the techniques of data analysis. Bruck et al. (1998) noted that some studies involved children's recollections of pleasant or neutral events and others involved unpleasant events. Some studies involved pre-event bias, some involved post-event suggestion, and some involved both (Leichtman & Ceci, 1995). Others have theorized that developmental suggestibility effects are negatively correlated with the "representational" mind. That is, an increase in children's ability to reason about conflicting mental representations is associated with a decrease in vulnerability to suggestibility (Welch-Ross, Diecedue, & Miller, 1997).

For example, when shown a white fish that subsequently is placed behind a red filter, three-year-old children will say that the fish looks red and it truly is red. At age five, children show the capacity to consider simultaneous pieces of information (Flavell, Flavell, & Green, 1986). Three-year-old children who are shown a crayon box will say that it contains crayons. When they discover it contains candles, they will say that they previously believed there were candles inside (Gopnik & Astington, 1988). Young preschool children believe there is a direct correspondence between reality and the way the world is represented in the mind. Older children recognize that the mind is more than a mere repository of information that is directly "copied" from reality. By the age of five, children understand that appearance does not always represent reality. They recognize the same person can represent an object or event differently at two different points in time, and that two people can represent a single object or event differently from one another (Welch-Ross, Diecedue, & Miller, 1997).

FACTORS UNDERLYING SUSCEPTIBILITY TO SUGGESTIBILITY

Suggestibility is multiply determined by cognitive, social, motivational, and personality factors in children (Ceci & Bruck, 1993; Goodman & Reed, 1986) and by interviewer characteristics (Bruck et al., 1998). Cognitive and social influences have been demonstrated, but less is understood about how cognitive factors influence social factors and vice versa. Although data suggest that cognitive and social factors interact with the type of information suggested, the cumulative and interactive effects are not well understood. In addition, there are other biological and developmental influences on suggestibility such as memory capacity, information processing capacity, and physiological arousal or stress. It is possible that susceptibility to suggestibility is related to memory functioning problems (Ceci & Bruck, 1993). There are encoding and retrieval opportunities for memory distortion (Brainerd et al., 1990). Age differences in responses to suggestibility might occur because younger children encode "weaker traces" that are more vulnerable to disintegration or overwriting, and they encode more verbatim representations (compared to the interpretive or gist representations of older children and adults). Researchers have demonstrated that weaker memory traces (as measured by the failure to report details in the first instance) are altered more easily with suggestions than strong memory traces (King & Yuille, 1987; Warren, Hulse-Trotter, & Tubbs, 1991).

Linguistic capacity is a second factor that underlies suggestibility (Ceci & Bruck, 1993). It is related to vulnerability to suggestion in adult and child samples (Loftus & Zanni, 1975; Dale, Loftus, & Rathbun, 1978). For example, individuals are more responsive to suggestions embedded in questions with definite articles (such as, "Did you see the car?) compared to those with indefinite articles (such as, "Did you see a car?). Although no studies have examined linguistic capacity in a detailed manner, theory would suggest that linguistic limitations explain why younger children sometimes are more vulnerable to suggestion than older children. Linguistic capabilities probably have a bimodal influence. If children fail to comprehend a complex question, they might reply, "I don't know," because the question is complex, not because they lack the information needed for an accurate response. Conversely, young children lacking sufficient syntactic or semantic linguistic development might resist suggestions to which older children succumb because of better language facility (Ceci & Bruck, 1993).

An individual's fund of knowledge (factual knowledge and representations of that knowledge in long-term memory) is a third factor underlying suggestibility. Knowledge is semantic and scripted. Semantic knowledge is an individual's repository of declarative, procedural, and associative meanings of concepts and world knowledge. Representation in long-term memory plays an important role in the interpretation of semantic knowledge. Implausible details are more difficult to recall than plausible details unless the details or the event is so novel that it appears bizarre

(Ceci & Bruck, 1993). Scripted knowledge enhances memory reconstruction by providing a template or expected sequence of events. Individuals use scripts, usually unconsciously, to fill in memory gaps (Myles-Worsley, Cromer, & Dodd, 1986). Scripts sometimes interfere with memory accuracy if an expected routine detail is absent from the real event. The scripts of preschool children are less flexible than those of older children (Hudson & Nelson, 1986). Preschool children have difficulty recalling discrepant or unexpected details in relation to scripts. If discrepant or unexpected details are present, younger children are likely to incorporate them into the script rather than regarding them as discrepant from the script (Hudson & Nelson, 1986). Therefore, younger children may be more vulnerable to some types of suggestion because of the immaturity and inflexibility of their script knowledge (Ceci & Bruck, 1993). Scripts also can produce faulty assumptions about the meaning of a behavior. Therefore, older children with more elaborate scripts make more false attributions than younger children about the meaning of an ambiguous event. For example, compared to third graders, sixth graders and college students were more likely to assume that a student's request to another student for the time was a pretext for cheating (Lindberg, 1991).

The capacity to distinguish fantasy from reality is a component of suggestibility that might explain developmental differences in vulnerability to suggestibility (Ceci & Bruck, 1993). On some tasks, such as asking children to group toys into fantasy figures and real figures, children as young as five are quite accurate (Morison & Gardner, 1978). However, the behavior of children sometimes reflects difficulty sustaining conceptual groupings. One study revealed that children were able to state accurately whether ghosts, monsters, and witches were real. But when told there was a monster in a box (and statistically comparing responses to children who were told there was a rabbit in a box), four out of twelve four-year-old children would not let an adult leave the room even after they were shown that the box was empty. None of the comparison sample children and none of the six-year-old children were frightened of the "monster" (Harris, Brown, Marriott, Whittall, & Harmer, 1991).

Interview structure affects suggestibility (Ceci & Bruck, 1993). Children are more likely than adults to change their answer in response to repeated questions within single interviews, presuming they must not have provided the correct response the first time. In Moston's (1987) study, the effect of repeated questions within an interview were more dramatic for six-year-old children, with accurate responses falling from 60 percent to 39 percent. In older children, it fell from 69 percent to 54 percent. Poole and White (1991) found that question type interacts with suggestibility. Repeated questions, within and across interviews, had little effect on children's or adults' responses. When specific yes-no questions were used, four-year-old children were most likely to change their responses, within and across interviews, compared to older participants. By contrast, repeated questions across interviews sometimes enhance the accuracy of children's recollections. Several studies found that children recalled about 10 percent more information in response to repeated interviews compared to a single interview (Baker-Ward, Hess, & Flannagan, 1990; Brainerd et al., 1990, Tucker, Merton, & Luszcz, 1990). Some studies have not replicated this result (Dent & Stephenson, 1979; Ornstein et al., 1992).

Whether children respond to suggestions sometimes depends upon their assessment of the questioner's credibility. Children are less suggestible when provided misleading information by another child compared to that provided by an adult (Ceci et al., 1990). Children also are more resistant to suggestions about salient actions compared to peripheral details (Rudy & Goodman, 1991; Saywitz et al., 1991). Children as young as age four resist suggestions about salient actions (Tobey & Goodman, 1992). Resistance is lost, however, when interviewers are insistent or selective in their approach to questions. In a study that challenged the view that the effects of suggestibility are less powerful for personal and salient actions compared to peripheral details, three groups of five-year-old children were given post-event suggestions in two phases after a visit to a pediatrician. In phase one, children were given one of three types of feedback following a routine Diphtheria Pertussin Tetanus (DPT) inoculation: pain-affirming feedback, pain-denying feedback, or neutral feedback. One week later, the groups of children did not differ in their reports of the severity of pain or duration of crying. In phase two, children were visited one year after the inoculation. During three separate visits, they were given additional pain-denying or neutral feedback, and either misleading or accurate information about the actions of the pediatrician and the assistant. In the pain-denying feedback condition, children reported they cried less and felt less pain compared to children in the neutral feedback condition. Children in the misleading information condition made more false allegations about the actions of the pediatrician and the assistant compared to children who were given accurate information (Bruck, Ceci, Francoeur, & Barr, 1995).

Although the prevalence of interview bias and stereotype inducement is unknown, researchers have demonstrated that a number of interviewers use techniques that either wittingly or unwittingly could bias the interview process or encourage children to respond to stereotyped depictions of events or individuals. Bruck et al. (1998) examined transcripts made available by judges, attorneys, parents, and medical and mental health professional. They found frequent examples of possible bias and stereotype induction, with some cases involving blatant examples and veiled (or actual) threats. Researchers have demonstrated that interviewers tend to rely on specific and leading questions, to repeat information known or thought to be true from records prior to the child's own disclosure of the information, to characterize behaviors or individuals as "bad" or as "doing bad things," or to selectively reinforce certain responses (Hulse, 1994; Warren, Woodall, Hunt, & Perry, 1996).

Social and motivational factors influence suggestibility (Ceci & Bruck, 1993). Interpretations of the meaning of conversations or questions are constrained by social conventions such as expectations of cooperation, expectations of compliance with authority figures, assumptions that adults speak the truth, and failure to expect deception. In a study of five- and six-year-old children's reports and recollections of the behavior of a janitor involved in an ambiguous task with toys, children were interviewed after one hour and after one week in one of three ways: neutral or non-leading, with incriminating statements suggesting the janitor was playing on the job and was bad, and with exculpating statements suggesting the janitor cleaned well and was good. Children were interviewed by experimenters and by parents. In response to neutral interview questions, children consistently gave accurate accounts of the janitor's behavior. In response to suggestive questions, children shifted their accounts in the direction of the suggestions as the interviews progressed. The suggestion effect was particularly dramatic when children responded to interpretive questions concerning whether the janitor was cleaning or playing with the toys when he performed six actions such as touching a doll or hitting a drum. At the end of the interviews, children gave inaccurate accounts to their parents even though they had no reason to mislead their parents. The suggestions persisted even though parents interviewed children in a non-leading manner (Thompson, Clarke-Stewart, & Lepore, 1997).

It is possible the emotional tone of the interviewer influences suggestibility. Although it is important to use reasonable measures to develop rapport, interviewers sometimes have been criticized for encouraging and reinforcing the content of children's responses to questions (Raskin & Yuille, 1989). In a study of children's responses to either familiar or unfamiliar individuals, researchers found a significant difference in children's responses to questions of an "opinionated" interviewer relative to questions posed by a "neutral" interviewer. Children in the incriminating interview condition made more cued recall errors and endorsed more biased interpretations of a confederate's actions compared to children in the neutral interview condition. Whether the confederate was a familiar or an unfamiliar individual had no effect on children's responses or their propensity to provide more inaccurate information in the "opinionated" interviewer condition (Lepore & Sesco, 1994). In another study, children of all ages provided a greater frequency of accurate responses to interviewers with whom they felt comfortable, but comfort level did not decrease the frequency of inaccurate responses relative to interviews in which children felt less comfortable (Goodman et al., 1990; Saywitz et al., 1992).

Suggestibility is influenced by children's perceptions of the omniscience of adults (Ceci & Bruck, 1993). Even when information is personally important or salient, some children respond to suggestions by adults with inaccurate information (such as misidentification of their father in a picture of an unfamiliar adult male). However, many children resist suggestions even when adults make them (Lewis, Wilkins, Baker, & Woobey, 1995). In a study of the responses of first-graders, third-graders and adults to authoritative versus non-authoritative and adult versus child speakers, adult speakers rated authoritative sources as more credible, whereas children rated adults as more credible regardless of their authoritative versus non-authoritative approach to a subject (Ackerman, 1983). Compared to adults, children are more likely to respond to nonsensical questions asked by adults (Hughes & Grieve, 1980), because they assume that questions asked by adults must have an answer. The child's level of familiarity with the adult might lessen the impact of the omniscience factor.

When parents were given inaccurate information about an event, they nonetheless elicited relatively accurate information from preschool children compared to interviews conducted by an unfamiliar female. Children's free recall accuracy suffered when they were interviewed by unfamiliar females provided with misleading or biased information about the child's play activities of a research assistant, but not when interviewed by biased versus unbiased mothers (Goodman, Sharman, Golden, & Thomas, 1991). Children are influenced by their parents' statements, however. In a study comparing three- and four-year-old children to five- to seven-year-old children, both groups gave accurate information in response to a non-suggestive interview about their interactions with an experiment confederate, Mr. Science. Three months later, a portion of the children heard their parents read a story about Mr. Science. The story described events that the children experienced with Mr. Science, but it also described events the children did not experience. The children made many erroneous reports in response to a second interview (the sample cell sizes in the second recruitment of participants were too small to compare the older to the younger children) (Poole & Lindsay, 1995).

In a study of children's beliefs about memory and suggestibility, researchers demonstrated that children show developmental differences in their awareness of the fallibility of memory and their vulnerability to suggestibility (O'Sullivan, Howe, & Marche, 1996). Most children believed that central events of a story would be retained more easily than peripheral details. Preschool and first grade children believed memory was invulnerable to suggestion from a sibling or parent. Third grade children believed that suggestion could adversely affect memory. Most preschool children believed that retroactive interference would not adversely affect memory, but most first and third grade children thought that it would. Older children believed that they were less vulnerable to suggestibility if memories had been retained for several months compared to retention of only one day.

Suggestibility and False Memories of Maltreatment

It is well established that even a single exposure to misleading information can produce false memories for suggested events (Loftus, 1993; Zaragoza & Lane, 1994). Although participants of all ages remember seeing suggested items, the magnitude of the effect is greater for first-grade children compared to third- and fifth-grade-children (Ackil & Zaragoza, 1995). Repeated exposure to misleading information exaggerates the harmful effects of suggestion (Zaragoza & Mitchell, 1996). Hypotheses concerning the underlying mechanisms of suggestibility that results in false memories of an event or for some of the details of an event include five possible causal mechanisms (Ceci & Bruck, 1993). The first two explanations reflect memory storage problems. The original memory trace for the event is changed or overwritten by suggestions, or it is unchanged but rendered irretrievable because of the interference of post-event suggestions. The third explanation is a gap-filling strategy: misleading information is accepted to compensate for the absence of memory for the original event. The fourth is a memory retrieval problem: the individual has simultaneous access to accurate information and to the misleading information, but chooses the inaccurate version of the event because of source monitoring problems. The fifth is a problem of social influence or the need for social approval.

In a study that contrasted suggestibility with attempts to implant false memories or erase real memories, researchers found only a significant effect in a "changed memory" condition compared to the "implanted" and "erased" memory conditions (Pezdek & Roe, 1997). Eighty four-year-old children and 80 ten-year-old children were either touched in a specific way or were not touched at all. Later, experimenters suggested that a different touch, a completely new touch, or no touch at all had occurred. The researchers concluded it is less likely that an event can be implanted or erased from memory, compared to suggestions that change or reinterpret the event. The results were consistent across both age groups. When the memory contains personally significant or embarrassing information, implanting false memories is difficult (Rudy & Goodman, 1991; Pezdek, 1995). It is possible to implant false memories in the laboratory and in the context of psychotherapy (Hyman, Husband, & Billings, 1995; Loftus, 2000). False memories are not as permanent as real memories. The content is more likely to be recanted after a two-year delay compared to memory for real events (Huffman, Crossman, & Ceci, 1997). Although later recovery of true traumatic childhood memories usually also contains inaccurate information (Loftus, 1997; Woodall, 1998), the degree of inaccuracy is not as substantial as debate over the controversy might suggest (Harris, 1996; Lamb, Sternberg, & Esplin, 1995).

Suggestibility and Disavowals or Denials of Maltreatment

Most of the suggestibility research described above has focused on children's responses to suggestions that an event occurred, or that it occurred in a particular way. However, some of the research studies contained an assessment of whether children respond to suggestions that an event did not occur when, in actuality, it did (errors of omission) (Bruck et al., 1995; Pezdek & Roe, 1997; Saywitz et al., 1991; Thompson et al., 1997). Children appear to make errors of omission in response to suggestions in a manner comparable to their errors of commission. It is likely that some nondisclosures of abuse are influenced by suggestions.

Failure to disclosure maltreatment also occurs for other reasons. Some scholars have theorized that repression of truly traumatic memories is rare (Bowers & Farvolden, 1996). In an interview of patients reporting memories of child maltreatment, a majority of them reported some degree of continuous recall. A little over half (53 percent) said they had never forgotten the traumatic events, some reported a mixture of continuous and delayed recall (17 percent), and some reported amnesia followed by delayed recall (16 percent). Statistical analyses revealed that participants with and without delayed recall did not differ in reporting corroboration of their memories from other sources. In the sample of individuals with delayed recall, the majority of them cited idiosyncratic, trauma-specific reminders or crises that precipitated recall. Only 28 percent cited psychotherapy as the factor that precipitated recall (Herman & Harvey, 1997).

The prevalence of false memories of abuse is much smaller than the prevalence of child maltreatment. False memories and accompanying false accusations of child maltreatment detract from and trivialize the problem of genuine reports of child maltreatment (Bowers & Farvolden, 1996; Loftus, 1993). Many critics of repressed traumatic memories have focused heavily on the problem of "recovered" memories, usually occurring in the context of psychotherapy. Criticisms of recovered memories, although frequently valid, suffer from problems of generalization from the laboratory to clinical setting. It is possible that a sizable majority of so-called recovered memories have at least some degree of validity. In an outpatient sample, researchers found a relationship between the extent to which memory was delayed and age of onset of trauma, duration, and degree of maltreatment. In that sample, 74 percent of participants obtained corroborating evidence from other sources when asked to do so (Herman & Schatzow, 1987). In a non-clinical sample of 1,712 individuals asked to provide self-report data on child maltreatment, only a small minority reported temporarily forgetting childhood sexual abuse. Forgetting was unassociated with victim or abuse characteristics, but it was associated with a suggestion from someone else that the individual might have suffered childhood abuse (Epstein & Bottoms, 1998).

Critics of recovered memories tend to neglect other facets of unreported trauma, such as non-disclosures that occur in the context of fear, embarrassment, confusion, or other negative elements that often accompany failure to report maltreatment (Bander, Fein, & Bishop, 1982). Non-disclosures also occur because of pathological processes and object relationships (such as identification with the aggressor) and use of dissociation and other primitive defense mechanisms (Davies, 1996; Green, 1993, 1998). Disclosing maltreatment is difficult for most children. Child victims of intrafamilial abuse are in a "double bind." In cases of intrafamilial child maltreatment, the family unit dually threatens and promotes the physical and emotional survival of the child. The family dynamic often involves overt and subtle messages that children must yield their autonomy and maintain family loyalty. They are given messages about their potential abandonment should they reveal the abuse. The child who threatens family loyalty often gets "scapegoated" or targeted for escalating maltreatment. The physical and emotional pain of maltreatment becomes muted over time because chronic maltreatment becomes an "expected" or seemingly "ordinary" occurrence in a cruel or exploitative family system (Maddock, 1988).

Although the relevance to children is unclear, researchers have shown that the structure and content of questions facilitated true disclosures in adults when they were asked to provide self-report data that researchers could compare to documented histories of child maltreatment (however, the researchers did not include a comparison sample to assess whether the same questions might result in false reports in adults who were not victimized in childhood). The study showed that adults were reluctant reporters of past histories of victimization (West, Williams, & Siegel, 2000). Finkelhor (1998) conducted a national survey of 2,000 youth, examining whether younger children (ages 10 to 11) were more reluctant reporters compared to older children (ages 12 to 16). He found comparable self-report rates of family and non-family assaults in both groups, but the younger group showed a lower rate of self-reported sexual abuse. Hamby and Finkelhor (2000) found that simple, behaviorally specific language facilitates better distinctions in children's self reports of different forms of maltreatment.

STRATEGIES FOR ENHANCING CANDOR, CENTRAL DETAILS, AND RELIABILITY IN CHILDREN'S REPORTS

When six- to ten-year-old children are told it is acceptable to reply, "I don't know," the accuracy of their responses to misleading questions does not increase (Moston, 1987). When six- and eight-year-old children are provided with specific instructions on how to articulate their lack of comprehension of a question, along with rehearsal of asserting a lack of comprehension, they show a marked increase in accurate responding and a decrease in responding to questions that young children would not be expected to comprehend (Saywitz, Snyder, & Nathanson, 1999). Use of an innocuous staged event, followed by a review of interview rules and demonstration of the rules in a "practice" interview also enhances accuracy in seven- to 12-year-old children's reports (Geiselman, Saywitz, & Bornstein, 1993; Saywitz et al., 1992). Researchers have shown that adults show a reduction in suggestibility if they are warned (either before or after receiving post-event information) that some of the information might contain inaccuracies (Christiaansen & Ochalek, 1983; Greene, Flynn, & Loftus, 1982). Children benefit from similar warnings that some questions will be "misleading or tricky" (Warren et al., 1991). The effect is small across age groups (ages seven, 12, and adult in the Warren et al. study), improving accuracy by only about 5 percent. It also helps to warn children that cognitive frameworks contain stereotypes that might impede the accuracy of their answers (Koblinsky & Cruse, 1981).

Sternberg and colleagues (1996) developed a somewhat standardized approach to rapport-building procedures designed to elicit spontaneous information from children. Carter, Bottoms, and Levine (1996) described the components of supportive interviewing techniques designed to increase children's resistance to suggestion, such as using a warm but non-leading interview style. Saywitz and Snyder (1996) developed a procedure to expand children's spontaneous reports by teaching them a narrative elaboration procedure. The procedure involves the use of reminder cards, training in how to use the reminder cards, and pictorial cues and organizational strategies to trigger memory. Prior to being asked to provide an account of an incident, the interviewer teaches the child that their narrative account should include some basic elements and details, including the participants, the setting, any actions, any conversation, and their recollection of affective states of the individuals in their account. The child is given simple drawings on five cards depicting each basic aspect of the narrative. The five basic aspects of the narrative were based on cognitive studies of children's scripts and schemata. Children are asked to rehearse narrating with each card, using a practice event to demonstrate their capacity to benefit from the technique. Children in the Saywitz and Snyder (1996) study of an abbreviated form of the narrative elaboration procedure demonstrated a 53 percent improvement in spontaneous recall over a control group of children who did not receive the procedure.

The narrative elaboration procedure has been shown to increase the accuracy of true reports of children (compared to children who received cue cards without training in their use) without increasing the frequency of reports of false information. Researchers have cautioned that there tends to be a large standard deviation in groups of children using the narrative elaboration procedure. A small number of children using the procedure provided false information (during a two-week follow-up interview) for a fictitious event compared to their responses concerning the staged event. No narrative elaboration study has included a sample of preschool aged children (Camparo, Wagner, & Saywitz, 2001).

Another structured technique designed to increase children's report of details is the cognitive interview, developed by Geiselman and colleagues (1984). The original technique, developed for questioning of adult crime victims, was adapted for children by Saywitz and colleagues (1992). When using the technique, the child is asked to mentally recreate the environmental, cognitive, physiological, personal context and affective states of the event. The individual is asked to report all information, regardless of the completeness or perceived importance of the information. The child has several opportunities for retrieval, providing the account in chronological order and reversed chronological order. They are asked to change perspectives, providing an account of the event from the perspective of an observer or a different vantage point. Distractions are minimized because the interviewer is not allowed to interrupt the child, the child is asked to close his or her eyes. The child is asked to use mental imagery.

The cognitive interview procedure is not particularly effective with children under age six. Young children misunderstand some of the instructions and they do not understand the change-of-perspective step in the interview (Geiselman, 1999; Memon, Cronin, Eaves, & Bull, 1993). Some studies have shown that the cognitive interview reduces vulnerability to suggestibility (Memon & Bull, 1991; Milne, Bull, Koehnken, & Memon, 1995). Other studies have shown that although the technique increases recall accuracy, it is no better than control conditions involving standard interview instructions in reducing susceptibility to misleading suggestions (Hayes & Delamothe, 1997; McCauley & Fisher, 1995; Milne & Bull, 1996). The cognitive interview is no better than non-standardized techniques, such as using visual props, in enhancing free recall in children aged seven to ten (Miller, Fremouw, Aljazireh, & Perker, 1996).

SUMMARY

1. Developmental perspectives are important to the understanding of children's experiences in care and protection cases.
2. The impact of foster placements is a relatively new area of research. Preliminary studies suggest kinship placements and foster care training have a positive impact on child outcomes. Foster care training is negatively related to risk of multiple placements.
3. Features of children's linguistic development are linked to case rulings relevant to child witness competency, judicial and jury interpretations of the credibility of child witnesses, children's comprehension of the meaning of an oath, case rulings and statutes addressing the confrontation clause, and the development of hearsay exceptions specific to child witnesses.
4. Specialized knowledge of children's linguistic development is central to the construction of valid and reliable interview techniques for children.
5. Suggestibility is a situational and interactive process that is affected by age, individual susceptibility, interview variables, social and motivational factors. When other factors are taken into account, age is a less robust predictor of suggestibility than previously thought; however, there does appear to be at least a mild to moderate negative correlation between age and suggestibility.
6. Suggestibility studies are relevant to care and protection matters as a basis for understanding possible influences on cases. However, the generalizability of empirical demonstrations of suggestibility is limited in care and protection matters because of sampling issues, limits in generalizability, and ethical constraints in studying the unique manifestations, chronicity, or severity of suggestive influences that might be relevant to some care and protection matters.

7. Failure to report maltreatment probably is a much greater problem for child interviews in care and protection cases. Most studies that illustrate the impact of failure to report child maltreatment are retrospective, suffering from problems inherent to self-report data. However, studies with external corroboration of maltreatment are emerging.

8

Evaluation Methodology

Research and Practice

This chapter outlines the steps and procedures of conducting a parenting evaluation in the context of care and protection proceedings. Using a systematic approach, recommendations are made for ways to establish a reasonable approach to methodology across cases. The use of consistent methodology within referral questions and the use of multimodal assessment (or multiple methods of gathering or corroborating relevant data) enhance the reliability and validity of evaluation results. Good methodology should allow for flexibility to accommodate different degrees of breadth or comprehensiveness of evaluations, and it should be adaptable to a variety of referral questions. Care and protection evaluation approaches and reports range from brief to comprehensive, based on the nature of referral question(s), the number of parties involved in an evaluation, formal requests from judges and attorneys for reports of a particular size or scope, and the resources available for the evaluation. Parenting evaluations typically include a clinical interview of the parent(s), observations of the parent(s) with the child (when indicated), a clinical interview of the child, gathering collateral information and relevant records, and psychological testing when indicated. Psychological testing might include measures that assess general functioning, measures related to specific symptoms or behaviors, and/or measures that contain risk factors or hypothesized psychological correlates of behaviors or risk factors.

This first section of this chapter focuses on steps for evaluating the caregiver(s), including obtaining informed consent, explaining the referral question(s) and the limits of confidentiality, and gathering and reviewing records and collateral data. Next, the content and empirical basis for child maltreatment risk assessment and assessment of amenability to treatment is reviewed. Research on the correlates of child maltreatment is expanded upon for the purpose of illustrating how it is integrated into evaluation practices. Hypothesized risk factors relevant to child maltreatment are described along with an analysis of hypothesized causal links between risk factors and child maltreatment. The benefits and limitations of risk assessment are described. Research and case examples are reviewed that are relevant to the link between risk factors and treatable conditions. The degree to which a risk factor or condition is treatable depends upon many features such as the static versus dynamic nature of the problem and the severity of the problem. It also depends upon the relative weight of the condition as an explanatory or exacerbating factor for child maltreatment.

Particular attention is given to behavioral, mental, and neurological conditions identified in judicial analyses of causal explanations for protracted involvement with child protective services and for treatment failures that eventuate in termination of parental rights. Because potentiating factors are not limited to behavioral, neurological or mental health conditions, other factors are examined. Common potentiating factors (such as attributional style) might be seen in varying degrees across cases regardless of the presence of one or more of the above-mentioned conditions or disorders. These factors, when they are known and measurable, enhance the predictive validity of a risk assessment relevant to child maltreatment because they are less amorphous constructs than the broad constructs of mental illness, mental deficiencies, or organic impairment. However, the same caveat is in order in assessing the relative weight of any of these underlying factors. Given these caveats, advice is offered for integrating risk factors and analyzing parental amenability to rehabilitation, while respecting the limits of the predictive validity of assessment.

The third section focuses on interviewing the child. It begins with preliminary steps, interview techniques, and other assessment techniques for children. It provides information about how to conduct a first appointment with a child and how to conduct a multimodal assessment of a child.

It reviews how to gather historical information, making decisions about the use of interview props or tools, how to ask children questions about their behavior and symptoms, balancing the interview with questions relevant to vulnerabilities and resilience in children, how to question children about parents and adaptations to placements, and the utility and limitations of considering children's self reports of historical information and other interview content. It describes available studies relevant to the use and misuse of general and specific psychological assessment measures in care and protection matters. The usefulness of records and collateral information is discussed.

EVALUATING CAREGIVERS

Preliminary Steps and the First Appointment

Notification of Limits of Confidentiality

Prior to initiating any evaluation, informed consent should be sought based upon prevailing regulations and practice standards. In the initial session and in all sessions thereafter, the individual being interviewed should be told the limits of confidentiality prior to being asked any interview questions (American Psychological Association Committee on Professional Practice Standards, 1998). Explanations of the limits of confidentiality should be given in concrete and straightforward terminology, with the opportunity for questions. Asking the individual to paraphrase the notification usually provides useful data concerning their comprehension of the notification. If the individual does not comprehend the notification, formal steps should be taken to determine whether the evaluation should proceed. Examples include contacting the referring attorney, or notifying the court if the evaluation was court ordered. The explanation of the limits of confidentiality should include a clear explanation of the referral question, the individuals who are a party to the evaluation, who will view the report, the lack of confidentiality, who "owns" the report, provisions (or lack thereof due to judicial restrictions in some jurisdictions) for release of the report to individuals who are not a party to the legal proceeding, and the difference between medical records and forensic records. When more than one party is evaluated in the context of one case or one forensic assessment report, the evaluator should explain restrictions in releases, namely that one party cannot authorize release of the full report unless all other parties similarly sign releases. Individuals should be told they are under no obligation to participate in the evaluation, they may decline any further questions if they agree to the evaluation but later change their mind, they may refrain from answering certain questions if they wish to keep information private, and that nothing they say will remain "off the record." They should be told their statements potentially will appear in the evaluator's written report and that they also might be summarized during court testimony. The notification of the limits of confidentiality applies not only to the party being interviewed, but to all individuals who are interviewed during the evaluation process, including collateral contacts.

If the individual shows a lack of comprehension of the notification, certain aspects of the notification might need to be repeated in simpler language. It sometimes is helpful to ask what the individual has been told about the reason for the evaluation, especially when evaluating children. Children might not have been told anything, or they might have relatively complete information. The level of disclosure to the child about the legal context (for example, that the evaluation might be used as evidence in a hearing concerning parental rights termination), should be weighed against concern for unduly alarming or worrying young children. The disclosure about the lack of confidentiality, however, should be complete (Koocher & Keith-Spiegel, 1990).

The notification of the limits of confidentiality provides the interviewee with important knowledge about what to expect during the evaluation process. It also provides an opportunity for the evaluator to explain the expected number and duration of evaluation sessions, the scope of the referral question, and the evaluation methodology (Oberlander, 1995a). Some evaluators worry that the notification of the limits of confidentiality will sacrifice the validity or reliability of self-report data. Although the situations are not directly parallel, similar concerns were raised after the *Miranda* notification of rights was required prior to police interrogations. Some researchers found that the notification had little if any effect on the interviewee's willingness to provide a statement, but others continue to worry about the chilling effect on statements (for a brief description of confidentiality issues and their relationship to evaluation methodology, see Oberlander, 1995a; for a description of articles concerning the impact of the *Miranda* notification on suspects' statements see Oberlander & Goldstein, 2001; Oberlander, Goldstein, & Goldstein, 2002). To date, there is no empirical research on the effects of a notification of the limits of confidentiality on the willingness of interviewee's to provide critical personal information of direct relevance to the referral question. Regardless of concerns of the possible effect on willingness to divulge personal information, the notification must be given to satisfy ethical and legal standards. In most jurisdictions, the evaluation data would be redacted (in part or in whole) or completely rendered inadmissible if appropriate notification was omitted.

Evaluation Methodology and the External Validity of Assessment Measures and Behavioral Indices of Theoretical Constructs

In making plans for an evaluation strategy, careful attention should be given to limitations in the external validity of assessment measures. No approach to a forensic evaluation has been empirically demonstrated to be perfectly valid or reliable (Barnum, 1997; Budd & Holdsworth, 1996). Contemporary theories and research studies on parenting behavior continue to focus predominantly on optimal parenting rather than minimal parenting competence (Budd, Poindexter, Felix, & Naik-Polan, 2001; Jacobsen, Miller, & Kirkwood, 1997). Few valid behavioral indicators of psychological constructs (e.g., warmth, nurturance, responsiveness) have been developed (Budd & Holdsworth, 1996). There is little consensus, either clinically or legally, on the criteria used to determine minimal parenting competence (Budd et al., 2001; Melton et al.; 1997). Psychological assessment measures, even when specific to parenting behaviors, typically were not designed for forensic contexts or purposes (Brodzinsky, 1993; Budd & Holdsworth, 1996). Although measures might in fact have theoretical applicability to evaluations for the court, there is little supplementary normative data for population samples of families involved in care and protection matters.

On the other hand, there also is little supporting empirical basis for conducting evaluations without turning to psychological assessment measures or measures of parenting behaviors. Even when supplementary norms are not available for specific populations, measures sometimes provide valid, reliable, and clinically meaningful data because of the relationship of the measures to variables that are commonly found across populations or situations. Although approaches to care and protection cases take many forms, it is common for psychologists to use some form of psychological testing in evaluations of parental functioning, caregiving behaviors and skills, quality of parent-child relationship, substance abuse, and general functioning (Budd et al., 2001). Most researchers and clinicians recommend a multimodal approach to assessment, applying the tradition of seeking converging data in forensic assessment (American Professional Society on the Abuse of Children, 1990; American Psychological Association, 1999; American Psychological Association Committee on Professional Practice and Standards, 1998; Jacobsen et al., 1997; Wolfe, 1988).

A Caveat against Universal Evaluation Recommendations

The literature contains suggestions for core features of care and protection evaluations. However, this book takes a different approach, suggesting consistency or uniformity of methodology should be based on referral questions within the legal context, not solely on the legal context itself. Scholars who make recommendations for use of particular methods across cases usually assume the band of possible referral questions is narrow. However, in care and protection matters, there is a broad expanse of possible referral questions, making it cumbersome or unsuitable to adhere to a particular methodology across cases. For example, some scholars recommend the consistent use of multi-session approaches in care and protection evaluations (Azar et al., 1998, Budd et al., 2001). Although it is a reasonable recommendation for comprehensive evaluations, one could easily imagine specific referral questions that could be addressed in a single evaluation session. In addition, some court clinic contexts and funding sources do not provide resources for multi-session evaluations. Therefore, referral questions sometimes are limited to critical, but highly focused, questions or content areas to accommodate clinical demands in light of limitations in funding resources for evaluations. Similarly, some scholars advocate for the use of home visits as a standard method of observational data (Budd et al., 2001; Jacobsen et al., 1997). Although home visits provide fruitful information, especially in circumstances of alleged neglect, they probably are not a necessary feature of all care and protection evaluations. Nor would the required inclusion of them be pragmatic for evaluators who must operate in conditions of limited funding, geographic expanse, potential danger to them in some neighborhoods or homes, or scheduling problems. Although methodology recommendations certainly are worthwhile, consistency or uniformity across cases or legal contexts is not as useful as a reasonable degree of uniformity within referral questions. Methodology should be individually crafted to address the referral question (Oberlander, 1998). Evaluation methodology must remain flexible to accommodate referral questions of differing breadth, limitations in resources and other pragmatic concerns, court docket schedules, care and protection deadlines, and statutory time limitations. The evaluator must craft questions and choose methodology sagaciously to assure that reliability and validity are not sacrificed because of resource or time limitations.

Scholars have made recommendations concerning evaluation methodology (American Psychological Association Committee on Professional Practice and Standards, 1998; Azar et al., 1998; Barnum, 1997; Melton et al., 1997; Wolfe, 1988), most of which were clinically derived. Because of obvious ethical concerns in applied research, it would be impossible to experimentally manipulate evaluation measures or features of methodology in the context of real cases. Nevertheless, enough is known about approaches to clinical and forensic assessment to offer recommendations for the basic features of common referral questions in care and protection matters (American Psychological Association Committee of Professional Practice and Standards, 1998). Even when recommendations for standards of practice and evaluation methodology have been developed and published, consistent evaluation approaches rarely have been demonstrated (Budd et al., 2001; Keilin & Bloom, 1986; Liss & McKinley-Pace; Oberlander, 1995a, 1995b). Deviations from those approaches, however, are not necessarily an indicator of invalidity or poor evaluation quality. More specific studies are needed to determine whether deviations reflect reasonable and necessary accommodations to individual cases, compromises to quality, or a combination of both reasons.

MULTIMODAL ASSESSMENT: THE CAREGIVER

The Clinical Interview

The degree of clinical interview comprehensiveness that is necessary in an evaluation is determined by the referral question. Some interviews might address an extensive range of historic and current factors, with an in depth focus on particular spheres of functioning, and other interviews might be highly specific to one or two areas of functioning or historical factors (Ownby, 1997; Schwartz, 1987). Regardless of the nature of the content area or domain of functioning, it is important to include questions designed to inquire about positive historical factors or strengths in functioning (Budd & Holdsworth, 1996). Focusing only on deficits in functioning carries the risk of neglecting important mitigating information or compensatory skills. It also carries the risk of alienating the interviewee. A strong clinical interview balances inquiry into both positive and negative features of functioning (Schwartz, 1987).

HISTORICAL INFORMATION. Clinical interviews ordinarily progress from emotionally neutral topics, such as educational and occupational history, to more sensitive areas, such as mental health problems or substance abuse problems (Ownby, 1997; Schwartz, 1987). In care and protection evaluation practice, however, it is useful to begin with the parent's perspective of their history of involvement with the child protective service system. Interviewees otherwise tend to report frustration because they perceive the interview questions as peripheral to the central topic of their child protective service system involvement and their parenting. There is a cathartic quality to interviewees' accounts of their involvement with the child protective service system. Many times they report that the evaluation provided them with their first opportunity to described what happened. This approach can ease tension in the evaluation and aid the rapport building process, but finesse is required so that the interviewee does not mistakenly conclude that the evaluator is an advocate just by virtue of listening (Crenshaw & Barnum, 2001).

The interviewee's first account of the history of child protective service involvement usually lacks some or many details central to the actual maltreatment (Coburn, 2000; Crenshaw & Barnum, 2001). It is helpful to ask follow up questions and to ask for another full account later in the interview. Sometimes details will be gathered in different phases of the interview. Inconsistencies across accounts or between accounts and data in records should be noted. In some cases it is useful to point them out, seeking clarification and providing an opportunity for the interviewee to acknowledge details that were left out or that possibly were distorted. Usually a curious or inquisitive approach is sufficient to elicit such an acknowledgment, but some situations call for more direct or confrontational approaches. Confrontational approaches should be used with caution when there is a question of mental retardation or suggestibility in the interviewee (Sgroi, 1989). It is reasonable, however, to approach a topic more than one time if there is inconsistency or if the interviewee avoids responding to the topic in some way. Multiple inquiries of adults help the evaluator to determine whether the interviewee will divulge or acknowledge relevant information concerning the allegations of child maltreatment (this approach is less useful when there is concern about inaccuracies in records to which the interviewee's account would be compared). To avoid the risk of acquiescence, caution should be used in asking multiple questions within single interviews to adults with cognitive limitations (Cairns & Paris, 1971; Sigelman et al., 1981).

Other interview content depends upon the nature of the inquiry. If the referral question contains a relatively broad request for information about parenting abilities or risk of harm, the interview concerning historical data in most cases would be fairly comprehensive, including content areas relevant to risk. If the interview question is limited to a specific band of parenting skills or a specific kind of risk (for example, risk related only to substance abuse relapse potential), then there is less need for comprehensive historical data. When comprehensive data are needed, usual areas of inquiry include family of origin history, important adulthood relationships including current family relationships, dating and marital history, the decision process (or lack thereof) to bear children, educational history, occupational history, mental health history, medical history (including neurological data), psychosexual history, substance use history, violence history, and criminal history (Dolan & Doyle, 2000). The depth of inquiry into any area depends in part on a preliminary review of records that guide interview content, and information that the individual might divulge in the course of an interview (Douglas et al., 1999; Dutton & Kropp, 2000).

The depth of a specific inquiry sometimes hinges upon whether the referral question includes a request for data about past treatment responses or prognosis in future interventions. For example, for a parent with a history of substance abuse problems relevant to risk of child maltreatment, the interview questions should cover not only patterns of alcohol and drug use, but the individual's history of sobriety, the past duration of periods of sobriety, factors that potentiated and hindered sobriety, the effectiveness or lack thereof of past rehabilitation efforts, the individual's current status (level of participation and stage of treatment) in rehabilitation, the individual's motivating influences for remaining sober, options available for reducing urges to drink or use drugs, relapse prevention plans, and other relevant information (Bernardi et al., 1989; Famulero et al., 1986; Miller, 1990). Asking about the treatment modality used in rehabilitation has bearing on follow up questions. If a self-help group is the main treatment modality, it is important to inquire about the nature and frequency of the self-help meetings, the steps or stages of the self-help process, the use of sponsors, and the type of meetings attended. If relapse prevention is the main treatment modality, it is important to inquire about the phase of relapse prevention planning, whether the plan is committed to memory or readily available in written form, the level of detail in the plan, the adaptability of the plan to different settings, and other relevant questions. Interview proficiency also depends upon the interviewer's level of knowledge about the addictive potential and differential impact of various illicit or licit substances on the individual's functioning.

For each specific content area, it is important to become proficient in interview methods designed to elicit reliable and valid information. For example, both motivational (Marlatt, 1996; Miller, 2000) and confrontational (Schneider, Casey, & Kohn, 2000) interview methods have been developed for use with individuals who have a history of substance abuse. Motivational interviewing techniques have been developed to address both substance abuse risk and its relationship to harm to self and others (Marlatt, Blume, & Parks, 2001). Regardless of the method chosen, interview skill acquisition is essential to a successful assessment (Tappin et al., 2000). Some interview techniques are easily generalized across content domains and others are less easily adapted to new content domains (Martino, Carroll, O'Malley, & Rounsavilee, 2000; Van Horn & Bux, 2001). Sometimes comorbidity of conditions, such as substance abuse and serious mental illness, has implications for interviewing techniques (Swanson, Pantalon, & Cohen, 1999). For example, if an interviewee is particularly skilled in confrontational approaches to interviewing individuals with substance abuse problems, adaptations might be required for an interviewee with comorbid posttraumatic stress disorder that results in fragile or avoidant responses to such approaches.

RISK ASSESSMENT RESEARCH AND THE IMPLICATIONS FOR INTERVIEW CONTENT. Risk assessment originated out of concern for the post-institutionalization behavior of individuals with mental illness or criminal justice involvement who had histories of violence. Much of the recent violence risk assessment research has maintained this focus (Monahan et al., 2000; Novaco, 1994; Steadman et al., 2000). The relative degree of concordance among evaluators of violence risk is unknown, but when concordance exists, there is a high correspondence to the likelihood of later violence, at least in inpatient psychiatric samples (McNeil et al., 2000). The level of concordance and the specificity of risk communication depend upon the format within which the clinician is asked to make a prediction. Clinicians reach different levels of concordance based upon whether they employ probability formats or frequency formats of prediction (Slovic et al., 2000). Researchers have questioned the generalizability of violence risk research to other clinical populations. Most existing actuarial risk assessment tools are based on main effects regression analyses. Some researchers have proposed using a classification tree rather than a main effects regression approach. Using decision thresholds for identifying high versus low risk cases (instead of risk/no risk), enhances the external validity and clinical applicability of actuarial measures (Steadman et al., 2000).

The classification tree approach was supported with empirical data from the MacArthur Violence Risk Assessment Study, based on a sample of risk factors identified in 939 patients recently discharged from psychiatric hospitals (Steadman et al., 2000). The Iterative Classification Tree (ICT) is an actuarial tool that was developed in the MacArthur research study. It assesses 106 risk factors (designed for use with psychiatric inpatients). It the original study, it classified 72.6 percent of the sample as low risk (less than half the sample's base rate of violence) or high risk (more than twice the sample's base rate of violence (Monahan et al., 2000), thereby showing some clinical utility in clarifying which patients might carry a heightened risk of violence relative to other patients. Thus far, it is unclear whether these approaches are comparable to or superior to more traditional violence assessment tools such as the HCR-20 (Webster, Douglas, Eaves, & Hart, 1997), the Psychopathy Checklist-Revised (Hare, 1991, 1998) or the Psychopathy Checklist Screening Version (Hart, Cox, & Hare, 1994) in their classificatory and predictive utility (cf. Douglas, Ogloff, Nicholls, & Grant, 1999). Regardless of the risk assessment approach that is used, it is important to note that much of what is known about violent conduct in individuals is based on population samples other than parents involved in care and protection matters. Studies of parents involved in maltreatment, however, have isolated similar risk factors (Dubowitz, 1999; Hanson, 1998; Haskett et al., 1995). Although much of the research on inpatient psychiatric samples probably is generalizable to care and protection samples, the degree of generalizability for specific risk factors or for cumulative risk is unknown. Researchers studying inpatient psychiatric populations and criminal populations tend to focus on physical violence (Monahan et al., 2000), but care and protection matters include individuals at risk of sexual violence and neglect (Dubowitz, 1999; Hanson, 1998; Haskett et al., 1995).

Specific studies of risk associated with child maltreatment have been based on small sample sizes and a small dimension of variables relative to the violence risk studies cited above (Murphy et al., 1991; Milner & Gold, 1986; Milner, Robertson, & Rogers, 1990). Nonetheless, some wide-scope studies are beginning to appear that are relevant to risk in maltreating parents (Widom, 1989a, 1989b; Wolfe, 1985, 1987, 1988). When factors are identified, their relevance to specific populations of maltreating parents, such as mentally retarded parents, might be limited (Roszkowski, 1984). Similarly, the weight and relevance of risk factors differ when comparing physical violence, neglect, and sexual offending.

Advances in risk assessment research have been seen in the area of domestic violence risk. Some of this research has taken place in the context of child maltreatment investigations. For example, in a small sample of 15 caseworkers, simply introducing a questionnaire about domestic violence resulted in a 100 percent increase in the number of battered women identified during child maltreatment investigations (Magen, Conroy, Hess, Panciera, & Simon, 2001). Although it was based on a small sample size, this research suggests that simply asking direct questions heightens the probability of identifying factors relevant to risk. Campbell, Sharps, and Glass (2001) questioned the wisdom of applying general risk assessment methods to individuals at risk of intimate partner homicide by virtue of their history of victimization by domestic violence (among other factors). Some researchers have suggested that risk should be specific to the nature and target(s) of violent behavior, hypothesizing that domestic violence shows a different manifestation and risk configuration than other forms of violence (Dutton & Kropp, 2000). By contrast, other researchers have suggested that violence risk variables carry the same predictive valence regardless of the population of interest. Webster and colleagues (1997) have shown that the variables on the HCR-20 are equally predictive in populations with and without an appreciable psychiatric disorder.

PHYSICAL ABUSE RISK ASSESSMENT RESEARCH AND THE IMPLICATIONS FOR INTERVIEW CONTENT. Researchers have developed instruments specific to child abuse potential (Milner, 1986, 1991). Studies have shown that stress, family resources, and social support (either independently or collectively) are predictive of child abuse potential (Burrell, Thompson, & Sexton, 1994; Casanova, Domanic, McCanne, & Milner, 1992). Physical abuse is a low-frequency act that usually occurs in a private setting. Because of problems with self-report data, it is difficult to demonstrate in applied research whether personality features or behaviors, such as hostility, criticism, or threats, have any potent predictive or discriminative validity for physical abuse (Wolfe, 1985, 1987, 1988). Based on a review of the literature, Jacobsen and colleagues (1997) provided an example of risk factors that have at least a moderate link to risk of physical abuse. Examples include untreated major mood or thought disorders, failure to acknowledge a mental illness or the need for treatment, a history of violent outbursts of temper, active drug or alcohol addiction, a childhood history of abuse, other adverse childhood experiences (such as a hostile and rejecting family environment, harsh or unfair discipline, placement in foster care or multiple placements, parental discord, institutional upbringing), few ties to neighbors or community agencies, violent relationships with spouses or dating partners, gross misperceptions about the child or child development, gross misperceptions about useful or appropriate discipline strategies, unrealistic expectations of children, difficulty discerning and responding to cues from the child, insecure parent-child attachment, role reversals, "scapegoating" the child, extreme worry about the child's well being, high levels of parenting stress or social isolation, a hazardous home environment, and a history of violent behavior.

In a descriptive study of parents facing termination of parental rights, Schetky and colleagues (1979) identified many historical factors that might be relevant to risk, including a history of victimization by maltreatment, frequent separations or losses, frequent moves, institutionalization at some point while growing up, poor relationships with or attachments to parents, few support figures in the family or community, alcohol or drug abuse, one or more psychiatric admissions, a history of arrest and incarceration, and mental retardation. Descriptive studies, however, do not illustrate the predictive utility (or lack thereof) of hypothesized risk factors. In a more formal analysis of variables predicting judicial decisions to separate the child from the family, Dalgleish and Drew (1989) demonstrated that judges (in Queensland, Australia) consider risk variables related to severity of abuse, parenting, and the family social system their analysis of risk to the child. Variables contributing to the predictive value of the equation included severity of abuse, salient aspects of parenting, salient aspects of the marital relationship, and the parents' lack of cooperation. (The study unfortunately did not specify what was meant by "salient aspects.") The researchers concluded that "at risk" or "perceived risk" variables have a common meaning across child protection workers and judges, but the predictive value of any individual variable is moderate at best. Because of inconsistency in the explicitness of judicial opinions and in data provided to the court by child protection workers, the researchers were unable to offer suggestions for standards of unacceptable risk.

Other hypothesized risk factors include the deliberateness with which the individual harmed the child in the past, the extent of harm to the child, the frequency of harm to the child, and patterns of allowing perpetrator access to the child. Factors include adequacy of supervision, safety of the home environment, and age and visibility of the child, the caregiver's age and maturity, the mental and social development of the child (which is linked to their capacity to report on their own behalf), the level of fear the child expresses about the caregiver or the home environment, the presence of other adequate caregivers, the level of stress on the caregiver, the availability of supports, the caregiver's history of childhood maltreatment or victimization in adulthood by acts such as domestic violence. Also potentially relevant to risk are the mental and emotional well being of the caregiver, the physical health of the caregiver, the caregiver's criminal history, the caregiver's history of substance abuse relevant to maltreatment, the caregiver's history of mental illness or neurological illness or impairment relevant to maltreatment, cognitive appraisals of caregiver-child conflict, attributions of blame and responsibility, anger management skills, the caregiver's recognition of the problem, the caregiver's capacity to select suitable substitute caregivers, the caregiver's response to the child's misconduct, the nature of the caregiver-child relationships, appropriate assignment of family roles, and the nature of family conflict (Moncher, 1996; Murphy et al., 1991; Milner & Gold, 1986; Milner, Robertson, & Rogers, 1990; Widom, 1989a, 1989b; Wolfe, 1985, 1987, 1988). Much attention has been given to substance abuse in maltreating families. Gaudin (1994) reported that substance or alcohol abuse is a factor in 80 to 90 percent of child maltreatment cases.

Some of the above risk factors are classified as "static." They are aspects of the caregiver's history and they cannot be modified. Others are classified as "dynamic." Examples of dynamic risk factors include the caregiver's degree of acknowledgment of the problem, the intensity of relevant symptoms, and the individual's justification for the maltreatment. Dynamic risk factors have the potential to change with the passage of time, with treatment interventions, or with personal motivation, among other things (Borum, 1996; Miller, 2000; Hanson & Harris, 2000). The potency and individual relevance of specific risk factors is difficult to identify when applying aggregate group data to individual clinical cases. Less is known about the desistance of risk in maltreating parents compared to other clinical populations whose risk has been studied over time. Common problems in violence prediction that have been examined in forensic assessment (Borum, Otto, & Golding, 1993) probably are applicable to care and protection evaluations, but the extent of generalizability has not been empirically demonstrated.

SEXUAL ABUSE RISK ASSESSMENT RESEARCH AND THE IMPLICATIONS FOR INTERVIEW CONTENT. Risk assessment for sexual offending is different from that of other violent offending (Hanson & Thornton, 2000). Although some of the predictors overlap between groups of violent offenders and sexually violent offenders, risk of child sexual abuse is more directly linked to aberrations in psychosexual history than violence risk. Some researchers hypothesize the most potent predictive factors are a reduction in family boundaries and individual autonomy, and a misdirection of sexuality. Child sexual abuse is defined in the law based on age of consent, onset of puberty, sexual maturity, effective consent, community standards, age differentials, and type of sexual activity (Goldstein, 1999). Sexual abuse, however, is not necessarily sexually motivated (Finkelhor, 1984). Rather, it is related to cognitive distortions in identification and affiliation, "power and control" issues, hostility, and aggression (Sgroi, 1982, 1989). It is a mistake, however, to ignore the sexual component of sexual abuse. All sexual behavior, even when it is socially conventional and innocuous, is motivated to some degree by nonsexual needs (Finkelhor, 1984). Sexual acts can be characterized by the degree to which the sexual element is low versus high, and the degree to which the desire to punish or humiliate is high versus low. In pedophilic behavior, in contrast to rape, evidence suggests there often is a strong erotic component (Groth, 1979).

Psychopathological models of deviant sexual arousal and deviant social and cognitive functioning have been developed to explain sexual offending. Theories probably overemphasize psychopathology because they are based on unrepresentative samples of convicted offenders (Finkelhor, 1984; Gelles, 1973). Researchers studying sexual offenders of children seek to explain why individuals find relating to a child emotionally gratifying and congruent, why sexual arousal takes place in the presence of a child, why the individual's efforts to obtain sexual gratification by more socially sanctioned methods is blocked, and why the individual is undeterred by conventional social inhibitions from sexual relations with a child (Finkelhor, 1984). Theories to explain these factors include arrested psychological development, low self esteem, low efficacy, a sense of inadequacy and immaturity, shame and humiliation based on childhood experiences, identification with the aggressor, symbolic mastery over childhood trauma, imprinting and conditioning from childhood sexual victimization, and socialization that values dominance and power (Groth, Hobson, & Gary, 1982). Sex offenders of children are often described as timid, unassertive, inadequate, awkward, poorly socially skilled, and moralistic (Goldstein, Kant & Hartman, 1973).

Stress in combination with alcohol or other substance abuse has been cited as a potent predictor of disinhibition. Social and cultural factors, such as victim blame and the reluctance of the legal system to prosecute and punish offenders, contributes to disinhibition (Armstrong, 1983; McIntyre, 1981). Some theorists believe there is a distinction between sex offenders who prefer boys and those who prefer girls. There may be differences in the nature and the relative contribution of risk factors based on the gender of the offender (Finkelhor, 1984; Howells, 1981). Typologies have been developed based on the level of fixation for a particular form of offending compared to offending that depends on degree of regression in the offender (Groth, Hobson, & Gary, 1982). Separate theories have been used to explain incest offenders compared to other sex offenders against children (Langevin, 1983). More unified theories classify incest offenders as a subtype of offenders against children (Groth, 1979; Howells, 1981; Waterman, 1986). Both groups of theorists agree that incest offenders differ in some ways from other sex offenders against children. The disagreement is over the degree of shared features between the groups (Finkelhor, 1984).

Most theories and treatment programs require offenders to acknowledge that they have a problem, and to implement various methods of self control to prevent relapse (Abel, Rouleau, & Cunningham-Rathner, 1986; Prentky & Bird, 1997; Quinsey, Rice, & Harris, 1995). Treatment programs focus on characteristic compulsive thoughts and urges, cognitive distortions and rationalizations, justifications and minimizations, involvement in antisocial conduct outside the sexual domain, ruminations and fantasies during masturbation, interest in deviant sexual themes, post-offense transient guilt, temporary regaining of control, and dissipation of guilt over time. Treatment programs focus on assertiveness skill deficits, social skill deficits, insufficient arousal to nondeviant stimuli, deficits in sexual knowledge and dysfunction, and the cyclical nature of sex offending (Abel et al., 1986; Barlow, Abel, Blanchard, Bristow, & Young, 1977; Johnson, 1995). Although movement through a cycle of abuse involves common phases and features, an individual seldom progresses through a "cycle of offending" one step at a time, start to finish, nor does the triggering of the cycle always result in a sex offense outcome (Lane, 1997b). Nonetheless, recidivism is a common occurrence. By the time an offender reaches adulthood, the average pedophile or incest offender has attempted over 25 child molestations

(DeFrancis, 1969). Most pedophilic and incest offenders admit to prior offenses (Studer, Cleeland, Aylwin, Reddon, & Monro, 2000). The level of violence used against children is especially high in paraphiliacs who select child victims unknown to them (DeFrancis, 1969).

Examples of phases or steps in a sex offending cycle include triggers, personalization distortions (victim stance), negative anticipation, hopelessness distortions, avoidance, externalizing distortions (blaming others), power and control, increased need to distort or control, fantasy, offense setup, sexual abuse, reinforcing distortions (affirming adequacy), fugitive thinking, control distortions (such as thinking one is immune from getting caught or facing consequences), reframing, and suppression distortions (thinking the abuse is not a problem). The offense setup phase involves planning, victim selection, grooming and stalking, opportunity, justification, objectification of the victim, super-optimism, and a decision to act (Lane, 1997b). It is important to have collateral data and documentation against which to gauge an individual's response to assessment questions relevant to risk. The data assist the evaluator in determining the interviewee's candor, degree of acknowledgment of the problem, areas of denial or minimization, attributions of responsibility, and sexual abuse behavior patterns.

Areas in inquiry relevant to sex offending risk recommended by Lane (1997a) include candor, self initiation of disclosure, recall of details, degree of aggression or overt violence in offenses, frequency and duration of offenses, length and progression of history of sexual offending, offense characteristics other than sexual aggression, number of victims in relation to victim access, victim selection characteristics, preferred victim type, victim blame, appraisal of victim harm, personal responsibility for offending behavior, precipitating factors, degree of arousal and habituation, other exploitative or addictive behavior, family system functioning, stability of school or employment, stability of social relationships, non-offending sexual history, past victimization, external and internal motivation for rehabilitation, response to confrontation, treatment history and response, criminal arrests and convictions, and current access to victims. Inquiry into related factors includes ability to form and maintain healthy relationships, capacity for intimacy, social competence, trauma history, self concept, capacity for empathy, substance abuse history, depression, suicidal ideation, family roles and structure, intellectual capacities, and the quality of expression and management of anger and conflict.

Theoreticians agree with Lane's (1997a) analytical and behavioral framework, although they sometimes classify risk factors differently. They caution that there is limited empirical basis for structured interview techniques or specialized instruments that cover the above content areas.

Nonetheless, active research programs relevant to risk assessment in sex offenders show promise (Boer, Wilson, Gauthier, & Hart, 1997; Hatch-Maillette, Scalora, Huss, & Baumgartner, 2001; Lanyon, 2001b). Preliminary research study outcomes have shown that dynamic risk factors appear to have a greater relationship to sex offending recidivism than static risk factors, even after controlling for pre-existing static risk factor differences (Hanson & Harris, 2000).

NEGLECT RISK ASSESSMENT RESEARCH AND THE IMPLICATIONS FOR INTERVIEW CONTENT.   Assessing risk in neglectful parents is probably the most difficult risk analysis. There is enormous heterogeneity among neglectful families (Gaudin & Dubowitz, 1997). Neglect commonly co-occurs with other forms of maltreatment, adding complexity to risk equations. Neglect may not represent as discrete a set of risk variables as have been identified for physical or sexual abuse. The enormous variability among neglecting families may mask between-group differences in the relevance or potency of risk variables (Dubowitz, 1999). Neglect is associated with blunted affect, apathetic interaction styles between parents and children, passive-dependent interactive styles between parents and children, non-reciprocal relationships among family members, cycling between passive and aggressive behavior (Crittenden, 1988), chaos and poor planning, impulsive actions in parents, and conflict-laden relationships between parents (Kadushin, 1988). Social isolation, poor social support, poor social skills, and rejection by the community sometimes are indicators of neglect (Gaudin & Polansky, 1986; Polansky, Ammons, & Gaudin, 1985). Analyses of verbal and nonverbal behavior in neglectful families indicate that neglectful mothers are critical, show little positive attention, provide little stimulation and nurturance, are less responsive and sensitive, speak less, use short and less complete sentences, issue more demands, and express less acceptance (Crittenden & Bonvillian, 1984; Gaudin, 1994). Not all studies have shown similar results, however (Gaudin & Dubowitz, 1997). Difficulty emotionally connecting with others, apathy and futility, disorganization, depression, hostility, poor socialization, and hopelessness are personality variables that have been identified in neglectful mothers. There is little research on personality variables in neglectful fathers, but socio-demographic data suggest children of single parents and children in family units having different fathers are vulnerable to greater paternal neglect (Dubowitz, 1999).

MITIGATING FACTORS.   In an assessment of the characteristics of care and protection evaluation reports in one jurisdiction (Cook County, Illinois), researchers found that evaluators had a greater tendency to identify or report weaknesses relative to strengths in parents. The tendency was present regardless of who conducted the evaluation (psychiatrist, psychologist, or other individual) (Budd et al., 2001). Violence risk assessment studies have revealed that mitigating factors influence the desistance of risk (Monahan et al., 2000; Novaco, 1994; Steadman et al., 2000). Age and maturation also contribute to the desistance of risk (Grisso, 1986). Therefore, it is important to consider mitigating factors when analyzing risk of child maltreatment. Possible mitigating factors include social support, good parenting role models, acknowledgment of parenting problems, recognition of the impact of past parenting problems on the child's development and functioning, and adherence to recommended interventions (Jacobsen et al., 1997). Other factors include: Substance abuse recovery, abatement of mental health symptoms, identification of compensatory strategies, utilization of community resources, positive reports of rehabilitation progress, stable and consistent visitation with the child, recognition of the impact of separation on the child, separation from abusive partners, and a strong post-reunification after-care plan.

THE CAREGIVER'S RELATIONSHIP WITH THE CHILD.   Areas of inquiry into the caregiver's relationship with the child include the strength and quality of the relationship, the presence and degree of emotional closeness, parental perceptions of the child (and child perceptions of the parent), the parent's ability to promote appropriate development in the child, and parental responsiveness to the child's needs (Stahl, 1994). The family plays a role in assisting children through developmental stages, culminating in identity formation in the adolescent years. In care and protection assessments, it is important to retain focus on current features of the parent-child relationship. When more than one child is involved in the care and protection petition, it is important to individualize the assessment of the parent's skills to each child and to report the quality of the parent's relationship to each child (Budd et al., 2001).

Data concerning the caregiver's relationship with the child come from many sources, including self-report data from the parent, self-report data from the child, observational data, collateral reports, and relevant records. Interview content for the parent might consist of a description of the child, the activities of the child, chores and other expectations of the child, parental awareness of preferred foods or activities of the child, what the parent wishes he or she could change about the child, how the parent responds when the child seeks attention, concerns for the relationship with the child, a description of how the parent tries to talk to the child or negotiate conflict with the child, reports of "close calls" of maltreatment, daily routines, and awareness of the child's friendships and surroundings (Oberlander, 1995a; Stahl, 1994). Empirical research has shown that parental discourse about child behavior and development yields meaningful data about the strength and nature of the parent-child relationship

(Laible & Thompson, 2000). Structured self-report measures of parent-child attachment sometimes facilitate the assessment (see below). As long as appropriate caveats are made during the interpretation process, they sometimes can be adapted for use as semi-structured interview measures. Relationship and parent-child interaction observation strategies are described below.

THE CAREGIVER'S VISITATION OF THE CHILD. The decision strategies that agencies use to determine the nature and extent of contact between parents and children in foster or residential care are somewhat idiosyncratic. Although agencies might form internal standards, there is little consensus across agencies about the appropriate criteria for determining the frequency of contact, whether or not contact should be supervised, who qualifies as an appropriate candidate for a visitation supervisor, and whether supervised visitation should take place in a natural setting or in a formal visitation center. Similarly, there is little information concerning the predictive utility of parent-child visitation reports or observations for determining the quality or safety of the relationship. Children with histories of trauma reported a variety of responses to visitation, suggesting that although standardization of visitation criteria might be a complex endeavor, it would help promote objectivity in the visitation observation process (Johnston & Straus, 1999).

Because of the relative novelty of formal visitation centers, agencies are struggling to help child protective service workers and judges understand the limitations in their resources and roles (Theonnes & Person, 1999). Because of resource limitations and scheduling problems, most visitation centers have requested that the court limit their role to supervision of parent-child visitation rather than asking supervisors to attend hearings as fact witnesses or expert witnesses. Similarly, although it might be appropriate to request observational data, evaluators should not ask visitation supervisors to reach conclusions about the appropriateness of visitation or the appropriateness of reunification versus termination goals (nor should that question be posed to other collaterals). The demand for supervised visitation steadily exceeds the supply, and some policy researchers have suggested programs should be made universally available by enacting legislation for their creation, regulation and funding. Regulations would help clarify the role of visitation supervisors (Clement, 1998).

In a study of parental perceptions of visitation centers, parents had mixed reports of their visitation centers experiences (Pearson & Theonnes, 2000). Some parents prefer visitation center supervisors to other supervisors because they are trained remain neutral during supervision, because they feel less awkward with a professional supervisor compared to other supervisors, and because it is easier to reschedule missed appointments.

Complaints about visitation centers include geographic distance from the caregiver's home or the child's foster home, formality that contributes to the discomfort of being scrutinized, scheduling inflexibility, and insufficient numbers of staff members to meet the demands for supervised visitation sessions. Regardless of the method of visitation supervision, keeping foster children connected to biological parents through visitation and other forms of contact is essential for reunification. It helps maintain family relationships during out-of-home placement and it has the potential to facilitate the child's adaptation to out-of-home placement (Cantos et al., 1997). In a survey of 650 foster parents, results suggested that training and support of foster parents increased the involvement of foster parents in promoting biological parent-child visitation (Sanchirico & Jablonka, 2000).

There is little empirical data relevant to factors that facilitate or impede parental compliance with visitation. Reviews of case files for 676 families in one visitation agency showed that half of the families ceased visitation without stating their reasons for exiting the program (Pearson & Theonnes, 2000). These data are troubling in light of findings that visiting mothers showing a tenfold increase in likelihood of reunification compared to mothers who visit infrequently or not at all (Davis, Lanksverk, Newton, & Ganger, 1996). Based on an analysis of case outcomes in the legal system, Huffaker (2001) concluded that visitation rights are heavily linked to judicial views of whether a parent has been successful in his or her substance abuse rehabilitation efforts or has failed in the endeavor.

THE CAREGIVER'S RELATIONSHIPS WITH HELPING SOURCES. Referral questions sometimes address the impact of social isolation on parenting. Especially in cases of neglect, social isolation sometimes is a prominent feature of child maltreatment. The caregiver's capacity to develop relationships with helping sources, positive support individuals, mentors, and non-neglectful parenting role models might be a main goal of the child protective service intervention plan. When the caregiver's relationship to helping sources is examined, it is useful to inquire into both breadth of contacts and depth of contacts (Jacobson & Frye, 1991). The reasons for limitations in depth, quality, or persistence of constructive relationships should be examined (Mitchell et al., 1982; Nitz et al., 1995). Current data should be compared to historical data. For example, sometimes caregivers might initiate new helping or support relationships during the pendency of care and protection matters because they are making a meaningful attempt to develop relationship skills. Other attempts might be transient or superficial, to mollify child protective service workers. Collateral reports from helping sources sometimes help clarify the caregiver's motivations, quality of relatedness and intentions. Reports also clarify whether the caregiver is developing skill in knowing how and when to use helping resources and how and when to recognize when formal helping resources no longer are necessary because of independent social skill development (Procidano & Heller, 1983).

SELF REPORT OF READINESS OF REUNIFICATION (OR RELEASE OF THE CHILD FOR ADOPTION). Parental reports of readiness for reunification help clarify the parent's own appraisal of skills and limitations in parenting, the degree to which the parent has met intervention goals, the degree to which the parent has addressed the original problem of maltreatment, and the realistic nature of the parent's appraisal of readiness to regain custody of the child (Bandura et al., 1977; Hoffman, 1983; Smith & O'Leary, 1995). Parents who have difficulty identifying personal strengths and weaknesses at this phase of the assessment probably have had equal difficulty doing so in the context of treatment and other interventions (Azar et al., 1998). The parent's report of treatment progress relevant to reduction of risk of child maltreatment can be compared to collateral reports and records of treatment progress.

Psychological Assessment

When assessment measures are administered by trained professionals with knowledge of the strengths and limitations of data, psychological assessment has the potential to yield useful and relevant data. If measures are used out of context, over-interpreted, or otherwise misinterpreted, the data can be a serious drawback to the utility of forensic assessment because of misleading and unfounded conclusions (Jacobsen et al., 1997). The methodological utility of any assessment measure or procedure is based upon the psychometric attributes of the technique, namely its reliability and validity (Anastasi, 1982; Matarazzo, 1990). Although not an exhaustive list, types of reliability and validity include: inter-rater reliability, test-retest reliability, content validity, construct validity, criterion validity and predictive validity. Inter-rater reliability reflects agreement among independent raters or evaluators. Test-retest reliability is an indicator of the stability of a measure over time. Content validity is an indicator of the extent to which test items are drawn from relevant domains. Construct validity is an indicator of the extent to which test items are drawn from relevant concepts or correlates of a particular behavior. Criterion validity is the correlation of the assessment results with other measures of the same or related factors. Predictive validity is an indicator of how well the measure predicts or forecasts subsequent behaviors or event.

When choosing psychological assessment measures, it is best to begin with theoretically or logically derived hypotheses concerning behavioral features or possible causal or explanatory variables that are relevant to the referral question. The evaluator should carefully consider the degree to which the measure demonstrably corresponds to the behavior or set of behaviors of interest (Brodzinsky, 1993; Dalgleish & Drew, 1989). It is unproductive to use traditional measures indiscriminately (Brodzinsky, 1993). However, traditional measures can be quite useful if they are selected carefully based on research or theory supporting a relationship between the indices and specific behaviors of concern in a parent's history or current functioning. To be relevant to parenting, indices usually need to be specific to a particular behavior or set of behaviors of concern. Nonetheless, sometimes the use of global indices, such as intelligence quotient, diagnostic status, or personality functioning might be used as explanatory data for parenting problems, maltreatment risk, or suitability of interventions. In order to serve as explanatory factors, those data would need to be linked to the behavior(s) of concern. For example, if two measures yield data that support a diagnosis of mental illness, the mental illness alone, although possibly relevant, would not be a sufficient explanation for compromises to parenting.

Many measure revisions include an option for computer-aided scoring and test interpretation. Research thus far has shown that computer-generated interpretations should be viewed as a valuable adjunct to, but not a substitute for, clinical judgment (Grove, Zald, Lebow, Snitz, & Nelson, 2000; Snyder, 2000). Readers easily recognize when a report contains computer-generated information because of abrupt changes in prose, structure, and use of technical or jargon terms. Although they might value actuarial data, many readers place little stock in the prose of computer-generated interpretations compared to integrated interpretations by clinicians (Hanson, Claiborn, & Kerr, 2001). Because readers benefit from examples, actuarial data is best illustrated with both summary scores and descriptive examples of the meaning of the data (Grisso, 1986).

INDICES OF PSYCHOLOGICAL FUNCTIONING. Psychological assessment data are useful in evaluating the relationship between current and premorbid functioning, specific potential that could contribute to the development of adequate parenting competence, specific deficits that might impair adequate parenting competence, global functioning problems that might be relevant to deficiencies in parenting, reasons why a particular parenting intervention is ineffective or inappropriate for a parent, intervention strategies that might be suitable for a particular parent, problems and deficits that might explain intractability, skills and compensatory strategies, and the individual bases (and therefore stability or lack of expected stability) for parenting skills and deficiencies. Cognitive and intellectual assessment measures provide useful information relevant to the parent's overall abilities, differential strengths and weaknesses, capacity to communicate, and level of word knowledge. Nonverbal cognitive and intellectual assessment measures provide useful information relevant to the parent's nonverbal abilities and maturity, capacity for alternative modes of expression and understanding, and differential strengths and weaknesses in nonverbal communication. Achievement and basic skills assessment measures provide information about the possible reasons a parent might struggle with a particular intervention. Neuropsychological assessment measures provide data concerning a parent's abstraction abilities and capacity for attention, concentration, and self-report narratives. They aid in differential diagnosis between brain injury or impairment and factors attributable to cognitive or personality functioning. Personality or psychopathology assessment measures provide data about personality functioning, psychopathology, dissimulation, malingering, and clarification of the correlation between assessment data and parental self-report data of functioning and social relationships. Adaptive behavior scales provide data about the general skills and functioning of parents in communication, social, and daily skill domains. Assessment measures supplement other assessment data, but they should not be interpreted to "prove" or "disprove" allegations of child maltreatment. Data should be integrated with objective information contained in the parent's history (Brodzinsky, 1993; Matarazzo, 1990; Tallent, 1993).

In making a determination of the appropriateness of using measures of overall functioning, it is important to remember that not all parents with cognitive limitations or mental health problems have parenting deficits or engage in child maltreatment. Similarly, not all parents who engage in child maltreatment have cognitive limitations or mental health problems. If functioning is impaired in some fashion, it is only relevant if there is a demonstrable link between the impairment and child maltreatment (Grisso, 1986; Jacobsen et al., 1997).

Limited intellectual functioning of a parent, as assessed by intelligence quotient and scales of adaptive behavior, is insufficient by itself to warrant termination of parental rights (Grisso, 1986), but the indices serve as a framework for understanding specific functioning limitations. If there is concern that limited cognitive functioning is related to parenting deficits, an assessment of IQ and adaptive behavior would be relevant in some cases. An example of an index of adaptive behavior is the Vineland Adaptive Behavior Scale (Sparrow, Balla, & Cichetti, 1984). The Vineland or another measure of adaptive behavior, in combination with an IQ assessment, might be essential in a case with no prior documentation of mental retardation, especially if there are strong indicators that the mental retardation probably was linked to past acts of child maltreatment. For cases with strong documentation of the diagnosis, however, assessment might be indicated only if there is a need for clarification of specific strengths and weaknesses in current functioning. Assessment data might clarify whether a caregiver would benefit from a particular type of training, support services, supervision and/or substituted judgment (e.g., a limited-purpose guardian *ad litem*) for some spheres of functioning.

When global measures of functioning are indicated, they typically should be accompanied by an assessment of relevant parenting behaviors or functions that might be impaired due to cognitive limitations. Some compromised skills or behaviors might respond to interventions and others might not, depending upon the parent's capacity to develop compensatory strategies, and depending upon the specificity and relevance of interventions for the deficits. Although legal protections have increased for parents who are mentally retarded or "borderline" in their intellectual functioning, some parents are deemed by the court to be at risk of harming their children because of problems with judgment, reasoning, and information processing (Budd & Greenspan, 1984; Budd & Holdsworth, 1996). Analyses of judgment, reasoning, and information should not be based on IQ scores alone. It is shortsighted to extrapolate only from IQ subscale scores (Beebe, Pfiffner, & McBurnett, 2000).

Although neuropsychological deficits are an uncommon causal variable explaining parenting deficiencies, neuropsychological assessment measures occasionally are used to determine whether impairments in memory functioning or other neurological processes might account for or partially account for parenting problems. Assessment measures are used to aid the process of differential diagnosis between neuropsychological deficits and other possible explanatory factors. Those distinctions sometimes are important because some forms of impairment respond better to treatment than others, depending upon etiological factors. As with any other type of formal assessment, the choice of neuropsychological assessment measures should be drawn from reasonably formed hypotheses about possible causal variables that might partially or wholly account for parenting deficiencies or patterns of maltreatment.

Similarly, because mental illness sometimes is causally related to parenting deficits, diagnostic and personality assessment measures sometimes are indicated. The need for assessment measures depends in part on the degree and credibility of prior documentation of mental health problems. Formal psychological assessment might not be necessary if the referral question focuses on diagnostic concerns and if diagnoses are credibly documented in records. The recency of records would be important for mental health problems of an episodic nature. Psychological assessment might be indicated if the nuances of mental health problems and the relationship to parenting deficits needed to be better understood. Data relevant to mental health functioning are useful in determining whether there is a causal link between deficits in mental health functioning and deficits in specific areas of parental functioning (Budd & Holdsworth, 1996; Grisso, 1986). Although epidemiological studies have shown only a modest relationship between mental health problems and parenting problems, studies specific to care and protection samples of parents have yielded more robust data relevant to actual or probable mental health problems in parents who severely maltreated children (Taylor et al., 1991). Although diagnosis alone is not an automatic indicator of potential for maltreatment, the most common diagnoses in mothers with histories of severe maltreatment were schizophrenia and severe depression. The most common diagnoses in fathers were character disorders and severe depression (Taylor et al., 1991). Although it is useful to determine diagnostic status, there are no characteristic patterns of symptoms associated with child maltreatment (Wolfe, 1985).

Evaluators sometimes use personality and symptom measures in care and protection evaluations. They should be included only after giving due concern to the examinee's reading level and cultural background. Measures that sometimes are used in care and protection evaluations (Brodzinsky, 1993; Budd & Holdsworth, 1996) include the MMPI-2 (Butcher, Dahlstrom, Graham, Tellegen, & Kaemmer, 1989), the MCMI-II and the MCMI-III (McCann & Dyer, 1996), the Personality Assessment Inventory (Morey, 1999; Morey & Glutting, 1994; Rogers, Sewell, Morey, & Ustad, 1996) (also available in a Spanish version), the Rorschach Inkblot Test (Rorschach, 1942), the Brief Psychiatric Rating Scale (Overall, 1988; Overall & Gorham, 1962), and the Symptom Checklist 90-Revised (Derogatis, 1983). Although published studies have described the use of the above measure in care and protection evaluations, this list does not preclude the use of other personality or diagnostic measures, as long as they are reliable and valid in light of the referral question. If the focus of the assessment is current symptom severity, checklists such as the Beck Depression Inventory (Beck, Ward, Mendelson, Mock, & Erbaugh, 1961), the Hamilton Depression Inventory (Reynolds & Kobak, 1995) or the Trauma Symptom Inventory (Briere, 1995) sometimes are useful.

Specific measures target indices of behaviors or personality constructs related to areas of functioning or risk (such as substance abuse risk), and others target realms of parenting behavior (see below). Substance use measures are used in care and protection evaluations (Budd & Holdsworth, 1996) to gather data relevant to use patterns, treatment response, and ongoing risk. Examples of indices of substance use are the Michigan Alcoholism Screening Test (Selzer, 1971) and the Substance Abuse Subtle Screening Inventory, third edition (Miller, Roberts, Brooks, & Lazowski, 1998; Lazowski, Miller, Boye, & Miller, 1998). Other instruments also are available. Because substance abuse is common in care and protection matters, familiarity with the strengths and limitations of such measures is important.

When there are questions about how to interpret behavior in light of cultural differences, The Stephenson Multigroup Acculturation Scale (Stephenson, 2000) might aid evaluators in examining the caregiver's level of ethnic society immersion relative to dominant society immersion. The scale was developed from the acculturation literature and published instruments revealing common domains of language knowledge, language use, language preference, interaction with ethnic and dominant societies, and food and media use preferences. The item pool was generated by an ethnically diverse research team of community professionals and consultants. Of the 95 items that remained in the scale after small-scale field tests, 47 measured immersion in dominant society and 48 measured ethnic society immersion. The factor structure, internal consistency, and construct validity were analyzed, with an evaluation of whether the factor structure was robust across samples and provided a good fit with a new sample. Factor analysis yielded two factors, as predicted, and the factor structure was consistent across samples. Convergent and discriminant validity were analyzed in relation to two other acculturation instruments, yielding expected correlations and relationships with generational status. It is the first acculturation scale developed for use across ethnic groups. There are some limitations in the clinical utility of the measure. Stephenson (2000) recommended replication with larger representative samples and adaptation of the measure for non-English speaking samples.

INDICES AND CORRELATES OF PARENTING BEHAVIOR. Care and protection evaluations focus on the assessment of minimal parenting competence rather than ideal parenting abilities (Budd & Holdsworth, 1996). Because definitions of minimal parenting competence are legally derived, they sometimes do not translate well into theories or techniques that lend themselves to scientific scrutiny. Because it is based on a set of legal concepts that vary from state to state, minimal parenting competence rarely is behaviorally based in a manner conducive to the development of specific measures of parenting abilities with content or construct validity. The relevance of existing measures to care and protection matters must be determined on a case-by-case basis, using theory to guide hypotheses and to choose appropriate measures in specific cases.

On a case-by-case basis, evaluators might find certain measures useful because of their face validity in measuring the domain of parenting abilities that are of interest in specific cases. Measures specific to parenting usually have a high level of face validity and some measures have demonstrated predictive validity in certain samples of parents. Whether using measures of parenting abilities or clinical interviews, most experts recommend that an assessment of parenting abilities should be based on a functional set of behaviors in a specific context. The evaluator should assess what the parent understands, believes, knows, does, and is capable of doing in relation to the specific parenting needs of a particular child, including any special needs the child might have (Green et al., 1980; Grisso, 1986).

Assessment measures specific to parenting behaviors include measures of couple adjustment, parenting stress, perceived social support, parenting knowledge and skills, parenting attitudes and beliefs, parental expectations of children and parents, knowledge of child development trajectories and principals, self report of the parental-child relationships, observation rating scales, and self-report measures of personality or behavioral indices in the context of parenting (Reis, 1989). Specific measures with obvious content usually suffer from reporting bias (especially social desirability responding), limitations in general and supplementary normative data, and limitations in supporting research relevant to cultural diversity (Milner, 1991). Although there are an abundance of self-report measures of parental attitudes and beliefs, many of them either have poor reliability and validity, or an insufficient research base to determine their reliability and validity (Grusec & Walters, 1991; Holden & Edwards, 1989), especially in care and protection samples. In analyzing the reliability and validity of a scale, including its relevance to the referral question, evaluators should consider the conceptual basis for the scale, the degree of attention to operational definitions of the constructs measured by the scale or subscales, its psychometric development and properties (standardization, reliability, and norms), construct validation, predictive or classificatory utility, and the potential of the scale or subscale scores to provide data that reflects parent-child congruency (Grisso, 1986).

Measures of infant-child attachment sometimes are relevant to care and protection evaluation referral questions. They should be interpreted with caution because most of them were developed for research purposes rather than clinical assessment purposes. The Adult Attachment Interview (Main & Goldwyn, 1994) is a semi-structured interview that probes for relationship descriptions, descriptions of current relationships with parents, and attachment-related early childhood memories. The coding system yields three adult attachment classifications: autonomous or secure, dismissing, and preoccupied. Results have been replicated and are supported by meta-analytic results. Meta-analysis suggests it predicts quality of infant-parent attachment and parental responsiveness to the infant's attachment signals (van IJzendoorn, 1995). Classifications remain stable over time (George et al., 1985; Main & Goldwyn, 1994).

Related to the concept of attachment assessment is the assessment of object relations. Measuring the impact of childhood experiences on adult functioning from a different theoretical vantage point than the Adult Attachment Inventory, the Bell Object Relations-Reality Testing Inventory

(Bell, Billington, & Becker, 1986) is a 90-item true-false self-report questionnaire forming two scales: reality testing and object relations (with oblique factor analysis revealing four dimensions: alienation, insecure attachment, egocentricity and social incompetence). It was designed to assess the individual's capacity to develop and maintain satisfying relationships. Split-half reliability is .78 to .90. It has been shown to be relatively free of response bias due to age, gender, or social desirability. The readability of the measure has not been reported.

Theories of socioemotional development emphasize the intensely emotional experience of parenting (Thompson, 1993). Theorists believe that negative emotions reflect and contribute to parenting problems. In examining the relationship between emotions and parenting, researchers have found support for intense emotional features in parent-child relationships and interactions (Dix, 1991). Functional analysis has yielded an average of 3.5 to 15 conflict-laden interactions between parents and young children per hour (Dunn & Munn, 1985; Lee & Bates, 1985), with more frequent conflicted interactions seen in aggressive families (Patterson, 1982). Even parents with no identifiable serious parenting problems report fear of loss of control of their anger (Frude & Goss, 1979). Mothers of young children report high rates of depression (Patterson, 1980). Parental warmth is a consistent predictor of positive developmental outcomes for children. Parental hostility consistently predicts unfavorable outcomes (Grusec & Lytton, 1988).

Regardless of the level of initial dysfunction in the family, hostile emotions between adults or between adults and children are predictive of poor outcomes (Radke-Yarrow, Richters, & Wilson, 1988). Parents with high levels of stress or low levels of parenting support use harsh and erratic discipline (Dix, 1991; McLoyd, 1990). Stress is strongly correlated with negative emotion and social support is strongly correlated with positive emotion (Riley & Eckenrode, 1986; Barrera, 1988). Chronic and intense negative emotions are common in parents of families with identifiable family dysfunction (Susman, Trickett, Iannotti, Hollenbeck, & Zahn-Waxler, 1985; Trickett & Kuczynski, 1986). Nonetheless, some researchers have suggested that some negative emotional experiences, if they are not chronic or intense, might be adaptive for parenting (Johnson & McGillicuddy-Delisi, 1983; Zahn-Waxler, Radke-Yarrow, & King, 1979).

Intense emotions interact with cognitive appraisals of events, influencing the nature of parental engagement with a child. The specific positive or negative emotions that are activated are linked to parental appraisals or expectancies of problem or conflict outcomes. Parents' emotions depend upon the nature of their concerns, their appraisals of whether and why their concerns have been promoted or frustrated, and their appraisals of available options and resources for (or obstacles to) promoting their concerns. Once emotions are activated, they are transformed into an engagement process that orient and organize behavioral tendencies (Dix, 1991). The engagement process then leads to the regulation process. Within the regulation process, humans control emotions and expressions rather than simply responding reflexively. Individuals attempt to comprehend their feelings, they evaluate how others might react to the available options for emotional expression, and they initiate thoughts or actions to augment or inhibit their emotional expressions. Individuals develop skills to promote desirable emotions and to suppress or cope with undesirable emotions, especially those that might undermine their concerns (Dix, 1991; Hochschile, 1979).

Dix (1991) provides guidance for content areas relevant to clinical interviews and choices of parenting assessment measures. Based on an analysis of socioemotional research relevant to parenting behavior, Dix (1991) concluded that (a) parents' emotions are aroused or activated when parent-child interactions occur that are relevant to significant concerns; (b) the nature and intensity of emotions that parents experience depend upon compatibility of parental concerns and behaviors with child behaviors and concerns; (c) parental emotions are more positive if they coordinate interactions with their children so that mutually satisfactory behaviors and outcomes take place (when compatibility is not plausible, parents might choose cooperative or forceful strategies to elicit child compliance); (d) the nature and intensity of parental emotions depend upon the extent to which parents have the capacity to formulate and select concerns that their children are able and willing to promote and to elicit child behaviors that allow the promotion of parental concerns; and (e) which emotions are activated depends on parental appraisals of why behaviors that promote or violate concerns are occurring and the degree of parental control in meeting parental concerns. Over time, parents and children develop shared mental representations of events, stable representations of each others, and interdependent behavioral tendencies that determine the frequency and ease with which dyads attain compatibility and resolve incompatibility. Once aroused, the emotions that parents feel when children promote or violate parental concerns influence the engagement process. The impact on parental functioning depends upon how well parents understand and can control their emotions (Dix, 1991).

Although measures of the emotional features of parent-child interactions yield helpful self-report and observational data for specific points in time, the etiologies and persistence of chronic and intense negative emotional experiences are not well understood (Dix, 1991). Because of the subjectivity of emotional phenomena, it is difficult to objectively quantify emotional experiences, expressions, and the impact on parental functioning (Thompson, 1993). It is equally difficult to make predictions about the enduring nature of the impact of emotions because temperamental dimensions (such as activity level, adaptability and distractibility) show high variability. Although the dimensions of temperament are important, they are not linked to individual dispositions or behavioral tendencies in a highly robust manner (Thompson, 1990, 1993). Similarly, attachment theory does not robustly predict the impact of emotional phenomena. Although attachment researchers have demonstrated a broad association between parental sensitivity and secure attachment, less is known about features of early care that predict attachment security or alternative attachments. Influences that predict parental emotions or behaviors that promote secure attachment are not well understood. Much is known about parent-infant attachment, but less is known about attachment beyond infancy. Researchers have just begun to focus on conditions that promote continuity and change in attachment and on the emotional features of attachment that influence parenting behaviors (Thompson, 1993). Emotions, whether positive or negative, and whether chronic and intense or relatively transient and weak, are related to both adaptive and maladaptive functioning. Therefore, it is important to refrain from over-interpreting measures or indicators of the emotional features of parenting (Dix, 1991).

When the emotional features of parenting are relevant to the referral question, the evaluator might choose to administer measures of emotional functioning relevant to parenting behaviors. The Parenting Stress Index (Abidin, 1986; 1990; Loyd & Abidin, 1985) measures the degree of stress parents report in relation to specific spheres of parenting and parent-child interactions. It is available in a long and a short form. It was designed to assess parental reactions to child illness or disability, but it has been used in program evaluations studies of abusive parents. Internal consistency of the subscales and domains ranged from .7 to .95 (Abidin, 1986, 1990). Thus far, there have been no studies of its predictive validity for child maltreatment. There is a predictive relationship between level of parental stress and appropriateness of heath care mothers seek for their children (Abidin & Wilfong, 1989). The Parenting Stress Index is available in a Spanish version (Solis & Abidin, 1991) and it yields the same three factors seen in research with Anglo-American mothers, namely child characteristics, parent characteristic, and child-parent interaction. The Parental Stress Scale (Berry & Jones, 1995) is an 8-item brief rating scale with test-retest reliability of .81, normed on 385 mostly middle class parents recruited through school, day care programs and a university. Although factor analysis revealed a four-factor solution, the majority of variance loads on one factor: whether parenting is pleasant and rewarding. It correlates .75 with the Parenting Stress Index.

The Arizona Social Support Interview Schedule is a self-report scale of the number and types of individuals with whom the parent interacts in specified areas (obtaining material aid, sharing private feelings, enjoying leisure activities). It also measures the number of individuals with whom the parent is in conflict (Barrera, 1981). The Perceived Social Support Questionnaire, measures perceptions of support but not actual contacts (Procidano & Heller, 1983). The Interpersonal Network Questionnaire (Pearson, 1987) is a self-report scale of number, type, and perceived quality of interactions with support figures. The Perceived Adequacy of Resources Scale (Rowland, Dodder, & Nickols, 1985) is a self-report scale of stress related to limited resources.

The most extensively researched self-report instrument relevant to parents who engage in child maltreatment is the Child Abuse Potential Inventory (Milner, 1986, 1990). It is a 160-item, self-administered, forced-choice questionnaire, with a third-grade reading level. There is a Spanish version of the instrument (de Paul, Arruabarrena, & Milner, 1991; Milner, 1986). It assesses global personality and interaction characteristics related to parenting behaviors. It measures personal and interpersonal characteristics that are similar to those of parents known to physically abuse their children. It has validity indices for detecting fake good, fake bad, and random response patterns. Research has shown it is a useful screening measure for parents suspected of physical child abuse (Milner, 1986, 1994). Internal consistency ratings range from .74 to .98. Test-retest reliability does not vary with age, gender, level of education, or race (Milner, 1986). It has predictive validity across a span of about six months, but it unfortunately has a high false positive rate (Milner, Robertson, & Rogers, 1990). It has strong construct validity (Haskett, Scott, & Fann, 1995).

The Parent Opinion Questionnaire (Azar et al., 1984) is a rating scale that assesses the extent to which a parent holds unrealistic expectations of a child's developmental capacities. There are significant differences in Parent Opinion Questionnaire scores in samples of abusive and non-abusive parents (Azar et al., 1984; Azar & Rohrbeck, 1986). The Parenting Alliance Inventory is a 20-item self-report scale that assesses the degree to which parents believe that they have a sound cooperative relationship with the child's other parent. It has high internal consistency and it correlates significantly with established measures of marital satisfaction, parenting stress, and parenting style. It also correlates with measures of children's positive adjustment and social competence (Abidin, 1992; Abidin & Brunner, 1995). The Parenting Alliance Measure is a 20-item self-report scale that assesses the strength of the perceived alliance between the parents. It was normed on a somewhat larger sample than the PAI (1,224 parents, compared to 512 parents in the PAI sample). Multigroup confirmatory factor analysis showed that it measures the same constructs for mothers and fathers. Factor analysis yielded a two-factor model. The user can convert normative raw scores to percentiles and standardized t scores (Konold & Abidin, 2001). The Dyadic Adjustment Scale also assesses self-reported conflict between couples (Spanier, 1989).

The Block Child Rearing Practice Report (Block, 1965, 1986) is a 91-item scale scored in a seven-stage Q-sort. It also has been adapted for use as a 6-point Likert scale for faster administration time. Test-retest reliability co-efficients are inconsistent, rating from .38 to .85. Factor analysis yielded four factors: restrictiveness, nurturance, authoritarian parenting and authoritative parenting. The Alabama Parenting Questionnaire (Shelton, Frick, & Wootton, 1996) is a 42-item self-rating scale with test-retest reliability of .69 to .89, based on a sample of 124 clinic-referred parents compared to community volunteer families similar in age, gender and socioeconomic status (but not matched). Subscales were rationally derived: involvement, positive parenting, poor monitoring and supervision, inconsistent discipline, corporal punishment, and other discipline (the sample size was too small to conduct factor analysis).

The Parent-Child Relationship Inventory (Gerard, 1994) assesses parental attitudes toward parenting and children. It is a 78-item, self report questionnaire, with a fourth grade reading level. It has seven content scales and two validity indices (social desirability and inconsistency). The normative sample consisted of 1,139 parents recruited from schools and day-care centers. Separate norms were developed for male and female caregivers. Test-retest reliability was moderate to strong after one week (ranging from .68 to .93), but did not remain as high after five months (.44 to .79). There were some generalization weaknesses in the normative sample because of race and age differences in results The Parenting Inventory: Young Children (Fox, 1992; Fox & Bentley, 1992) is a rating scale that measures the developmental expectations and behavior of parents with children between the ages of one and four. It was normed on a representative urban sample of 1,056 mothers and found to have substantial item-construct correlations or content validity. It is useful as an empirically derived, descriptive classification system of specific parental behaviors and developmental expectations. It has concurrent validity with the Developmental Questionnaire and parental scores are unrelated to measures of social desirability (Peters & Fox, 1993). Some measures have no normative data relevant to samples of maltreating parents (or possible maltreating parents), but they nonetheless yield data relevant to parental perceptions, expectations, and tolerance for problematic child behavior. Examples include the Child Behavior Checklist (Achenbach, 1991) and the Eyberg Child Behavior Inventory (Eyberg & Ross, 1978), both of which include parent rating form versions.

Because of the relationship between the use of physical discipline and risk for physical child abuse, measures of parental attitudes about discipline sometimes are used. The Parenting Scale (Arnold, O'Leary, Wolff, & Acker, 1993) is a 30-item self-report inventory measuring poor discipline choices in parents of young children. It is applicable to parents hypothesized to be harsh and over-reactive, lax, and garrulous in parenting. Mothers in a clinic sample obtained significantly higher scores than mothers in a non-clinical sample, and the assessment showed good test-retest reliability. Scores on the Parenting Stress Index were correlated with observational measures of poor discipline and child misbehavior (Arnold et al., 1993). In an assessment of the relationship between Parenting Scale scores and self-report data in 40 mothers identified as either harsh and over-reactive or lax and permission, greater statistical sensitivity was found in the identification of harsh and over-reacting mothers compared to the other group (Smith & O-Leary, 1995). The Psychological Maltreatment Rating Scale (Brassard, Hart, & Hardy, 1993) was developed to assess mothers at risk of psychological maltreatment. It has been described as "moderately reliable and valid" in its discrimination between maltreating and comparison parents, and in predicting child protective service involvement, maternal use of personal resources, and maternal use of social support. It contains one factor of emotional abuse (hostile behavior/psychological neglect) and two factors of positive parenting.

Observation Methods and Home Visits

Conducting parent-child observation sessions in care and protection evaluations sometimes yields fruitful data relevant to the parent-child relationship. Observed sessions are a useful aspect of multimodal assessment; however, parent-child observation sessions are heavily influenced by the effects of social desirability responding. Most parents are on their best behavior during observed sessions. For very young children, conjoint sessions can be illustrative when children cannot otherwise express their feelings or thoughts about the caregiver. Observed sessions yield less incremental data for older children who have the linguistic capabilities to describe their view of the relationship, but they are useful when there is obvious conflict between the child and the caregiver. In the latter instance, observed sessions help illustrate how much of the conflict is initiated by the parent and how much it might be a function of adolescent developmental issues with autonomy and independence (Stahl, 1994). Observed sessions can be significantly useful in rare instances in which the parent cannot emit appropriate conduct even during an observed session. When conducting observed parent-child sessions, the evaluator has a choice of using unstructured methods, semi-structured methods (Whitten, 1994), or structured methods with observational rating scales.

Observational rating scales have been developed for research purposes. They usually require extensive training for reliable use. When they are used in a non-standardized manner for clinical purposes, the likelihood of misinterpretations increase (Budd & Holdsworth, 1996; Wolfe, 1988). It is difficult to control for reactivity effects when administering observational methods of assessment (Haynes & Horn, 1982). Examples of rating scales based on observations of parent-child interactions include the Dyadic Parent-Child Interaction Coding System II (Eyeberg, Bessmer, Newcomb, Edward, & Robinson, 1994), the Home Observation for the Measurement of the Environment (Caldwell & Bradley, 1984), the Nursing Child Assessment Satellite Training measure (Barnard et al., 1989), the Parent-Caregiver Involvement Scale (Farran, Kasari, Comfort, & Jay, 1986), and the Strange Situation (Ainsworth et al., 1978).

The Dyadic Parent-Child Interaction Coding System has objective scoring criteria. Extensive training is required for reliable use. Neglectful mothers are more critical and provide less positive attention to their children than comparison mothers in laboratory interactions, as rated on the Dyadic Parent-Child Interaction Coding System (Aragona & Eyberg, 1981). The Home Behavior Q-set (Waters & Deane, 1985) is a 90-item Q-sort completed by the evaluator during a home observation. It examines a broad set of attachment behaviors over a relatively long time frame, emphasizing proximity-seeking and exploring behaviors. The Home Observation for the Measurement of the Environment scale, a similar measure, yielded significant group differences between adolescent mothers and older mothers (Coll, Hoffman, & Oh, 1987). The Nursing Child Assessment Satellite Training has objective scoring criteria. Extensive training is required for reliable use. Adolescent and "at risk" mothers scored lower than mothers with healthy infants on the measure (Bernard et al., 1989).

The Parent-Caregiver Involvement Scale is a 9-point rating scale of the degree of maternal sensitivity observed over extended periods of unstructured interaction. In the development of the scale, there was an explicit attempt to separately quantify frequency of responding and quality of responding (Farin, Kasari, Comfort, & Jay, 1986). It includes components of maternal sensitivity identified by early attachment researchers, such as alertness to infant signals, accuracy or appropriateness of interpretation and response, promptness of response, flexibility of attention and behavior, appropriateness of level of control, negotiation of conflict, and flexibility of attention and behavior (Ainsworth et al., 1978). The Strange Situation (Ainsworth et al., 1978) is a structured observational session, with raters coding observations of the infant or child's reaction to separation from the parent, interaction with a stranger, and reunion with the parent. Objective scoring criteria are provided. It has high inter-rater reliability and modest to high test-retest reliability. Aggregate studies have demonstrated that maltreated children are more likely to be classified as insecurely attached to their parents compared to matched controls (Youngblade & Belsky, 1990). Other observational systems have been designed for use in specific situations. For example, the Bethlem Mother-Infant Interaction Scale is a system with good inter-rater reliability, used to aid the assessment of the impact of post-partum depression on maternal functioning. In one sample of patients, it showed good predictive validity in determining which mothers were likely to be separated from their infants due to compromised parenting secondary to mental health problems (Hipwell & Kumar, 1996).

Indices for Risk of Harm

Assessment measures that are used as supplements to clinical interview methods of violence risk assessment include the Hare Psychopathy Checklist-Revised (Hare, 1991; 1998), the Hare Psychopathy Checklist: Screening Version (Hart, Cox, & Hare, 1994), the Historical, Clinical and Risk Management-20 or HCR-20 (Webster et al., 1997), and the Violence Risk Appraisal Guide (Harris, Rice, & Quinsey, 1993; Quinsey, Harris, Rice, & Cormier, 1999; Rice & Harris, 1995, 1997). Measures used as supplements to sex offender risk assessment interviews include the Abel and Becker Cognition Scale for intellectually disabled sex offenders (Abel, Becker, & Cunningham-Rathner, 1984; Kolton, Boer, & Boer, 2001), the Minnesota Sex Offender Screening Tool-Revised (Epperson et al., 1998), the Rapid Risk Assessment for Sex Offense Recidivism (Hanson, 1997, 1998), the Sex Offender Risk Appraisal Guide (Quinsey, Rice, & Harris, 1995), the Sexual Violence Risk-20 (Boer, Hart, Kropp, & Webster, 1997), the Static-99 (Hanson & Thornton, 1999, 2000), and the Structured Anchored Clinical Judgment-Minimum scale (Grubin, 1998). Cautious interpretation should be used when these measures are administered in care and protection assessment. Although they are relevant to risk of physical violence and sexual abuse, they were normed on populations of criminal defendants and forensic psychiatric patients. Most of the measures were normed only on males. Confidence intervals typically are not known, there is a potential for overprediction, estimates are based on aggregate data, and the norms usually are specific to a given population at a specific time (e.g., at time of discharge from an inpatient psychiatric or correctional facility). Some specific supplementary norms for clinical samples of individuals are available for some of the scales, but there are no published norms specific to individuals involved in care and protection actions for any of the psychopathy or sex offender scales described above. Nonetheless, with appropriate caveats, their use is clinically acceptable and probably would meet admissibility standards because of the hypothesized constancy of the main features of risk matrices across groups of offenders in the general categories of physical violence and sexual violence (Groth et al., 1982; Hanson, 1998; Haskett et al., 1995; Slovic et al., 2000).

Research on the HCR-20 and the Psychopathy Checklist-Revised have shown good reliability and predictive validity (for recidivism) in forensic psychiatric settings (Dernevik, 2000; Dolan & Doyle, 2000) in North American, British, and Swedish samples (Hare, Clark, Grann, & Thornton, 2000). Risk factors are similar for men and women with mental disorders, but the nature of violence is somewhat different between the genders (Strand & Belfrage, 2001). A comparative study illustrated that the Psychopathy Checklist-Revised has somewhat better predictive validity than the HCR-20 (Dolan & Doyle, 2000), and least in one sample of mentally disordered offenders. In an analysis of the predictive validity of the HCR-20 and the Violence Risk Appraisal Guide, data with 358 personality disordered offenders and 202 violent offenders diagnosed with schizophrenia indicated better predictive validity for both scales in personality disordered sample relative to the mentally ill sample (Grann, Belfrage, & Tengstreom, 2000). The Violence Risk Appraisal Guide was developed on a sample of 618 adult male patients at a maximum security forensic hospital. Scores are divided into nine categories, each with a corresponding estimate of violent recidivism. It has a 75 percent hit rate in accurately identifying violent recidivism. There is an abundance of research on the above measures. Interested readers may wish to consult further resources (Abel et al., 1984; Hare, 1998; Hart et al., 1994; Kolton et al., 2001; Quinsey et al., 1999; Webster et al., 1997).

Malingering, Embellishments, Dissimulation and Underreporting

In care and protection evaluations of caregivers, there usually is greater concern about dissimulation and underreporting compared to concern about malingering and embellishment. In rare cases, there is concern about an hysterical or fabricated trauma history in the caregiver (Pfefferbaum, Allen, Lindsey, & Whittlesey, 1999). Dissimulation and underreporting are much more common. Because of the high stakes in care and protection evaluations, it is not surprising that caregivers would attempt to present themselves in a socially desirable manner (Budd & Holdsworth, 1996). A few standardized assessment measures (Minnesota Multiphasic Personality Inventory, 2e; Dissimulation Scale-Revised subscale of the MMPI-2, Child Abuse Potential Inventory, Parenting Stress Index) contain validity indices for "fake good" and "fake bad" presentations (Abidin, 1986; Butcher et al., 1989; Milner, 1986). These validity indices provide useful information about the individual's approach to the assessment, alerting the evaluator to possible distortions in responses to assessment items.

Most validity indices developed for forensic instruments have applicability to malingering in incarcerated and inpatient samples of defendants (Lanyon, 2001a). Measures to detect malingering produce stronger effect sizes (fewer false positive and false negative results) than measures designed to detect social desirability responding (Viswesvaran & Ones, 1999). Many social desirability measures have greater applicability to samples of job applicants than other population samples (Ellingson, Sackett, & Hough, 1999). However, supporting theory for the use of social desirability responding measures is based on broad constructs of personality functioning, with applicability to many population samples (Merydith & Wallbrown, 1991). Some studies have been conducted on populations that bear similarity to care and protection samples. Preliminary studies suggest that victims of aggression show a lesser tendency to give socially desirable responses (to minimize reports of aggression) than perpetrators of aggression in inter-partner relationships (Riggs, Murphy, & O'Leary).

No research studies have linked the social desirability distortions to specific parenting behaviors that might be of concern (Budd & Holdsworth, 1996). Even when there are many assessment data indicators of dissimulation or social desirability responding, the motivation for responding as such might be due to fairly innocuous factors such as impression management, it might be due to self-deception or repression, or it might be related to more deceptive practices of attempts to conceal psychopathology (Becker & Cherny, 1992). Interpretation of validity indices should be appropriately limited to their actual meaning. The manuals for administration for each of the above measures contain information about the uses and limitations of validity indices (Abidin, 1986; Butcher et al., 1989; Milner, 1986).

MULTIMODAL ASSESSMENT: COLLATERAL INTERVIEWS AND RECORDS

Records and Collateral Reports

Records and collateral reports are a useful adjunct to interview data and an invaluable method for corroborating parent and child reports of information relevant to the referral question (Oberlander, 1995a, 1995b; Ogloff, 1999). Records frequently contain rich data, but caution should be used in gleaning information from records because they are subject to error, incompleteness and bias (Budd & Holdsworth, 1996). Critical data in records that might be persuasive in forming opinions should be corroborated or checked for accuracy (Grisso, 1986). Information should be gathered from multiple sources, including documentation and collateral interviews.

CHILD PROTECTIVE SERVICE RECORDS. Child protective service records should be reviewed with several goals in mind. First, the original allegations of child maltreatment usually are documented, along with investigation records and summaries, and an indication of why the allegations were supported. Records of allegations and investigations are useful because they help illustrate whether a case has retained focus on the original maltreatment, they are a good indicator of the degree to which the caregiver's report of maltreatment comports with or deviates from documentation of maltreatment, and they illustrate the frequency with which there have been supported episodes of child maltreatment. If the records are descriptive and reliable, they can be used to gauge caregiver progress in acknowledging the frequency and severity of maltreatment, a necessary step toward seeking meaningful intervention (Borum, 1996; Hanson & Harris, 2000).

Second, child protective service records usually contain a service plan or intervention plan for the caregivers and the children (Oberlander, 1998). If only one caregiver is accused of maltreatment, a second caregiver might be included because of concern about tolerance of maltreatment or pathological passivity toward the maltreating caregiver. Children are included in service plans, with interventions designed to help the child recover from the effects of maltreatment and remain safe from any further maltreatment. The service plan is a useful starting point to evaluate certain referral questions. For example, if the referral question involves an assessment of the caregiver's amenability to intervention, the caregiver's progress toward learning methods for refraining from maltreatment, or the child's recovery from trauma, the service plan can be used for several purposes. A caregiver with little recollection of the service plan is unlikely to have taken the plan seriously. An evaluation of a caregiver might clarify whether the service plan includes services that are relevant to the caregiver's level of cognitive functioning or deficits in parenting abilities. It also might clarify whether potentially effective interventions have been neglected in the service plan, or whether superfluous interventions are included. Contact with service providers might help the evaluator determine whether interventions such as parenting training are relevant to the parenting deficits that led to the maltreatment. For example, a parenting class that teaches infant care is not appropriate for a parent who was neglectful of the supervision needs of an eight-year-old child. Similarly, a parent who committed a sexual offense against a child might show little improvement in the behavior of concern if sex offender treatment is not a component of the service plan.

Third, child protective service records sometimes contain important documentation of parental self reports of child maltreatment, visitation plans (and changes over time in visitation plans), parental adherence to visitation schedules, observations of parental visitation of children, and observations of children's reactions to visitation commencement or termination. Records sometimes contain information relevant to the parent-child relationship, the parent's participation in and response to interventions, and any past or pending criminal actions against the parent that might be relevant to features of or risk of child maltreatment (Oberlander, 1998).

OTHER RECORDS.   Other records that potentially are useful include records of participation in or response to rehabilitation efforts, psychiatric treatment records, psychological evaluation records, substance abuse rehabilitation records, educational and vocational records, medical records, visitation center records, and police investigation reports relevant to child maltreatment or substance abuse-related offenses (Grisso, 1986). Indirect indices of caregiver response to intervention include documentation that the parent is attending and engaging in recommended interventions (Budd & Holdsworth, 1996). Nonattendance or poor participation should not be interpreted at face value. The caregiver's explanation for failure to attend or effectively use recommended interventions should be examined (Azar, 1992). Sometimes the court will allow the evaluator to have access to prior care and protection evaluations. Records should be examined for their relevance to the referral question.

COLLATERAL REPORTS.   After obtaining appropriate releases of information to collect collateral information, the evaluator should determine the scope of questions appropriate to each collateral contact. Possible sources of information include teachers, religious instructors, child care workers, foster parents or residential placement staff members, grandparents or other relatives, child maltreatment investigators for the state, physicians (including internists, psychiatrists and pediatricians), mental health service providers, substance abuse rehabilitation providers, and caregiver-child visitation supervisors (Enfield, 1987; Kuehnle, 1996). In some circumstances, collecting information concerning substance abuse rehabilitation for adults or psychotherapy of children will require a special release because of statutorily defined higher levels of privilege for that information.

Prior to collecting information from collateral sources, each source should be warned that the conversation is not confidential. They should be given a full disclosure concerning the possibility that their information will appear in the forensic evaluation report. Depending upon whether the release of information form provides for a one-way release or a two-way exchange of information, care should be used in explaining the reason for the conversation. Even when releases provide for a two-way exchange of information, only information sufficient to give the collateral source a context for the conversation should be provided. Some collateral sources, especially nonprofessionals, are unaware of confidentiality issues and boundary concerns. They unwittingly might ask intrusive questions about the parties to the case or the evaluation results. Evaluators should refrain from speaking freely about the details of the evaluation. A release for an exchange of information is not intended to compromise the evaluation process by placing the evaluator in a dual role of reporter of information to collateral sources, even when those sources are professionals. The evaluator should politely decline to answer such questions from collateral sources, explaining that the context limits a two-way free exchange of information.

Although most collateral sources are careful to provide accurate information, they often need encouragement to speak in descriptive terms rather than conclusive terms (Oberlander, 1998). A source might, for example, say that a child was "frequently anxious." The individual should be encouraged to describe what is meant by "frequently" and "anxious" by describing how many times per day or per week the anxiety was observed, and by describing behavioral manifestations of anxiety. Caution should be used when encouraging descriptive information, however. A general encouraging question such as, "What are your reasons for saying the child was frequently anxious?" is reasonable, but suggestive or leading questions are not. Finally, the evaluator should be alert to the possibility that not all collateral sources will provide forthright or valid information. They sometimes simply lack the sophistication required to provide relevant data in their responses to questions. Of greater concern are deliberate attempts to deceive the examiner. Collateral sources sometimes have a relationship with the caregiver or child that makes it difficult for them to refrain from intentionally or unintentionally minimizing or embellishing information (Stahl, 1994; Williams et al., 2000). In the worst of circumstances, they provide inaccurate or misleading information for which they have been remunerated in some fashion.

Sometimes an evaluator does not want to limit individuals from providing information if the parties to the evaluation strongly believe the information is important. The evaluator might suspect that the information has little utility, either because of possible unreliability of information, the superfluous nature of the information, or other possible compromises to the usefulness of the information. Stahl (1994) recommends avoiding talking to (or at least over-reliance on talking to) close family, friends and relatives because of their tendency to "choose sides" or to get caught up in the legal issues. To prevent the parties to the case from feeling as though their collateral sources have been disregarded, he invites them to ask their friends, family, and relatives to write letters to him, delineating relevant issues of concern. This approach limits the number of calls the evaluator must make, without excluding sources that might potentially provide relevant data. Letters yielding useful data can be followed up with telephone calls.

EVALUATING SUBSTITUTE CAREGIVERS IN ADOPTION READINESS REFERRALS

This section briefly reviews assessment content relevant to evaluating substitute caregivers in adoption readiness referrals. Adoption readiness referrals sometimes are made in the context of care and protection petitions. When evaluating parental fitness, the evaluator should focus on the adoptive parent's commitment to the child, relationship or potential for a healthy relationship with the child, acceptance of blended families and cultural differences (if relevant), willingness to honor the child's cultural heritage and identity, awareness of resources for blended families, knowledge and skills in meeting the child's special needs, knowledge and skill in facilitating the child's adaptation to termination of the biological parent's rights and the transition to a new family, willingness to adhere to the conditions of an open adoption arrangement if such an arrangement is ordered by the court, skill in crisis and conflict management, skill in parenting children with histories of maltreatment, and awareness and willingness to use helping sources should the adoptive parent face obstacles to promoting the child's adaptation or functioning (Brodzinsky & Schechter, 1990; Glidden, 1991).

The evaluator should be familiar with factors that promote adoptee adjustment, adoption outcome studies, children's subjective experiences of foster care and adoption, the dynamics of adopting children from residential placements, adoption and identity formation, adjustment in trans-racial adoptions, factors that are common in disrupted and failed adoptions, and post-adoption strategies for promoting positive adaptation. Evaluating potential adoptive parents in the context of care and protection petitions sometimes is complicated by "rescue" fantasies or dynamics in some adoptive parents and even in some evaluators (Heineman, 2001). Sometimes such dynamics are recognizable and easily dealt with through interventions or support services. Other times they carry the risk of resulting in a failed adoption, especially when the "rescue" fantasies hinder a careful assessment of the match between the adoptive resource and the child, or the degree of acknowledgment and acceptance that the adoption resource has for the child's special needs and behavior concerns (Frank, 1980; Glidden, 1991). Motivational influences for adopting should be explored, especially if there is concern that the need to adopt might be based in pathological rather than healthy factors. More comprehensive information relevant to evaluating substitute caregivers can be found in other resources (Ames & Chisholm, 2001; Brodzinsky & Schechter, 1990).

EVALUATING CHILDREN

The First Appointment

Three main goals in the first appointment with a child are to set the child at ease, to develop an understanding of the child's language abilities, and to provide a notification of the limits of confidentiality that is suitable to the child's comprehension. It is important to find a way to obtain relevant information from children without seeming like an interrogator. It is helpful to begin with innocuous questions, but the questions should not be so innocuous, off topic, or disjointed that they confuse the child's understanding of the purpose of the evaluation. It also is important to refrain from asking questions that heighten their anxiety over loyalty bonds with their parents. For example, pointedly asking a child about his or her reunification or termination preferences usually is inadvisable. At the same time, the evaluator must be alert to the possibility that some children hold a clear preference about whom they want to raise them. A balancing act is required so that the evaluator avoids direct questions, but is ready to listen if the child wishes to express those preferences (Stahl, 1994). If the child expresses a preference, it is useful to remind the child that adults will make the decision. A reminder helps allay any subsequent guilt or anxiety that a child might experience if he or she believes the stated preference carries significant weight in the decision-making process (Oberlander, 1995a).

Rapport is difficult to define, but it contains elements of trust, empathy, positive regard, understanding, harmony, and accord (Barker, 1990). In forensic evaluations, a neutral stance sometimes is preferable to warmth and supportiveness (Lepore & Sesco, 1994; Raskin & Yuille, 1989; Thompson et al., 1997), but it is nonetheless important to help children feel at ease (Goodman et al., 1990; Saywitz et al., 1992). With respect to the rapport-building process, the following suggestions have been made. Establish an office environment that is child-centered. Chairs should be the appropriate height for children. Colorful decor helps children feel at home. There should be enough child-centered objects in the office to make it appear interesting, but not so many that the child is distracted. Allow the child time to get accustomed to the evaluator and to the context. Be attentive to issues of personal space, boundaries, and bodily integrity. Try not to crowd or hover over the child. Be prepared with small incentives such as stickers for "trying hard to pay attention," but do not allow the child to confuse the reward with "providing particular answers." Allow the child to ask questions. Do not inadvertently set the stage for an expectation that the child is required to "disclose" maltreatment. For example, do not introduce yourself as someone who talks to children to whom "bad things" have happened. Do not remind the child that he or she previously told others certain information. Give the child permission to tell you something different and help the child understand it should be something real (Greenberg, 1990; Oberlander, 1995b). Although building rapport is an important step in any evaluation, appropriate care should be used in the choice of rapport-building strategies because of concerns about gathering trustworthy interview data.

Specific recommendations for use of language appropriate to the child's level of linguistic development were described in the previous chapter. Although the recommendations are fairly straightforward, their use is not. Speaking in the language of children is difficult because it involves learning a novel skill after having successfully mastered and highly practiced an old skill. "Unlearning" old habits must accompany learning of new habits. When stress increases, the tendency is to revert to old habits, as might be the case when managing the behavior of an active or traumatized child in an assessment session. Speech and language habits are highly ingrained by the time a person reaches adulthood. Therefore, the structure and content of questions appropriate for children should be practiced and mastered prior to engaging in clinical interviews of children, especially young children.

Specific standards have not been developed that require audio- or video-recording of interviews with children. There is a trend toward recommendations for standards of practice that would required the use of an electronic recording device in interviews in which children might give accounts of maltreatment (Lamb et al., 1994; Perry & Wrightsman, 1991; Yuille, Hunter, Joffe, & Zaparniuk, 1993). Because of controversy over the capacity of evaluators to record complete and central information in written form, it is good practice to record the interview in some form. Audio- or video-recording usually requires special permission that should be incorporated in the process for informed consent (Kuehnle, 1996). Informed consent should specify the circumstances under which the recording might be released to other individuals. For evaluators who have not used recording devices in the past, they should practice conducting mock interviews with recording devices prior to using them in live interviews. Evaluators should have available an alternative recording device in the event of device failure. In live interviews, the child should be made aware of the presence and use of recording devices. An explanation for their use should be given in language comprehensible to the child. In some circumstances, electronic recording devices might interfere with the rapport-building process. A contingency plan should be available for children who are intimidated by recording devices to the degree that it would compromise their willingness to provide information.

There are many benefits to electronic recording, the most important of which are increases in the completeness of information, preserving information that might be used as legal evidence of abuse, promoting proper interview techniques, recording nonverbal accompaniments to verbal statements (in videotapes), and precluding or at least minimizing repeated interviews (Kuehnle, 1996; Saywitz, 1994). Disadvantages include intrusiveness and possible compromises to children's willingness to divulge information, logistical complications of obtaining appropriate equipment and rooms conducive to proper use of the equipment, ensuring adequate technical quality of the recording, loss of data through equipment malfunctions, frivolous hyper-focus on the interviewer's technique at the expense of focus on the allegations of maltreatment, and release of the recording to inappropriate sources such as the media (Berliner, 1992). In the absence of electronic recording, detailed written documentation is the minimum practice standard (American Professional Society on the Abuse of Children, 1990). Much of the literature on use of electronic recording devices has focused on child interviews. Their use might also be appropriate for other interviews.

Multimodal Assessment: The Child

The Clinical Interview

HISTORICAL INFORMATION.   The degree to which children should be asked about historical data depends upon the child's age, level of linguistic development, and reporting capacity (Yuille et al., 1993). When children cannot credibly report historical information, parent interviews, foster parent interviews or other interviews are needed to gather developmental data. When children can report information, it sometimes is useful to compare children's reports of historical data to other reports (Poole & Lamb, 1998). Inconsistency of data across reporters sometimes is an indicator of malingering or dissimulation in one or more reporters. Sometimes the inconsistency occurs for more innocuous reasons. For example, older children sometimes recall relevant details that caregivers have forgotten or cannot recall with sufficient specificity. On the other hand, they sometimes reveal relevant historical information that a parent or another adult interviewee might have neglected purposefully. Even when children can report information, an interview with the caregiver usually is necessary to gather relevant developmental data that the child would not know, such as developmental milestones in infancy and early childhood (Saywitz, 1994). As with other interviews, the comprehensiveness with which historical data are obtained depends upon the nature of the referral question.

Even when a child appears to be a credible historian, data of significant relevance to the evaluation that she or he solely provides should be checked for accuracy when possible. Sometimes an evaluator must make a decision about whether to include information of central relevance that is uncorroborated. Its inclusion would depend upon the possible salience of the information for the factfinder and hearsay provisions. It is not good practice to reach conclusions based on uncorroborated data (Jacobsen et al., 1997; Wolfe, 1988). Appropriate caveats should be used in reports if the evaluator believes it is important to include historical data for which the child is the sole source (Saywitz & Camparo, 1998).

Depending on the referral question, relevant historical data in child interviews include developmental milestones, a description of family structure and relationships, educational history (academic and behavioral functioning), chore and job history (for adolescents), mental health history, medical history (including neurological data), substance use history (usually relevant only for preadolescents and adolescents), history of attention problems or conduct problems, and juvenile justice history if relevant (Oberlander, 1995a, 1995b; Sattler, 1998). Content areas, the degree of breadth and the degree of depth should be tailored to the referral question. When the extent of necessary content is unclear from the referral question (for example, in cases in which the etiology of a child's functioning problems is enigmatic), it is better to cover a broad base of historical data than to neglect information that might be relevant.

INTERVIEWING CHILDREN ABOUT RECOLLECTIONS OF MALTREATMENT. There is no foolproof method for determining a child's capacity to provide reliable and valid reports of maltreatment. It is important to try to minimize influences that might result in data that is not credible. It is equally important to remember that the highest standards do require the evaluator to determine a child's credibility. Specialty guidelines advise against conclusions about truth-telling capabilities in children (American Psychological Association Committee on Professional Practice and Standards, 1998). Estimates might be possible based on relevant indicators, but specific determinations of truthfulness or lack thereof is beyond the state of forensic assessment science and practice. Although it is not appropriate to make judgments about credibility or truthfulness in children, estimates of children's capacities to report trauma sometimes are requested. Estimates should be based on empirically sound data. For example, Heiman (1992) recommends examining children's accounts of maltreatment for the following features: development of a context, the provision of idiosyncratic words or data, inclusion of peripheral or unnecessary information, explicit details, details that exceed the child's developmental level, a progression of "grooming" for maltreatment (for example, seduction, isolation, or escalation of threats or aggression), other engagement processes, strategies to discourage the child from reporting the maltreatment (for example, secrecy, threats, coercion, pressure, bribes, or rewards), affective responses or details that are congruent with the reported maltreatment, consistency of salient details, varied and rich description rather than a rehearsed litany, provision of a narrative from a child's perspective, and details of attempts to resist or avoid the maltreatment.

There are no pathognomonic signs of maltreatment, nor is there evidence that a certain type of response to interview questions, interview tools, objective assessment techniques or projective assessment techniques establishes that a child has been maltreated. Neither maltreatment nor the identification of a perpetrator can be confirmed or disconfirmed solely by the presence or absence of psychological symptoms or patterns of behavior (Oberlander, 1995b). Similarly, there is no foolproof method for detecting deception in evaluations. It is useful alert to possible signs of false reports of maltreatment. For example, children or parents might misinterpret innocuous events. A hypervigilant parent might become convinced that another adult's innocuous behavior represents maltreatment. A delusional parent might develop paranoid ideation about maltreatment. A delusional child might develop a false idea that he or she was maltreated. Caught up in the emotional contagion of false allegations, a child might yearn to be the center of attention. A maltreated child might transpose the allegation from a true perpetrator to another individual. Fabrication might occur in children motivated by external or internal incentives. Inadvertent distortion of memory or indoctrination can result from suggestive or coercive interview techniques. (Nurcombe & Parlett, 1994). There is little research on minimizing outright deception in interviews, but there is much information about minimizing the effects of suggestibility. The most fundamental approach is to craft clear and non-suggestive questions.

INTERVIEW TOOLS.   Common interview tools in child maltreatment interviews include children's drawings and anatomically detailed dolls. Children's drawings originally were developed to assess intelligence and later were expanded to assess personality and psychopathology. Research provides little empirical support for the validity of drawings as freestanding indicators of any of these global purposes (Poole & Lamb, 1998; Miller, Veltkamp, & Johnson, 1987). Drawings have questionable reliability and validity if they are used to elicit disclosures. However, they are useful as a tool of clarification. They can clarify the details of the abuse, who was present, where the abuse occurred, what took place, what clothing was present, and exposure of sexually relevant body parts. If a child can draw an abuse scene, the drawing might allay doubts that the child merely has memorized a description suggested by an adult. The child's emotional response to drawing the alleged perpetrator or the abuse scene might be of significance. Drawings potentially can provide a permanent record of the child's report of maltreatment (Miller et al., 1987; Oberlander, 1995b; Smith & Dumont, 1995).

Anatomically detailed dolls have questionable reliability and validity if they are used to elicit disclosures. However, they are useful as a tool of clarification of verbalizations through demonstration. The dolls are not standardized assessment tools. They should not be confused with psychological assessment tests or measures. They are an unstandardized tool that may or may not contain directions or suggestions for a consistent approach to their administration. There are many brands and varieties of dolls. They vary in their anatomical correctness and level of detail. They vary in their instructions for use and typically have no coding criteria or rules. The procedures used with the dolls vary widely, including number of sessions, number of dolls, matching doll race with victim race, conducting a body-part survey, and presenting the dolls dressed or undressed. There are no methodologically strong studies that demonstrate differential responses of sexually abused and non-abused children to the dolls. The sexual play of an alleged victim might be in response to demand characteristics, that is, the sexual nature of the dolls, and not previous abuse. There is a high false positive rate among three-year-old children. Chronically abused children might reject the dolls increasing the likelihood of false negative conclusions (Koocher et al., 1995; Kuehnle, 1996; Oberlander, 1995b).

BEHAVIOR DISORDERS AND TRAUMA REACTIONS IN CHILDREN. Interview data should focus on symptoms and behaviors relevant to empirically based descriptions and diagnostic criteria for child behavior disorders and trauma reactions (Heiman, 1992). Many evaluators find it helpful to base questions on semi-structured and standardized diagnostic assessment instruments to the degree possible so that questions are drawn from research and diagnostic criteria for behavior disorders and trauma reactions. Because clinical interviews have a higher margin of error than research and diagnostic instruments, instruments should be used as a guide. An example includes the NIMH Diagnostic Interview Schedule for Children, Version IV (NIMH DISC-IV). Researchers have demonstrated its reliability for many diagnostic categories, and they have made suggestions for administration formats that are "user friendly" in clinical settings (Edelbrock, Crnic, & Bohnert, 1999; Friman et al., 2000; Johnson, Barrett, Dadds, Fox, & Shortt, 1999; Schaffer, Fisher, Lucas, Dulcan, & Schwab-Stone, 2000).

Some research and diagnostic instruments are inefficient in clinical practice because of their time-consuming nature (e.g., the Diagnostic Interview Schedule for Children takes up to three hours to administer) and because of possible child fatigue in responding to questions that might be useful in research but irrelevant for clinical purposes. Nonetheless, they provide examples of diagnostic interview questions and they contain relevant content domains (American Medical Association, 1985; Corwin, 1990; Friedrich, 1990). Use of a semi-structured and standardized approach should not preclude spontaneous reports from children or others. Idiographic descriptions of behaviors, symptoms, and experiences sometimes have diagnostic relevance and significance (Corwin, 1990; Friedrich, 1990).

Measuring the impact of child maltreatment frequently is more complicated than simply rendering a diagnosis. Referring attorneys sometimes prefer descriptive information about the impact of trauma so that they can provide behavioral descriptions to judges rather than distilled information such as diagnostic entities or symptom checklist outcomes. Children sometimes have idiosyncratic responses to child maltreatment that cannot be characterized by existing symptom clusters or diagnostic entities. Therefore, it sometimes is appropriate to provide descriptive data, to illustrate the full impact of child maltreatment (Page 1999).

CHILDREN WITH SPECIAL NEEDS.   The challenges of interviewing children with disabilities are similar to those of interviewing very young children (Milne & Bull, 1996; Poole & Lamb, 1998). Intelligence in part determines children's capacities to describe maltreatment (Fundudis, 1989). Few studies have focused attention on how cognitive impairment impedes children's reporting capacities (Westcott & Jones, 1999). The interviewer should expect difficulty with narratives, susceptibility to suggestion and social desirability responding (usually in the form of acquiescence) (Sigelman, Budd, Spanhel, & Shoenrock, 1981). Because of an expectation that adults will structure their interactions, children with mental and/or physical disabilities might be especially likely to succumb to implicit demands (Westcott & Jones, 1999).

BILINGUAL CHILDREN.   Special interview techniques sometimes are required for bilingual children. Interpreters should be used when indicated. The evaluator might need to refer the case to an evaluator who speaks the predominant language of the child and family. Although the decision to refer is relatively straightforward in individual cases and in regions where evaluators who speak the language of concern are available, the decision to refer is less straightforward when there are few or no evaluators who speak the language of concern. The decision also is less straightforward when there are many parties to the case, all with different degrees of bilingual capabilities. Consultation and interpreters might be a better choice in those instances. When interpreters are used in forensic evaluations, the court sometimes requires the use of court-certified interpreters. In regions where there is a dearth of interpreters in the language of concern, the evaluator might need to make a decision about whether to accept the referral or turn it down, using ethical principals and prevailing practice standards to guide the decision.

THE CHILD'S VIEW OF THE CAREGIVER, ADAPTATION TO PLACEMENT, AND SUBSTITUTE CAREGIVERS. Children rarely can respond in an abstract manner to questions about their perceptions of their relationship or visitation with the caregiver. Even when they have the capacity to respond in a meaningful way, their responses might be tainted by loyalty binds with the caregiver. Children might be susceptible to recency effects if the interview concerning their relationship and visitation with the caregiver falls on the heels of a parent-child visit (Dyer, 1999; Schutz, Dixon, Lindenberger, & Ruther, 1989). They should not be asked directly to compare their relationship with the caregiver to other relationships because of the potential for heightening loyalty conflicts, and because of children's limited capacities to make such comparisons (Schutz et al., 1989).

Children sometimes can provide relevant data about the caregiver-child relationships and visitation when asked indirect questions, such as who is in their family, what are their favorite family activities, what they do during visits, what they recall about important events such as birthdays or holidays, with whom they prefer to play favorite games or activities, to whom they talk about school or other aspects of their daily routine, what happens when they become ill, what they know about rules and discipline in the caregiver's home or during visitation, what makes them angry, what makes them sad, what makes them happy, and what makes them scared. Depending upon the age and linguistic capacities of the child, answers might be brief or they might contain rich detail (Schutz et al., 1989). Similar approaches should be used for asking the child about his or her adaptation to placement and relationships with substitute caregivers (Howes & Segal, 1993; Stovall & Dozier, 2000). The evaluator sometimes learns relevant information from naturally occurring events, such as a child's separation from a parent or reunion with a substitute caregiver after a conjoint observation with the parent (Dyer, 1999).

The evaluator should be prepared for a variety of responses from children, even in response to indirect questions about the relationship and visitation with the caregiver. Children sometimes are capable of expressing information that has high consistency with the way that adults view their relationships, expectations, and visitation quality (Bush & Goldman, 1982). However, they also are alert to threats to the stability of their placement and probing interview questions. They might react with distress or become uncommunicative. They might have internally conflicted views of their relationships and visitation because of ambivalence toward caregivers and substitute caregivers (Dyer, 1999; Crittendon, 1988). They are influenced by pleasant and unpleasant exchanges in recent visits, even though their overall view might contradict their view after such a visit (Dyer, 1999). Sometimes children might seem eager to reunify with the parent, but their eagerness simply is a function of indiscriminant attachment behavior (George & Solomon, 1996).

In rare cases in which children show the emotional capacity to discuss their custodial preferences, their responses should not be taken at face value. Children might not weigh the same data as adults in expressing a preference for who should be their custodian. For example, they might wish to return to their school and their friends even if such a return would compromise their safety (Stahl, 1994). Children might give indiscriminant responses because they prefer both possibilities, or because they are ambivalent about all of the caregivers in their history. They might express impossible preferences, such as wanting to live with a parent and a foster parent (Oberlander, 1995a). Symmetrical questions about parents and foster parents sometimes illustrate when a child is giving indiscriminant positive responses regardless of which relationship is the topic at hand (Dyer, 1999).

Psychological Assessment

INDICES OF PSYCHOLOGICAL FUNCTIONING. Global assessment measures for children are relevant when the referral question contains inquiries into the child's global abilities in order to understand strengths and weaknesses in a child's innate resources. For example, in order to understand a child's specific strengths or weaknesses in capacity to report previous trauma or maltreatment, it sometimes is useful to compare specific child statements and patterns of communication to global indices of functioning such as intellectual assessment data, expressive and receptive language assessment data, developmental assessment data, or memory assessment data. The choice of global assessment measures would depend upon the hypothesized relationship between clinically observed communication strengths and weaknesses and etiological factors that might explain the strengths and weaknesses. Global assessment measures are not necessary across cases. Their use depends upon the nature of issues to be understood. Global measures sometimes also are useful if there is a need for an explanation of a child's poor or failed response to a particular treatment approach. Behavior scales and checklists sometimes clarify the nature and severity of a child's current behavior and mental health problems. If prior data exists from other assessments, the data can be used to compare the child's current functioning to past baselines or periods of florid symptoms or problems.

The Eyberg Child Behavior Inventory (Eyberg & Ross, 1984) measures parental ratings of the extent and type of child behavior problems. It has good test-retest reliability for classifying child behavior problems, and norms were developed on a large sample. The Child Behavior Checklist (Achenbach, 1991) measures parental ratings of the extent and type of child behavior problems. Parental ratings can be compared to foster parent ratings, teacher ratings, or other raters. It has good test-retest reliability and factor-analytic support for classifying child behavior problems. The Behavior Assessment Scale for Children (Reynolds & Kamphaus, 1992) yields similar data, but it also contains subscales for domains of positive or adaptive behavior. The Devereux Scales of Mental Disorders (Naglieri, LeBuffe, & Pfeiffer, 1994) is a 110-item scale used to identify the presence and severity of emotional problems and psychopathology in children ages five to 18. If the focus of the assessment is current symptom severity, checklists such as the Child Depression Inventory (Kovacs, 1992), the Reynolds Child Depression Scale (Reynolds, 1987), and the Trauma Symptom Checklist for Children (Briere, 1996) sometimes are useful. The Child Sexual Behavior Inventory, designed for ratings of children aged two to 12, is completed by the mother or primary female caregiver. It was designed to measure the frequency of child sexual behaviors across the course of the past six months. Norms were based on a sample of 1114 children (Friedrich, 1992). The Checklist for Child Abuse Evaluation (Petty, 1990) is a checklist of symptoms and behaviors that are associated with the impact of child maltreatment. Some behavior scales and checklists provide data relevant to the child's reporting patterns (such as patterns of under-emphasizing or over-emphasizing symptoms and behaviors). As with adult evaluations, assessment data should be interpreted in the context of relevant historical data (Brodzinsky, 1993; Matarazzo, 1990; Tallent, 1993).

INDICES OF THE PARENT-CHILD RELATIONSHIP. When the referral question includes an assessment of infant temperament as a variable relevant to possible goodness of fit between a parent and a child, rating scales of infant temperament sometimes are useful. Most measures of infant temperament require ratings by parents. Parental ratings sometimes are questionable because of problems with self-report data and because some parents in the context of care and protection evaluations have had only limited recent contact with their children, making it difficult for them to provide accurate ratings based on contemporary views of the infant of concern. Examples of infant temperament rating scales include the Emotionality, Activity Sociability Questionnaire (Buss & Plomin, 1984), the Infant Behavior Questionnaire (Rothbart, 1981), the Infant Characteristics

Questionnaire (Bates, Freeland, & Lousbury, 1979), and the Infant Temperament Questionnaire-Revised (Carey & McDevitt, 1978).

The Manchester Child Attachment Story Task (MCAST) is a doll-
play vignette that assesses constructs relevant to infant and adult attachment research. It is designed to identify and classify the child's internal
representations of attachment relationships. It was validated on a non-
clinical population of 53 children aged 5.2 to 7.7 years, with good inter-
rater reliability and content validity. Patterns of attachment representations
showed stability over time (Green, Stanley, Smith, & Goodwyn, 2000). In
another non-clinical sample, ratings on the MCAST showed an association with "unresolved" status on concurrent maternal Adult Attachment
Interview scores and with independent teacher ratings of classroom behavior. Measures of child temperament were predictive of style of engagement during the interview, but not with the attachment ratings (Goldwyn,
Stanley, Smith, & Green, 2000). The Separation Anxiety Test (Kalgsbrun &
Bowlby, 1976) takes only 10 minutes to administer. The child is presented
with six pictures. The child responds with feelings and thoughts about what
the child in the picture might do next. There are rules for administration and
prompts. Coding categories scored by blind raters resulted in inter-rater
reliability of .84 to 1.00. The original classification scheme was based on
74 second-born children from middle-class families in Cambridge, United
Kingdom, recruited through play groups, newspapers, and health visits.
Classification was based on the child's adaptation to the mother.

The Children's Reports of Parental Behavior (Schaefer, 1965) assesses
children's perceptions of parental behaviors and attitudes. The constructs
upon which the instrument was based were derived from theories and
research in developmental psychology. Item construction was assisted by
expert ratings of item clarity, item relevance to the concept of concern,
and relevance to female and male caregivers. The instrument has been
revised several times (Margolies & Weintraub, 1977; Schludermann &
Schludermann, 1970), and multiple versions bear the same title. All four
versions contain self-administered item statements about the child's perceptions of parental behavior, feelings or attitudes. The child responds to
each item on a 3-point scale, reporting whether the item is "like," "somewhat like," or "not like" the parent of concern. It has been used in research studies with children ranging from age seven to young adulthood.
Reading assistance is necessary for young children. The reading level of
the measure has not been reported. Research on the factor structure of the
measure consistently has yielded three factors: "acceptance versus rejection," "psychological autonomy versus psychological control," and "firm
versus lax discipline." Results are interpreted to reflect parental behavior
and attitudes as reported or perceived by the child; however, the measure

does not include validity scales to assess possible under-reporting, hyper-responding, or other motivational biases in reporting (such as a child's desire for a continued relationship with the caregiver). Cautious interpretation is necessary because scores do not necessarily reflect actual parental attitudes or behaviors. Test-retest reliability showed no difference between female caregiver and male caregiver forms, and no differences at one week retesting compared to five week retesting. Test-retest correlations ranged from .66 to .92 for the factor scores. Internal consistency coefficients were in the range of .60 to .90. There are no data on the advantages of using one of the revised versions over other versions, nor have data been published that allows comparison of a child's scores to a normative sample. Its advantage over clinical interview methods is the standardized approach, reducing interview biases such as subtle cues from the interviewer (Grisso, 1986).

Suggestibility, Malingering, Embellishments, Dissimulation and Underreporting

Although a few validity indices have been adapted for use with adolescents, there are no specific validity indicators to detect deceptive, influenced or biased responding in preschool- or elementary-school aged children. Most evaluators rely upon clinical methods of minimizing misleading interview questions and remaining vigilant about patterns in children's deception. To briefly review, interview methods for minimizing the impact of influence include providing the child with specific instructions on how to convey a lack of comprehension of a question, asking the child to practice saying he or she does not understand the question (Saywitz et al., 1999), using an innocuous staged event to determine a child's capacity to convey a lack of question comprehension, and reviewing and demonstrating interview rules in a "practice" interview (Geiselman et al., 1993; Saywitz et al., 1992). It helps to warn children that some questions will be "tricky." It also helps to warn them not to rely upon "guesses" that might fit a stereotype (Koblinsky & Cruse, 1981; Warren et al., 1991). Using a warm, but non-leading interview style has been recommended (Carter et al., 1996). Procedures such as the cognitive interview or the narrative elaboration procedure might be useful for some children. They are advantageous because they provide a structured approach to minimizing the influence of suggestibility. When they are used, their strengths and limitations should be noted. The examiner should gain experience with standardized interview techniques before using them in care and protection evaluations. They should not be used with age groups for which there is no supporting research base (Camparo et al., 2001; Geiselman, 1999; Memon et al., 1993; Saywitz and Snyder, 1996).

MULTIMODAL ASSESSMENT: COLLATERAL INTERVIEWS AND RECORDS

Similar to the approach used with adults, the child's interview and assessment data should be supplemented with data from collateral contacts and records. Records of relevance include documentation of the child's self report of maltreatment (usually contained in child protective services investigation records, but sometimes also found in medical records, mental health records or police investigation records), records of the child's functioning and adaptation to placement, records of the child's relationship with caregivers and substitute caregivers, educational records, medical records, mental health records, and any other relevant records.

SUMMARY

1. Evaluation methodology, data interpretation, and procedures for reaching recommendations with utility can be derived from codes of ethics and standards of practice.
2. Multimodal assessment is the primary buffer against data misinterpretation, over-interpretation, or under-interpretation.
3. Interpreting interview data and assessment data in the context of the examinee's history is the primary mechanism for meaningful data interpretation. Highlighting the strengths and limitations of data is an integral aspect of data interpretation.
4. Risk assessment matrices should include factors identified in empirical research on risk assessment that are relevant to samples of parents, especially those whose characteristics are similar to care and protection samples of parents. Analyses of child maltreatment risk in care and protection samples should include caveats about the dearth of empirical studies specifically relevant to the population of interest.
5. Further research is needed to better understand the degree of correspondence (or possible discordance) in static and dynamic risk factors between violence risk studies relevant to adult inpatient psychiatric and correctional samples, and factors identified in child maltreatment risk studies.
6. Although there are many existing measures and methods designed to assess the nature and quality of the parent-child relationship, standardized approaches with fairly uniform applicability to care and protection samples would depend upon the referral question. Data interpretation and recommendations relevant to parent-child relationships should be made with appropriate caution.

7. Dissimulation is an issue endemic to care and protection evaluations. Methods for detecting dissimulation that are specific to care and protection samples have not been developed. Evaluators should make reasonable efforts to detect dissimulation and other influences on the reliability and validity of data, but with the knowledge that false positive and false negative rates specific to care and protection samples are unknown.

8. Methods for minimizing the influence of suggestibility and other impediments to reliability and validity should be used when indicated. Many care and protection cases involve children with cognitive limitations and other special needs. The relevance of procedures should be judged on a case-by-case basis. Appropriate modifications to interview or assessment methods should be made only when the integrity of data would not be compromised. Novel procedures should not be used if there are no normative data or empirical demonstrations of their appropriate use with special populations.

9. The breadth of interview content and indications for the use of formal assessment measures are drawn from the referral question.

9

Data Integration and Interpretation

This chapter contains recommendations for data interpretation and report writing. The evaluation report is the most widely recognized form of integrating and disseminating information and recommendations to child protective service representatives, to attorneys and to the court. Compared to less formal methods of communicating results, a well-written report provides the advantage of documentation of the purpose of the evaluation, the limits of confidentiality, sources of information (records and collaterals), the evaluation methodology, a description of the data and reasoning process upon which the evaluator relied to render conclusions or opinions, the evaluation outcome, and any associated recommendations. This chapter provides suggestions for ways to analyze and synthesize evaluation data and other sources of information. Common interpretive topics relevant to care and protection matters are described, with ways to address the topics in light of the referral question. Suggestions are provided for report structure, content, flow and organization. Although there is no uniform way to write a care and protection report, this chapter contains ideas for organizing the basic features that are common to evaluation reports, and ways to avoid common problems in report writing. Some suggestions are given for the pragmatic aspects of preparation for expert testimony, but the reader might wish to turn to other resources for a full review of expert testimony (cf., Melton et al., 1997; Ogloff, 1999).

INTEGRATING THE DATA

The most fundamental key to a quality report is to integrate and interpret the data in light the original referral question. Theory is the basis for data interpretation. Interpretations should be made within a theoretical context, but it is rare that theory would be described at length in the interpretive process. Theory should serve as a template that might be manifest or latent, depending on the need to articulate it in specific cases. Data integration and interpretation is facilitated by the organization that a referral question brings to the assessment process. A basic format for organizing data interpretation is to review the referral question, review the reliability and validity of the data that were gathered in the assessment process, address the referral question with data that is judged to be valid and reliable, consider supporting and contradicting data, entertain competing explanations or hypotheses, and make a conclusion as to why competing hypotheses either are viable or why they were ruled out. The second most fundamental issue in data integration is to consider possible influences on the evaluation process and results. The primary influences in care and protection matters are social desirability responding in caregivers and family loyalty bonds in children. Other influences should be considered if they are relevant. The data integration and interpretation should address all relevant influences on the data.

The third fundamental key to a quality report is cogency and the fourth is descriptive information. The third point need not be sacrificed in favor of the fourth. It is possible to write a cogent report containing rich descriptive data. To maintain cogency, it is useful to follow a structure for the interpretation section. A suggested structure for comprehensive evaluation reports is to devote about one paragraph to each of the following points (points in the list below would be included only if relevant to the referral question): (a) answer the referral question, elaborating on supporting logic in the points that follow; (b) address competing hypotheses; (c) make a conclusion concerning the most viable hypothesis; (d) describe the caregiver's functioning; (e) describe the child's functioning and level of development; (f) describe the parent-child relationship; (g) describe etiological factors hypothesized to be related to maltreatment, specifying the explanatory reasons for the link to maltreatment; (h) describe risk factors and mitigating factors for future maltreatment, adding appropriate caveats concerning limitations in the predictive utility of risk matrices; and (i) address amenability to treatment. In some cases, elaboration on developmental concerns or theoretical bases for conclusions will be necessary.

For brief evaluations, the strategy above should be tailored to the relevant issues. For example, in a report on the impact of child maltreatment on the child's current functioning, the interpretation section might include one paragraph for each of the following points: descriptive data about current functioning, conclusions about diagnostic clusters of symptom and behaviors (if relevant), a comparison to documentation of past functioning, an analysis of the link (if any) to child maltreatment as an etiological factor, and the child's prognosis. Although cogency is important in both comprehensive and brief evaluation reports, the evaluator should include all data that is needed to meet admissibility standards. Some evaluators also prefer to write with testimony in mind, so that key points and supporting data are written in a manner that facilitates smooth testimony. Other evaluators prefer to use different organizational strategies, addressing the highlights in the report, but reserving elaboration for verbal testimony. It is important to base such judgments on personal experience and jurisdictional expectations. Each evaluator must develop a strategy that is acceptable to the court, acceptable to referring parties, useful to the evaluator, respectful of the parties involved, and feasible.

Reviewing the Reliability and Validity of the Data

Even advanced psychological assessment measures, such as measures of intelligence, personality, or memory, are not totally objective. There is always a subjective component to data analysis and interpretation (Matarrazo, 1990). The inevitability of at least some degree of subjectivity does not preclude the reasonable integration of psychological assessment data, historical data, collateral data, interview data, or data from records (Brodzinsky, 1993; Matarrazo, 1990). Psychological assessment is a one-to-one relationship with statutorily defined or implied professional responsibilities. Assessment techniques can be used for both harmful and helpful purposes and their use cannot be separated from their validity, from the training and competence of the evaluator, and from the evaluator's professional ethics (Matarrazo, 1990).

Matarrazo (1990) contends that too many clinical opinions are based solely on test scores. Although one way to obtain converging data is to look for correspondence between interview data and test scores, the data take on more significance when there is further corroboration, or when the data are consistent with documentation of earlier functioning. Opinions should be based not only on psychological test scores, but they should be integrated with objective information contained in the individual's history, such as school transcripts, medical records, mental health treatment records and other relevant records. Records often provide highly useful data that can be used to establish baseline functioning for behaviors or constructs of concern. Multimodal assessment, using either records or other forms of assessment to bolster conclusions, can guard against measurement error due to unreliability. For example, even when test-retest reliability is high, such as .90 for each of the three IQ scores of the WAIS or WISC, or between .7 and .9 for each of the subscales, it still is not 1.00. Therefore, using a single examination score to reach a judgment of impairment entails some degree of risk. Conclusions withstand challenges to reliability and validity when they are based on more than one point of data, such as combining an IQ score with other indices of intellect, or comparing current scores to past scores or other indices of intellectual functioning. The practice of psychological assessment is an activity by which the evaluator integrates assessment results with relevant information from the personal, educational, mental health, and occupational histories.

In addition, the evaluator might sometimes wish to conduct an up-to-date search of relevant behavioral sciences literature as a buffer against erroneous conclusions that an impairment or deficit exists that might be explained by other influences or might be equally present in samples of healthy individuals. Relevant base rate information that is not contained in assessment manuals might be found. Published information, found in test manuals and in subsequent studies, on the psychometric properties of scales and subscales sometimes is critically important in the appropriate interpretation of a test score in order to reach a conclusion that is anchored in the individual's life history. Such preparation is not meant simply to respond to cross-examination, but to seek assurance that the interpretation is clinically and legally meaningful and relevant. In evaluating the reliability and validity of the data, it is important to consider the cultural relevance of the data (Budd & Holdsworth, 1996). Normative data relevant to cultural status should be reported if available. Appropriate caveats should be given in the absence of such data. Cultural context, socioeconomic concerns, and other potential influences on the meaning of the data should be considered (Dana, 1993).

DESCRIBING LEVELS OF FUNCTIONING, PARENTING ABILITIES, AND PARENT-CHILD RELATIONSHIPS

Most referral questions require at least some attention to the level of functioning of the caregiver(s) and the child, and a summary of data relevant to the caregiver-child relationship (Barrera, 1988; Creasey & Jarvis,

1994). The breadth and depth of descriptive information on these topics will depend upon the referral question. For example, a brief description of overall functioning, parenting abilities, and the parent-child relationship might be all that is necessary in an evaluation that was designed to address a highly focused question relevant to one or two aspects of parental risk to a child. A more comprehensive description would be merited in cases in which the purpose of the evaluation is to gather data relevant to overall parental fitness and risk of maltreatment (Barnum, 1997; Murphy et al., 1991). When comprehensive descriptions are indicated, the evaluator should use an organizational framework to present the data, show careful attention to the distinction between descriptions and conclusions, and emphasize central points without sacrificing necessary attention to thoroughness.

Descriptions of a child's attachment to a parent should be included with caution due to the fact that attachment is an amorphous construct. It is illustrative to describe it in a manner that includes visitation patterns and observations; children's reactions before, during, and after visits; other forms of contact between visits; and deliberateness of parental efforts to increase visitation. The evaluator should consider whether the parent had ample opportunity over a long periods of time to establish and maintain a consistent visitation schedule, and then failed to do so. It is useful to include descriptions of whether the attachment is meaningful to the child, pathological, or non-existent in the child's view. In some cases, reports may need to highlight concern that a child might remain attached to the parent even when the attachment is destrictive to the child. The parent's level of responsibility to the child during the pendency of the care and protection matter should be described. It is worth highlighting data that suggest a child is thriving in substitute care relative to prior parental care, but developmental advances in the child should be taken into account.

DESCRIBING RISK AND MEDIATORS OF RISK OF CHILD MALTREATMENT

Causal inferences often are a central feature of the interpretive process concerning risk and mediators of risk (Grisso, 1986). Causal inferences imbue meaning into parental strengths and limitations. For example, a parental manifestation of a desirable trait or adequate abilities might reflect a strength in one parent, but the same data might reflect dissimulation in another parent (Grisso, 1986; Melton et al., 1997). There are many possible causal explanations for deficiencies in parenting, including situational stress or crises, evaluation-related stress, parental ambivalence about regaining custody, lack of knowledge or information about adequate parenting, substance abuse problems, mental health problems, psychopathy or character problems, factitious disorder by proxy and other maladaptive caretaking patterns, cognitive limitations, neurological impairment, adult conduct problems, or other factors (Dyer, 1999; Grisso, 1986).

Factors in the literature that are linked to child maltreatment potential should be considered. Some examples of potentially relevant factors include: compromised empathy and degrees of desirability of parenting, ambivalence in the parenting role, immaturity in parenting because of youthful status or developmental limitations, reduced stress tolerance capacity, disinhibition of aggression or avoidance (neglect), poor management of acute crisis and provocation, the development of an habitual pattern of arousal and aggression, blockage of adaptive coping, overcoming external inhibitors to maltreatment, and skill in breaking down the child's resistance to maltreatment (Bauer & Twentyman, 1985). Other factors were reviewed in the previous chapter. Similarly, factors relevant to risk desistance should be considered (Monahan et al., 2000). Examples include an abatement of the interfering effects of mental illness, use of resources to compensate for parenting weaknesses, effective substance abuse rehabilitation, effective parenting training, access to strong social support, and other factors. To the degree that it is possible to render conclusions about risk of child maltreatment, risk should be characterized in relationship to parenting skills and limitations.

Describing Amenability and Non-Amenability to Treatment and Reunification

Caregiver Amenability to Interventions

Referral questions concerning caregiver amenability to rehabilitation sometimes precede the development of service plans by child protective service agencies and sometimes are requested subsequent to them. For referrals that are made subsequent to the development of a service plan, the evaluator should first determine if sufficient time has elapsed for the caregiver to enroll in the recommended rehabilitation and to obtain some benefit from them. The nature of the recommended treatment sometimes has bearing on the amount of time that would be expected prior to seeing any treatment benefit. For example, for a caregiver who recently became sober after a period of sustained insobriety, a two-week period would need to pass prior to expecting sufficient cognitive clarity to benefit from the educational aspects of rehabilitation (Marlatt, Blume, & Parks, 2001). Depending upon the supporting base of empirical literature for a particular treatment method, it might be relatively straightforward or quite difficult to determine the expected length of time necessary for treatment benefit to become apparent, and the expected duration of sustained post-treatment benefits (Aronen & Kurkela, 1996). Similarly, in order to judge the suitability of one treatment method compared to another, it is important to be aware of empirical literature that demonstrates the relative efficacy of different methods for specific populations of concern (Webster-Stratton & Hammond, 1997).

Judgments about amenability should be based on what is known in the literature about the efficacy and predictive validity (treatment outcome) of various treatment methods, the applicability of the methods to samples of caregivers in care and protection actions, the applicability of the rehabilitation method to the individual's gender or level of education, the applicability of a rehabilitation method to a particular individual, the individual's attendance and participation in the rehabilitation, the judgments of rehabilitation providers who act as collateral reporters, the caregiver's self-assessment of rehabilitation impact, and the caregiver's ability to demonstrate or describe what they have learned from rehabilitation (Eiden & Reifman, 1996; Coley, 2001). Evaluators should avoid judgments about amenability that are based on middle-class values or assumptions about parenting (Mohit, 1996; Nicholson & Blanch, 1994). Amenability might depend upon the availability of support, monitoring or supervision. For example, case management sometimes is a useful adjunct for parents with cognitive limitations or serious mental illness (Mohit, 1996; Coley, 2001).

Most treatment outcome studies are based on pure clinical samples of individuals, or individuals with one specific problem. Outcome research is more valid when samples of patients with comorbidity are screened out. The relative dearth of outcome research on individuals with comorbid mental illnesses or dual diagnoses is problematic when evaluators need to make amenability judgments in complex cases. Although the treatment outcome literature certainly has applicability to some individuals involved in care and protection actions, it frequently lacks specificity to individuals with multiple and complex diagnostic concerns, or environmental complications such a poor neighborhood quality, and low socioeconomic status (Hipwell & Kumar, 1996; Morey, 1999). Similarly, much is known about expectations of treatment compliance and treatment progress in samples of substance abusers (Marlatt et al., 2001), but less is known about expected treatment progress when substance abuse interacts with the stress of legal actions, or with other expected complications (Mejta & Lavin, 1996). Theorists and researchers have developed methods for predicting the expected path of progress for patients in psychotherapy, using a normative estimate of the overall pattern of patient improvement and specifying expected patterns of change in specific domains (such as subjective well being, symptom remediation, and functioning) (Leuger et al., 2001), but supplementary norms for specific populations rarely are calculated, usually because of insufficient sampling techniques and insufficient numbers of individuals in research outcome studies. Methods for rating progress in inpatient samples of individuals with complex problems show promise, but norms have not been developed outside of particular facilities (Schalock, Sheehan, & Weber, 1993).

Although studies lack specificity to care and protection populations, much is known about factors that facilitate measurable treatment outcome. Treatments that target specific behavioral indicators usually are more effective in the short term (Piper & Joyce, 2001). For some mental illnesses, the duration of untreated symptoms predicts treatment outcome. For example, duration of untreated psychosis is negatively correlated with treatment outcome, as measured at six months follow up in an early psychosis program (Black et al., 2001). Symptom management approaches lend themselves to better measurement of treatment outcome than process or relationship approaches for anxiety disorders, including posttraumatic stress disorder and social phobia (Borkovec, Castonguay, & Newman, 1997), but ease of outcome measurement might not always correlate with efficacy across time. Depending upon the severity of the trauma that precipitated the disorder, process or insight-oriented approaches to treatment sometimes are disorganizing for the patient. Such approaches depend upon the patient's innate cognitive abilities related to capacity for insight, but they also depend upon the severity of disorganizing symptoms (e.g., hyperarousal or thought problems) of the mental illness. Insight or awareness can increase with treatment of manic episodes, but there is a "ceiling" on insight or awareness for most schizophrenic patients (McEvoy & Wilkinson, 2000). For individuals with serious and persistent mental illness, good treatment programs are comparable in their level of effectiveness. For example, comparisons of clubhouse model programs, consumer self-help groups, social skills training, and vocational skills training yielded similar effects for quality of life, patient satisfaction and frequency of psychiatric hospitalization (Accordineo & Herbert, 2000).

Studies that target comorbid mental illness and substance abuse problems in adults have indicated that substance abuse addiction severity is the most potent predictor of treatment outcome, with pre-existing mental illness having little relationship to substance abuse outcomes or relapse despite its prevalence as a comorbid factor (Marsden, Gossop, Stewart, Rolfe, & Farrell, 2000; McNamara, Schumacher, Milby, Wallace, & Usdan, 2001). However, character pathology and associated problems are predictive of poor outcomes, with antisocial character pathology having a particularly pronounced effect on risk of relapse (Galen, Brower,

Gillespie, & Zucker, 2000; Thomas, Melchert, & Banken, 1999). Polysubstance abuse, especially alcohol plus a drug of choice, is more predictive of poor treatment outcome than abuse of single substances (Heil, Badger, & Higgins, 2001). The predictive effect of addiction severity is mediated by employment (Marlatt et al., 2001). Positive outcome in self-help approaches such as Alcoholics Anonymous are linked to the individual's commitment to self-help practices, meeting attendance, and subjective impressions of the principals of the approach (Tonigan, Miller, & Connors, 2000).

In most care and protection cases, the maltreatment itself is the treatment target. Even when maltreatment is causally related to mental illness or substance abuse, it makes sense to target the maltreatment behaviors. Some treatment outcome studies provide useful data that is relevant to maltreatment in care and treatment cases. For example, in a sample of 36 incest perpetrators attending court-ordered treatment, researchers found that criminal prosecution was unrelated to treatment compliance and attendance, but it was negatively related to improved empathy and trends toward slightly higher ratings of treatment progress. Patients with more severe scores of personality disturbance (based on MMPI scores) showed less treatment completion and attainment of empathy for the victim (Chaffin, 1992). Based on an analysis of treatment outcome studies, researchers have concluded that cognitive-behavioral approaches to sex offender treatment are more effective than psychodynamic or purely behavioral approaches (Polizzi, MacKenzie, & Hickman, 1999; Wood, Grossman, & Fichtner, 2000); however, they are not optimal for individuals with high levels of self-centeredness, secrecy, minimization, and destructive influences in group treatment settings (Barker & Beech, 1993). Treatment effectiveness varies among categories of sex offending (Marques, Day, Nelson, & Miner, 1989). Overall effectiveness is difficult to measure, especially when seduction, victim grooming, or secrecy are involving. Most outpatient sex offender treatment outcome data are based on arrests or recidivism. Patients who complete sexual offender treatment tend to have more years of education, no history of sexual victimization, no history of violent (non-sex-offender) convictions, low likelihood of diagnosis of antisocial personality disorder, and lower levels of "minimizing" or "excusing" sexual crimes (Geer, Becker, Gray, & Krauss, 2001).

Treatment outcomes studies relevant to reducing violence risk have produced positive but mixed results (Griffin, Steadman, & Heilbrun, 1991), and their applicability to care and protection samples (as contrasted with criminal justice system or forensic inpatient samples) is not well established. Anger management is a popular approach to the treatment of violent offenders. Researchers draw a conceptual distinction between anger and aggressive or violent behavior (Dahlen & Deffenbacher, 2001). Anger management treatment outcome studies specific to samples of abusing parents (Grotberg, Feindler, White, & Stutman, 1991) and samples of learning disabled and mentally retarded adults (Gilmour, 1998; Howells, Rogers, & Wilcock, 2000) have been conducted, with preliminary results suggesting treatment gains are maintained when there is adequate support and follow up (Rose, 1996; Rossiter et al., 1998). Most studies illustrating treatment effectiveness have not been conducted with randomized trials using a control group comparison format (Reilly & Shopshire, 2000), making most treatment outcome conclusions tentative. Studies that have included comparison groups have not yielded particularly robust results when reduction in violence was the criterion variable (Watt & Howells, 1999). When subcategories of individuals committing acts of reactive aggression are compared to those committing premeditated acts, there is a more robust effect for the reactive group. Reductions in attitudes of vengeance are seen in the reactive aggression subtype (Holbrook, 1997).

The following treatment principles have been suggested as a method for evaluating potential treatment effectiveness for individuals with histories of violence (Heilbrun & Griffin, 1999). There should be a distinct assessment phase, with a separation between the goals of treatment planning the goals of the legal system concerning jurisdiction or case disposition. Treatment should address both clinical symptoms (of mental illness, substance abuse or both) and functional deficits (in the care and protection matters, functional deficits might include aspects of parenting). Treatment should be designed to restore the individual's mental health functioning and to remediate deficits. There should be a logical connection between symptoms, risk factors for target behavior classes (such as physical abuse, sexual abuse or neglect), and interventions. The decision to recommend short-term focused treatment versus long-term multimodal treatment should be based on the individual's functioning deficits. There should be a structure for smooth communication between treatment providers and case managers who must make periodic judgments about case status. Criteria for gauging treatment progress should be case-specific, but standardized whenever feasible. Individuals should be explicitly advised about requirements of confidentiality, duty to protect, and child maltreatment reporting requirements. Evaluators should have ready access to legal advice when questions arise that might require immediate consultation. Treatment criteria for gauging progress should be manifestly stated in treatment contracts. Contracts should include components such as medication compliance (when relevant), session attendance, session participation, abstinence from alcohol and drugs, blood or urine screening (if indicated), disallowance of possession of items that might increase risk (such as weapons, pornography, or other accelerants of risk), provisions for transportation to and from appointments, adherence to court-ordered no-contact rules, and consequences for violating the treatment contract (Heilbrun & Griffin, 1999).

With respect to parent education techniques, records and collateral data help to clarify whether the training program meets the specific parenting training needs of the parent in question (Fox & Hennick, 1996). In order for caregivers to benefit, the treatment must meaningfully address behaviors of concern without requiring broad or nebulous criteria for measuring behavior change. For example, in an evaluation of parent management training interventions, Cavell (2001) suggested that better progress might be seen in parents if the treatment helped the parent target specific behavior (such as acts of physical aggression and verbal coercion in children) rather than general parenting efforts to gain overall child noncompliance. He based his recommendation on an analysis of cultural differences in parental interpretations of child noncompliance, and ease of targeting specific behaviors compared to broad bands of behavior. Other researchers have found that parenting programs that emphasize specific child management skills are less effective (at lest for parents with substance abuse problems) than interventions that target more comprehensive problems such as multiple and chronic life problems, insufficient supports, poor coping skills, already damaged relationships with children, and repetitive patterns of relating to children based on the caregiver's history of trauma (Mejta & Lavin, 1996).

Although it is not a causal explanation for child maltreatment, difficult temperament has been shown to relate to child behavior problems and parental distress. To enhance treatment relevance and efficacy, treatment methods targeting caregiver management of child behavior also should take the child's temperamental characteristics into account (Sheeber & Johnson, 1994). The effectiveness of treatment methods based on attachment theory are enhanced when the caregiver is provided with concrete or step-wise methods of making connections between the caregiver's internal attachment representations, his or her past and present relationships, and the caregiver's understanding of the child's needs and feelings (Erickson, Korfmacher, & Egeland, 1992). Even when concepts are simplified, the appropriateness of using treatment methods based on attachment theory would depend upon the caregiver's capacity to examine those relationships and connections, and to make behavior change corresponding to that awareness.

Treatment Outcome Studies of Children

With the exception of treatment outcome studies for attention deficit hyperactivity disorder, treatment outcome research for children is not as advanced as research on adults (Brown & Ievers, 1999). Some treatment outcomes studies for mentally ill children have addressed comorbidity. In one study of the treatment effectiveness of cognitive-behavioral therapy, comorbidity was not associated with differences in treatment outcome (Kendall, Brady, & Verduin, 2001). The need for inpatient versus community-based treatment is linked to recency and severity of stressful life events and chronic adversities in child psychiatric populations (Sandberg, McGuinness, Hillary, & Rutter, 1998). Low IQ and a marked lack of individualized care in early childhood is related to the duration of hospitalization (Castle, Bredenkamp, Beckett, & Rutter, 1999). Outcome studies of attachment disorders in children have shown little decrease in symptom severity and level of impairment in children with severe deprivation histories (O'Connor & Rutter, 2001).

Children's perceptions of treatment outcomes are heavily influenced by parental perceptions (Chesson, Harding, Hart, & O'Loughlin, 1997), but children's reports of the link between trauma and the onset of mental illness often are inconsistent with parental reports. Children's perceptions of treatment outcome also are influenced by their awareness and understanding of the function of clinics and hospitals. In an inpatient sample, most young children were not informed about an impending psychiatric hospital admission, few understood that the treatment unit was a hospital, and few were able to provide a clear reason for their admission (Chesson et al., 1997).

The Availability of Relevant Rehabilitation Resources

Current knowledge on the effectiveness of interventions in child maltreatment is limited, but research suggests that home health visitors, self-help counseling, family therapy, and group therapy are promising interventions (Dubowitz, 1990). In one sample of neglectful parents, those who were provided with both individual and group treatment relevant to the maltreatment showed a better treatment response than those who were provided only with individual therapy (no data were collected for a group-therapy-only sample) (Iwaniec, 1997). Most agencies must make intervention recommendations based on both efficacy and cost-effectiveness, sometimes limiting the repertoire of agency-funded techniques available to individuals (Dubowitz, 1990). Some statutes require that amenability judgments must take into account the availability of resources. Availability frequently is linked to funding and it sometimes is linked to geographic accessibility. Even when funding sources are available (such as public funding or insurance funding), limits frequently are placed on the number of sessions and the variety of interventions for which funding is approved. Recommendations for modifications should be based on research that supports the effectiveness of the intervention for a particular parent, but they also should be based on pragmatic concerns linked to availability.

Estimating the Length of Time Needed for Successful Rehabilitation

Estimating the length of time needed for successful rehabilitation is a difficult task, but it sometimes is a key component of the referral question. Referring sources are interested in the duration of necessary treatment in order to consider the possible effectiveness of treatment within statutorily defined time limits for care and protection matters prior to initiating a termination petition. Prior to accepting such a referral question, the evaluator should make clear the limitations in the behavioral sciences literature relevant to the length of time necessary for a particular individual to obtain observable and measurable treatment effects. Although some preliminary data are available describing outcomes, less is known about predicting the length of time necessary for a parent to benefit from effective techniques (Aronen & Kurkela, 1996).

DESCRIBING THE CHILD'S PARENTING NEEDS

Some referral questions address the issue of goodness of fit between a parent and a child. A parent might have adequate abilities to parent a child with no special needs or special health problems, but the same parent might have difficulty parenting a child whose behavior, mental health, or physical health is compromised. Some children have behavior patterns that require a high level of structure, discipline or control, and others behave well with considerable autonomy. Differences sometimes are related to children's developmental status or age, other differences are more idiosyncratic (Lindsey, 2001). The goodness of fit component usually requires an analysis of support resources or substitute caregivers that are available to the parent. A parent with significant problems understanding how to respond to a child's special needs might not be at risk of harm to the child if other adults are available to fulfill those responsibilities. Other available adults might compensate for certain functional deficits in the parent. On the other hand, sometimes parents are involved with other adults who place a great demand on their time and attention, thereby exacerbating maltreatment potential (Grisso, 1986).

Parenting needs of children are based on their developmental status. For example, parents need an adequate grasp of developmental information in order to meet the needs of a particular child at a particular developmental level. A parent's ability to respond to developmental concerns, in the context of statutory emphasis on minimal parenting competence, sometimes is difficult to gauge. Although the following information is not exhaustive, it illustrates the breadth of information a parent must have available in order to understand infant and child development. The evaluator must make reasoned judgments about how a parent's need for developmental information relates to minimal parenting abilities. In infancy and toddlerhood, children learn concrete information and the safety and nurturing qualities of caregivers and environments (Bowlby, 1988; Stahl, 1994). Basic trust is established via the relationship with primary caregivers and surrogates. Following the development of trust and attachment comes a process wherein the child develops autonomy and the foundation for a sense of self. During this process, the child engages in tantrums, demanding behavior and stubbornness (Stahl, 1994). Parents need basic comprehension of developmental milestones to understand when an infant or toddler is ready to achieve a variety of neurological, sensory, and motor integrative milestones (Greenspan & Greenspan, 1991).

In the preschool years, children show sex role identification and an understanding of emotions (Barrett & Campos, 1987). They develop a growing sense of time, relationships and language (Stahl, 1994). Behavioral indicators of attachment become more apparent (Ainsworth & Bell, 1974). There is a strong need for predictability, consistency and structure. Preschoolers respond to stress and trauma with nightmares, whining, separation anxiety, confusion, aggression and regression. The grade school years are filled with a variety of tasks of growth and development, including increased involvement in the world, an ongoing need for structure and rules, a need for activities, and an increase in loyalty conflicts. Grade school children tend to replay conflicts with their peers. Some preliminary abstraction abilities might be emerging. The child begins to notice inconsistencies in the caregiver's behavior (Stahl, 1994).

Children's reactions to separations from their parents are different at different developmental stages. By age three or four, physical separations no longer present a serious threat to the child and tend not produce intense emotional reactions. At different stages, children show different developmental capacities to mentally represent an absent parent, discuss and impending or past separation, and plan for a reunion with the parent (Kobak, 1999). Children progress from a need for physical proximity to a need for availability and responsiveness (Bowlby, 1988). The decline of separation distress does not mean the importance of an attachment relationship declines. The sophistication of a child's representation and cognitive schemata or mapping for a caregiver and a caregiver's whereabouts increases with age. Children's capacity to tolerate absence might hinge on their mental representation of the caregiver's overall availability in a specific instance or across the course of the child's life. Emotional reactions to attachment disruptions also show a developmental progression. Manifest behavioral indicators of separation anxiety gradually are replaced with more subtle features of sadness, anger, and fear. Indicators also include distorted emotional communication and symptomatic expressions of separation and loss (Kobak, 1999). In summary, when evaluators consider data in light of legal standards of goodness of fit, developmental features, individual variables, and dyadic process variables are relevant.

RENDERING OPINIONS

When opinions are requested as part of the referral process, they usually are centered on the degree of congruency between a parent's abilities and the needs of the child. Another commonly requested opinion is the best dispositional option for the child (whether temporary or permanent). Grisso (1986) refers to this type of interpretation as "judgmental and dispositional characteristics." When the court considers the admissibility of clinical opinion testimony by psychologists, the law relies on a broad relevancy approach. If the opinion is relevant to a factual issue in question in the proceedings, the court will admit the opinion or testimony if the probative value is not outweighed by the danger of prejudice or jury confusion. The evaluators must be qualified as the person to offer the opinion as an expert, but there are no requirements placed on the quality of testimony. When the opinion and testimony is based on scientific knowledge, the law relies on either *Frye v. United States* (1923) or *Daubert v. Merrell Dow Pharmaceuticals, Inc.* (1993), depending upon the jurisdiction. Under either analysis, the court usually is concerned with the reliability of scientific evidence, general acceptance within the relevant field of science, whether the theory or technique is testable or has been tested, whether the theory or technique has been subjected to peer review or publication, and what the known or potential error rate is for the technique (Lavin & Sales, 1998).

INTERPRETATIONS AND RECOMMENDATIONS IN REPORTS AND TESTIMONY

REPORT COGENCY

The evaluation report is both a clinical and a forensic document, the primary purpose of which is to describe and interpret relevant data. The process of creating a report is a literary one requiring skill in organization, integration, and synthesis of data (Burns & Quintar, 2001). The process also is an inferential one, requiring a cautious and conservative approach to decisions about the appropriate level of interpretation and conclusion. Prior to preparing the written document, it is helpful to personally review the distinction between describing data, interpreting of data, making conclusive statements (such as rendering diagnoses or reaching conclusions about risk of harm), using qualifiers to conclusions (such as "moderate" risk or "serious" risk), rendering opinion(s), using statutory language in phrasing opinions, and using ultimate issue language in phrasing opinions (Oberlander, 1995a, 1995b). The evaluator should return to the original referral question(s), which might or might not necessitate an expert opinion. For example, some evaluations are requested to aid the discovery of parental attitudes, feelings, traits, and parent-child interactions. Some are requested to help the parties (especially children) articulate their feelings, experiences and preferences. Some are requested to aid the court in focusing on selected factors (or moving away from immaterial factors) relevant to statutory criteria designed to guide judicial decisions. Some referral questions are concerned with the child's current functioning or developmental potential (Grisso, 1986).

The report must be carefully planned and it must be meaningful to the reader. Meaningfulness is directly linked to responding to the referral question in the report (Burns & Quintar, 2001), and it also depends upon the report writer's familiarity with relevant theory and empirical research (Schwartz, 1987). Awareness of legal decision-making patterns also is important. For example, reports that place too much emphasis on diagnoses, personality characteristics, or general intellectual functioning of parents neglect the law's concerns about the impact of those factors on parenting abilities. The concept of competence requires a description of how limitations relate to parenting, if at all (Grisso, 1986).

Many report-writers find it useful to adhere to a report format outline. Sometimes several outlines are useful to address the needs of report-writers for both brief and comprehensive assessments (Burns & Quintar, 2001). Some evaluators craft individual outlines for a handful of commonly recurring referral questions, using them as a template to promote organization and efficiency in report writing. Systematic approaches to report structure, content and style promote clarity, thoroughness and utility or meaningfulness (Ownby, 1997). Outlines aid the organization process and clarity of style.

Even when evaluations are comprehensive, the reader appreciates it when the report is not overly demanding of the reader's time (Tallent, 1993). Some evaluators prefer lengthy reports because they facilitate testimony preparation by helping the attorney craft questions for direct examination and by helping the evaluator recall the details of the data. But overly lengthy reports lose their effectiveness if the reader loses sight of the main points. Some readers become frustrated with ambiguity in reports. The writer should try to avoid ambiguous terminology or phrasing (Ownby, 1997). However, if evaluation results are inconclusive because of ambiguity of a family dynamic, a treatment response, or another pertinent issue to the referral question, the writer should introduce the source of the ambiguity, explaining why the evaluation did not clarify the issue. Sometimes the data produce an "I don't know" answer to referral questions, at least in the immediate situation. Explaining to the court that the data revealed that a question has no immediate answer sometimes is a source of frustration and sometimes is a source of relief to the referring party and/or the court, depending upon the nature of delivery, the context of the information, or the status of the case. Despite any frustration parties might feel over the results, an inconclusive report builds the evaluator's reputation for objectivity and scientific integrity.

WRITING FOR THE READERS: THE NEXUS OF PSYCHOLOGY, CHILD PROTECTIVE SERVICES, AND THE LAW

Basic features of forensic assessment reports include: the circumstances of the referral, the purpose of the evaluation, the way in which informed consent was obtained, the interviewee's comprehension of the notification of the limits of confidentiality (and any means for compensating for a lack of comprehension if relevant), sources of data (documents and collateral contacts), clinical interviews (a list of all interviewee's, dates, and duration of interviews), psychological assessment techniques (a list of all measures, or multiple lists if the evaluation included more than one individual), a review the aspects of each document that bear upon the referral question(s), a summary of each interview (using verbatim excerpts when needed for illustrative purposes), psychological assessment results, data interpretation, a summary, and recommendations. The summary might include formal opinions if they are relevant and indicated. Some reports might include appendices of psychological assessment scores, expanded transcripts of interviews, diagrams or drawings (Nurcombe & Parlett, 1994).

The most common readers of care and protection evaluation reports are attorneys and judges. From the standpoint of the reader, what is required is thoroughness without wordiness, relevance to the legal issues in question, logic, plain language, an organized format (standardized when indicated because of jurisdictional requirements), use of headings, avoidance of repetition of information, and phrasing that satisfies legal requirements when indicated (for example, some courts require opinions to be rendered with specific language such as, "To a reasonable degree of psychological certainty, I offer the following opinion . . . ") (Nurcombe & Parlett, 1994). The most common complaints of lawyers about forensic reports are insufficient clarity and use of jargon (Marchevsky, 1998). Eliminating jargon does not necessarily mean the writer must use simple language. The audience for forensic reports primarily is attorneys and judges, so complex language (but not jargon) need not be avoided altogether. However, clear language usually is appreciated not only by attorneys and judges, but also by the participants in forensic evaluations (children and caregivers) and other individuals whom the judge might allow to read all or part of reports. Attorneys commonly review the report with their client prior to court hearings. Simple language facilitates this process and minimizes the possibility of miscomprehension of the report.

Time Limitations in Statutes and the Predictive Validity of Forensic Evaluations

It is important to be cautious in the interpretation of the meaning of caregiver-child attachment, features of relationships, functioning strengths and deficiencies, risk factors and mediators of risk. Time limitations in statutes actually facilitate accuracy of risk assessment by shortening the reach of predictive analyses. Nonetheless, risk assessment, even in the short term, always includes at least some margin of error. Although researchers have made consistent findings in identifying relevant factors, child maltreatment is a low base rate phenomenon. Risk analyses and opinions should go no further than forecasting the immediate and foreseeable consequences of reunification or termination on the child's functioning. In termination cases, the final judicial analysis comes down to the degree of risk to children that society is willing to assume, relative to the rights of parents. Balanced against the right of the state to intervene and limit those rights. A judicial decision to terminate parental rights is a decision that the risk of serious harm to the child outweighs parental rights, justifying the state's intervention in severing the relationship (Grisso, 1986).

Attachment Issues: Real Time, Statutory Time, and Child Time

Everyone who is involved in a care and protection evaluation must struggle with the relationship between real time, statutory time limitations and a child's developmental status and its bearing on the child's sense of the passage of time. Real time, or the notion that one month is one month, must be gauged against court docket limitations and the tendency in busy jurisdictions for matters to be continued despite the potential for frustration of the parties to the case, despite the potential impact on the parent-child relationship, and despite impending statutory deadlines for shifting the burden of proof or introducing a state child protective service agency's obligation to seek termination. Evaluators must be prepared to listen to both reasonable and dubious explanations from parents and others with respect to their ability to meet agency demands for required interventions within the specified amount of time or relative to impending court dates. Sometimes judgments about the impact of the parent-child separation will be complicated by court docket schedules and other delays in legal proceedings. In very busy jurisdictions, there sometimes is a threat that the evaluation results will be "cold" by the time the proceeding actually goes to hearing. Most significant is the impact upon the child of the passage of time. The length of care and protections matters, from initiation to adjudication, might represent a significant portion of the amount of time that the child has been alive. Amount of time in out-of-home placement sometimes equals or exceeds the amount of time the children spent with their parents. Children's comprehension of the meaning of separations from their parents sometimes might be significantly impacted by their memories (or lack thereof) of their parents and their sense of how much time has passed relative to the perceptions of adults.

The Relationship between the Report and Expert Testimony

Preparing for Daubert Challenges

Evaluation methodology should be crafted to address the referral question and to satisfy the rigorous demands of the court for reliable and valid measures and techniques. If appropriate measures are taken prior to implementing the evaluation methodology, then preparation for *Daubert* challenges should be relatively straightforward. Some attorneys turn to published critiques of psychological and psychiatric methodology to challenge experts (e.g., Faust & Ziskin, 1988; Kutchins & Kirk, 1986; Robins, 1985; Ziskin & Faust, 1988). Although the challenges can be personally stressful to the individual evaluator, some psychologists contend the process of legal and other challenges has strengthened the specialties of forensic assessment and psychological assessment by promoting even more rigorous analysis of the reliability and validity of measures and techniques (Matarazzo, 1990; Nicholson & Norwood, 2000).

There is scientific merit to the published critiques designed to help attorneys pose challenges to the reliability and validity of forensic assessment methodology and techniques. Nonetheless, some of the critiques have been frowned upon for their one-sided nature, promoting legal challenges to the reliability and validity of techniques rather than scientifically objective analyses of the strengths and weaknesses of the techniques. It is important to be familiar with the limitations of critiques, and to consult a variety of sources to prepare for *Daubert* challenges (e.g., Borum & Grisso, 1995; Grove, 1987; Hare, 1998; Kleinmuntz, 1990; Kutchins & Kirk, 1986; Matarazzo, 1978, 1983, 1985, 1986; Meehl, 1973; Robins, 1985; Weiner, 1992). General critiques are available along with critiques of specific forensic assessment methodologies and report-writing strategies (Borum & Grisso, 1996; Enfield, 1987; Weiner, 1985) and specific measures such as the MMPI-2 and MCMI-II (studies relevant to forensic assessment are not yet available for the MCMI-III) (Ben-Porath & Graham, 1995; Berry, 1995; Craig, 1999; Dyer, 1997; Heilbrun & Heilbrun, 1995; McCann & Dyer, 1996; Ogloff, 1995; Otto & Collins, 1995; Pope, Butcher, & Seelen, 2000; Weiner, 1993, 1995; Wise, 2001) and the Rorschach Inkblot Method (Meloy, Hansen, & Weiner, 1997; Weiner, Exner, & Sciara, 1996).

Preparing for Direct Expert Testimony and Cross Examination

Preparation for court testimony in some ways is an idiosyncratic process. It is important to know your own best methods of anxiety reduction, study and preparation, and organization. Evaluators have made suggestions that might be of use. Those suggestions include discarding nothing; using contact sheets to document all conversations, telephone calls, and procedures; keeping records of all interviews (including tests, dates, and duration); and keeping billing records current. Some evaluators find it useful to keep case records in folders with tabbed sections for (a) copies of laws, statutes and regulations; (b) scientific articles relevant to the case; (c) legal documents relevant to the case; (c) other documents; (d) case notes; (e) psychological assessment raw data and results; (f) telephone messages and other notes; (g) letters pertinent to the case; (h) informed consent documents and release of information forms; (i) the forensic evaluation report; and (j) other information (Nurcombe & Parlett, 1994). Some evaluators find it useful to schedule a one- to two-hour pretrial conference with the retaining attorney. Others find this method redundant if there has been sufficient contact in the process of the case. Pretrial conferences for friend-of-the-court evaluations can prove distracting or unnecessarily lengthy if they turn into a "mini-trial" of direct and cross examination of the expert. However, they can be useful to testimony preparation if the parties to the conference reach prior consensus about the structure, content and duration of the conference. One of the best methods for preparation is to remain positive about the motives and views of all parties to a proceeding, and to view testimony and cross-examination as an opportunity and a challenge by worthy parties with interesting and legitimate questions.

SUMMARY

1. Key approaches to data integration and organization of presentation include providing a specific answer to referral questions (even

when the answer is "inconclusive" or "I don't know"), using theory as a template for data integration and interpretation, interpreting data in light of the examinee's history, and describing the strengths and limitations of the data.

2. If a referral question includes a request for information relevant to risk of child maltreatment, risk factors should be described in terms of their static and dynamic nature. Mediators of risk should be identified along with risk factors.

3. Some factors relevant to parental or caregiver risk of child maltreatment vary depending upon the form of maltreatment.

4. Recommendations for service plan interventions and modifications in interventions should take into account statutory concerns about the availability of services. Specific recommendations tend to be more useful than general recommendations. For example, a recommendation for a specific type of substance abuse treatment (relevant to a parent or caregiver's specific cognitive and social functioning) usually is more helpful than a broad recommendation for "substance abuse treatment." Similarly, "parenting training" is usually less helpful than a description of the specific skills and abilities that a parent needs.

5. Recommendations concerning parental or caregiver amenability to rehabilitation should be given within the context of statutory time frames for service provision (but with appropriate recognition that statutory time frames might vary depending on provisions for extensions when progress is made, delays in scheduled hearings on dockets, and other influences on actual time frames). Recommendations concerning amenability should take into account the strengths and limitation of treatment outcome literature for any given intervention.

6. Interpretations and recommendations for children should be made in the context of their level of developmental maturity, any compromises to their capacity to benefit from a particular intervention, and any special needs they might have.

References

Abel, G. G., Becker, J. V., & Cunningham-Rathner, J. (1984). Complications, consent, and cognitions in sex between children and adults. *International Journal of Law & Psychiatry, 7*, 89–103.

Abel, G. G., Rouleau, J. L., & Cunningham-Rathner, J. (1986). Sexually aggressive behavior. In W. Curran, L. McGarry, & S. Shah (Eds.), *Forensic psychiatry and psychology: Perspectives and standards for interdisciplinary practice.* Philadelphia: F. A. Davis.

Abidin, R. R. (1986). *Parenting Stress Index (PSI) manual* (2nd ed.). Charlottesville, VA: Pediatric Psychology Press.

Abidin, R. R. (1992). The determinants of parenting behavior. *Journal of Clinical Child Psychology, 21*, 407–412.

Abidin, R. R., & Brunner, J. F. (1995). Development of a Parenting Alliance Inventory. *Journal of Clinical Child Psychology, 24*, 31–40.

Abidin, R. R., & Wilfong, E. (1989). Parenting stress and its relationship to child health care. *Child Health Care, 18*, 114–116.

Accordino, M. P., & Herbert, J. T. (2000). Treatment outcome of four rehabilitation interventions for persons with serious mental illness. *Journal of Mental Health Counseling, 22*, 268–282.

Ackil, J. E., & Zaragoza, M. S. (1995). Developmental differences in suggestibility and memory for source. *Journal of Experimental Child Psychology, 60*, 57–83.

Adler, N. E., Boyce, T., Chesney, M. A., Cohen, S. Folkman, S. Kahn, R. L., & Syme, S. L. (1994). Socioeconomic status and health: The challenge of the gradient. *American Psychologist, 49*, 15–24.

Adoption of Carla, 623 N.E. 1118 (Mass. S.J.C.) (1993).

Adorno, T. W., Frenkel-Brunswik, E., Levinson, D. J., & Sanford, R. N. (1950). *The authoritarian personality.* New York: Harper & Row.

Achenbach, T. M. (1991). *Manual for the Child Behavior Checklist/4–18 and 1991 profile*. Burlington, VT: University of Vermont.

Ackerman, B. (1983). Speaker bias in children's evaluation of the external consistency of statements. *Journal of Experimental Child Psychology, 35*, 111–127.

Ainsworth, M. D. S. (1967). *Infancy in Uganda: Infant care and the growth of attachment*. Baltimore: Johns Hopkins University Press.

Ainsworth, M. D. S. (1989). Attachments beyond infancy. *American Psychologist, 44*, 709–716.

Ainsworth, M. D. S., & Bell, S. M. (1974). Mother-infant interaction and the development of competence. In K. Connolly & J. Bruner (Eds.), *The growth of competence*. New York: Academic Press.

Ainsworth, M. D. S., Blehar, M. C., Waters, E., & Wall, S. (1978). *Patterns of attachment: A psychological study of the Strange Situation*. Hillsdale, NJ: Erlbaum.

Alaska v. Jackson, 776 P.2d 320 (Alaska Ct.App.1989).

Allison v. State, 256 Ga. 851, 353, W.E.2d 805 (1987).

Allison, D. B., & Roberts, M. S. (1998). *Disordered mother or disordered diagnosis? Munchausen by proxy syndrome*. Hillsdale, NJ: Analytic Press.

Altemeier, W., O'Connor, S., Vietze, P., Sandler, H. M., & Sherrod, K. B. (1982). Antecedents of child abuse. *Behavioral Pediatrics, 100*, 823–829.

Altemeyer, B. (1988). *Enemies of freedom: Understanding right-wing authoritarianism*. San Francisco: Jossey-Bass.

Amato, P. R., & Keith, N. (1991). Parental divorce and adult well-being: A meta-analysis. *Journal of Marriage and the Family, 53*, 43–58.

Amato, P. R., Loomis, L. S., & Booth, A. (1995). Parental divorce, marital conflict, and offspring well-being during early adulthood. *Social Forces, 73*, 895–915.

American Academy of Psychiatry and the Law. (1995). *Ethics guidelines for the practice of forensic psychiatry*. Bloomfield, CT: Author.

American Humane Association (1985). *National analysis of official child abuse and neglect reports*. Denver: Author.

American Humane Association. (1988). *Highlights of official child neglect and child abuse reporting, 1986*. Denver: Author.

American Medical Association (1985). AMA diagnostic and treatment guidelines concerning child abuse and neglect. *Journal of the American Medical Association, 254*, 796–800.

American Professional Society on the Abuse of Children. (1990). *Guidelines for the psychosocial evaluation of suspected sexual abuse in young children*. Chicago, IL: Author.

American Psychiatric Association. (1994). *Diagnostic and statistical manual of mental disorders* (4th ed.). Washington, DC: author.

American Psychiatric Association. (2000). *Diagnostic and statistical manual of mental disorders* (4th ed., text revision). Washington, DC: author.

American Psychological Association. (1999). *Standards for educational and psychological testing* (2nd ed.). Washington, DC: Author.

American Psychological Association. (2002). Ethical principles of psychologists and code of conduct. *American Psychologist, 57*, 1060–1073.

American Psychological Association. (1993). Record keeping guidelines. *American Psychologist, 48*, 984–986.

American Psychological Association, Committee on Professional Practice and Standards. (1998). *Guidelines for psychological evaluations in child protection matters*. Washington, DC: Author.

Ames, E. W., & Chisholm, K. (2001). Social and emotional development in children adopted from institutions. In D. B. Bailey & J. T. Bruer et al. (Eds.), *Critical thinking about critical periods* (pp. 129–148). Baltimore, MD: Brookes.

Ammaniti, M. (1994). Maternal representations during pregnancy and early infant-mother interaction. In M. Ammaniti & D. S. Stern (Eds.), *Psychoanalysis and development: Representations and narratives* (pp. 79–96). New York: New York University Press.

Anastasi, A. (1982). *Psychological testing.* New York: MacMillan.

Anstone, N., & McLanahan, S. (1994). Family structure, residential mobility, and school dropout: A research note: *Demography, 31,* 575–584.

Aponte, J. F., & Crouch, R. T. (1995). The changing ethnic profile of the United States. In J. F. Aponte, R. Y. Rivers, & J. Wohl (Eds.), *Psychological interventions and cultural diversity* (pp. 1–18). Boston: Allyn and Bacon.

Aragona, J. A., & Eyberg, S. M. (1981). Neglected children: Mothers' report of child behavior problems and observed verbal behavior. *Child Development, 52,* 596–602.

Aronen, E. T., & Kurkela, S. A. (1996). Long-term effects of an early home-based intervention. *Journal of the American Academy of Child & Adolescent Psychiatry, 35,* 1665–1672.

Aries, P. (1962). *Centuries of childhood.* New York: Vintage.

Armstrong, I. (1983). *The home front.* New York: McGraw Hill.

Arnold, D. S., O'Leary, S. G., Wolff, L. S., & Acker, M. M. (1993). The Parenting Scale: A measure of dysfunctional parenting in discipline situations. *Psychological Assessment, 5,* 131–136.

Asher, R. (1951). Munchausen's syndrome. *Lancet, 1,* 339–341.

Ashworth, K., Hill, M., & Walker, R. (1994). Patterns of childhood poverty: The dynamics of spell. *Journal of Policy Analysis and Management, 13,* 658–680.

Ayoub, C. C., Deutsch, R. M., & Kinscherff, R. (2000). Munchausen by proxy: Definition, identification, and evaluation. In R. M. Reece et al. (Eds.), *Treatment of child abuse: Common ground for mental health, medical, and legal practitioners* (pp. 213–226). Baltimore, MD: Johns Hopkins University Press.

Azar, S. T. (1992). Legal issues in the assessment of family violence involving children. In R. T. Ammerman & M. Hersen (Eds.), *Assessment of family violence. A clinical and legal sourcebook* (pp. 47–70). New York: Wiley.

Azar, S. T., & Benjet, C. L. (1994). A cognitive perspective on ethnicity, race and termination of parental rights. *Law and Human Behavior, 18,* 249–268.

Azar, S. T., Lauretti, A. F., & Loding, B. V. (1998). The evaluation of parental fitness in termination of parental rights cases: A functional-contextual perspective. *Clinical Child and Family Psychology Review, 1,* 77–100.

Azar, S. T., Robinson, D. R., Hekimian, E., & Twentyman, C. T. (1984). Unrealistic expectations and problem-solving ability in maltreating and comparison mothers. *Journal of Consulting and Clinical Psychology, 54,* 867–868.

Azar, S. T., & Rohrbeck, C. A. (1986). Child abuse and unrealistic expectations: Further validation of the Parent Opinion Questionnaire. *Journal of Consulting and Clinical Psychology, 54,* 1867–1868.

Baker-Ward, L., Hess, T., & Flannagan, D. (1990). The effects of involvement on children's memory for events. *Cognitive Development, 5,* 55–69.

Balint, M. (1959). *Thrills and regressions.* London: Hogarth Press.

Baltimore City Department of Social Services v. Bouknight, 493 U.S. 549 (1990), 51, 500n.62.

Bandura, A. (1965). Influences of models' reinforcement contingencies on the acquisition of imitative responses. *Journal of Personality and Social Psychology, 1,* 589–595.

Bandura, A. (1977). Self-efficiency: Toward a unifying theory of behavioral change. *Psychological Review, 84,* 191–215.

Bandura, A. Ross, D., & Ross, S. (1961). Transmission of aggression through imitation of aggressive models. *Journal of Abnormal and Social Psychology, 63,* 575–582.

Bandura, A. Ross, D., & Ross, S. (1963). Imitation of film mediated aggressive models. *Journal of Personality and Social Psychology, 3,* 54–62.

Bandura, A., & Walters, R. H. (1963). *Social learning and personality development*. New York: Holt, Rinehart, & Winston.

Barker, M., & Beech, T. (1993). Sex offender treatment programmes: A critical look at the cognitive-behavioural approach. *Issues in Criminological & Legal Psychology, 19*, 37–42.

Barker, P. (1990). *Clinical interviews with children and adolescents*. New York: Norton.

Barlow, D. H., Abel, G. G., Blanchard, E. B., Bristow, A., & Young, L. A. (1977). Heterosocial skills checklist for males. *Behavior Therapy, 8*, 229–239.

Barnard, K. E., Hammond, M. A., Booth, C. L., Bee, H. L., Mitchell, S. K., & Spieker, S. J. (1989). Measurement and meaning of parent-child interaction. In F. Morrison, C. Lord, & D. Keating (Eds.), *Applied developmental psychology* (Vol. III, pp. 40–76). New York: Academic Press.

Barnett, D., Manly, J., & Cicchetti, D. (1993). Defining child maltreatment. The interface between policy and research. In D. Cicchetti & S. Toth (Eds.), *Child abuse, child development, and social policy*. Norwood, NJ: Ablex.

Barnum, R. (1997). A suggested framework for forensic consultation in cases of child abuse and neglect. *Journal of the American Academy of Psychiatry and Law, 25*, 581–593.

Barrett, K., & Campos, J. J. (1987). Perspectives on emotional development. II. A functionalist approach to emotions. In J. D. Osofsky (Ed.), *Handbook of infant development* (2nd ed., pp. 555–578). New York: Wiley.

Barrera, M. (1981). Social support in the adjustment of pregnant adolescents: Assessment issues. In B. H. Gottlieb (Ed.), *Social networks and social support* (pp. 69–95). Beverly Hills: Sage.

Barrera, M. (1988). Models of social support and life stress: Beyond the buffering hypothesis. In L. J. Cohen (Ed.), *Life events and psychological functioning* (pp. 211–236). Beverly Hills, CA: Sage.

Barth, R. P., & Berry, M. (1988). *Adoption and disruption: Rates, risks, and responses*. New York: Aldine De Gruyter.

Bates, J. E., Freeland, C. A., & Lousbury, M. L. (1979). Measure of infant difficultness. *Child Development, 50*, 794–803.

Bauer, W. D., & Twentyman, C. T. (1985). Abusing, neglectful, and comparison mothers' responses to child-related and non-child-related stressors. *Journal of Consulting and Clinical Psychology, 53*, 335–343.

Baumrind, D. (1968). Child care practices anteceding three patterns of preschool behavior. *Genetic Psychology Monographs, 75*, 43–88.

Baumrind, D. (1971). Current patterns of parental authority. *Developmental Psychology Monographs (Part 2), 4*, 99–102.

Baumrind, D. (1985). Familial antecedents of adolescent drug use: A developmental perspective. In C. L. Jones & R. J. Battjes (Eds.), *Etiology of drug abuse: Implications for prevention* (Research Monograph 56, pp. 13044). Rockville, MD: National Institute on Drug Abuse.

Baumrind, D. (1989). Rearing competent children. In W. Damon (Ed.), *New direction for child development: Child development, today and tomorrow* (pp. 349–378). San Francisco: Jossey-Bass.

Baumrind, D. (1991a). The influence of parenting style on adolescent competence and substance use. *Journal of Early Adolescence, 11*, 56–95.

Baumrind, D. (1991b). Parenting styles and adolescent development. In R. Learner, A. C. Peterson, & J. Brooks-Gunn (Eds.), *The encyclopedia on adolescence* (pp. 746–758). New York: Garland.

Beck, A. T., Rush, A. J., Shaw, B. F., & Emery, G. (1979). *Cognitive therapy of depression*. New York: Guilford Press.

Beck, A. T., Ward, C. H., Mendelson, M., Mock, J., & Erbaugh, J. (1961). An inventory for measuring depression. *Archives of General Psychiatry, 4*, 561–571.

Becker, G., & Cherny, S. S. (1992). A five-factor nuclear model of socially desirable responding. *Social Behavior & Personality, 20*, 163–191.

Beckerman, A. (1998). Charting a course: Meeting the challenge of permanency planning for children with incarcerated mothers. *Child Welfare, 77*, 513–529.

Beebe, D. W., Pfiffner, L. J., & McBurnett, L. J. (2000). Evaluation of the validity of the Wechsler Intelligence Scale for Children—Third Edition Comprehension and Picture Arrangement subtests as measures of social intelligence. *Psychological Assessment, 12*, 97–101.

Bell, M. B., Billington, R., & Becker, B. (1986). A scale for the assessment of object relations: Reliability, validity, and factorial invariance. *Journal of Clinical Psychology, 15*, 733–741.

Belsky, J. (1980). Child maltreatment: An ecological integration. *American Psychologist, 35*, 320–335.

Belsky, J. (1984). Determinants of parenting: A process model. *Child Development, 55*, 83–96.

Belsky, J. (1993a). Etiology of child maltreatment: A developmental-ecological analysis. *Psychological Bulletin, 114*, 413–434.

Belsky, J. (1993b). Promoting father involvement: An analysis and critique. *Journal of Family Psychology, 7*, 287–292.

Belsky, J. (1996). Parent, infant, and social-contextual antecedents of father-son attachment security. *Developmental Psychology, 32*, 905–913.

Belsky, J. (1999). Modern evolutionary theory and patterns of attachment. In J. Cassidy & P. R. Shaver (Eds.), *Handbook of attachment: Theory, research, and clinical applications* (pp. 141–161). New York: Guilford.

Belsky, J., & Pensky, E. (1988). Developmental history, personality and family relationships: Toward an emergent family system. In R. Hinde & J. Stevenson-Hinde (Eds.), *Relationships within families* (pp. 153–202). Cambridge, England: Cambridge University Press.

Belsky, J., & Rovine, M. (1990). Patterns of marital change across the transition to parenthood: Pregnancy to three years postpartum. *Journal of Marriage and the Family, 52*, 5–19.

Belsky, J., Steinberg, L., & Draper, P. (1991). Childhood experience, interpersonal development and reproductive strategy: An evolutionary theory of socialization. *Child Development, 62*, 647–670.

Belsky, J., & Vondra, J. (1989). Lessons from child abuse: The determinants of parenting. In D. Cicchetti & V. Carlson (Eds.), *Child maltreatment*. New York: Cambridge University Press.

Belsky, J., Woodworth, S., & Crnic, K. (1996). Trouble in the second year: Three questions about family interaction. *Child Development, 67*, 556–578.

Ben-Porath, Y. S., & Graham, J. R. (1995). Scientific bases of forensic applications of the MMPI-2. In Y. S. Ben-Porath, & J. R. Graham (Eds.), *Forensic applications of the MMPI-2: Applied psychology* (Vol. 2: Individual, social, and community issues, pp. 1–17). Thousand Oaks, CA: Sage.

Benedek, T. (1959). Parenthood as a developmental phase: A contribution to the libido theory. *Journal of the American Psychoanalytic Association, 7*, 389–417.

Benedek, T. (1970). The psychobiological approach to parenthood. In E. J. Anthony & T. Benedek (Eds.), *Parenthood: Its psychology and psychopathology* (pp. 109–136). Boston: Little, Brown and Company.

Benjamin, L. R., Benjamin, R., & Rind, B. (1996). Dissociative mothers' subjective experience of parenting. *Child Abuse & Neglect, 20*, 933–942.

Benoit, D., & Parker, K. (1994). Stability and transmission of attachment across three generations. *Child Development, 65*, 1444–1456.

Berkowitz, C. D. (1991). Child sexual abuse. *Report of the Twenty-second Ross Roundtable on Critical Approaches to Common Pediatric Problems*, 2–8.

Berlin, L. J., Brooks-Gunn, J., Spiker, D., & Zaslow, M. J. (1995). Examining observational measures of emotional support and cognitive stimulation in Black and White mothers of preschoolers. *Journal of Family Issues, 16*, 664–686.

Berlin, R., & Davis, R. B. (1989). Children from alcoholic families: Vulnerability. In T. F. Dugan & R. Coles (Eds.), *The child in our homes: Studies in the development of resiliency* (pp. 81–108). New York: Brunner/Mazel.

Berliner, L. (1992). Should investigative interviews of children be videotaped? *Journal of Interpersonal Violence, 7*, 277–288.

Berliner, L., & Barbieri, M. (1984). The testimony of the child victim of sexual assault. *Journal of Social Issues, 40*, 125–137.

Bernardi, E., Jones, M., & Tennant, C. (1989). Quality of parenting in alcoholism and narcotic addicts. *British Journal of Psychiatry, 154*, 677–682.

Bernet, W. (1993). False statements and the differential diagnosis of abuse allegations. *Journal of the American Academy of Child and Adolescent Psychiatry, 32*, 903–910.

Berry, D. T. R. (1995). Detecting distortion in forensic evaluations with the MMPI-2. In Y. S. Ben-Porath & J. R. Graham (Eds.), *Forensic applications of the MMPI-2: Applied psychology* (Vol. 2: Individual, social, and community issues, pp. 82–102). Thousand Oaks, CA: Sage.

Berry, J. O., & Jones, W. H. (1995). The Parental Stress Scale: Initial psychometric evidence. *Journal of Social and Personal Relationship, 12*, 463–472.

Besharov, D. J. (1985). The legal framework for child protection. In C. M. Mouzakitis, R. Varghese et al. (Eds.), *Social work treatment with abused and neglected children* (pp. 148–167).

Besharov, D. J. (1990). *Recognizing child abuse: A guide for the concerned.* New York: Free Press.

Bishop, S. J., & Leadbeater, B. (1999). Maternal social support patterns and child maltreatment: Comparison of maltreating and nonmaltreating mothers. *American Journal of Orthopsychiatry, 69*, 172–181.

Black, H. C., & Garner, B. A. (1999). *Black's law dictionary* (7th ed.). St. Paul, MN: West Group.

Black, K., Peters, L., Rui, Q. Milliken, H., Whitehorn, D., & Kopala, L. C. (2001). Duration of untreated psychosis predicts treatment outcome in an early psychosis program. *Schizophrenia Research, 47*, 215–222.

Black, M., Schuler, M., & Nair, P. (1993). Prenatal drug exposure: Neurodevelopmental outcome and parenting environment. *Journal of Pediatric Psychology, 18*, 605–620.

Blackenhorn, D. (1995). *Fatherless America: Confronting our most urgent social problem.* New York: Basic Books.

Blanch, A., Nicholson, J., & Purcell, J. (1994). Parents with severe mental illness and their children: The need for human services integration. *The Journal of Mental Health Administration, 21*, 388–396.

Blassingame, J. (1972). *The slave community: Plantation life in the antebellum South.* New York: Oxford University Press.

Block, J. (1965). *The child rearing practices report.* Berkeley, CA: University of California, Institute of Human Development.

Block, J. H. (1986). *The child rearing practice report (CRPR): A set of Q items for the description of parental socialization attitudes and values.* Berkeley, CA: University of California.

Block, K. H., & Potthast, M. J. (1998). Girl scouts beyond bars: Facilitating parent-child contact in correctional settings. *Child Welfare, 77*, 561–578.

Blume, E. S. (1991). *Secret survivors. Uncovering incest and its aftereffects in women.* New York: Ballantine.

Boer, D. R., Hart, S. D., Kropp, P. R., & Webster, C. D. (1997). *Manual for the Sexual Violence Risk-20*. Odessa, FL: Psychological Assessment Resources.

Boer, D. P., Wilson, R. J., Gauthier, C. M., & Hart, S. D. (1997). Assessing risk of sexual violence: Guidelines for clinical practice. In C. D. Webster & M. A. Jackson (Eds.), *Impulsivity: Theory, assessment, and treatment* (pp. 326–342). New York: Guilford.

Bolton, F., & Laner, R. (1981). Maternal maturity and maltreatment. *Journal of Family Issues, 2,* 485–508.

Bond, M. H., & Wang, S. (1983). China: Aggressive behavior and the problem of maintaining order and harmony. In A. P. Goldstein & M. H. Segall (Eds.), *Aggression in global perspective* (pp. 58–74). New York: Pergamon.

Boone v. State, 282 Ark. 274, 668 S.W.2d 17 (1984).

Borgida, E., Gresham, A. W., Swim, J., Bull, M. A., & Gray, E. (1989). Expert testimony in child sexual abuse cases: An empirical investigation of partisan orientation. *Family Law Quarterly, 23,* 433–449.

Borkovec, T. D., Castonguay, L. G., & Newman, M. G. (1997). Measuring treatment outcome for posttraumatic stress disorder and social phobia: A review of current instruments and recommendations for future research. In H. H. Strupp et al. (Eds.), *Measuring patient changes in mood, anxiety, and personality disorders: Toward a core battery* (pp. 117–154). Washington, DC: American Psychological Association.

Borum, R., Otto, R., & Golding, S. (1993). Improving clinical judgment and decision making in forensic evaluation. *Journal of Psychiatry & Law, 21,* 35–76.

Bousha, D. M., & Twentyman, C. T. (1984). Mother-child interactional style in abuse, neglect, and control groups: Naturalistic observations in the home. *Journal of Abnormal Psychology, 93,* 106–114.

Bowlby, J. (1956). The growth of independence in the young child. *Royal Society of Health Journal, 76,* 587–591.

Bowlby, J. (1969). *Attachment and loss: Vol. 1, Attachment.* New York: Basic Books.

Bowlby, J. (1973). *Attachment and loss: Vol. 2, Separation.* New York: Basic Books.

Bowlby, J. (1980). *Attachment and loss: Vol. 3, Loss: Sadness and depression.* New York: Basic Books.

Bowlby, J. (1988). *A secure base: Parent-child attachment and health human development.* London, England: Routeledge.

Bowlby, J., Ainsworth, M. D. S., Boston, M., & Rosenbluth, D. (1956). The effects of mother-child separation: A follow-up study. *British Journal of Medical Psychology, 49,* 211–247.

Bozett, F. W. (1989). Gay fathers: A review of the literature. In F. W. Bozett, (Ed.), *Homosexuality and the family* (pp. 137–162). New York: Harrington Park Press.

Brainerd, C., Reyna, V. F., Howe, M. L., & Kingma, J. (1990). Development of forgetting and reminiscence. *Monographs of the Society for Research in Child Development, 55,* 1–93.

Brand, E., Clingempeel, W. G., & Bowen-Woodward, K. (1988). Family relationships and children's adjustment in stepmother and stepfather families. In E. M. Hetherington & J. D. Aresteh (Eds.), *Impact of divorce, single-parenting, and stepparenting on children* (pp. 299–324). Hillsdale, NJ: Erlbaum.

Brassard, M. R., Hart, S. N., & Hardy, D. B. (1993). The Psychological Maltreatment Rating Scales. *Child Abuse & Neglect, 17,* 715–729.

Brazelton, T. B. (1981). *On becoming a family.* New York: Delacorte Press/Lawrence.

Bretherton, I. (1985). Attachment theory: Retrospect and prospect. In I. Bretherton & E. Waters (Eds.), Growing points of attachment theory and research. *Monographs of the Society for Research and Development, 50* (1–2, Serial No. 209), 3–35.

Bretherton, K., & Watson, M. W. (Eds.). (1990). *Children's perspectives on the family: New directions for child development* (Serial No. 48). San Francisco: Jossey-Bass.

Breznitz, Z., & Sherman, T. (1987). Speech patterning of natural discourse of well and depressed mothers and their young children. *Child Development, 58*, 395–400.

Briere, J. (1995). *Trauma Symptom Inventory (TSI): Professional manual*. Odessa, FL: Psychological Assessment Resources.

Briere, J. (1996). *Trauma Symptom Checklist for Children*. Odessa, FL: Psychological Assessment Resources.

Brodzinsky, D. M. (1987). Adjustment to adoption: A psychosocial perspective. *Clinical Psychology Review, 7*, 25–47.

Brodzinsky, D. M. (1993). On the use and misuse of psychological testing in child custody evaluations. *Professional Psychology: Research and Practice, 24*, 213–219.

Brooks-Gunn, J., Britto, P. R., & Brady, C. (1999). Struggling to make ends meet: Poverty and child development. In M. E. Lamb (Ed.), *Parenting and child development in "nontraditional" families* (pp. 279–304). Mahwah, NJ: Erlbaum.

Brooks-Gunn, J., & Duncan, G. J. (1997). The effects of poverty on children. *Future of Children, 7*, 55–71.

Brooks-Gunn, J., Duncan, G. J., & Aber, J. L. (Eds.). (1997). *Neighborhood poverty: Context and consequences for children. Vol. 1. Six studies of children in families in neighborhoods*. New York: Russell Sage Foundation Press.

Brooks-Gunn, J., Klebanov, P. K., & Duncan, G. J. (1996). Ethnic differences in children's intelligence test scores: Role of economic deprivation, home environment, and maternal characteristics. *Child Development, 67*, 396–408.

Brown, R. T., & Ievers, C. E. (1999). Psychotherapy and pharmacotherapy treatment outcome research in pediatric populations. *Journal of Clinical Psychology in Medical Settings, 6*, 63–88.

Brownell, A., & Shumaker, S. A. (1984). Social support: An introduction to a complex phenomenon. *Journal of Social Issues, 40*, 1–9.

Bruck, M., Ceci, S. J., Francoeur, E., & Barr, R. (1995). "I hardly cried when I got my shot!" Influencing children's reports about a visit to their pediatrician. *Child Development, 66*, 193–208.

Bruck, M., Ceci, S. J., & Hembrooke, H. (1998). Reliability and credibility of young children's reports: From research to policy and practice. *American Psychologist, 53*, 136–151.

Budd, K. S., & Greenspan, S. (1984). Mentally retarded mothers. In E. A. Blechman (Ed.), *Behavior modification with women* (pp. 477–506). New York: Guilford.

Budd, K. S., & Holdsworth, M. J. (1996). Issues in clinical assessment of minimal parenting competence. *Journal of Clinical Child Psychology, 25*, 2–14.

Budd, K. S., Poindexter, L. M., Felix, E. D., & Naik-Polan, A. T. (2001). Clinical assessment of parents in child protection cases: An empirical analysis. *Law and Human Behavior, 25*, 93–108.

Bugental, D., Blue, J., & Lewis, J. (1990). Caregiver beliefs and dysphoric affect directed to difficult children. *Developmental Psychology, 26*, 631–638.

Bugental, D. B., Blue, J., Cortez, V., Fleck, K., & Rodriguez, A. (1992). Influences of witnessed affect on information processing in children. *Child Development, 63*, 774–786.

Bugental, D. B., & Cortez, V. L. (1988). Physiological reactivity to responsive and unresponsive children as moderated by perceived control. *Child Development, 59*, 686–693.

Bugental, D. B., Mantyla, S. M., & Lewis, J. (1989). Parental attributions as moderators of affective communication to children at risk for physical abuse. In D. Cicchetti & V. Carlson (Eds.), *Child maltreatment: Theory and research on the causes and consequences of child abuse and neglect* (pp. 254–279). Cambridge: Cambridge University Press.

Bulkley, J. A. (1988). Legal proceedings, reforms, and emerging issues in child sexual abuse cases. *Behavioral Sciences and the Law, 6*, 153–180.

Bulkley, J. A. (1992). The prosecution's use of social science expert testimony in child sexual abuse cases: National trends and recommendations. *Journal of Child Sexual Abuse, 1*, 73–93.

Bumpass, L. L., & Sweet, J. A. (1989). *Children's experience in single-parent families: Implications of cohabitation and marital transitions* (NSFH Working Paper No. 3). Madison: University of Wisconsin, Center for Demography and Ecology.

Burchinal, M. R., Follmer, A., & Bryant, D. M. (1996). The relations of maternal social support and family structure with maternal responsiveness and child outcomes among African American families. *Developmental Psychology, 32*, 1073–1083.

Burgdoff, K. (1980). *Natural study of the incidence and severity of child abuse and neglect.* Washington, DC: National Center on Child Abuse and Neglect, U. S. Department of Health and Human Services.

Burgess, R. L. (1994). The family in a changing world: A prolegomenon to an evolutionary analysis. *Human Nature, 5*, 203–221.

Burgess, R. L., & Conger, R. D. (1978). Family interaction in abusive, neglectful, and normal families. *Child Development, 49*, 1163–1173.

Burgess, R. L., & Draper, P. (1989). The explanation of family violence: The role of biological, behavioral, and cultural selection. In L. Ohlin & M. Tonry (Eds.), *Family violence* (pp. 59–116). Chicago: University of Chicago Press.

Buriel, R., & De Ment, T. (1997). Immigration and sociocultural change in Mexican, Chinese, and Vietnamese American families. In A. Booth, A. C. Crouter, & N. Landale (Eds.), *Immigration and the family* (pp. 165–200). Mahwah, NJ: Erlbaum.

Burlingham, D., & Freud, A. (1944). *Infants without families.* London: Allen & Unwin.

Burns, W. J., & Quintar, B. (2001). Integrated report writing. In W. I. Dorfman & M. Hersen (Eds.), *Understanding psychological assessment: Perspectives on individual differences* (pp. 353–371). New York: Kluwer/Plenum.

Burrell, B., Thompson, B., & Sexton, D. (1994). Predicting child abuse potential across family types. *Child Abuse & Neglect, 18*, 1039–1049.

Burton, L. M. (1992). Black grandparents rearing children of drug-addicted parents: Stressors, outcomes, and social service needs. (1992). *The Gerontologist, 32*, 744–751.

Burton, R. V. (1976). Honesty and dishonesty. In T. Lickona (Ed.), *Moral development and behavior: Theory, research, and social issues* (pp. 173–197). New York: Holt, Rinehart and Winston.

Burton, R. V. (1984). A paradox in theories and research in moral development. In W. M. Kurtines & J. L. Gewirtz (Eds.), *Morality, moral behavior, and moral development* (pp. 193–207). New York: Wiley and Sons.

Burton, R. V., & Strichartz, A. F. (1991). Children on the stand: The obligation to speak the truth. *Developmental and Behavioral Pediatrics, 12*, 121–128.

Bush, M., & Goldman, H. (1982). The psychological parenting and permanency principles in child welfare: A reappraisal and critique. *American Journal of Orthopsychiatry, 52*, 223–235.

Bushnell, I. W. R. (2001). Mother's face recognition in newborn infants: Learning and memory. *Infant & Child Development, 10*, 67–74.

Buss, A. H., & Plomin, R. (1984). *Temperament: Early developing personality traits.* Hillsdale, NJ: Erlbaum.

Bussey v. Commonwealth, 697 S.W.2d 139 (Ky.1985).

Bussey, K., Lee, K., & Grimbeek, E. J. (1993). Lies and secrets: Implications for children's reporting of sexual abuse. In G. S. Goodman & B. L. Bottoms (Eds.), *Child victims, child witnesses: Understanding and improving testimony* (pp. 147–168). New York: Guilford.

Butcher, J., Dahlstrom, W., Graham, J., Tellegen, A., & Kaemmer, B. (1989). *Minnesota Multiphasic Personality Inventory-2 (MMPI-2): Manual for administration and scoring.* Minneapolis: University of Minnesota Press.

Bycer, A., Breed, L. D., Fluke, J. E., & Costello, T. (1984). *Unemployment and child abuse and neglect reporting.* Denver, CO: American Humane Association.

Caffey, J. (1946). Multiple fractures in the long bones of infants suffering from chronic subdural hematoma. *American Journal of Radiology, 56.*

Cairns, R. B., & Paris, S. G. (1971). Informational determinants of social reinforcement effectiveness among retarded children. *American Journal of Mental Retardation, 76*, 361–369.

Caldwell, B. M., & Bradley, R. H. (1984). *Home Observation for the Measurement of the Environment: Administration manual* (rev. ed.). Little Rock: University of Arkansas.

Camparo, L. B., Wagher, J. T., & Saywitz, K. J. (2001). Interviewing children about real and fictitious events: Revisiting the narrative elaboration procedure. *Law & Human Behavior, 25*, 63–80.

Campbell, J. C., Sharps, P., & Glass, N. (2001). Risk assessment for intimate partner homicide. In G. F. Pinard & L. Pagani (Eds.), *Clinical assessment of dangerousness: Empirical contributions* (pp. 136–157). New York: Cambridge University Press.

Campos, J. J., Campos, R. G., & Barrett, K. C. (1989). Emergent themes in the study of emotional development and emotion regulation. *Developmental Psychology, 25*, 394–402.

Cantos, A. L., Gries, L. T., & Slis, V. (1997). Behavioral correlates of parental visiting during family foster care. *Child Welfare, 76*, 309–329.

Cantwell, H. B. (1981). Sexual abuse of children in Denver, 1979: Reviewed with implications for pediatric intervention and possible prevention. *Child Abuse & Neglect, 5*, 75–85.

Carey, S., & Williams, T. (2001). The role of object recognition in young infants' object segregation. *Journal of Experimental Child Psychology, 78*, 55–60.

Carey, W. B., & McDevitt, S. C. (1978). Revision of the Infant Temperament Questionnaire. *Pediatrics, 61*, 735–739.

Carter, C., Bottoms, B., & Levine, M. (1996). Linguistic and socioemotional influences on the accuracy of children's reports. *Law and Human Behavior, 20*, 335–358.

Carver, L. J., Bauer, P. J., & Nelson, C. A. (2000). Associations between infant brain activity and recall memory. *Developmental Science, 3*, 234–246.

Casanova, G. M., Domanic, J., McCanne, T. R., & Milner, J. S. (1992). Physiological responses to nonchild related stressors in mothers at risk for child abuse. *Child Abuse & Neglect, 16*, 31–44.

Cassidy, J. (1994). Emotion regulation: Influences of attachment relationships. In N. Fox (Ed.), Biological and behavioral foundations of emotion regulation. *Monographs of the Society for Research in Child Development, 59*, 228–250.

Cassidy, J. (1999). The nature of the child's ties. In J. Cassidy & P. R. Shaver (Eds.), *Handbook of attachment: Theory, research, and clinical applications* (pp. 3–20). New York: Guilford.

Cassidy, J., & Shaver, P. R. (Eds.). (1999). *Handbook of attachment: Theory, research, and clinical applications.* New York: Guilford.

Castle, J., Groothues, C., Bredenkamp, D., Beckett, C., O'Connor, T., & Rutter, M. (1999). Effects of qualities of early institutional care on cognitive attainment. E.R.A. Study Team. English and Romanian adoptees. *American Journal of Orthopsychiatry, 69*, 424–437.

Caudill, O. B., & Pope, K. S. (1995). *Law and mental health professionals: California.* Washington, DC: American Psychological Association.

Cavell, T. A. (2001). Updating our approach to parent training. 1: The case against targeting noncompliance. *Clinical Psychology: Science and Practice, 8*, 299–318.

Ceci, S. J. & Bruck, M. (1993). Suggestibility of the child witness: A historical review and synthesis. *Psychological Bulletin, 113*, 403–439.

Ceci, S. J., Toglia, M., & Ross, D. (1990). The suggestibility of preschoolers' recollections: Historical perspectives on current problems. In R. Fivush & J. Hudson (Eds.), *Knowing and remembering in young children* (pp. 285–300). New York: Cambridge University Press.

Center for Adoption Research and Policy. (1997). *Case statement to explore a campaign for the Center for Adoption Research and Policy at the University of Massachusetts.* Worcester, MA: Author.

Chaffin, M. (1992). Factors associated with treatment completion and progress among intrafamilial sexual abusers. *Child Abuse & Neglect, 16,* 251–264.

Chandler, M., Fritz, A., & Hala, S. (1989). Small scale deceit: Deception as a marker of two-, three-, and four-year-olds' early theories of mind. *Child Development, 60,* 1263–1277.

Chupsky v. Wood, 26 Kan. 650, 42, 499n.12, 511n.32 (1881).

Chase-Lansdale, P. L., Brooks-Gunn, J., & Zamsky, E. S. (1994). Young African-American multigenerational families in poverty: Quality of mothering and grandmothering. *Child Development, 65,* 373–393.

Chasnoff, I. J., (1988). Drug use in pregnancy: Parameters of risk. *Pediatric Clinics of North America, 35,* 1408–1412.

Chavkin, W., & Kandall, S. R. (1990). Between a rock and a hard place. *Pediatrics, 85,* 221–225.

Cherlin, A. (1992). *Marriage, divorce, remarriage.* Cambridge, MA: Harvard University Press.

Cherlin, A., & Furstenberg, F. F. (1994). Stepfamilies in the United States: A reconsideration. In J. Blake & J. Hagen (Eds.), *Annual review of sociology* (pp. 359–381). Palo Alto, CA: Annual Reviews.

Cherlin, A., Kiernan, D., & Chase-Lansdale, P. L. (1995). Parental divorce in childhood and demographic outcomes in adulthood. *Demography, 32,* 299–318.

Chesson, R., Harding, L., Gart, C., & O'Loughlin, V. (1997). Do parents and children have common perceptions of admission, treatment and outcome in a child psychiatric unit? *Clinical Child Psychology & Psychiatry, 2,* 251–270.

Chilcoat, H. D., Breslau, N., & Anthony, J. C. (1996). Potential barriers to parent monitoring: Social disadvantage, marital status, and maternal psychiatric disorder. *Journal of the American Academy of Child and Adolescent Psychiatry, 35,* 1673–1682.

Christiaansen, R. E., & Ochalek, K. (1983). Editing misleading information from memory: Evidence for the coexistence of original and postevent information. *Memory and Cognition, 11,* 467–475.

Christianson, S., Goodman, J., & Loftus, E. F. (1992). Eyewitness memory for stressful events: Methodological quandaries and ethical dilemmas. In S. Christianson (Ed.), *The handbook of emotion and memory: Research and theory* (pp. 217–241). Hillsdale, NJ: Erlbaum.

Cicchetti, D., & Carlson, V. (Eds.). (1989). *Child maltreatment: Theory and research on the causes and consequences of child abuse and neglect.* Cambridge, England: Cambridge University Press.

Cicchetti, D., & Toth, S. (1995). A developmental psychopathology perspective on child abuse and neglect. *Journal of the American Academy of Child and Adolescent Psychiatry, 34,* 541–565.

Clement, D. A. (1998). A compelling need for mandated use of supervised visitation program. *Family & Conciliation Courts Review, 36,* 294–316.

Clement, M. J. (1993). Parenting in prison: A national survey of programs for incarcerated women. *Journal of Offender Rehabilitation, 19,* 89–100.

Cobb, R. J., Davila, J., & Bradbury, T. N. (2001). Attachment security and marital satisfaction: The role of positive perceptions and social support. *Personality & Social Psychology Bulletin, 27,* 1131–1143.

Coburn, W. J. (2000). The organizing forces of contemporary psychoanalysis: Reflections on nonlinear dynamic systems theory. *Psychoanalytic Psychology, 17,* 750–770.

Cohen, R. L., & Harnick, M. A. (1980). The susceptibility of child witnesses to suggestion. *Law and Human Behavior, 4,* 201–210.

Cohen, T. (1995). Motherhood among incest survivors. *Child Abuse & Neglect, 19,* 1423–1429.

Coley, R. L. (2001). (In)visible men: Emerging research on low-income, unmarried, and minority fathers. *American Psychologist, 56,* 743–753.

Coll. C. T. G., Hoffman, J., & Oh, W. (1987). The social ecology and early parenting of Caucasian adolescent mothers. *Child Development, 58,* 955–963.

Collins, W. A., Wellman, H., Keniston, A., & Westby, S. (1978). Age-related aspects of comprehension and inferences from a televised dramatic narrative. *Child Development, 49,* 389–399.

Committee on Ethical Guidelines for Forensic Psychologists (1991). Specialty guidelines for forensic psychologists. *Law & Human Behavior, 15,* 655–665.

Commonwealth v. Allen, 1996 665 N.E.2d 105 (Mass.Ct.App.1996).

Commonwealth v. Callahan, 1998 Mass. Super. LEXIS 586 (1998).

Commonwealth v. Corbett, 26 Mass.App.Ct. 773, 533 N.E.2d 207 (1989).

Commonwealth v. Caracino 33 Mass.App.Ct. 787 (1993).

Commonwealth v. Snow, 30 Mass.App.Ct. 433 (1991).

Connelly, C., & Straus, M. (1992). Mother's age and risk for physical abuse. *Child Abuse & Neglect, 16,* 709–718.

Cook-Fong, S. K. (2000). The adult well-being of individuals reared in family foster care placements. *Child & Youth Care Forum, 29,* 7–25.

Corwin, D. (1990). Early diagnosis of child sexual abuse: Diminishing the lasting effects. In G. Wyatt & G. Powell (Eds.), *Lasting effects of child sexual abuse.* Newbury, CA: Sage.

Courage, M. L., & Howe, M. L. (2001). Long-term retention in 3.5-month-olds: Familiarization time and individual differences in attentional style. *Journal of Experimental Child Psychology, 79,* 271–293.

Cox, M. J., Owen, M. T., Henderson, V. K., & Margand, N. A. (1992). Prediction of infant-father and infant-mother attachment. *Developmental Psychology, 28,* 474–483.

Coy v. Iowa, 487 U.S. 1012 (1988).

Craig, R. J. (1999). Testimony based on the Millon Clinical Multiaxial Inventory: Review, commentary, and guidelines. *Journal of Personality Assessment, 73,* 290–304.

Creasey, G. L., & Jarvis, P. A. (1994). Relationships between parenting stress and developmental functioning among two-year-olds. *Infant Behavior and Development, 17,* 423–429.

Crenshaw, W., & Barnum, D. (2001). You can't fight the system: Strategies of family justice in foster care reintegration. *Family Journal: Counseling & Therapy for Couples & Families, 9,* 29–36.

Crittenden, P. M. (1981). Abusing, neglecting, problematic, and adequate dyads: Differentiating by patterns of interaction. *Merrill-Palmer Quarterly, 27,* 1–18.

Crittenden, P. M. (1985). Maltreated infants: Vulnerability and resilience. *Journal of Child Psychology and Psychiatry, 26,* 85–96.

Crittenden, P. M. (1988). Distorted patterns of relationship in maltreating families: The role of internal representational models. *Journal of Reproductive and Infant Psychology, 6,* 183–199.

Crittenden, P. M., & Ainsworth, M. D. S. (1989). Child maltreatment and attachment theory. In D. Cicchetti & V. Carlson (Eds.), *Child maltreatment: Theory and research on the causes and consequences of child abuse and neglect* (pp. 432–464). New York: Cambridge University Press.

Crittenden, P. M., & Bonvillian, J. D. (1984). The relationship between maternal risk status and maternal sensitivity. *American Journal of Orthopsychiatry, 54,* 250–262.

Crouch, J. L., & Milner, J. S. (1993). Effects of child neglect on children. *Criminal Justice and Behavior, 20,* 49–65.

Currie, J. M. (1997). Choosing among alternative programs for poor children. *The Future of Children, 7,* 113–131.

Cushman, P. (1991). Ideology obscured: Political uses of the self in Daniel Stern's infant. *American Psychologist, 46*, 206–219.

Cutler, B. L., & Penrod, S. D. (1995). *Mistaken identification: The eyewitness, psychology, and the law.* New York: Cambridge University Press.

Dahlen, E. R., & Deffenbackher, J. L. (2001). Anger management. In W. J. Lyddon & J. V. Jones (Eds.), *Empirically supported cognitive therapies: Current and future applications* (pp. 163–181). New York: Springer.

Dale, P. S., Loftus, E. F., & Rathbun, L. (1978). The influence of the form of the question on the eyewitness testimony of preschool children. *Journal of Psycholinguistic Research, 7*, 269–277.

Dalgleish, L. I., & Drew, E. C. (1989). The relationship of child abuse indicators to the assessment of perceived risk and to the court's decision to separate. *Child Abuse & Neglect, 13*, 491–506.

Daly, D. L., & Dowd, T. P. (1992). Characteristic of effective, harm-free environments for children in out-of-home care. *Child Welfare, 71*, 487–496.

Daly, M., & Wilson, M. (1981). Child maltreatment from a sociobiological perspective. *New Directions in Child Development: Developmental Perspectives on Child Maltreatment, 11*, 92–112.

Dana, R. H. (1993). *Multicultural assessment perspectives for professional psychology.* Boston: Allyn & Bacon.

Daubert v. Merrell Dow Pharmaceuticals, Inc., 509 U.S. 579, 113 S.Ct. 2786 (1993).

Davenport Bost v. Van Nortwick, 82 CVD 887 N.C. Court of Appeals (1994).

Davies, E., & Seymour, F. (1997). Child witnesses in the criminal courts: Furthering New Zealand's commitment to the United Nations Convention on the Rights of the Child. *Psychiatry, Psychology and Law, 4*, 13–24.

Davies, G. M., Tarrant, A., & Flin, R. (1989). Close encounters of a witness kind: Children's memory for a simulated health inspection. *British Journal of Psychology, 80*, 415–429.

Davis, D. L. (1984). Medical misinformation: Communication between outport Newfoundland women and their physicians. *Social Science & Medicine, 18*, 273–278.

Davis, D. L., Joakimsen, L. M. (1997). Nerves as status and nerves as stigma: Idioms of distress and social action in Newfoundland and Northern Norway. *Qualitative Health Research, 7*, 370–390.

Davis, I. P., Landsverk, J., Newton, R., & Ganger, W. (1996). Parental visiting and foster care reunification. *Children & Youth Services Review, 18*, 363–382.

Davies, J. M. (1996). Dissociation, repression and reality testing in the countertransference: The controversy over memory and false memory in the psychoanalytic treatment of adult survivors of childhood sexual abuse. *Psychoanalytic Dialogues, 6*, 189–218.

Davis v. State, 527 So.2d 962 (Fla. Dist.Ct.App.1988).

de Paul, J., Arruaberrena, I., & Milner, J. S. (1991). Validacion de una version Espanola del Child Abuse Potential Inventory para su uso en Espana. *Child Abuse & Neglect, 15*, 495–504.

DeFrancis, V. (1969). *Protecting the child victim of sex crimes committed by adults.* Denver: American Humane Association.

Delfini, L. F., Bernal, M. C., & Rosen, P. M. (1976). Comparison of normal and deviant boys in their homes. In L. A. Hamerlynck, L. C. Handy, & L. J. Mash (Eds.), *Behavior modification and families. 1. Theory and research.* New York: Brunner/Mazel.

Dent, H. R., & Stephenson, G. M. (1979). An experimental study of the effectiveness of different techniques of questioning child witnesses. *British Journal of Social and Clinical Psychology, 18*, 41–51.

Derdeyn, A. P. (1976). Child custody contests in historical perspective. *American Journal of Orthopsychiatry, 133*, 1369–1376.

Derdeyn, A. P., & Scott, E. (1984). Joint custody: A critical analysis and appraisal. *American Journal of Orthopsychiatry, 54*, 199–209.

Dernevik, M. (2000). Preliminary findings on reliability and validity of the Historical-Clinical-Risk assessment in a forensic psychiatric setting. *Psychology Crime & Law, 4*, 127–137.

Derogatis, L. J. (1983). *Symptom Checklist-90 Revised.* Towson, MD: Clinical Psychometric Research.

Derryberry, D., & Rothbart, M. K. (1984). Emotion, attention, and temperament. In C. E. Izard, J. Kagan, & R. B. Zajonc (Eds.), *Emotions, cognition, and behavior* (pp. 132–166). Cambridge: Cambridge University Press.

DeShaney v. Winnebago County Department of Social Services, 489 U.S. 189 (1989), 17, 50, 495n.15, 500n.58, 546n.119.

Dienski, H. (1986). A comparative approach to the question of why human infants develop so slowly. In T. Filed, A. M. Sostek, P. Vietze, & P. H. Liederman (Eds.), *Primate ontogeny, cognition, and social behavior* (pp. 149–168). Hillsdale, NJ: Erlbaum.

Disbrow, M. A., Doerr, H., & Caulfield, C. (1977). Measuring the components of parents' potential for child abuse and neglect. *International Journal of Child Abuse and Neglect, 1*, 279–296.

Dix, T. (1991). The affective organization of parenting: Adaptive and maladaptive processes. *Psychological Bulletin, 110*, 3–25.

Dix, T., & Reinhold, D. P. (1991). Chronic and temporary influences on mothers' attributions for children's disobedience. *Merrill Palmer Quarterly, 37*, 251–271.

Dodge, K. A., Pettit, G. S., & Bates, J. E. (1994). Socialization mediators of the relation between socioeconomic status and child conduct problems. *Child Development, 65*, 649–665.

Dolan, M., & Doyle, M. (2000). Violence risk prediction: Clinical and actuarial measures and the role of the Psychopathy Checklist. *British Journal of Psychiatry, 177*, 303–311.

Doran v. United States, 205 F.2d 717 (1953).

Dornbusch, S., Ritter, P., Liederman, P., Roberts, D., & Fraleigh, M. (1987). The relation of parenting style to adolescent school performance. *Child Development, 58*, 1244–1257.

Douglas, K. S., Ogloff, J. R. P., Nicholls, T. L., & Grant, I. (1999). Assessing risk for violence among psychiatric patients: The HCR-20 violence risk assessment scheme and the Psychopathy Checklist: Screening Version. *Journal of Consulting & Clinical Psychology, 67*, 917–930.

Downey, G., & Coyne, J. C. (1990). Children of depressed parents: An integrative review. *Psychological Review, 108*, 50–76.

Drake, B., & Pandey, S. (1996). Understanding the relationship between neighborhood poverty and specific types of child maltreatment. *Child Abuse & Neglect, 20*, 1003–1018.

DSS V. Lail, 517 S.E.2d 463 (S.C.App. 1999).

DuBois, W. E. B. (1899). *The Philadelphia Negro.* Philadelphia: University of Pennsylvania.

Dubowitz, H. (1990). Costs and effectiveness of interventions in child maltreatment. *Child Abuse & Neglect, 14*, 177–186.

Dubowitz, H. (1999). The families of neglected children. In M. E. Lamb (Ed.), *Parenting and child development in "nontraditional" families* (pp. 327–345). Mahwah, NJ: Erlbaum.

Dubowitz, H., Hampton, R. L., Bithoney, W. G., & Newberger, E. H. (1987). Inflicted and noninflicted injuries: Differences in child and familial characteristics. *American Journal of Orthopsychiatry, 57*, 525–535.

Dubowitz, H., Zuckerman, D. M., Bithoney, W. G., & Newberger, E. H. (1989). Child abuse and failure to thrive: Individual, familial, and environmental characteristics. *Violence & Victims, 4*, 191–201.

Duncan, G. J., & Brooks-Gunn, J. (Eds.). *Consequences of growing up poor.* New York: Russell Sage Foundation.

Duncan, G. J., & Rogers, W. (1988). Longitudinal aspects of childhood poverty. *Journal of Marriage and the Family, 50,* 1007–1021.

Duncan, G. J., Yeung, W., Brooks-Gunn, J., & Smith, J. R. (1998). How much does childhood poverty affect the life chances of children? *American Sociological Review, 63,* 406–423.

Dunn, J., & Munn, P. (1985). Becoming a family member: Family conflict and the development of social understanding the second year. *Child Development, 56,* 480–492.

Dutton, D. G., & Kropp, P. R. (2000). A review of domestic violence risk instruments. *Trauma Violence & Abuse, 1,* 171–181.

Duvall, E. M. (1971). *Family development.* Philadelphia: Lippincott.

Dwyer, J. G. (1997). Setting standards for parenting—By what right? *Child Psychiatry and Human Development, 27,* 165–177.

Dyer, F. J. (1997). Application of the Millon inventories in forensic psychology. In T. Millon (Ed.), *The Millon inventories: Clinical and personality assessment* (pp. 124–139). New York: Guilford.

Dyer, F. J. (1999). *Psychological consultation in parental rights cases.* New York: Guilford.

Eckenrode, J., Laird, M., & Doris, J. (1993). School performance and disciplinary problems among abused and neglected children. *Developmental Psychology, 29,* 53–62.

Edelbrock, C., Crnic, K., & Bohnert, A. (1999). Interviewing as communication: An alternative way of administering the Diagnostic Interview Schedule for Children. *Journal of Abnormal Child Psychology, 27,* 447–453.

Edelman, M. W. (1987). *Families in peril: An agenda for social change.* Cambridge, MA: Harvard University Press.

Edin, K., & Lein, L. (1997). *Making ends meet: How single mothers survive welfare and low-wage work.* New York: Russell Sage Foundation.

Egami, Y., Ford, D. E., Greenfield, S. F., & Crum, R. M. (1996). Psychiatric profile and sociodemographic characteristics of adults who report physically abusing or neglecting children. *American Journal of Psychiatry, 153,* 921–928.

Egeland, B., & Farber, I. A. (1984). Infant-mother attachment: Factors related to its development and changes over time. *Child Development, 55,* 753–771.

Egeland, B. Jacobvitz, D., & Papatola, K. (1987). Intergenerational continuity of abuse. In R. Gelles & J. Lancaster (Eds.), *Child Abuse & Neglect: Biosocial dimensions* (pp. 255–276). Chicago: Aldine.

Egeland, B., Sroufe, L. A., & Erickson, M. (1993). The developmental consequences of different patterns of maltreatment. *Child Abuse & Neglect, 7,* 459–469.

Eiden, R. D., & Reifman, A. (1996). Effects of Brazelton demonstrations on later parenting: A meta-analysis. *Journal of Pediatric Psychology, 21,* 857–868.

Eisenstadt v. Baird, 405 U.S. 438 (1972).

Elder, G. H. (1974). *Children of the Great Depression: Social change in life experience.* Chicago: University of Chicago Press.

Ellingson, J. E., Sackett, P. R., & Hough, L. M. (1999). Social desirability corrections in personality assessment measurement: Issues of applicant comparison and construct validity. *Journal of Applied Psychology, 84,* 155–166.

Ellis, A. (1977). *Reason and emotion in psychotherapy.* Secaucus, NJ: Citadel Press.

Emanuel, S. L. (1999). *Constitutional law* (17th ed.). Larchmont, NY: Emanuel Publishing Corp.

Emery, R., & Laumann-Billings, L. (1998). An overview of the nature, causes, and consequences of abusive family relationships: Toward differentiating maltreatment and violence. *American Psychologist, 53,* 121–135.

Endicott, J., & Spitzer, R. L. (1978). A diagnostic interview: The Schedule of Affective Disorders and Schizophrenia. *Archives of General Psychiatry, 35,* 837–844.

Enfield, R. (1987). A model for developing the written forensic report. In P. A. Keller, & S. R. Heyman (Eds.), *Innovations in clinical practice: A sourcebook* (Vol. 6, pp. 379–394). Sarasota, FL: Professional Resource Exchange.

Epperson, D. L., Kaul, J. D., Huot, S. J., Hesselton, D., Alexander, W., & Goldman, R. (1998). Final Report on the Development of the Minnesota Sex Offender Screening Tool-Revised (MnSOST-R). Presented at the Annual Research and Treatment Conference of the Association for the Treatment of Sexual Abusers, Vancouver, British Columbia.

Epstein, M., Markowitz, R., Gallo, D., Holmes, J., & Gryboski, J. (1987). Munchausen syndrome by proxy: Considerations in diagnosis and confirmation by video surveillance. *Pediatrics, 80,* 220–224.

Epstein, M. A., & Bottoms, B. L. (1998). Memories of childhood sexual abuse: A survey of young adults. *Child Abuse & Neglect, 22,* 1217–1238.

Erickson, M. E., & Egeland, B. (1987). A developmental view of the psychological consequences of maltreatment. *School Psychology Review, 16,* 156–168.

Erickson, M. E., Egeland, B., & Pianta, R. C. (1989). The effects of maltreatment on the development of young children. In D. Cicchetti & V. Carlson (Eds.), *Child maltreatment: Theory and research on the causes and consequences of child abuse and neglect* (pp. 647–684). New York: Cambridge University Press.

Erickson, M. F., Korfmacher, J., & Egeland, B. R. (1992). Attachments past and present: Implications for therapeutic intervention with mother-infant dyads. *Development and Psychopathology, 4,* 495–507.

Erikson, E. H. (1963). *Childhood and society* (2nd ed.). New York: Norton.

Erikson, E. H. (1982). *The life cycle completed.* New York: Norton.

Eyberg, S., Bessmer, J., Newcomb, K., Edward, D., & Robinson, E. (1994). *Dyadic Parent-child Interaction Coding System. II: A manual.* Unpublished manuscript. University of Florida, Gainsville, Department of Clinical/Health Psychology.

Eyberg, S., & Ross, A. W. (1978). Assessment of child behavior problems: The validation of a new inventory. *Journal of Clinical Child Psychology, 7,* 113–116.

Fagara v. State, 514 So.2d 295 (Miss.1987).

Fagot, B. I., & Pears, K. C. (1996). Changes in attachment during the third year: Consequences and predictions. *Development and Psychopathology, 8,* 325–344.

Falk, P. J. (1989). Lesbian mothers: Psychosocial assumptions in family law. *American Psychologist, 44,* 941–947.

Famularo, R., Kinscherff, R., Bunshaft, D. Spivak, G., & Fenton, T. (1989). Parental compliance to court-ordered treatment interventions in cases of child maltreatment. *Child Abuse & Neglect, 13,* 507–514.

Famularo, R., Kinscherff, R., & Fenton, T. (1992). Parental substance abuse and the nature of child maltreatment. *Child Abuse & Neglect, 16,* 475–483.

Famulero, R., Stone, K., Barnum, R., & Wharton, R. (1986). Alcoholism and severe child maltreatment. *American Journal of Orthopsychiatry, 36,* 481–485.

Fanshel, D. (1972). *Far from the reservation: The transracial adoption of American Indian children.* Metuchen, NJ: Scarecrow Press.

Faust, D., & Ziskin, J. (1988). The expert witness in psychology and psychiatry. *Science, 241,* 31–35.

Feher, T. (1988). The alleged molestation victim, the rules of evidence, and the Constitution: Should children really be seen and not heard? *American Journal of Criminal Law, 14,* 227.

Fenichel, O. (1955). The economics of pseudologia phantastica. In H. Fenichel & D. Rapaport (Eds.), *the Collected Papers, Second Series,* p. 133. London: Routledge and Kegan Paul.

Ferenczi, S. (1993). On the definition of introjection. In G. H. Pollack (Ed.), *Pivotal papers on identification* (pp. 53–55). Madison, CT: International Universities Press.

Fiegelman, W., & Silverman, A. R. (1983). *Chosen children*. New York: Praeger.

Field, T. (1995). Infants of depressed mothers. *Infant Behavioral Development, 18*, 1–13.

Field, T. M., Widmayer, S. Adler, S., & De Cubas, M. (1990). Teenage parenting in different cultures, family constellations, and caregiving environments: Effects of infant development. *Infant Mental Health Journal, 11*, 158–174.

Finkelhor, D. (1979). *Sexually victimized children*. New York: Free Press.

Finkelhor, D. (1984). *Child sexual Abuse: New theory and research*. New York: Free Press.

Finkelhor, D. (1986). Sexual abuse: Beyond the family system approach. In T. S. Trepper & M. J. Barrett (Eds.), *Treating incest: A multiple systems perspective* (pp. 53–65). New York: Haworth Press.

Finkelhor, D. (1998). A comparison of the responses of preadolescents and adolescents in a national victimization survey. *Journal of Interpersonal Violence, 13*, 362–382.

Finkelhor, D. (1990). Early and long-term effects of child sexual abuse: An update. *Professional Psychology: Research and Practice, 21*, 325–330.

Fischbach v. State, 1996WL 145968 (Del.1996).

Fischer, C. T. (1970). Levels of cheating under conditions of informative appeal to honesty, public affirmation of values, and threats of punishment. *Journal of Educational Research, 64*, 12–16.

Fisher, P. A., & Chamberlain, P. (2000). Multidimensional treatment foster care: A program for intensive parenting, family support, and skill building. *Journal of Emotional & Behavioral Disorders, 8*, 155–164.

Fiske, S. T., & Taylor, S. E. (1991). *Social cognition*. New York: McGraw-Hill.

Fivush, R. (1993). Developmental perspectives on autobiographical recall. In G. Goodman & B. Bottoms (Eds.), *Child victims, child witnesses: Understanding and improving testimony*, pp. 1–24. New York: Guilford.

Fivush, R., & Hammond, N. R. (1989). Time and again: Effects of repetition and retention interval on 2-year-olds' event recall. *Journal of Experimental Child Psychology, 47*, 259–273.

Flanagan v. State, 625 So.2d 827 (Fla. 1993).

Flavell, J. H., Flavell, E. R., & Green, F. L. (1986). Development of knowledge about the appearance-reality distinction. *Monographs of the Society for Research in Child Development, 60* (1, Serial No. 212).

Fleagle, J. G. (1988). *Primate adaptation and evolution*. New York: Academic Press.

Flin, R., Boon, J., Knox, A., & Bull, R. (1992). Children's memories following a five-month delay. *British Journal of Psychology, 83*, 323–336.

Fonagy, P. (1999). Psychoanalytic theory from the viewpoint of attachment theory and research. In J. Cassidy & P. R. Shaver (Eds.), *Handbook of attachment: Theory, research, and clinical applications* (pp. 595–624). New York: Guilford.

Fonagy, P., Steele, H., & Steele, M. (1991). Maternal representations of attachment during pregnancy predict the organization of infant-mother attachment at one year of age. *Child Development, 62*, 891–905.

Fonagy, P., & Target, M. (1997). Attachment and reflective function: Their role in self-organization. *Development and Psychopathology, 9*, 679–700.

Fontana, V. (1973). The diagnosis of the maltreatment syndrome in children. *Pediatrics, 51*, 780–782.

Forehand, R., & Atkeson, B. (1977). Generality of treatment effects with parents as therapists: A review of assessment and implementation procedures. *Behavior Therapy, 8*, 575–593.

Forehand, R., & Kotchick, B. A. (1996). Cultural diversity: A wake-up call for parent training. *Behavior Therapy, 27*, 187–206.

Fox, L., Long, S. H., & Langlois, A. (1991). Patterns of language comprehension deficits in abused and neglected children. *Journal of Speech and Hearing Disorders, 53*, 239–244.

Fox, R. A. (1992). Development of an instrument to measure the behaviors and expectations of parents of young children. *Journal of Pediatric Psychology, 17,* 231–239.

Fox, R. A. & Bentley, K. S. (1992). Validity of the Parenting Inventory: Young Children. *Psychology in the Schools, 29,* 101–107.

Fox, R. A., & Hennick, E. P. (1996). Evaluating a training program for parental educators. *Psychological Reports, 79,* 1143–1150.

Fox, R. A., Platz, D. L., Bentley, K. S. (1995). Maternal factors related to parenting practices, developmental expectations, and perceptions of child behavior problems. *The Journal of Genetic Psychology, 156,* 431–441.

Fracasso, M. P., Busch-Rossnagal, N. A., & Fisher, C. B. (1994). The relationship of maternal behavior and acculturation in the quality of attachment in Hispanic infants living in New York City. *Hispanic Journal of Behavioral Sciences, 16,* 143–154.

Frank, G. (1980). Treatment needs of children in foster care. *American Journal of Orthopsychiatry, 50,* 256–263.

Frankel, K. A., & Harmon, R. J. (1996). Depressed mothers: They don't always look as bad as they feel. *Journal of the American Academy of Child and Adolescent Psychiatry, 35,* 289–298.

Freud, A. (1965). *Normality and pathology in childhood: Assessments of development.* New York: International Universities Press.

Freud, S. (1957). Five lectures on psycho-analysis. In J. Strachey (Ed. and Trans.), *The standard edition of the complete psychological works of Sigmund Freud* (Vol. 11, pp. 3–56). London: Hogarth Press. (Original work published 1910).

Freud, S. (1961). The ego and the id. In J. Strachey (Ed. and Trans.), *The standard edition of the complete psychological works of Sigmund Freud* (Vol. 19, pp. 19–27). London: Hogarth Press. (Original work published 1923).

Freud, S. (1981). Analysis terminable and interminable. In J. Strachey (Ed. and Trans.), *The standard edition of the complete psychological works of Sigmund Freud* (Vol. 23, pp. 216–253). London: Hogarth Press. (Original work published 1937).

Friedrich, W. (1990). *Psychotherapy of sexually abused children and their families.* New York: Norton.

Friedrich, W. N. (1992). *Child Sexual Behavior Inventory.* Odessa, FL: Psychological Assessment Resources.

Friman, P. C., Handwerk, M. L., Smith, G. L., Larzelere, R. E., Lucas, C. P., & Shaffer, D. M. (2000). External validity of conduct and oppositional defiant disorders determined by the NIMH Diagnostic Interview Schedule for Children. *Journal of Abnormal Child Psychology, 28,* 277–286.

Frodi, A. M., & Lamb, M. E. (1980). Child abusers' responses to infant smiles and cries. *Child Development, 51,* 238–241.

Fromuth, M. E., (1986). The relationship of childhood sexual abuse with later psychological and sexual adjustment in a sample of college women. *Child Abuse & Neglect, 10,* 5–15.

Frudi, N., & Goss, A. (1979). Parental anger: A general population survey. *Child Abuse & Neglect, 3,* 331–333.

Frye v. U.S., 293 F. 1013, 1014 (D.C.Cir.1923).

Fulero, S. M. & Finkel, N. J. (1991). Barring ultimate issue testimony: An "insane" rule? *Law and Human Behavior, 15,* 495–507.

Fundudis, T. (1989). Children's memory and the assessment of possible child sex abuse. *Journal of Child psychology & Psychiatry & Allied Disciplines, 30,* 337–346.

Furstenberg, F. F. (1988). Child care after divorce and remarriage. In E. M. Hetherington & J. D. Aresteh (Eds.), *Impact of divorce, single parenting, and stepparenting on children* (pp. 245–261). Hillsdale, NJ: Erlbaum.

Furstenberg, F., & Brooks-Gunn, J. (1987). *Adolescent mothers in later life.* New York: Cambridge University Press.

Furstenberg, F., Brooks-Gunn, J., & Levine, J. (1990). The children of teenage mothers: Patterns of early childbearing in two generations. *Family Planning Perspectives, 22*, 54–61.

Furstenberg, F. F., & Teitler, J. (1994). Reconsidering the effects of marital disruption: What happens to children of divorce in early adulthood? *Journal of Family Issues, 15*, 173–190.

Gabel, S. (1992). Children of incarcerated and criminal parents: Adjustment, behavior, and prognosis. *Bulletin of the American Academy of Psychiatry and the Law, 20*, 33–45.

Gadsden, V. L. (1999). Black families in intergenerational and cultural perspective. In M. E. Lamb (Ed.), *Parenting and child development in "nontraditional" families* (pp. 221–246). Mahwah, NJ: Erlbaum.

Gaensbauer, T. J. (1995). Trauma in the preverbal period: Symptoms, memories, and developmental impact. *Psychoanalytic Study of the Child, 50*, 122–149.

Galen, L. W., Brower, K. J., Gillespie, B. W., & Zucker, R. A. (2000). Sociopathy, gender, and treatment outcome among outpatient substance abusers. *Drug & Alcohol Dependence, 61*, 23–33.

Galinsky, E. (1971). *Between generations: The six stages of parenthood.* New York: Berkeley.

Ganong, L. H., & Coleman, M. (1994). *Remarried family relationships.* Thousand Oaks: Sage.

Garb, H. N. (2000). Computers will become increasingly important for psychological assessment: Not that there's anything wrong with that! *Psychological Assessment, 12*, 31–39.

Garbarino, J., & Kostelny, K. (1992). Child maltreatment as a community problem. *Child Abuse & Neglect, 16*, 455–464.

Garber, J., & Dodge, K. A. (Eds.). (1991). *The development of emotion regulation and dysregulation.* Cambridge: Cambridge University Press.

Garcia Coll, C. T., Meyer, E. C., & Brillon, L. (1995). Ethnic and minority parenting. In M. H. Bornstein (Ed.), *Handbook of parenting: Biology and ecology of parenting* (Vol. 2, pp. 189–210). Mahwah, NJ: Erlbaum.

Gaudin, J. M. (1994). *Child neglect: A guide for intervention (The User Manual Series).* Washington, DC: U. S. Department of Health and Human Services.

Gaudin, J. M., & Dubowitz, H. (1997). Family functioning in neglectful families: Recent research. In J. Berrick & N. Barth (Eds.), *Child Welfare Research Review* (Vol. 2, pp. 28–26). New York: Columbia University Press.

Gaudin, J. M., & Polansky, N. A. (1986). Social distancing of the neglectful family: Sex, race, and social class influence. *Children and Youth Services Review, 8*, 1–12.

Gaudin, J. M., Polansky, N. A., Kilpatrick, A. C., & Shilton, P. (1993). *Family structure and functioning in neglectful families* (Final report: National Center on Child Abuse and Neglect, Grant No. 90 CA-1400). Washington, DC: National Clearing House on Child Abuse and Neglect.

Geer, T. M., Becker, J. V., Gray, S. R., & Krauss, D. (2001). Predictors of treatment completion in a correctional sex offender treatment program. *International Journal of Offender Therapy & Comparative Criminology, 45*, 302–313.

Geiger, B. (1996). *Fathers as primary caregivers.* Westport, CT: Greenwood.

Geiselman, R. E. (1999). Commentary on recent research with the cognitive interview. *Psychology Crime & Law, 5*, 197–202.

Geiselman, R. E., & Fisher, R. P. (1985). *Interviewing victims and witnesses of crime. Research in Brief.* Washington, DC: National Institute of Justice.

Geiselman, R. E., Fisher, R. P., Firstenberg, I., Hutton, L. A., Sullivan, S., Avetissian, I., & Proski, A. (1984). Enhancement of eyewitness memory: An empirical evaluation of the cognitive interview. *Journal of Police Science and Administration, 12*, 74–80.

Geiselman, R. E., Saywitz, K. J., & Bornstein, G. K. (1993). Effects of cognitive questioning techniques on children's recall performance. In G. S. Goodman, & B. L. Bottoms (Eds.),

Child victims, child witnesses: Understanding and improving testimony (pp. 71–93). New York: Guilford.

Geller, J., & Johnston, C. (1995). Predictors of mothers' responses to child noncompliance: Attributions and attitudes. *Journal of Clinical Child Psychology, 24,* 272–278.

Gelles, R. (1973). Child abuse as psychopathology. *American Journal of Orthopsychiatry, 43,* 611–621.

Genty, P. M. (1998). Permanency planning in the context of parental incarceration: Legal issues and recommendations. *Child Welfare, 77,* 543–559.

George, C., Kaplan, N., & Main, M. (1985). *Adult Attachment Interview.* Unpublished manuscript, University of California, Berkeley.

George, C., & Solomon, J. (1989). Internal working models of caregiving and security of attachment at age six. *Infant Mental Health Journal, 10,* 222–237.

George, C., & Solomon, J. (1996). Representational models of relationships: Links between caregiving and attachment. *Infant Mental Health Journal, 17,* 198–216.

George, C., & Solomon, J. (1999). Attachment and caregiving: The caregiving behavioral system. In J. Cassidy, & P. R. Shaver (Eds.), *Handbook of attachment: Theory, research, and clinical applications* (pp. 649–670). New York: Guilford.

Gibbs, P., & Mueller, U. (2000). Kinship foster care moving to the mainstream: Controversy, policy, and outcomes. *Adoption Quarterly, 4,* 57–87.

Gil, D. (1973). *Violence against children.* Cambridge, MA: Harvard University Press.

Gilmour, K. (1998). An anger management programme for adults with learning disabilities. *International Journal of Language & Communication Disorders, 33,* 403–408.

Glendening v. State, 536 So. 2d 212 (Fla.1988).

Glick, P. C. (1989). Remarried families, stepfamilies, and stepchildren: A brief demographic profile. *Family Relations, 38,* 24–27.

Glidden, L. M. (1991). Adopted children with developmental disabilities: Post-placement family functioning. *Children and Youth Services Review, 13,* 363–377.

Golden, O. (2000). The federal response to child abuse and neglect. *American Psychologist, 55,* 1050–1053.

Goldman, R. L. (1994). Children and youth with intellectual disabilities: Targets for sexual abuse. *International Journal of Disability, Development & Education, 41,* 89–102.

Goldstein, R. D. (1999). *Child abuse and neglect: Cases and materials.* St. Paul, MN: West.

Goldstein, J., Freud, A., & Solnit, A. J. (1979). *Beyond the best interests of the child.* New York: The Free Press.

Goldstein, J., Solnit, A. J., Goldstein, S., & Freud, A. (1996). *The best interests of the child: The least detrimental alternative.* New York: Free Press.

Goldstein, M. J., Kant, H. S., & Hartman, J. J. (1973). *Pornography and sexual deviance.* Los Angeles: University of California Press.

Goldwyn, R., Stanley, C., Smith, V., & Green, J. (2000). The Manchester Child Attachment Story Task: Relationship with parental AAI, SAT and child behaviour. *Attachment & Human Development, 2,* 71–84.

Goodman, G. S. (Ed.). (1984). The child witness. *Journal of Social issues, 40.*

Goodman, G., Aman, C., & Hirschman, J. (1987). Child sexual abuse and physical Abuse: Children's testimony. In S. Ceci, M. Toglia, & D. Ross (Eds.), *Children's eyewitnesses memory,* pp. 1–23. New York: Springer-Verlag.

Goodman, G. S., Hirschman, J., Hepps, D., & Rudy, L. (1991). Children's memory for stressful events. *Merrill-Palmer Quarterly, 37,* 109–158.

Goodman, G. S., Quas, J., Batterman-Faunce, J. M., Riddlesberger, M., & Kuhn, J. (1994). Predictors of accurate and inaccurate memories of traumatic events experienced in childhood. *Consciousness and Cognition, 3,* 269–294.

Goodman, G. S., & Reed, R. S. (1986). Age differences in eyewitness testimony. *Law and Human Behavior, 10*, 317–332.

Goodman, G. S., Rudy, L., Bottoms, B. L., & Aman, C. (1990). Children's concerns and memory: Issues of ecological validity in the study of children's eyewitness testimony. In R. Fivush & J. Hudson (Eds.), *Knowing and remembering young children: Emory symposia in cognition* (Vol. 3, pp. 249–284). New York: Cambridge University Press.

Goodman, G. S., Sharma, A., Golden, M., & Thomas, S. (1991, April). *The effects of mothers' and strangers' interviewing strategies on children's reporting of real-life events.* Paper presented at the biennial meeting of the Society for Research in Child Development, Seattle, WA.

Gopkik, A., & Astington, J. W. (1988). Children's understanding of representational change and its relation to the understanding of false belief and the appearance-reality distinction. *Child Development, 59*, 26–37.

Gordon, B. N., Schroeder, C. S., Ornstein, P. A., & Baker-Ward, L. E. (1995). Clinical implications of research on memory development. In T. Ney (Ed.), *True and false allegations of child sexual Abuse: Assessment and case management* (pp. 99–124). Philadelphia, PA: Brunner/Mazel.

Gottman, J. S. (1990). Children of gay and lesbian parents. In F. W. Bozett & M. B. Sussman, (Eds.), *Homosexuality and family relations* (pp. 177–196). New York: Harrington Park Press.

Grann, M., Belfrage, H., & Tengstroom, A. (2000). Actuarial assessment of risk for violence: Predictive validity of the VRAG and the historical part of the HCR-20. *Criminal Justice & Behavior, 27*, 97–114.

Graziano, A. M. (1994). Why we should study subabusive violence against children. *Journal of Interpersonal Violence, 9*, 412–419.

Grbich, C. (1992). Societal response to familial role change in Australia: Marginalisation or social change? *Journal of Comparative Family Studies, 23*, 79–94.

Green, A. H. (1998). Factors contributing to the generational transmission of child maltreatment. *Journal of the American Academy of Child & Adolescent Psychiatry, 37*, 1334–1336.

Green, A. H. (1993). Child sexual abuse: Immediate and long-term effects and intervention. *Journal of the American Academy of Child and Adolescent Psychiatry, 32*, 890–902.

Green, J., Stanley, C., Smith, V., & Goldwyn, R. (2000). A new method of evaluating attachment representations in the young school-age children: The Manchester Child Attachment Story Task (MCAST). *Attachment & Human Development, 2*, 48–70.

Greenberg, M. A., & Stone, A. A. (1992). Emotional disclosure about traumas and its relation to health: Effects of previous disclosure and trauma severity. *Journal of Personality and Social Psychology, 63*, 75–84.

Greenberg, S. (1990). Conducting unbiased sexual abuse evaluations. *Preventing Sexual Abuse*, 8–14.

Greene, B. (1990). Sturdy bridges: Role of African-American mothers in the socialization of African-American children. In J. P. Knowles & E. Cole (Eds.), *Woman-defined motherhood* (pp. 205–225). New York: Harrington Park Press.

Greene, B. (1995). African-American families: A legacy of vulnerability and resilience. *National Forum, 75*, 29–32.

Greene, E., Flynn, M. A., & Loftus, E. F. (1982). Inducing resistance to misleading information. *Journal of Verbal Learning and Verbal Behavior, 21*, 207–219.

Greenspan, S. I. (1992). *Infancy and early childhood: The practice of clinical assessment and intervention with emotional and developmental challenges.* Madison, CT: International Universities Press.

Greenspan, S. I., & Greenspan, N. T. (1991). *The clinical interview of the child* (2nd ed.). Washington, DC: American Psychiatric Press.

Griffin v. State, 526 So.2d 752 (Fla.Dist.Ct.App.1988).

Griffin, P. A., Steadman, H. J., & Heilbrun, K. (1991). Designing conditional release systems for insanity acquittees. *Journal of Mental Health Administration, 18*, 231–241.

Grisso, T. (1986). *Evaluating competencies: Forensic assessments and instruments.* New York: Plenum.

Grisso, T. (1998). *Forensic evaluation of juveniles.* Sarasota, Florida: Professional Resource Press.

Griswold v. Connecticut, 381 U.S. 479 (1965).

Grotberg, E. H., Feindler, E. L., White, C. B., & Stutman, S. S. (1991). Using anger management for prevention of child abuse. In P. A. Keller & S. R. Heyman (Eds.), *Innovations in clinical practice: A source book* (Vol. 10, pp. 5–21). Sarasota, FL: Professional Resource Press.

Grotevant, H. D., & Kohler, J. K. (1999). Adoptive families. In M. E. Lamb (Ed.), *Parenting and child development in "nontraditional" families* (pp. 161–190). Mahwah, NJ: Erlbaum.

Grotevant, H. D., & McRoy, R. G. (1997). The Minnesota/Texas Adoption Research Project: Implications of openness in adoption for development and relationships. *Applied Developmental Science, 1*, 166–184.

Grotevant, H. D., & McRoy, R. G. (1998). *Openness in adoption: Exploring family connections.* Newbury park, CA: Sage.

Groth, N. (1979). *Men who rape.* New York: Plenum.

Groth, N. A., Hobson, W., & Gary, T. (1982). The child molester: Clinical observations. In J. Conte & D. Shore (Eds.), *Social work and child sexual abuse.* New York: Hawthorn.

Grove, W. M. (1987). The reliability of psychiatric diagnosis. In C. G. Last & M. Hersen (Eds.), *Issues in diagnostic research* (pp. 99–119). New York: Plenum.

Grove, W. M., Zald, D. H., Lebow, B. S., Snitz, B. E., & Nelson, C. (2000). Clinical versus mechanical predictions: A meta-analysis. *Psychological Assessment, 12*, 19–30.

Grubin, D., (1998). *Sex offending against children: Understanding the risk.* Police Research Paper Series Paper 99. London: Home Office.

Grusec, J. E., & Lytton, H. (1988). *Social development.* New York: Springer-Verlag.

Grusec, J. E., & Walters, G. C. (1991). Psychological abuse and childrearing belief systems. In R. H. Starr, & D. A. Wolfe (Eds.), *The effects of child abuse and neglect: Issues and research* (pp. 186–202). London: Guilford.

Gudjonsson, G. H. (1992). *The psychology of interrogations, confessions, and testimony.* London: Wiley.

Gutman, H. G. (1976). *The Black family in slavery and freedom 1750–1925.* New York: Vintage Books.

Hadden v. State, 690 So. 2d 573 (1997).

Hairston, C. F. (1998). The forgotten parent: Understanding the forces that influence incarcerated fathers' relationships with their children. *Child Welfare, 77*, 617–637.

Hall, G. C. N. (1992). Sexual aggression against children: A conceptual perspective of etiology. *Criminal Justice and Behavior, 19*, 8–23.

Hamby, S. L., & Finkelhor, D. (2000). The victimization of children: Recommendations for assessment and instrument development. *Journal of the American Academy of Child & Adolescent Psychiatry, 39*, 829–840.

Hanson, R. K. (1997). *The development of a brief actuarial risk scale for sexual offense recidivism.* Department of the Solicitor General of Canada, Public Works and Government Services Canada, cat. No. JS4-1/1997-4E.

Hanson, R. K., (1998). What do we know about sex offender risk assessment? *Psychology, Public Policy & the Law, 4*, 50–72.

Hanson, R. K., & Harris, A. J. R. (2000). Where should we intervene? Dynamic predictors of sexual assault recidivism. *Criminal Justice & Behavior, 27*, 6–35.

Hanson, R. K., & Thornton, D. (1999). *Static-99: Improving actuarial assessments for sex offenders*. Ottawa, Ontario, Canada: Department of the Solicitor General of Canada.

Hanson, R. K., & Thornton, D. (2000). Improving risk assessments for sex offenders: A comparison of three actuarial scales. *Law & Human Behavior, 24*, 119–136.

Hanson, T. L., McLanahan, S., & Thomson, E. (1997). Economic resources, parental practices, and children's well-being. In G. Duncan & J. Brooks-Gunn (Eds.), *Consequences of growing up poor* (pp. 190–238). New York: Russell Sage Foundation.

Hanson, W. E., Claiborn, C. D., & Kerr, B. (2001). Differential effects of two test-interpretation styles in counseling: A field study. In C. E. Hill (Ed.), *Helping skills: The empirical foundation* (pp. 401–412). Washington, DC: American Psychological Association.

Hare, R. D. (1991). The Hare PCL-R Manual. North Tonawanda, NY: Multi Health Systems.

Hare, R. D. (1998). The Hare PCL-R: Some issues concerning its use and misuse. *Legal & Criminological Psychology, 3*, 101–122.

Hare, R. D., Clark, D., Grann, M., & Thornton, D. (2000). Psychopathy and the predictive validity of the PCL-R: An international perspective. *Behavioral Sciences & the Law, 18*, 623–645.

Hare, J., & Richards, L. (1993). Children raised by lesbian couples: Does the context of birth affect father and partner involvement? *Family Relations, 42*, 249–255.

Harris, G. T., Rice, M. E., & Quinsey, V. L. (1993). Violent recidivism of mentally disordered offenders: The development of a statistical prediction instrument. *Criminal Justice and Behavior, 20*, 315–335.

Harkness, S., & Super, C. M. (1995). Culture and parenting. In M. H. Bornstein (Eds.), *Handbook of parenting: Biology and ecology of parenting* (Vol. 2, pp. 211–234). Mahwah, NJ: Erlbaum.

Harlow, H. F. (1962). The development of affectional patterns in infant monkeys. In B. M. Foss (Ed.), *Determinants of infant behavior* (Vol. 1, pp. 75–88). New York: Wiley.

Harlow, H. F., & Harlow, M. K. (1965). The affectional systems. In A. M. Schrier, H. F. Harlow, & F. Stollnitz (Eds.), *Behavior of non-human primates* (Vol. 2, pp. 287–334). New York: Academic Press.

Harrington, D., Dubowitz, H., Black, M. M., & Binder, A. (1995). Maternal substance use and neglectful parenting: Relations with children's development. *Journal of Clinical Child Psychology, 24*, 258–263.

Harris, A. (1996). False memory? False memory syndrome? The so-called false memory syndrome? *Psychoanalytic Dialogues, 6*, 155–187.

Harris, P., Brown, E., Marriott, C., Whittall, S., & Harmer, S. (1991). Monsters, ghosts and witches: Testing the limits of the fantasy-reality distinction in young children. *British Journal of Developmental Psychology, 9*, 105–123.

Harrison, A. O., Wilson, M. N., Pine, C. J., Chan, S. Q., & Buriel, R. (1990). Family ecologies of ethnic minority children. *Child Development, 61*, 347–362.

Harrison, K. (1997). Parental training for incarcerated fathers: Effects on attitudes, self-esteem, and children's self perceptions. *Journal of Social Psychology, 137*, 588–593.

Hart, S. D., Cox, D. N., & Hare, R. D. (1994). *Hare Psychopathy Checklist: Screening Version (PCL-SV)*. Odessa, FL: Psychological Assessment Resources.

Hartman, C., & Burgess, A. (1989). Sexual abuse of children: Causes and consequences. In D. Cicchetti & V. Carlson (Eds.), *Child maltreatment: Theory and research on the causes and consequences of child abuse and neglect* (pp. 95–128). Cambridge, MA: Cambridge University Press.

Harwood, R. L., & Miller, J. G. (1991). Perceptions of attachment behavior: A comparison of Anglo and Puerto Rican mothers. *Merrill-Palmer Quarterly, 37*, 583–599.

Harwood, R. L., Scholmerich, A., Ventura-Cook, E., Schulze, P., & Wilson, S. P. (1996). Culture and class influences on Anglo and Puerto-Rican mothers' beliefs regarding long-term socialization goals and child behavior. *Child Development, 67*, 2446–2461.

Haskett, M. E., Myers, L. W., Pirrello, V. E., & Dombalis, A. O. (1995). Parenting style as a mediating link between parental emotional health and adjustment of maltreated children. *Behavior Therapy, 26*, 625–642.

Haskett, M. E., Scott, S. S., & Fann, K. D. (1995). Child Abuse Potential Inventory and parenting behavior: Relationship with high-risk correlates. *Child Abuse & Neglect, 19*, 1483–1495.

Hatch-Maillette, M. A., Scalora, M. J., Huss, M. T., & Baumgartner, J. V. (2001). Criminal thinking patterns: Are child molesters unique? *International Journal of Offender Therapy & Comparative Criminology, 45*, 102–117.

Haugaard, J. J. (1993). Young children's classification of the corroboration of a false statement as the truth or a lie. *Law and Human Behavior, 17*, 645–659.

Haugaard, J. J. (2000). The challenge of defining sexual abuse. *American Psychologist, 35*, 1036–1039.

Haugaard, J. J., & Emery, R. E., (1989). Methodological issues in child sexual abuse research. *Child Abuse & Neglect, 13*, 89–101.

Haugaard, J. J., Reppucci, N. D., Laird, J. & Nauful, T. (1991). Children's definitions of the truth and their competency as witnesses in legal proceedings. *Law and Human Behavior, 15*, 253–271.

Hauser, R., & Sweeney, M. (1997). Does poverty in adolescence affect the life chances of high school graduates? In G. Duncan & J. Brooks-Gunn (Eds.), *Consequences of growing up poor* (pp. 541–595). New York: Sage.

Haveman, R., & Wolfe, B. (1994). *Succeeding generations on the effects of investments in children.* New York: Sage.

Haveman, R., & Wolfe, B. (1995). The determinants of children's attainments: A review of methods and findings. *Journal of Economic Literature, 33*, 1829–1878.

Hayes, B. K., & Delamothe, K. (1997). Cognitive interviewing procedures and suggestibility in children's recall. *Journal of Applied Psychology, 82*, 562–577.

Haynes, S. N. & Hron, W. F. (1982). Reactivity in behavioral observation: A review. *Behavioral Assessment, 4*, 369–385.

Heil, S. H., Badger, G. J., & Higgins, S. T. (2001). Alcohol dependence among cocaine-dependent outpatients: Demographics, drug use, treatment outcome and other characteristics. *Journal of Studies on Alcohol, 62*, 14–22.

Heilbrun, K., & Griffin, P. (1999). Forensic treatment: A review of programs and research. In R. Roesch, S. D. Hart, & J. R. P. Ogloff (Eds.), *Psychology and law: The state of the discipline* (pp. 242–274). New York: Kluwer Plenum.

Heilbrun, K., & Heilbrun, A. B. (1995). Risk assessment with the MMPI-2 in forensic evaluations. In Y. S. Ben-Porath, & J. R. Graham (Eds.), *Forensic applications of the MMPI-2: Applied Psychology* (Vol. 2: Individual, social, and community issues, pp. 160–178). Thousand Oaks, CA: Sage.

Heiman, M. L. (1992). Annotation: Putting the puzzle together: Validating allegations of child sexual abuse. *Journal of Child Psychology and Psychiatry, 33*, 311–329.

Heineman, T. V. (2001). Hunger pangs: Transference and countertransference in the treatment of foster children. *Journal of Applied Psychoanalytic Studies, 3*, 5–16.

Helfer, R. E. (1987). The developmental basis of child abuse and neglect: An epidemiological approach. In R. E. Helfer & R. S. Kempe (Eds.), *The battered child* (4th ed., pp. 60–80). Chicago: University of Chicago Press.

Helfer, R. E., & Kempe, R. S. (Eds.) (1987). *The battered child* (4th ed.). Chicago: University of Chicago Press.

Helfer, M. E., Kempe, R. S., & Krugman, R. D. (Eds.) (1997). *The battered child* (5th ed.). Chicago: University of Chicago Press.

Heller, M. (1996). Should breaking up be harder to do? The ramifications a return to a fault-based system would have upon domestic violence. *Virginia Journal of Social Policy and Law, 4,* 263–264.

Heller, M. C., Sobel, M., & Tanaka-Matsumi, J. (1996). A functional analysis of verbal interactions of drug-exposed children and their mothers: The utility of sequential analysis. *Journal of Clinical Psychology, 52,* 687–697.

Hendrick v. State, 257 Ga. 514-361 S.E.2d 169 (1987).

Herbert, J., & Hayne, H. (2000). Memory retrieval by 18–30-month-olds: Age-related changes in representational flexibility. *Developmental Psychology, 36,* 473–484.

Herman, J. L., & Harvey, M. R. (1997). Adult memories of childhood trauma: A naturalistic clinical study. *Journal of Traumatic Stress, 10,* 557–571.

Herman, J. L., & Schatzow, E. (1987). Recovery and verification of memories of childhood sexual trauma. *Psychoanalytic Psychology, 4,* 1–14.

Herrenkohl, E. C., & Herrenkohl, R. C. (1979). A comparison of abused children and their nonabused siblings. *Journal of the American Academy of Child Psychiatry, 18,* 260–269.

Herrenkohl, E. C., & Herrenkohl, R. C. (1981). Some antecedents and developmental consequences of child maltreatment. In R. Risley & D. Cicchetti (Eds.), *Developmental perspectives on child maltreatment* (pp. 57–76). San Francisco: Jossey-Bass.

Herrenkohl, E. C., Herrenkohl, R. C., & Toedtler, L. (1983). Perspectives on the intergenerational transmission of abuse. In D. Finkelhor, R. Gelles, G. Hotaling, & M. Straus (Eds.), *The dark side of families* (pp. 305–316). Beverly Hills, CA: Sage.

Herrerias, C. (1988). Prevention of child abuse and neglect in the Hispanic community: The MADRE Parent Education Program. *Journal of Primary Prevention, 9,* 104–119.

Hess, P. (1988). Case and context. Determinants of planned visit frequency in foster family care. *Child Welfare, 67,* 311–326.

Hess, P. M. (1987). Parental visiting of children in foster care: Current knowledge and research agenda. *Children & Youth Services Review, 9,* 29–50.

Hetherington, E. M. (1993). An overview of the Virginia longitudinal study of divorce and remarriage with a focus on early adolescence. *Journal of Family Psychology, 7,* 1–18.

Hetherington, E. M., & Stanley-Hagan, M. M. (1999). Stepfamilies. In M. E. Lamb (Ed.), *Parenting and child development in "nontraditional" families* (pp. 137–160). Mahwah, NJ: Erlbaum.

Hetherington, E. M., Clingempeel, W. G., Anderson, E. R., Deal, J., Stanley-Hagan, M., Hollier, E. A., & Lindner, M. (1992). Coping with marital transitions: A family systems perspective. *Monographs of the Society for Research in Child Development, 57*(2–3, Serial No. 227).

Hetherington, E. M., & Jodl, K. M. (1994). Stepfamilies as settings for child development. In A. Booth & J. Dunn (Eds.), *Stepfamilies: Who benefits? Who does not?* (pp. 55–79). Hillsdale, NJ: Erlbaum.

Hewitt, S. (1999). *Assessing preschool children with allegations of abuse.* Thousand Oaks, CA: Sage.

Hillson, J. J. C., & Kupier, N. A. (1994). A stress and coping model of child maltreatment. *Clinical Psychology Review, 14,* 261–285.

Hinde, R. A. (1979). *Towards understanding relationships.* London: Academic Press.

Hinde, R. A. (1982). *Ethnology.* New York: Oxford University Press.

Hindle, D. (2000). Assessing children's perspectives on sibling placements in foster or adoptive homes. *Clinical Child Psychology & Psychiatry, 5,* 613–625.

Hipwell, A. E., & Kumar, R. (1996). Maternal psychopathology and prediction of outcome based on mother-infant interaction ratings (BMIS). *British Journal of Psychiatry, 169,* 655–661.

Ho, D. Y. F. (1989). Continuity and variation in Chinese patterns of socialization. *Journal of Marriage and the Family, 51,* 149–163.

Hobbs, G. F., Hobbs, C. J., & Wynne, J. M. (1999). Abuse of children in foster and residential care. *Child Abuse & Neglect, 23,* 1239–1252.

Hochschild, A. R. (1979). Emotion work, feeling rules, and social structure. *American Journal of Sociology, 85,* 551–575.

Hoeffer, B. (1981). Children's acquisition of sex-role behavior in lesbian-mother families. *American Journal of Orthopsychiary, 5,* 536–544.

Hoffman-Plotkin, D., & Twentyman, C. T. (1984). A multimodal assessment of behavioral and cognitive deficits in abused and neglected preschoolers. *Child Development, 55,* 794–802.

Holbrook, M. I. (1997). Anger management training in prison inmates. *Psychological Reports, 81,* 623–626.

Holden, E. W., & Banez, G. A. (1996). Child abuse potential and parenting stress within maltreating families. *Journal of Family Violence, 11,* 1–12.

Holden, G. W., & Edwards, L. A. (1989). Parental attitudes toward child rearing: Instruments, issues, and implications. *Psychological Bulletin, 106,* 29–58.

Holzworth-Munroe, A., & Stuart, G. L. (1994). Typologies of male batterers: Three subtypes and the differences among them. *Psychological Bulletin, 116,* 476–497.

Hooper v. Rockwell, 334 S.C. 281, 315 S.E.2d (1999).

Hopf, C., (1993). Authoritarians and their families: Qualitative studies on the origins of authoritarian dispositions. In W. F. Stone, G. Lederer, & R. Christie (Eds.), *Strength and weakness: The authoritarian personality today* (pp. 119–143). New York: Springer-Verlag.

Howard, C. A. (1993). Factors influencing a mother's response to her child's disclosure of incest. *Professional Psychology: Research and Practice, 24,* 176–181.

Howells, K. (1981). Adult sexual interest in children: Considerations relevant to theories of etiology. In M. Cook & K. Howells (Eds.), *Adult sexual interest in children.* New York: Academic Press.

Howells, P. M., Rogers, C., & Wilcock, S. (2000). Evaluating a cognitive behavioural approach to teaching anger management skills to adults. *British Journal of Learning Disabilities, 28,* 137–142.

Howes, C., & Segal, J. (1993). Children's relationships with alternative caregivers: The special case of maltreated children removed from their homes. *Journal of Applied Developmental Psychology, 17,* 71–81.

Hudson, J., & Nelson, K. (1986). Repeated encounters of a similar kind: Effects of familiarity on children's autobiographic memory. *Cognitive Development, 1,* 253–271.

Hudson, J. A., & Sheffield, E. G. (1999). The role of reminders in young children's memory development. In L. Balter & C. Tamis-LeMonda (Eds.), *Child psychology: A handbook of contemporary issues* (pp. 193–214). Philadelphia, PA: Psychology Press/Taylor & Francis.

Huffaker, M. L. (2001). A parent's addiction: The judicial disposition of children to drug abusing parents. *Law & Psychology Review, 25,* 145–160.

Huffman, M. L., Crossman, A. M., & Ceci, S. J. (1997). "Are false memories permanent?": An investigation of the long-term effects of source misattributions. *Consciousness & Cognition: An International Journal, 6,* 482–490.

Huggins, S. L. (1989). A comparative study of self-esteem of adolescent children of divorced lesbian mothers and divorced heterosexual mothers. In F. W. Bozett, (Ed.), *Homosexuality and the family* (pp. 123–135). New York: Harrington Park Press.

Hughes, M., & Grieve, R. (1980). On asking children bizarre questions. *First Language, 1,* 149–160.

Hurd, E. P., Moore, C., & Rogers, R. (1995). Quiet success: Parenting strengths among African Americans. *Families in Society: The Journal of Contemporary Human Services, September,* 434–443.

Hyman, I. E., Husband, T. H., & Billings, F. J. (1995). False memories of childhood experiences. *Applied Cognitive Psychology, 9,* 181–187.

Idaho v. Wright, 497 U.S. 805 (1990).

In the Interest of G.C., A Minor Child, 735 A.2d 1236 (1997).

In the Matter of B.S.M, unpublished opinion, State of Minnesota, Court of Appeals, (1997).

In the Matter of Bryan L., 149 Misc.2d 899, 565 N.Y.S.2d 969 (Fam.Ct.1991).

In the Matter of the Adoption of J.M.H., a Minor, ND 99, 564 N.W.2d 623 (1997).

In re D.K., 245 N.W.2d 644 (S.D. 1976).

In re Doe children, 938 P.2d 178 Haw. Ct. App. (1977).

In re Gault, 387 U.S. 1 (1967).

In re Glenn G., 154 Misc.2d 677, 587 N.Y.S.2d 464 (N.Y.Fam.Ct.1992).

In re Harley C., 203 W. Va. 594, 509 S.E.2d 875 (1998).

In re J.M.P., 669 S.W.2d 298 (Mo.App.1984).

In re Jeffrey E., 557 A.2d 954 (Me.1989).

In re Jose Y., 177A.D.2d 580, 576 N.Y.S.2d 297 (1991).

In re K.L.M., 146 Ill.App.3d 489, 100 Ill. Dec. 197, 496 N.E.2d 1262 (1986).

In re Linda, 362 S.W.2d 782 (Mo.Ct.App.1962).

In re M.R., W.D., & C.J., 452 N.E.2d 1085 (Ind.Ct.App.1983).

In re Montgomery, 316 S.E. 246 N.C. Sup. Ct. (1984).

In re Pardee, 190 Mich App 243, 475 NW2d 870 (1991).

In re Rodney D., A Child Found to be Neglected In re M. Children, Children Found to be Neglected, 91 Misc.2d 677 398 N.Y.W.2d 511 (Fam.Ct.1977).

In re Scott G., 124 A.D.2d 928, 508 N.Y.S.2d 669 (1986).

In re Wachlin, 309 Minn. 370, 245 N.W.2d 183 (Minn.1976).

Insel, T. R. (1997). A neurobiological basis of social attachment. *American Journal of Psychiatry, 154,* 726–735.

Isely v. Capuchin Province, 877 F.Supp. 1055 (E.D.Mich.1995).

Isen, A. M., Means, B., Patrick, R., & Bowicki, G. (1982). Some factors influencing decision-making strategy and risk taking. In M. S. Clark & S. T. Fiske (Eds.), *Affect and cognition* (pp. 243–261). Hillsdale, NJ: Erlbaum.

Iwaniec, D. (1997). Evaluating parent training for emotionally abusive and neglectful parents: Comparing individual versus individual and group intervention. *Research on Social Work Practice, 7,* 329–349.

Izard, C. E. (1984). Emotion-cognition relationships and human development. In C. E. Izard, J. Kagan, & R. B. Zajonc (Eds.), *Emotions, cognition, and behavior* (pp. 17–37). Cambridge: Cambridge University Press.

Izard, C. E. (1991). *The psychology of emotions.* New York: Plenum.

Jackson, A. P. (1994). Psychological distress among single, employed, Black mothers and their perceptions of their young children. *Journal of Social Service Research, 19,* 87–101.

Jacobsen, T., Miller L. J., & Kirkwood, K. P. (1997). Assessing parenting competency in individuals with severe mental illness: A comprehensive services. *Journal of Mental Health Administration, 24,* 189–199.

Jacobson, S. W., & Frye, K. F. (1991). Effect of maternal social support on attachment: Experimental evidence. *Child Development, 62,* 572–582.

Jahoda, M. (1953). The meaning of psychological health. *Social Casework, 34,* 349–354.

Jahoda, M. (1958). *Current concepts of positive mental health.* New York: Basic Books.

Jason, J., & Andereck, N. (1983). Fatal child abuse in Georgia: The epidemiology of severe physical abuse. *Child Abuse & Neglect, 7,* 1–9.

Jackson, J. (Ed.). (1991). *Life in Black America.* Newbury Park, CA: Sage.

Jenny, C., Roesler, T. A., & Poyer, K. L. (1994). Are children at risk for sexual abuse by homosexuals? *Pediatrics, 94,* 41–44.

Johnson, J. E., & McGillicuddy-Delisi, A. (1983). Family environment factors and children's knowledge of rules and conventions. *Child Development, 54*, 218–226.

Johnson, M. K., & Foley, M. A. (1984). Differentiating fact from fantasy: The reliability of children's memory. *Journal of Social Issues, 40*, 33–50.

Johnson, S., Barrett, P. M., Dadds, M. R., Fox, T., & Shortt, A. (1999). The Diagnostic Interview Schedule for Children, Adolescents and Parent: Initial reliability and validity data. *Behaviour Change, 16*, 155–164.

Johnston, J. R., & Straus, R. B. (1999). Traumatized children in supervised visitation: What do they need? *Family & Conciliation Courts Review, 37*, 135–158.

Jones, D. C., & McGraw, J. M. (1987). Reliable and fictitious accounts of sexual abuse in children. *Journal of Interpersonal Violence, 2*, 27–45.

Jones, D. C., Swift, D. J., & Johnson, M. (1988). Nondeliberate memory for a novelty event among preschoolers. *Developmental Psychology, 24*, 641–645.

Kadushin, A. (1988). Neglect in families. In E. W. Nunnally C. S. Chilman, & F. M. Cox (Eds.), *Mental illness, delinquency, addictions, and neglect* (pp. 147–166). Newbury Park, CA: Sage.

Kahan, B., & Crofts Yorker, B. (1991). Munchausen syndrome by proxy: Clinical review and legal issues. *Behavioral Sciences and the Law, 9*, 73–83.

Kail, R. V. (1989). *The development of memory in children* (2nd ed.). New York: Freeman.

Kalichman, S. (2000). *Mandated reporting of suspected child abuse: Ethics, law and policy* (2nd ed.). Washington, DC: American Psychological Association.

Kalish, C. W., Weissman, M., & Bernstein, D. (2000). Taking decisions seriously: Young children's understanding of conventional truth. *Child Development, 71*, 1289–1308.

Kama v. State, 507 So.2d 154 (Fla.Dist.Ct.App.1987).

Kantrowitz, R. M., & Limon, S. M. (2001). *2002 Massachusetts Juvenile Law Sourcebook.* Boston: Massachusetts Continuing Legal Education.

Kaufman, J., & Zigler, E. (1987). Do abused children become abusive parents? *American Journal of Orthopsychiatry, 57*, 186–192.

Kazura, K. (2001). Family programming for incarcerated parents: A needs assessment among inmates. *Journal of Offender Rehabilitation, 32*, 67–83.

Keilin, W. G., & Bloom, L. J. (1986). Child custody evaluation practices: A survey of experienced professionals. *Professional Psychology: Research and Practice, 17*, 338–346.

Keith R., 123 Misc.2d 617, 621, 474 N.Y.S.2d 254, 258 (1984).

Kelley, M. L., & Tseng, H. M. (1992). Cultural differences in child rearing: A comparison of immigrant Chinese and Caucasian American mothers. *Journal of Cross-cultural Psychology, 23*, 444–455.

Kelley, M. L., Power, T. G., & Wimbush, D. D. (1992). Determinants of disciplinary practices in low-income Black mothers. *Child Development, 63*, 578–582.

Kelley, S. J. (1992). Parenting stress and child maltreatment in drug-exposed children. *Child Abuse & Neglect, 16*, 317–328.

Kempe, C., Silverman, F., Steele, B., Droegemueller, W., & Silver, H. (1962). The battered-child syndrome. *Journal of the American Medical Association, 181*, 17–24.

Kendall, P. C., Brady, E. U., & Verduin, T. L. (2001). Comorbidity in childhood anxiety disorders and treatment outcome. *Journal of the American Academy of Child & Adolescent Psychiatry, 40*, 787–794.

Kendall, P. C., & Urbain, E. (1982). Social-cognitive approaches to therapy with children. In J. R. Lachenmeyer & M. S. Gibbs (Eds.), *Psychopathology in Childhood* (pp. 298–326). New York: Gardner Press.

Kenrick, J. (2001). "Be a kid": The traumatic impact of repeated separations on children who are fostered and adopted. *Journal of Psychotherapy, 26*, 393–412.

Kent v. U.S., 383 U.S. 541 (1966).

Keri v. State, 179 Ga. App. 664, 347 S.E.2d 236 (1986).

Kermoian, R., & Liederman, P. H. (1986). Infant attachment to mother and child caretaker in an East African community. *International Journal of Behavioral Development, 9*, 455–469.

Kessen, W. (1965). *The child.* New York: Wiley.

Kim, S., McLeod, J. H., & Shantzis, C. (1992). Cultural competence for evaluators working with Asian-Americans. In M. Orlandi (Ed.), *Cultural competence for evaluators.* Washington, DC: U. S. Department of Health and Human Services.

King, M., & Yuille, J. (1987). Suggestibility and the child witness. In S. J. Ceci, M. Toglia, & D. Ross (Eds.), *Children's eyewitness memory* (pp. 24–35). New York: Springer-Verlag.

Kinscherff, R., & Ayoub, C. C. (2000). Legal aspects of Munchausen by proxy. In R. M. Reece et al. (Eds.), *Treatment of child abuse: Common ground for mental health, medical, and legal practitioners* (pp. 242–267). Baltimore, MD: Johns Hopkins University Press.

Kirkpatrick, M. (1996). Lesbians as parents. In R. P. Cabaj & T. S. Stein (Eds.), *Textbook of homosexuality and mental health* (pp. 353–370). Washington, DC: American Psychiatric Press.

Kirkpatrick, M., Smith, C., & Roy, R. (1981). Lesbian mothers and their children: A comparative survey. *American Journal of Orthopsychiatry, 51*, 545–551.

Kiser, L. J., Heston, J., Millsap, P. A., & Pruitt, D. B. (1991). Physical and sexual abuse in childhood: Relationship with post-traumatic stress disorder. *Journal of the American Academy of Child and Adolescent Psychiatry, 30*, 776–783.

Klagsbrun, M., & Bowlby, J. (1976). Responses to separation from parents: A clinical test for young children. *Projective Psychology, 21*, 7–26.

Klaus, M. H., Kennell, J. H., & Klaus, Ph. H. (1995). *Bonding.* Reading, MA: Addison-Wesley.

Klee, L., Kronstadt, D., & Zlotnick, C. (1997). Foster care's youngest: A preliminary report. *American Journal of Orthopsychiatry, 67*, 290–299.

Klein, M. (1980). On Mahler's autistic and symbiotic phases: An exposition and evolution. *Psychoanalysis and Contemporary Thought, 4*, 69–105.

Klein, N. C., Alexander, J. F., & Parsons, B. V. (1977). Impact of family systems intervention on recidivism and sibling delinquency: A model of primary prevention and program evaluation. *Journal of Consulting and Clinical Psychology, 45*, 469–474.

Kleinmuntz, B. (1990). Why we still use our heads instead of the formulas: Toward an integrative approach. *Psychological Bulletin, 107*, 296–310.

Klopfer, P. H. (1971). Mother love: What turns it on? *American Scientist, 59*, 404–407.

Kobak, R. (1999). The emotional dynamics of disruptions in attachment relationships: Implications for theory, research, and clinical intervention. In J. Cassidy, & P. R. Shaver (Eds.), *Handbook of attachment: Theory, research, and clinical applications* (pp. 21–43). New York: Guilford.

Koblinsky, S., & Cruse, D. F. (1981). The role of frameworks in children's retention of sex-related story content. *Journal of Experimental Child Psychology, 31*, 321–331.

Koblinsky, S. A., Morgan, K. M., & Anderson, E. A. (1997). African-American homeless and low-income housed mothers: Comparison of parenting practices. *American Journal of Orthopsychiatry, 6*, 37–47.

Kohn, M. L. (1977). *Class and conformity: A study of values* (2nd ed.). Chicago: University of Chicago Press.

Kolton, D. J., Boer, A., & Boer, D. P. (2001). A revision of the Abel and Becker Cognition Scale for intellectually disabled sexual offenders. *Sexual Abuse: Journal of Research & Treatment, 13*, 217–219.

Konold, T. R., & Abidin, R. R. (2001). Parenting alliance: A multifactor perspective. *Assessment, 8*, 47–65.

Koocher, G. P., & Keith-Spiegel, P. C. (1990). *Children, ethics, & the law: Professional issues and cases.* Lincoln: University of Nebraska Press.

Koocher, G. P., Goodman, G. S., White, C. S., Friedrich, W. N., Sivan, A. B., & Reynolds, C. R. (1995). Psychological science and the use of anatomically detailed dolls in child sexual abuse assessments. *Psychological Bulletin, 118,* 199–222.

Kotelchuck, M. (1982). Child abuse and neglect: Prediction and misclassification. In R. H. Starr (Ed.), *Child abuse prediction: Policy implications* (pp. 67–104). Cambridge, MA: Ballinger.

Kotre, J. (1984). *Outliving the self: Generativity and the interpretation of lives.* Baltimore, MD: Johns Hopkins University.

Kovacs, M. (1992). *Kovacs' Children's Depression Inventory.* North Tonawanda, NY: Multi-Health Systems.

Kovera, M. B., & Borgida, E. (1998). Exerpt scientific testimony on child witnesses in the age of *Daubert.* In S. J. Ceci & H. Hembrooke (Eds.), *Expert witnesses in child abuse case: What can and should be said in court* (pp. 185–215). Washington, DC: American Psychological Association.

Krugman, R., Lenherr, M., Betz, L., & Fryer, G. (1986). The relationship between unemployment and physical abuse of children. *Child Abuse & Neglect, 10,* 415–418.

Kuehnle, K. (1996). *Assessing allegations of child sexual abuse.* Sarasota, FL: Professional Resource Press.

Kutchins, H., & Kirk, S. A. (1986, Winter). The reliability of *DSM-III*: A clinical review. *Social Work Research and Abstracts, 22,* 3–12.

Laan, N. M. A., Loots, G. M. P., Janssen, C. G. C., & Stolk, J. (2001). Foster care for children with mental retardation and challenging behaviour: A follow-up study. *British Journal of Developmental Disabilities, 47,* 3–13.

LaFramboise, T. D. (1988). American Indian mental health policy. *American Psychologist, 43,* 388–397.

Lahey, B. B., Conger, R. D., Atkeson, B. M., & Treiber, F. A. (1984). Parenting behavior and emotional status of physically abusive mothers. *Journal of Consulting and Clinical Psychology, 52,* 1062–1071.

Laible, D. J., & Thompson, R. A. (2000). Mother-child discourse, attachment security, shared positive affect, and early conscience development. *Child Development, 71,* 1424–1440.

Lamb, M. E. (1997). The development of father-infant relationships. In M. E. Lamb (Ed.), *The role of the father in child development* (pp. 261–285). New York: Wiley.

Lamb, M. E. (Ed.). (1999). *Parenting and child development in "nontraditional" families.* Mahwah, NJ: Erlbaum.

Lamb, M. E., Frodi, M., Hwang, C.-P., Frodi, M., & Steinberg, J. (1982). Mother- and father-infant interaction involving play and holding in traditional and nontraditional Swedish families. *Developmental Psychology, 18,* 215–221.

Lamb, M. E., Gaensbauer, T. J., Malkin, C. M., & Schultz, L. A. (1985). The effects of child maltreatment on security of infant-adult attachment. *Infant Behavior and Development, 8,* 35–45.

Lamb, M. E., Sternberg, K. J., & Esplin, P. W. (1994). Factors influencing the reliability and validity of statements made by young victims of sexual maltreatment. *Journal of Applied Developmental Psychology, 15,* 255–280.

Lamb, M. E., Sternberg, K. J., & Esplin, P. W. (1995). Making children into competent witnesses: Reactions to the amicus brief In re Michaels. *Psychology, Public Policy & Law, 1,* 438–449.

Lamb, M. E., Sternberg, K. J., & Thompson, R. A. (1999). The effects of divorce and custody arrangements on children's behavior, development, and adjustment. In M. E. Lamb (Ed.), *Parenting and child development in "nontraditional" families* (pp. 125–136). Mahwah, NJ: Erlbaum.

Lamb, M. E., Thompson, R. A., Gardner, W., & Charnov, E. L. (1985). *Infant-mother attachment: The origins and developmental significance of individual differences in Strange Situation behavior.* Hillsdale, NJ: Earlbaum.

Lamborn, S. D., Mounts, N. S., Steinberg, L., & Dornbusch, S. M. (1991). Patterns of competence and adjustment among adolescents from authoritative, authoritarian, indulgent, and neglectful families. *Child Development, 62,* 1049–1065.

Landreth, G. L., & Lobaugh, A. F. (1998). Filial therapy with incarcerated fathers: Effects on parental acceptance of child, parental stress, and child adjustment. *Journal of Counseling and Development, 76,* 157–165.

Lane, S. (1997a). Assessment of sexually abusive youth. In. G. Ryan & S. Lane (Eds.), *Juvenile sexual offending: Causes, consequences, and correction* (pp. 219–166). San Francisco: Jossey-Bass.

Lane, S. (1997b). The sexual abuse cycle. In. G. Ryan and S. Lane (Eds.), *Juvenile sexual offending: Causes, consequences, and correction* (pp. 77–121). San Francisco: Jossey-Bass.

Langevin, R. (1983). *Sexual strands: Understanding and treating sexual anomalies in men.* Hillsdale, NJ: Erlbaum.

Langlois, J. H., Ritter, J. M., Casey, R. J., & Sawin, D. B. (1995). Infant attractiveness predicts maternal behaviors and attitudes. *Developmental Psychology, 31,* 464–472.

Lantrip v. Commonwealth, 713 S.W.2d 816 (Ky.1986).

Lanyon, R. I. (2001a). Dimensions of self-serving misrepresentations in forensic assessment. *Journal of Personality Assessment, 76,* 169–179.

Lanyon, R. I. (2001b). Psychological assessment procedures in sex offending. *Professional Psychology: Research & Practice, 32,* 253–260.

Laosa, L. M. (1980). Maternal teaching strategies in Chicano and Anglo-American families: The influence of culture and education on maternal behaviors. *Child Development, 51,* 759–765.

Lassiter v. Department of Social Services, 452 U.S. 18 (1981).

Laumann, L. A., & Elliott, R. (1992). Reporting what you have seen: Effects associated with age and mode of questioning on eyewitness reports. *Perceptual and Motor Skills, 75,* 799–818.

Lavin, M., & Sales, B. D. (1998). Moral justifications for limits on expert testimony. In S. J. Ceci & H. Hembrooke (Eds.), *Expert witnesses in child abuse case: What can and should be said in court* (pp. 59–81). Washington, DC: American Psychological Association.

Lawson, K. A., & Hays, J. R. (1989). Self-esteem and stress as factors in abuse of children. *Psychological Reports, 56,* 1259–1265.

Lay, K., Waters, E., & Park, K. A. (1989). Maternal responsiveness and child compliance: The role of mood as a mediator. *Child Development, 60,* 1505–1411.

Lazowski, L. E., Miller F. G., Boye, M. W., & Miller, G. A. (1998). Efficacy of the Substance Abuse Subtle Screening Inventory-3 (SASSI-3) in identifying substance dependence disorders in clinical settings. *Journal of Personality Assessment, 17,* 114–128.

Lee, C. L., & Bates, J. E. (1985). Mother-child interaction and age two years and perceived difficult temperament. *Child Development, 56,* 1314–1325.

Lee, V. E., Burkham, D. T., Zimiles, H., & Ladewski, B. (1994). Family structure and its effect on behavioral and emotional problems in young adolescents. *Journal of Research on Adolescence, 4,* 405–437.

Leger, D. W. Thompson, R. A, Merritt, J. A. B., & Joseph J. (1996). Adult perception of emotional intensity in human infant cries: Effects of infant age and cry acoustics. *Child Development, 67,* 3238–3249.

Leichtman, M., & Ceci, S. J. (1995). Effects of stereotypes and suggestions on preschoolers' reports. *Developmental Psychology, 31,* 568–578.

Lepore, S. J. (1991). Child witness: Cognitive and social factors related to memory and testimony. *Issues in Child Abuse Accusation, 3*, 65–89.

Lepore, S. J., & Sesco, B. (1994). Distorting children's reports and interpretations of events through suggestion. *Journal of Applied Psychology, 79*, 108–120.

Leuger, R. J., Howard, K. I., Martinovich, Z., Lutz, W., Anderson, E. E., & Grissom, G. (2001). Assessing treatment progress of individual patients using expected treatment response models. *Journal of Consulting & Clinical Psychology, 69*, 150–158.

Leutenegger, W. (1972). Newborn size and pelvic dimensions of Australopithecus. *Nature, 240*, 568–569.

Leventhal, J. (1981). Risk factors to child abuse: Methodologic standards in case control studies. *Child Abuse & Neglect, 6*, 113–123.

Levine, M., & Battistoni, L. (1991). The corroboration requirement in child sex abuse cases. *Behavioral Sciences and the Law, 9*, 3–20.

Levine, M., & Levine, A. (1992). *Helping children: A social history.* New York: Oxford University Press.

Levy v. Louisiana, 391 U.S. 68, 71 (1968).

Levy, R. J. (1989). Using "scientific" testimony to prove child sexual abuse. *Family Law Quarterly, 23*, 383–409.

Lewis, C., Wilkins, R., Baker, L., & Woobey, A. (1995). "Is this man your daddy?" Suggestibility in children's eyewitness identification of a family member. *Child Abuse & Neglect, 19*, 739–744.

Leyendecker, B., & Lamb, M. E. (1999). Latino families. In M. E. Lamb (Ed.), *Parenting and child development in "nontraditional" families* (pp. 247–262). Mahwah, NJ: Erlbaum.

Leyendecker, B., Lamb, M. E., Scholmerich, A., & Fracasso, M. P. (1995). The social worlds of 8- and 12-month-old infants: Early experiences in two subcultural contexts. *Social Development, 4*, 194–208.

Liang, B., & Bogat, G. A. (1992, August). *Culture, control and coping: A comprehensive model of social support.* Presented at the annual meeting of the American psychological Association, Washington, DC.

Liaw, F. R., & Brooks-Gunn, J. (1994). Cumulative risk and low-birth weight children's cognitive development and their determinants. *Developmental Psychology, 29*, 1024–1035.

Lin, C-Y. C., & Fu, V. R. (1990). A comparison of child-rearing practices among Chinese, immigrant Chinese, and Caucasian-American parents. *Child Development, 61*, 429–433.

Lindberg, M. (1991). A taxonomy of suggestibility and eyewitness memory: Age, memory process, and focus of analysis. In J. L. Doris (Ed.), *The suggestibility of children's recollections* (pp. 47–55). Washington, DC: American Psychological Association.

Lindsey, E. W. (2001). Foster family characteristics and behavioral and emotional problems of foster children: Practice implications for child welfare, family life education, and marriage and family therapy. *Family Relations: Interdisciplinary Journal of Applied Family Studies, 50*, 19–22.

Lipovsky, J. A., Tidwell, R., Crisp, J., Kilpatrick, D. G., Saunders, B. E., & Dawson, V. L. (1992). Child witnesses in criminal court: Descriptive information from three southern states. *Law and Human Behavior, 16*, 635–650.

Liss, M. B., & McKinley-Pace, M. J. (1999). Best interests of the child: New twists on an old theme. In R. Roesch, S. D. Hart, & J. R. P. Ogloff (Eds.), *Psychology and law: The state of the discipline* (pp. 341–368). New York: Kluwer Plenum.

Loftus, E. F. (1979). *Eyewitness testimony.* Cambridge, MA: Harvard University Press.

Loftus, E. F. (1993). Desperately seeking memories of the first few years of childhood: The reality of early memories. *Journal of Experimental Psychology: General, 122*, 274–277.

Loftus, E. F. (1997). Repressed memory accusations: Devastated families and devastated patients. *Applied Cognitive Psychology, 11*, 25–30.

Loftus, E. F. (2000). Remembering what never happened. In E. Tulving (Ed.), *Memory, consciousness, and the brain: The Tallinn Conference* (pp. 106–118). Philadelphia, PA: Psychology Press/Taylor & Francis.

Loftus, E. F., & Pickrell, J. E. (1995). The formation of false memories. *Psychiatric Annals, 25*, 720–725.

Loftus, E. F., & Zanni, G. (1975). Eyewitness testimony: The influence of wording of a question. *Bulletin of the Psychonomic Society*, 86–88.

Lorenz, K. (1935). *Der Kumpan in der Umwelt des Vogels. Journal of Ornithology, 83*, 137–213.

Loving v. Virginia, 388 U.S. 1, 87 S.Ct. 1817, 18 L.Ed.2d 1010 (1967).

Loyd, B. H., & Abidin, R. R. (1985). Revision of the Parenting Stress Index. *Journal of Pediatric Psychology, 10*, 169–177.

Lyon, T. D., & Saywitz, K. J. (1999). Young maltreated children's competence to take the oath. *Applied Developmental Science, 3*, 16–27.

Lyon, T. D., Saywitz, K. J., Kaplan, D. L., & Dorado, J. S. (2001). Reducing maltreated children's reluctance to answer hypothetical oath-taking competency questions. *Law and Human Behavior, 25*, 81–92.

Maccoby, E. E. (1980). *Social development: Psychological growth in the parent-child relationship.* San Diego, CA: Harcourt Brace Jovanovich.

Maccoby, E. E., & Martin, J. A. (1983). Socialization in the context of the family: Parent-child interaction. In P. H. Mussen (Series Ed.) & E. M. Hetherington (Vol. Ed.), *Handbook of child psychology: Vol 4. Socialization, personality, and social development* (pp. 1–101). New York: Wiley.

Macias v. State, 776 S.W.2d 255 (Tx.App.1989).

MacKinnon Lewis, C., Lamb, M., Arbuckly, B., Baradoran, L., & Volling, B. (1992). The relationship between biased maternal and filial attributions and the aggressiveness of their interactions. *Development and Psychopathology, 4*, 403–415.

MacPhee, D., Fritz, J., & Miller-Heyl, J. (1996). Ethnic variations in personal social networks and parenting. *Child Development, 67*, 3278–3295.

Maddock, J. W. (1988). Child reporting and testimony in incest cases: Comments on the construction and reconstruction of reality. *Behavioral Sciences & the Law, 6*, 201–220.

Magen, R. H., Conroy, K., Hess, P. M., Panciera, A., & Simon, B. L. (2001). Identifying domestic violence in child abuse and neglect investigations. *Journal of Interpersonal Violence, 16*, 580–601.

Mahler, M. S., & Furere, M. (1968). *On human symbiosis and the vicissitudes of individuation: Vol 1. Infantile psychosis.* New York: International Universities Press.

Mahler, M., Pine, F., & Bergman, A. (1975). *The psychological birth of the human infant: Symbiosis and individuation.* New York: Basic Books.

Main, M., & Goldwyn, R. (1984). Predicting rejection of her infant from other's representation of her own experience: Implications for the abused-abusing intergenerational cycle. *Child Abuse & Neglect, 8*, 203–217.

Main, M., & Goldwyn, R. (1994). *Adult attachment scoring and classification systems* (Version 5.3). Unpublished manual. Berkeley, CA: University of California Press.

Main, M., Kaplan, N., & Cassidy, J. (1985). Security in infancy, childhood and adulthood: A move to the level of representation. In I. Bretherton & E. Waters (Eds.), Growing points in attachment theory and research. *Monographs of the Society for Research in Child Development, 50* (1–2, Serial No. 209), 66–104.

Manassis, K., Bradley, S. Goldberg, S. Hood, J., & Swinson, R. P. (1994). Attachment in mothers with anxiety disorders and their children. *Journal of the American Academy of Child and Adolescent Psychiatry, 33*, 1106–1113.

Marchevsky, D. (1998). Current views of solicitors on psychiatric court reports. *Psychological Bulletin, 22*, 33–35.

Margolies, P., & Weintraub, S. (1977). The revised 6-item CRPBI as a research instrument. *Journal of Clinical Psychology, 33*, 472–476.

Marin, B. V., Holmes, D. L., Guth, M., & Kovac, P. (1979). The potential of children as eyewitnesses. *Law and Human Behavior, 3*, 295–306.

Marlatt, G. A. (1996). Commentary on replications of Marlatt's taxonomy: Lest taxonomy become taxidermy: A comment on the relapse replication and extension project. *Addiction, 91 (Supplement)*, 147–153.

Marlatt, G. A., Blume, A. W., & Parks, G. A. (2001). Integrating harm reduction therapy and traditional substance abuse treatment. *Journal of Psychoactive Drugs, 33*, 13–21.

Marques, J. K., Day, D. M., Nelson, C., & Miner, M. H. (1989). The Sex Offender Treatment and Evaluation Project: California's relapse prevention program. In Richard D. Laws (Ed.), *Relapse prevention with sex offenders* (pp. 247–267). New York: Guilford.

Marsden, J., Gossop, M., Stewart, D., Rolfe, A., & Farrell, M. (2000). Psychiatric symptoms among clients seeking treatment for drug dependence: Intake data from the National Treatment outcome Research Study. *British Journal of Psychiatry, 176*, 285–289.

Mart, E. G. (1999). Problems with the diagnosis of factitious disorder by proxy in forensic settings. *American Journal of Forensic Psychology, 17*, 69–82.

Martin, R. D. (1990). *Primate origins and evolution: A phylogenetic reconstruction.* Princeton: Princeton University Press.

Martin, T., & Bumpass, L. (1989). Recent trends in marital disruption. *Demography, 26*, 37–51.

Martino, S., Carroll, K. M., O'Malley, S. S., & Rounsaville, B. J. (2000). Motivational interviewing with psychiatrically ill substance abusing patients. *American Journal on Addictions, 9*, 88–91.

Maryland v. Craig, 497 U.S. 836 (1990).

Massachusetts Department of Social Services. (1989). *Substance abuse and family violence: Part I.* Boston, MA: author.

Matarazzo, J. D. (1978). The interview: Its reliability and validity in psychiatric diagnosis. In B. B. Wolman (Ed.), *Clinical diagnosis of mental disorders: A handbook* (p. 47–96). New York: Plenum.

Matarazzo, J. D. (1983). The reliability of psychiatric and psychological diagnosis. *Clinical Psychology Review, 3*, 103–145.

Matarazzo, J. D. (1985). Clinical psychological test interpretations by computer: Hardware outpaces software. *Computers in Human Behavior, 1*, 235–253.

Matarazzo, J. D. (1986). Computerized clinical psychological test interpretations: Unvalidated plus all mean and no sigma. *American Psychologist, 41*, 14–24, 94–96.

Matarazzo, J. D. (1990). Psychological assessment versus psychological testing: Validation from Binet to the school, clinic, and courtroom. *American Psychologist, 45*, 999–1017.

Matarazzo, J. D. (1990). Psychological assessment versus psychological testing: *Validation from Binet to the school, clinic, and courtroom. American Psychologist, 45*, 999–1017.

Matas, M., & Marriott, A. (1987). The girl who cried wolf: Pseudologia phantastica and sexual abuse. *Canadian Journal of Psychiatry, 32*, 305–309.

Matthews v. Lucas, 472 U.S. 495 (1976).

Mayhall, P. D., & Norgard, K. E. (1983). *Child abuse and neglect: Sharing responsibility.* New York: Wiley.

McAdoo, H. P. (1980). Factors related to stability in upwardly mobile Black families. *Journal of Marriage and the Family, 40*, 761–776.

McAdoo, H. P. (1986). Strategies used by Black single mothers against stress. In M. Simms & J. Malveaux (Eds.), *Slipping through the cracks: The status of Black women* (pp. 153–166). New Brunswick, NJ: Transaction Books.

McAdoo, H. P. (1991). Family values and outcomes for children. *Journal of Negro Education, 60*, 361–365.

McCann, J. T., & Dyer, F. J. (1996). *Forensic assessment with the Millon inventories*. New York: Guilford.

McCauley, M. R., & Fisher, R. P. (1995). Facilitating children's eyewitness recall with the revised cognitive interview. *Journal of Applied Psychology, 80*, 510–516.

McEvoy, J. P., & Wilkinson, M. L. (2000). The role of insight in the treatment and outcome of bipolar disorder. *Psychiatric Annals, 30*, 496–498.

McGuire, T. L., & Feldman, K. W. (1989). Psychologic morbidity of children subjected to Munchausen syndrome by proxy. *Pediatrics, 83*, 289–292.

McIntyre, A., & Keesler, F. (1986). Psychological disorders among foster children. *Journal of Clinical Child Psychology, 15*, 297–303.

McIntyre, K. (1981). Role of mothers in father-daughter incest: A feminist analysis. *Social Work, 26*, 462–466.

McLanahan, S., & Sandefur, G. (1994). *Growing up with a single parent: What hurts, what helps?* Cambridge, MA: Harvard University Press.

McLanahan, S., & Teitler, J. (1999). The consequences of father absence. In M. E. Lamb (Ed.), *Parenting and child development in "nontraditional" families* (pp. 83–102). Mahwah, NJ: Erlbaum.

McLeod, J. D., & Shanahan, M. J. (1993). Poverty, parenting, and children's mental health. *American Sociological Review, 58*, 351–366.

McLoyd, V. C. (1989). Socialization and development in a changing economy: The effects of paternal job and income loss on children. *American Psychologist, 44*, 293–302.

McLoyd, V. C. (1990). The impact of economic hardship on Black families and children: Psychological distress, parenting, and socioemotional development. *Child Development, 61*, 311–346.

McNamara, C., Schumacher, J. E., Milby, J. B., Wallace, D., & Usdan, S. (2001). Prevalence of nonpsychotic mental disorders does not affect treatment outcome in a homeless cocaine-dependent sample. *American Journal of Drug & Alcohol Abuse, 27*, 91–106.

McNichol, S., Shute, R., & Tucker, A. (1999). Children's eyewitness memory for a repeated event. *Child Abuse & Neglect, 23*, 1127–1139.

McNichol, T., & Tash, C. (2001). Parental substance abuse and the development of children in family foster care. *Child Welfare, 80*, 239–256.

McNiel, D. E., Lam, J. N., & Binder, R. L. (2000). Relevance of interrater agreement to violence risk assessment. *Journal of Consulting & Clinical Psychology, 68*, 1111–1115.

Meadow, R. (1977). Munchausen syndrome by proxy: The hinterland of child abuse. *Lancet, 2*, 343–345.

Meehl, P. E. (1973). Why I do not attend case conferences. In P. E. Meehl (Ed.), *Psychodiagnosis: Selected papers* (pp. 225–302). Minneapolis: University of Minnesota Press.

Mejta, C. L., & Lavin, R. (1996). Facilitating health parenting among mothers with substance abuse or dependence problems: Some considerations. *Alcoholism Treatment Quarterly, 14*, 33–46.

Mekos, D., Hetherington, E. M., & Reiss, D. (1996). Sibling differences in problem behavior and parental treatment in nondivorced and remarried families. *Child Development, 67*, 2148–2165.

Meloy, J. R., Hansen, T. L., & Weiner, I. B. (1997). Authority of the Rorschach: Legal citations during the past 50 years. *Journal of Personality Assessment, 69,* 53–62.

Melton, G. B. (1981). Children's competency to testify. *Law and Human Behavior, 5,* 73–85.

Melton, G. B. (1984a). Developmental psychology and law: The state of the art. *Journal of Family Law, 22,* 445–482.

Melton, G. B. (1984b). Child witnesses and the First Amendment: A psycholegal dilemma. *Journal of Social Issues, 40,* 109–123.

Melton, G. B. (Ed.) (1987). *Reforming the law: Impact of child development research.* New York: Guilford.

Melton, G. B. (1994). Doing justice and doing good: Conflicts for mental health professionals. *The Future of Children, 4,* 102–114.

Melton, G. B., Goodman, G. S., Kalichman, S. C., Levine, M., Saywitz, K. J., & Koocher, G. P. (1995). Empirical research on child maltreatment and the law. *Journal of Clinical Child Psychology, 24,* 47–77.

Melton, G. B., Petrila, J., Poythress, N. G., & Slobogin, C. (1997). *Psychological evaluation for the courts* (2nd ed.). New York: Guilford.

Melton, G. B., & Wilcox, B. L. (2001). Children's law: Toward a new realism. *Law and Human Behavior, 25,* 3–12.

Meltzoff, A. N. (1990). Infant imitation and memory: Nine-month-olds in immediate and deferred tests. In S. Chess & M. E. Hertzig (Eds.), *Annual progress in child psychiatry and child development* (pp. 3–17). Philadelphia, PA: Brunner/Mazel.

Memon, A., & Bull, R. (1991). The cognitive interview: Its origins, empirical support, evaluation and practical implications. *Journal of Community & Applied Social Psychology, 1,* 291–307.

Memon, A., Cronin, O., Eves, R., & Bull, R. (1993). The cognitive interview and child witnesses. *Issues in Criminological & Legal Psychology, 20,* 3–9.

Merritt, K., Ornstein, P. A., & Spicker, B. (1994). Children's memory for a salient medical procedure: Implications for testimony. *Pediatrics, 94,* 17–23.

Merydith, S. P., & Wallbrown, F. H. (1991). Reconsidering response sets, test-taking attitudes, dissimulation, self-deception, and social desirability. *Psychological Reports, 69,* 891–905.

Meyer v. Nebraska, 262 U.S. 390 (1923).

Miller, A. (1993). Social science, social policy, and the heritage of African American families. In M. B. Katz (Ed.), *The "underclass" debate: Views from history* (pp. 254–289). Princeton, NJ: Princeton University Press.

Miller, B. A. (1990). The interrelationships between alcohol and drugs and family violence. *National Institute on Drug Abuse Research Monograph Series, 103,* 177–207.

Miller, C. M., Fremouw, W. J., Aljazireh, L., & Perker, B. K. (1996). Two methods of recall enhancement for child and adult eyewitness testimony. *American Journal of Forensic Psychology, 14,* 67–84.

Miller, F. G., Roberts, J., Brooks, M. K., & Lazowski, L. E. (1998). *SASSI-3: Substance Abuse Subtle Screening Inventory.* Odessa, FL: Psychological Assessment Resources.

Miller, M. C. (2000). A model for the assessment of violence. *Harvard Review of Psychiatry, 7,* 299–304.

Miller, P. J., & Sperry, L. L. (1988). Early talk about the past: The origins of conversational stories of personal experience. *Journal of Child Language, 15,* 293–315.

Miller, T. W., Veltkamp, L. J., & Janson, D. (1987). Projective measures in the clinical evaluation of sexually abused children. *Child Psychiatry and Human Development, 18,* 47–57.

Miller, W. (2000). Motivational interviewing: IV. Some parallels with horse whispering. *Behavioural & Cognitive Psychotherapy, 28,* 285–292.

Milne, R., & Bull, R. (1996). Interviewing children with mild learning disability with the cognitive interview. *Issues in Criminological & Legal Psychology, 26,* 44–51.

Milne, R., Bull, R., Koehnken, G., & Memon, A. (1995). The cognitive interview and suggestibility. *Issues in Criminological & Legal Psychology, 22,* 21–27.

Milner, J. S. (1986). *The Child Abuse Potential Inventory: Manual* (2nd ed.). Webster, NC: Psytec.

Milner, J. S. (1990). *An interpretive manual for the Child Abuse Potential Inventory.* Webster, NY: Psytec.

Milner, J. S. (1991). Physical child abuse perpetrator screening and evaluation. *Criminal Justice and Behavior, 18,* 47–63.

Milner, J. S. (1994). Assessing physical child abuse risk: The Child Abuse Potential Inventory. *Clinical Psychology Review, 14,* 547–583.

Milner, J. S., & Gold, R. G. (1986). Screening spouse abusers for child abuse potential. *Journal of Clinical Psychology, 42,* 169–172.

Milner, J. S., Robertson, K. R., & Rogers, D. L. (1990). Childhood history of abuse and adult child abuse potential. *Journal of Family Violence, 5,* 15–34.

Milner, J. S., & Wimberley, R. C. (1980). Prediction and explanation of child abuse. *Journal of Clinical Psychology, 36,* 875–884.

Mitchell, R. E., Billings, A. G. & Moos, R. H. (1982). Social support and well-being: Implications for prevention programs. *Journal of Primary Prevention, 3,* 77–98.

Mnookin, R. H. (1975). Child custody adjudication: Judicial functions in the face of indeterminancy. *Law and Contemporary Problems, 39,* 226–293.

Moates v. State, 545 So.2d 224, 225 (Ala.Crim.App.1989).

Mohit, D. L. (1996). Management and care of mentally ill mothers of young children: An innovative program. *Archives of Psychiatric Nursing, 10,* 49–54.

Monahan, J., Steadman, H. J., Appelbaum, P. S., Robbins, P. C., Mulvey, E. P., Silver, E., Roth, L. H., & Grisso, T. (2000). Developing a clinically useful actuarial tool for assessing violence risk. *British Journal of Psychiatry, 176,* 312–319.

Monahan, J., & Walker, L. (1988). Social science research in law: A new paradigm. *American Psychologist, 43,* 465–472.

Moncher, F. J. (1996). The relationship of maternal adult attachment style and risk of physical child abuse. *Journal of Interpersonal Violence, 11,* 335–350.

Moore, D. R. (1982). Childhood behavior problems: A social learning perspective. In J. R. Lachenmeyer & M. S. Gibbs (Eds.), *Psychopathology in childhood* (pp. 211–243). New York: Gardner Press.

Moore, K., & Snyder, N. (1990). *Cognitive development among the children of adolescent mothers.* Washington, DC: Child Trends.

Morey, L. C. (1999). Personality Assessment Inventory. In M. E. Maruish (Ed.), *The use of psychological testing for treatment planning and outcome assessment* (2nd ed., pp. 1083–1121). Mahwah, NH: Erlbaum.

Morey, L. C., & Glutting, J. H. (1994). The Personality Assessment Inventory and the measurement of normal and abnormal personality constructs. In S. Strack & M. Lorr (Eds.), *Differentiating normal and abnormal personality,* (pp. 402–420). New York: Springer.

Morison, P., & Gardner, H. (1978). Dragons and dinosaurs: The child's capacity to differentiate fantasy from reality. *Child Development, 49,* 642–648.

Morse, S. J. (1978a). Crazy behavior, morals, and science: An analysis of mental health law. *Southern California Law Review, 51,* 527–645.

Morse, S. J. (1978b). Law and mental health professionals: The limits of expertise. *Professional Psychology, 8,* 389–399.

Morton, N., & Browne, K. D. (1998). Theory and observation of attachment and its relation to child maltreatment: A review. *Child Abuse & Neglect, 22,* 1093–1104.

Mosek, A., & Adler, L. (2001). The self-concept of adolescent girls in non-relative versus kin foster care. *International Social Work, 44*, 149–162.

Moston, S. (1987). The suggestibility of children in interview studies. *First Language, 7*, 67–78.

Muir, G. D. (2000). Early ontogeny of locomotor behaviour: A comparison between altricial and precocial animals. *Brain Research Bulletin, 53*, 719–726.

Mulsow, M. H., & Murry, V. M. (1996). Parenting on edge: Economically stressed, single, African American adolescent mothers. *Journal of Family Issues, 17*, 704–721.

Murphy, J. M., Jellinek, M., Quinn, D., Smith, G., Poitrast, F. G., & Goshko, M. (1991). Substance abuse and serious child mistreatment: Prevalence, risk, and outcome in a court sample. *Child Abuse & Neglect, 15*, 197–211.

Myers, J. E. B. (1995a). Taint hearings for child witnesses? A step in the wrong direction. *Baylor Law Review, 46*, 873–945.

Myers, J. E. B. (1995b). New era of skepticism regarding children's credibility. *Psychology, Public Policy & Law, 1*, 387–398.

Myers, J. E. B., Bays, J., Becker, J., Berliner, L., Corwin, D. L., & Saywitz, K. J. (1989). Expert testimony in child sexual abuse litigation. *Nebraska Law Review, 69*, 1–143.

Myers, N., Clifton, R. K., & Clarkson, M. G. (1987). When they were very young: Almost threes remember two years ago. *Infant Behavior and Development, 10*, 123–132.

Myles-Worsley, M., Cromer, C., & Dodd, D. (1986). Children's preschool script construction: Reliance on general knowledge after memory fades. *Developmental Psychology, 22*, 22–30.

Nadelson, T. (1979). The Munchausen spectrum: Borderline character features. *General Hospital Psychiatry, 11*–17.

Naglieri, J. A., LeBuffe, P. A., & Pfeiffer, S. I. (1994). *Devereux Scales of Mental Disorders.* Odessa, FL: Psychological Assessment Resources.

National Center on Child Abuse and Neglect. (1979). *Child abuse and neglect: State reporting laws.* (Available from the Clearinghouse on Child Abuse and Neglect Information, P.O. Box 118,2, Washington, DC, 20013.)

National Center on Child Abuse and Neglect. (1988). *State statutes related to child abuse and neglect: 1988.* (Available from the Clearinghouse on Child Abuse and Neglect Information, P.O. Box 118,2, Washington, DC, 20013.)

National Child Abuse and Neglect Reporting System. (1999). *Child maltreatment,* U.S. Department of Health and Human Services. Washington, DC: U.S. Government Printing Office.

Nelson, K. (1986). *Event knowledge: Structure and function in development.* Hillsdale, NJ: Erlbaum.

Nicholson, J., & Blanch, A. (1994). Rehabilitation for parenting roles for people with serious mental illness. *Psychosocial Rehabilitation Journal, 18*, 107–119.

Nicholson, R. A., & Norwood, S. (2000). The quality of forensic psychological assessments, reports, and testimony: Acknowledging the gap between promise and practice. *Law & Human Behavior, 24*, 9–44.

Nitz, K., Ketterlinus, R. D., & Brandt, L. J. (1995). The role of stress, social support, and family environment in adolescent mothers' parenting. *Journal of Adolescent Research, 10*, 358–382.

Novaco, R. W. (1994). Anger as a risk factor for violence among the mentally disordered. In J. Monahan & H. J. Steadman (Eds.), *Violence and mental disorder: Developments in risk assessment.* Chicago, IL: University of Chicago Press.

Nurcombe, B. (1986). The child as witness: Competency and credibility. *Journal of the American Academy of Child Psychiatry, 25*, 473–480.

Nurcombe, B., & Parlett, D. F. (1994). *Child mental health and the law.* New York: Free Press.

Oates, K., & Shrimpton, S. (1991). Children's memories for stressful and nonstressful events. *Medicine, Science, and the Law, 31*, 4–10.

Oberlander, L. B. (1995a). Ethical responsibilities in child custody evaluations: Implications for evaluation methodology. *Ethics and Behavior, 3*, 311–332.

Oberlander, L. B. (1995b). Psycholegal issues in child sexual abuse evaluations: A survey of forensic mental health professionals. *Child Abuse & Neglect, 19*, 473–490.

Oberlander, L. B. (1998, April). *Evaluating parenting capacity and allegations of child maltreatment.* Seminar presented at Contemporary Issues in Forensic Psychology: A Workshop Series of the American Academy of Forensic Psychology, San Juan, PR.

Oberlander, L. B. (1999, August). *Ethical responsibilities in child protection evaluations: Implications for evaluation methodology.* Paper presented at the annual convention of the American Psychological Association, Boston, MA.

Oberlander, L. B., Goldstein, A., & Goldstein, N. E. (2002). Competence to confess: Evaluating the validity of Miranda rights waivers and trustworthiness of confessions. In A. M. Goldstein (Ed.), *Comprehensive handbook of psychology* (Volume 11: Forensic Psychology).

Oberlander, L. B., & Goldstein, N. E. (2001). A review and update on the practice of evaluating Miranda comprehension. *Behavioral Sciences and the Law, 19*, 453–471.

Oberlander, L. B., Goldstein, N. E., & Ho, C. N. (2001). Competence to stand trial: Evaluation of preadolescents. *Behavioral Sciences and the Law, 19*, 545–564.

O'Connor, T. G., & Rutter, M. (2000). Attachment disorder behavior following early severe deprivation: Extension and longitudinal follow-up. English and Romanian Adoptees Study Team. *Journal of the American Academy of Child & Adolescent Psychiatry, 39*, 703–712.

Offerman-Zukerberg, J. (1992). The parenting process: A psychoanalytic perspective. *Journal of the American Academy of Psychoanalysis, 20*, 205–214.

Office of Inspector General, Department of Health and Human Services (1990). *Crack babies.* Washington, DC: U. S. Government Printing Office, 709–926:30010.

Ogbu, J. U. (1981). Origins of human competence: A cultural-ecological perspective. *Child Development, 52*, 413–429.

Ogbu, J. U. (1985). A cultural ecology of competence among inner-city Blacks. In M. B. Spencer, G. K. Brookins, & W. R. Allen (Eds.), *Beginnings: The social and affective development of Black children* (pp. 45–66). Hillsdale, NJ: Erlbaum.

Ogbu, J. U. (1992). Understanding cultural diversity and learning. *Educational Researcher, 21*, 5–14.

Ogloff, J. R. P. (1995). The legal basis of forensic applications of the MMPI-2. In Y. S. Ben-Porath, & J. R. Graham (Eds.), *Forensic applications of the MMPI-2: Applied Psychology* (Vol. 2: Individual, social, and community issues, pp. 18–47). Thousand Oaks, CA: Sage.

Ogloff, J. R. P. (1999). Ethical and legal contours of forensic psychology. In R. Roesch, S. D. Hart, & J. R. P. Ogloff (Eds.), *Psychology and law: The state of the discipline* (pp. 405–422). New York: Kluwer Plenum.

Onheiber, M. D. (1997). Toward a reorientation of values and practice in child welfare. *Child Psychiatry and Human Development, 27*, 151–165.

Oppenheim, E., & Bussiere, A. (1996). Adoption: Where do relatives stand? *Child Welfare, 75*, 471–487.

Orangeburg County Department of Social Services v. Harley, 393 S.E.2d 597 (S.C.App. 1990).

Orleans, M., Palisi, B. J., & Caddell, D. (1989). Marriage adjustment and satisfaction of stepfathers: Their feelings and perceptions of decision making and stepchildren relations. *Family Relations, 38*, 371–377.

Ornstein, P. A., Gordon, B. N., & Larus, D. (1992). Children's memory for a personally experienced event: Implications for testimony. *Applied Cognitive Psychology, 6*, 49–60.

O'Sullivan, J. T., Howe, M. L., & Marche, T. A. (1996). Children's beliefs about long-term retention. *Child Development, 67*, 2989–3009.

Otto, R. K., & Collins, R. P. (1995). Use of the MMPI-2/MMPI-A in child custody evaluations. In Y. S. Ben-Porath, & J. R. Graham (Eds.), *Forensic applications of the MMPI-2: Applied*

Psychology (Vol. 2: Individual, social, and community issues, pp. 222–252). Thousand Oaks, CA: Sage.

Otto, R. K., Ogloff, J. R. P., & Small, M. A. (1991). Confidentiality and informed consent in psychotherapy: Clinicians' knowledge and practices in Florida and Nebraska. *Forensic Reports, 4,* 379–389.

Ownby, R. L. (1997). *Psychological reports: A guide to report writing in professional psychology* (3rd ed.). New York: Wiley.

Page, T. (1999). The attachment partnership as conceptual base for exploring the impact of child maltreatment. *Child & Adolescent Social Work Journal, 16,* 419–437.

Palmore v. Sidoti, 466 U.S., 104 S.Ct. 1879, 80 L.Ed.2d 421 (1984).

Passman, R. H., & Mulhern, R. K. (1977). Maternal punitiveness as affected by situational stress: An experimental analogue of child abuse. *Journal of Abnormal Psychology, 86,* 565–569.

Patterson, C. J. (1995). Adoption of minor children by lesbian and gay adults: A social science perspective. *Duke Journal of Gender, Law, and Policy, 2,* 191–205.

Patterson, C. J., & Chan, R. W., (1996). Gay fathers. In M. E. Lamb (Ed.), *The role of the father in child development* (3rd ed., pp. 245–260). New York: Wiley.

Patterson, C. J. & Chan, R. W. (1999). Families headed by lesbian and gay parents. In M. E. Lamb (Ed.), *Parenting and child development in "nontraditional" families* (pp. 191–220). Mahwah, NJ: Erlbaum.

Patterson, G. R. (1980). Mothers: The unacknowledged victims. *Monographs of the Society for Research in Child Development, 45*(5, Serial No. 186).

Patterson, G. R. (1982). *Coercive family process.* Eugene, OR: Castalia.

Patterson, G. R., Littman, R. A., & Bricker, W. (1967). Assertive behavior in children: A step toward a theory of aggression. *Monographs of the Society for Research in Child Development, 32,* 1–43.

Patterson, G. R., & Reid, J. B. (1970). Reciprocity and coercion: Two facets of social systems. In C. Neuringer & J. L. Michael (Eds.), *Behavior modification in clinical psychology.* New York: Appleton-Century-Crofts.

Paul, J. P. (1986). *Growing up with a gay, lesbian, or bisexual parent: An explatoratory study of experiences and perceptions.* Unpublished doctoral dissertation, University of California at Berkeley.

Pearson, J., & Theonnes, N. (2000). Supervised visitation: The families and their experiences. *Family & Conciliation Courts Review, 38,* 123–142.

Pearson, J. E. (1987). The Interpersonal Network Questionnaire: A tool for social network assessment. *Measurement and Evaluation in Counseling and Development, 20,* 99–105.

Pecora, P. J. (1991). Investigating allegations of child maltreatment: The strengths and limitations of current risk assessment systems. *Child and Youth Services, 15,* 73–92.

Pelton, L. (1978). Child abuse and neglect: The myth of classlessness. *American Journal of Orthopsychiatry, 48,* 608–617.

Pennsylvania v. Ritchie, 480 U.S. 39, 1076 S.Ct. 989 (1987).

People v. Bowker, 203 Cal.App.3d 385, 249 Cal. Rptr. 886 (1988).

People v. Brown, 8, Cal.4th 746, 35 Cal.Rptr.2d 407, 883 P.2d 949 (1994).

People v. Caffero, 207 Cal.App.3d 678, 255 Cal. Rptr. 22 (1989).

People v. District Court In and For Summit County, 791 P.2d 682, 685 (Colo.1990).

People v. Draper, 150 Mich.App. 481, 389 N.W.2d 89 (1986).

People v. Gray, 187 Cal.App.3d, 231 Cal. Rptr. 658 (1986).

People v. Luna, 204 Cal.App.3d 776, 250 Cal. Rptr. 878 (1988).

People v. McNichols, 139 Ill.App.3d 947, 94 Ill.Dec. 375, 487 N.E.2d 1252 (1986).

People v. Michael M., 618 N.Y.S.2d 171 (Sup.Ct.1994).

People v. Phillips, 122 Cal.App.3d 69 (1981).

People v. Pointer, 151 Cal.App.3d 1128, 199 Cal.Rptr. 357 (1984).

People v. Pulido, 226 Cal.Rptr. 782 (Cal.Ct.App.1986).

People v. Roscoe, 168 Cal.App.3e 1983, 1098–99, 215 Cal. Rptr. 45, 48–49 (1985).

Perry, N. W., McAuliff, B. D., Tam, P., & Claycomb, L. (1995). When lawyers question children: Is justice served? *Law & Human Behavior, 19*, 609–629.

Perry, N. W., & Wrightsman, L. S. (1991). *The child witness.* Newbury Park, CA: Sage.

Peters, C. L., & Fox, R. A. (1993). Parenting Inventory: Validity and social desirability. *Psychological Reports, 72*, 683–689.

Peters, H. E., & Mullis, N. C. (1997). The role of family income and source of income in adolescent achievement. In G. Duncan & J. Brooks-Gunn (Eds.), *Consequences of growing up poor* (pp. 340–381). New York: Sage.

Peterson, B. E., Smirles, K. A., Wentworth, P. A. (1997). Generativity and authoritarianism: Implications for personality, political involvement, and parenting. *Journal of Personality and Social Psychology, 72*, 1202–1216.

Peterson, B. E., & Stewart, A. J. (1993). Generativity and social motives in young adults. *Journal of Personality and Social Psychology, 65*, 186–198.

Peterson, C. C., Peterson, J. L., & Seeto, D. (1983). Developmental changes in ideas about lying. *Child Development, 54*, 1529–1535.

Petty, J. (1990). *Checklist for Child Abuse Evaluation.* Odessa, FL: Psychological Assessment Resources.

Pezdek, K. (1995). *What types of false childhood memories are not likely to be suggestively implanted?* Paper presented at the meeting of the Society for Applied Research on Memory and Cognitive, University of British Columbia, Vancouver.

Pezdek, K., & Roe, C. (1997). The suggestibility of children's memory for being touched: Planting, erasing, and changing memories. *Law and Human Behavior, 21*, 95–106.

Pfefferbaum, B., Allen, J. R., Lindsey, E. D., & Whittlesey, S. W. (1999). Fabricated trauma exposure: An analysis of cognitive, behavioral, and emotional factors. *Psychiatry: Interpersonal & Biological Processes, 62*, 293–302.

Phares, V. (1992). Where's poppa? The relative lack of attention to the role of fathers in child and adolescent psychopathology. *American Psychologist, 47*, 656–664.

Phelps v. State, 439 So.2d 727 (Ala.Crim.App.1983).

Piaget, J. (1932/1962). *The moral judgment of the child.* New York: Free Press.

Piaget, J. *The construction of reality in the child.* New York: Basic Books.

Pianta, R., Egeland, B., & Erickson, M. F. (1989). The antecedents of maltreatment: Results of the mother-child interaction research project. In D. Cicchetti & V. Carlson (Eds.), *Child maltreatment: Theory and research on the causes and consequences of child abuse and neglect* (pp. 203–253). Cambridge, MA: Cambridge University Press.

Pianta, R. C., Marvin, R., Britner, P., & Borowitz, K. (1996). Mothers' resolution of their children's diagnoses: Organized patterns of caregiving representations. *Infant Mental Health Journal, 17*, 239–256.

Pierce v. Society of Sisters, 268 U.S. 510 (1925).

Pies, C. (1990). Lesbians and the choice to parent. In F. W. Bozett & M. B. Sussman (Eds.), *Homosexuality and family relations* (pp. 137–154). New York: Harrington Park Press.

Pipe, M. E., & Goodman, G. S. (1991). Elements of secrecy: Implications for children's testimony. *Behavioral Sciences and the Law, 9*, 33–41.

Piper, W. E., & Joyce, A. S. (2001). *Psychosocial treatment outcome.* In W. J. Livesley (Ed.), *Handbook of personality disorders: Theory, research, and treatment* (pp. 323–343). New York: Guilford.

Pleck, J. H. (1997). Paternal involvement: Levels, sources and consequences. In M. E. Lamb (Ed.), *The role of the father in child development* (3rd ed., pp. 66–103). New York: Wiley.

Polansky, N. A., Ammons, P. W., & Gaudin, J. M. (1985). Loneliness and isolation in child neglect. *Social Casework: The Journal of Contemporary Social Work, 66,* 38–47.

Polansky, N. A., Chalmers, M. A., Buttenweiser, E., & Williams, D. P. (1981). *Damaged parents.* Chicago: University of Chicago Press.

Polansky, N. A., Gaudin, J. M., Ammons, P. W., & Davis, K. B. (1985). The psychological ecology of the neglectful mother. *Child Abuse & Neglect, 9,* 265–275.

Polizzi, D. M., MacKenzie, D., & Hickman, L. J. (1999). What works in adult sex offender treatment? A review of prison- and non-prison-based treatment programs. *International Journal of Offender Therapy & Comparative Criminology, 43,* 357–374.

Poole, D., & Lamb, M. (1998). *Investigative interviews of children: A guide for helping professionals.* Washington, DC: American Psychological Association.

Poole, D. A., & Lindsay, D. S. (1995). Interviewing preschoolers: Effects of nonsuggestive techniques, parental coaching, and leading questions on reports of nonexperienced events. *Journal of Experimental Child Psychology, 60,* 129–154.

Poole, D., & White, L. T. (1991). Effects of question repetition on the eyewitness testimony of children and adults. *Developmental Psychology, 27,* 975–986.

Pope, K. S., Butcher, J. N., & Seelen, J. (2000). *The MMPI, MMPI-2 & MMPI-A in court: A practical guide for expert witnesses and attorneys* (2nd ed.). Washington, DC: American Psychological Association.

Popenoe, D. (1988). *Disturbing the nest: Family change and decline in modern societies.* New York: A. deGreyter.

Powe v. State, 597 So.2d 721 (Ala.1991).

Power, T. G., Kabayashi-Winata, H., & Kelley, M. L. (1992). Childrearing patterns in Japan and the United States: A cluster analytic study. *International Journal of Behavioral Development, 15,* 185–205.

Powers, P., Andriks, J. L., & Loftus, E. F. (1979). Eyewitness accounts of females and males. *Journal of Applied psychology, 64,* 339–347.

Prentky, R., & Bird, S. (1997). *Assessing sexual abuse: A resource guide for practitioners.* Brandon, VT: Safer Society Press.

Prince v. Massachusetts, 321 U.S. 158 (1944), 42, 133, 136, 496n.43, 499n.13, 516nn.2, 14.

Proch, K., & Hess, P. M. (1987). Parent-child visiting policies of voluntary agencies. *Children & Youth Services Review, 9,* 17–28.

Procidano, M. E., & Heller, K. (1983). Measures of perceived social support from friends and from family: Three validation studies. *American Journal of Community Psychology, 11,* 1–24.

Pruett, K. (1982). *The nurturing father.* New York: Warner.

Pryce, C. R. (1995). Determinants of motherhood in human and nonhuman primates: A biosocial model. In C. R. Pryce, R. D. Martin, & D. Skuse (Eds.), *Motherhood in human and nonhuman primates* (pp. 1–15). Basel: Karger.

Quinsey, V., Rice, M., & Harris, G. (1995). Actuarial prediction of sexual recidivism. *Journal of Interpersonal Violence, 10,* 85–105.

Quinsey, V. L., Harris, G. T., Rice, M. E., & Cormier, C. A. (1999). *The Violent Offender.* Washington, DC: American Psychological Association.

Radin, N. (1982). Primary caregiving and role-sharing fathers of pre-schoolers. In M. E. Lamb (Ed.), *Nontraditional families: Parenting and child development* (pp. 173–204). Hillsdale, NJ: Erlbaum.

Radin, N. (1994). Primary-caregiving fathers in intact families. In A. E. Gottfried & A. W. Gottfried (Eds.), *Redefining families: Implications for children's development* (pp. 55–97). New York: Plenum.

Radke-Yarrow, M., Richters, J., & Wilson, W. E., (1988). Child development in a network of relationships. In R. A. Hinde & J. Stevenson-Hinde (Eds.), *Relationships within families: Mutual influences* (pp. 48–67). London: Oxford University Press.

Rafkin, L. (1990). *Different mothers: Sons and daughters of lesbians talk about their lives.* Pittsburgh, PA: Cleis Press.

Rand, D., & Feldman, M. D. (1999). Misdiagnosis of Munchausen syndrome by proxy: A literature review and four new cases. *Harvard Review of Psychiatry, 7,* 94–101.

Raskin, D., & Yuille, J. (1989). Problems in evaluating interviews of children in sexual abuse cases. In S. J. Ceci, M. Toglia, & D. Ross (Eds.), *Children's eyewitness memory* (pp. 36–52). New York: Springer-Verlag.

Ray, S. A., & McLoyd, V. C. (986). Fathers in hard times: The impact of unemployment and poverty on paternal and marital relations. In M. Lamb (Ed.), *The father's role* (pp. 339–383). New York: Wiley.

Red Horse, J. G., Lewis, R., Feit, M., & Decker, J. (1978). Family behavior of urban American Indians. *Social Casework, Feb.,* 67–72.

Redding, R. E., Fried, C., & Britner, P. A. (2000). Predictors of placement outcomes in treatment foster care: Implications for foster parent selection and service delivery. *Journal of Child & Family Studies, 9,* 425–447.

Rees, R. L. (1979). *A comparison of children of lesbian and single heterosexual mothers on three measures of socialization.* California School of Professional Psychology, Berkeley.

Reese, E., & Fivush, R. (1993). Parental styles of talk about the past. *Developmental Psychology, 29,* 596–606.

Reilly, P. M., & Shopshire, M. S. (2000). Anger management group treatment for cocaine dependence: Preliminary outcomes. *American Journal of Drug & Alcohol Abuse, 26,* 161–177.

Reis, J. (1989). A comparison of young teenage, older teenage, and adult mothers on determinants of parenting. *The Journal of Psychology, 123,* 141–151.

Reyes, M. B., Routh, D. K., Jean-Gilles, M. M., Sanfilippo, M. D., & Fawcett, N. (1991). Ethnic differences in parenting children in fearful situations. *Journal of Pediatric Psychology, 16,* 717–726.

Reynolds, C. R., Hays, J. R., & Ryan-Arredondo, K. (2001). When judges, law, ethics, and rules of practice collide: A case study of assent and disclosure in assessment of a minor. *Journal of Forensic Neuropsychology, 2,* 41–52.

Reynolds, C. R., & Kamphaus, R. W. (1992). *Behavior Assessment System for Children.* Circle Pines, MN: American Guidance Service.

Reynolds, W. M. (1987). *Reynolds Child Depression Scale.* Odessa, FL: Psychological Assessment Resources.

Reynolds, W. M., & Kobak, K. A. (1995). Reliability and validity of the Hamilton Depression Inventory: A paper-and-pencil version of the Hamilton Depression Rating Scale Clinical Interview. *Psychological Assessment, 7,* 472–483.

Rice, M.E., & Harris, G.T. (1995). Violent recidivism: Assessing predictive validity. *Journal of Consulting and Clinical Psychology, 63,* 737–748.

Rice, M. E., & Harris, G. T. (1997). Cross-validation and extension of the Violence Risk Appraisal Guide for child molesters and rapists. *Law & Human Behavior, 21,* 231–241.

Ricketts, W. (1991). *Lesbians and gay men as foster parents.* Portland: National Child Welfare Resource Center, University of Southern Maine.

Riggs, D. S., Murphy, C. M., & O'Leary, K. D. (1989). Intentional falsification in reports of interpartner aggression. *Journal of Interpersonal Violence, 4,* 220–232.

Riley, D., & Eckenrode, J. (1986). Social ties: Subgroup differences in costs and benefits. *Journal of Personality and Social Psychology, 51,* 770–778.

Roback, D., Sanders, A. L., Lorentz, J., & Koestenblatt, M. (1980). Child-rearing practices reported by students in six cultures. *Journal of Social Psychology, 110,* 153–162.

Roberts, J. (1993). Abused children and foster care: The need for specialist resources. *Child Abuse Review, 2,* 3–14.

Robins, L. N. (1985). Epidemiology: Reflections on testing the validity of psychiatric interviews. *Archives of General Psychiatry, 42,* 918–924.

Robins, P. M., & Sesan, R. (1991). Munchausen syndrome by proxy: another women's disorder? *Professional Psychology: Research and Practice, 22,* 283–290.

Roder, B. J., Bushnell, E. W., Sasseville, A. M. (2000). Infants' preferences for familiarity and novelty during the course of visual processing. *Infancy, 1,* 491–507.

Roe v. Wade, 410 U.S. 113 (1973).

Rogers, R., & Ewing, C. P. (1989). Ultimate opinion proscriptions: A cosmetic fix and a plea for empiricism. *Law and Human Behavior, 13,* 357–374.

Rogers, R., Sewell, K. W., Morey, L. C., & Ustad, K. L. (1996). Detection of feigned mental disorders on the Personality Assessment Inventory: A discriminant analysis. *Journal of Personality Assessment, 67,* 629–640.

Rogler, L. (1994). International migrations: A framework for directing research. *American Psychologist, 49,* 701–708.

Rorschach, H. (1942). *Psychodiagnostics.* New York: Grune & Stratton.

Rose, J. (1996). Anger management: A group treatment program for people with mental retardations. *Journal of Developmental & Physical Disabilities, 8,* 133–149.

Rose, S. A., Feldman, J. F., & Jankowski, J. J. (2001). Attention and recognition memory in the 1st year of life: A longitudinal study of preterm and full-term infants. *Developmental Psychology, 37,* 135–151.

Rosenblatt, P. C. (1999). Multiracial families. In M. E. Lamb (Ed.), *Parenting and child development in "nontraditional" families* (pp. 263–278). Mahwah, NJ: Erlbaum.

Rosenblatt, P. C., Karis, T. A., & Powell, R. D. (1995). *Multiracial couples: Black and White voices.* Thousand Oaks, CA: Sage.

Rosenthal, J. A., & Groze, V. (1992). *Special needs adoption: A study of intact families.* New York: Praeger.

Roszkowski, M. J. (1984). Validity of the Similarities Ratio as a predictor of violent behavior: Data from a mentally-retarded sample. *Personality & Individual Differences, 5,* 117–118.

Rothbart, M. K. (1981). Measurement of temperament in infancy. *Child Development, 52,* 569–587.

Rothbaum, F., Weisz, J., Pott, M. Miyake, K., & Morelli, G. (2000). Attachment and culture: Security in the United States and Japan. *American Psychologist, 55,* 1093–1104.

Rovee-Collier, C., Hartshort, K., & DiRubbo, M. (1999). Long-term maintenance of infant memory. *Developmental Psychobiology, 35,* 91–102.

Rovee-Collier, C., & Hayne, H. (1987). Reactivation of infant memory: Implications for cognitive development. *Advances in Child Development and Behavior, 20,* 185–238.

Rowland, V. T., Dodder, R. A., & Nickols, S. Y. (1985). Perceived adequacy of resources: Development of a scale. *Home Economics Research Journal, 14,* 221–225.

Ruck, M. D. (1996). Why children think they should tell the truth in court: Developmental considerations for the assessment of competency. *Legal & Criminological Psychology, 1,* 103–116.

Rudy, L., & Goodman, G. S. (1991). Effects of participation on children's reports: Implications for children's testimony. *Developmental Psychology, 27,* 527–538.

Russell, D. (1983). The incidence and prevalence of intrafamilial and extrafamlial sexual abuse of female children. *Child Abuse & Neglect, 7,* 133–146.

Russell, G. (1989). Work/family patterns and couple relationships in shared caregiving families. *Social Behaviour, 4,* 265–284.

Russell, G. (1999). Primary caregiving fathers. In M. E. Lamb (Ed.), *Parenting and child development in "nontraditional" families* (pp. 57–81). Mahwah, NJ: Erlbaum.

Russell, G., & Radojevic, M. (1992). The changing role of fathers? Current understandings and future directions for research and practice. *Infant Mental Health Journal, 13,* 296–311.

Russell v. State, 289 Ark. 533, 712 S.W.2d 916 (1986).

Rutter, M., & O'Connor, T. G. (1999). Implications of attachment theory for child care policies. In J. Cassidy, & P. R. Shaver (Eds.), *Handbook of attachment: Theory, research, and clinical applications* (pp. 823–844). New York: Guilford.

Ryan, L., Ehrlich, J. M., & Finnegan, L. P. (1987). Infants of drug addicts: At risk for child abuse, neglect, and placement in foster care. *Neurotoxicology and Teratology, 9,* 315–319.

Sagatun, I. J. (1991). Expert witnesses in child abuse cases. *Behavior Sciences and the Law, 9,* 201–215.

Sagi, A. (1982). Antecedents and consequences of various degrees of parental involvement in childrearing: The Israeli project. In M. E. Lamb (Ed.), *Nontraditional families: Parenting and child development* (pp. 205–232). Hillsdale, NJ: Erlbaum.

Sameroff, A. J., Seifer, R., Baldwin, A., & Baldwin, C. (1993). Stability of intelligence from preschool to adolescence: The influence of social and family risk factors. *Child Development, 64,* 80–97.

Sameroff, A. J., Seifer, R., Barocas, R., Zax, M., & Greenspan, S. (1987). Intelligence quotient scores of 4-year-old children: Social and environmental risk factors. *Pediatrics, 79,* 343–350.

Sampson, R., & Morenoff, J. (1997). Ecological perspectives on the neighborhood context of urban poverty: Past and present. In J. Brooks-Gunn, G. J. Duncan, & J. L. Aber (Eds.), *Neighborhood poverty: Context and consequence for children: Vol. 2. Conceptual, methodological, and policy approaches to studying neighborhoods* (pp. 1–23). New York: Russell Sage Foundation Press.

Sanchirico, A., & Jablonka, K. (2000). Keeping foster children connected to their biological parents: The impact of foster parent training and support. *Child & Adolescent Social Work Journal, 17,* 185–203.

Sandberg, S., McGuinness, D., Hillary, C., & Rutter, M. (1998). Independence of childhood life events and chronic adversities: A comparison of two patient groups and controls. *Journal of the American Academy of Child & Adolescent Psychiatry, 37,* 728–735.

Sandberg, S., Rutter, M., Pickles, A., McGuinness, D., & Angold, A. (2001). Do high-threat life events really provoke the onset of psychiatric disorder in children? *Journal of Child Psychology & Psychiatry & Allied Disciplines, 42,* 523–532.

Sandler, J., Holder, A., Dare, C., & Dreher, A. U. (1997). *Freud's models of the mind: An introduction.* London: Karnac Books.

Sandler, J., & Sandler, A. M. (1998). *Object relations theory and role responsiveness.* London: Karnac Books.

Santosky v. Kramer, 455 U.S. 745 (1982).

Sattler, J. (1998). *Clinical and forensic interviewing of children and families: Guidelines for the mental health, education, pediatric and child maltreatment fields.* San Diego, CA: Jerome M. Sattler Publisher, Inc.

Saywitz, K. J. (1989). Court is a place to play basketball: Children's conceptions of the legal system. In S. Ceci, D. Ross, & M. Toglia, *Perspectives of children's testimony,* pp. 131–157. New York: Springer-Verlag.

Saywitz, K. J. (1994). Effects of a multidisciplinary interview center on the investigation of alleged child sexual abuse. *Violence Update, 5,* 3, 6.

Saywitz, K. J., & Camparo, L. (1998). Interviewing child witnesses: A developmental perspective. *Child Abuse & Neglect, 22,* 825–843.

Saywitz, K. J., Geiselman, R. E., & Bornstein, G. K. (1992). Effects of cognitive interviewing and practice on children's recall performance. *Journal of Applied Psychology, 77,* 744–756.

Saywitz, K. J., Goodman, G. S., Nicholas, E., & Moan, S. F. (1991). Children's memories of a physical examination involving genital touch: Implications for reports of child sexual abuse. *Journal of Consulting and Clinical Psychology, 59,* 682–691.

Saywitz, K. J., Jaenicke, C., & Camparo, L. (1990). Children's knowledge of legal terminology. *Law and Human Behavior, 14,* 523–535.

Saywitz, K., & Lyon, D. (1997). *Sensitively assessing children's testimonial competence.* (Final report to the National Center on Child Abuse and Neglect, Grant No. 90-CA-1553).

Saywitz, K. J., Mannarino, A. P., Berliner, L., & Cohen, J. A. (2000). Treatment for sexually abused children and adolescents. *American Psychologist, 55,* 1040–1049.

Saywitz, K. J., & Snyder, L. (1996). Narrative elaboration: Test of a new procedure for interviewing children. *Journal of Consulting and Clinical Psychology, 64,* 1347–1357.

Saywitz, K. J., Snyder, L., & Nathanson, R. (1999). Facilitating the communicative competence of the child witness. *Applied Developmental Science, 3,* 58–68.

Schaefer, E. (1965). Children's Reports of Parental Behavior: An inventory. *Child Development, 36,* 417–423.

Schaffer, D., Fisher, P., Lucas, C. P., Dulcan, M. K., Schwab-Stone, M. E. (2000). NIMH Diagnostic Interview Schedule for Children Version IV (NIMH DISC-IV): Description, differences from previous versions, and reliability of some common diagnoses. *Journal of the American Academy of Child & Adolescent Psychiatry, 39,* 28–38.

Schaffer, H. R. (1971). *The growth of sociability.* London: Penguin.

Schalock, R. L., Sheehan, M. J., & Weber, L. (1993). The use of Treatment Progress Scales in client monitoring and evaluation. *Journal of Mental Health Administration, 20,* 264–269.

Schetky, D. H., Angell, R., Morrison, C. V., & Sack, W. H. (1979). Parents who fail: A study of 51 cases of termination of parental rights. *Journal of the American Academy of Child Psychiatry, 18,* 366–383.

Schludermann, E., & Schludermann, S. (1970). Replicability of factors in children's report of parental behavior (CRPBI). *Journal of Psychology, 79,* 29–39.

Schmidt, E., & Eldridge, A. (1986). The attachment relationship and child maltreatment. *Infant Mental Health Journal, 7,* 264–273.

Schneider, R. J., Casey, J., & Kohn, R. (2000). Motivational versus confrontational interviewing: A comparison of substance abuse assessment practices at employee assistance programs. *Journal of Behavioral Health Services & Research, 27,* 60–74.

Schreier, H. A. (2000). Factitious disorder by proxy in which the presenting problem is behavioral or psychiatric. *Journal of the American Academy of Child & Adolescent Psychiatry, 39,* 668–670.

Schreier, H. A. (2001). Factitious disorder by proxy: Reply. *Journal of the American Academy of Child & Adolescent Psychiatry, 40,* 4–5.

Schreier, H. A., & Libow, J. A. (1993). *Hurting for love: Munchausen by proxy syndrome.* New York: Guilford.

Schuman, D. C. (1986). False allegations of physical and sexual abuse. *Bulletin of the American Academy of Psychiatry and the Law, 14,* 5–21.

Schutz, B. M., Dixon, E. B., Lindenberger, J. C., & Ruther, N. J. (1989). *Solomon's sword: A practical guide to conducting child custody evaluations.* San Francisco: Jossey-Bass.

Schwartz, N. H. (1987). Data integration and report writing. In R. S. Dean (Ed.), *Introduction to assessing human intelligence: Issues and procedures* (pp. 289–313). Springfield, IL: Charles C. Thomas.

Seagull, E. A. W. (1987). Social support and child maltreatment: A review of the evidence. *Child Abuse & Neglect, 11*, 41–52.

Seideman, R. Y., Williams, R., Burns, P., Jacobson, S., Weatherby, F., & Primeaux, M. (1994). Culture sensitivity in assessing urban Native American parenting. *Public Health Nursing, 11*, 98–103.

Selzer, M. L. (1971). The Michigan Alcoholism Screening Test (MAST): The quest for a new diagnostic instrument. *American Journal of Psychiatry, 3*, 176–181.

Seymour, C. (1998). Children with parents in prison: Child welfare policy, program, and practice issues. *Child Welfare, 77*, 469–493.

Sgroi, S. M. (1982). *Handbook of clinical intervention in child sexual abuse.* Lexington, MA: Lexington Books.

Sgroi, S. M. (Ed.). (1989). *Vulnerable populations: Sexual abuse treatment for children, adult survivors, offenders, and persons with mental retardation,* Vol. 2. Lexington, MA: Lexington Books/D. C. Heath and Company.

Shahzade v. Gregory, 923 F.Supp. 2896 (D.Mass.1996).

Shapiro, J. R., & Mangelsdorf, S. C. (1994). The determinants of parenting competence in adolescent mothers. *Journal of Youth and Adolescence, 23*, 621–641.

Sheeber, L. B., & Johnson, J. H. (1994). Evaluation of a temperament-focused, parent-training program. *Journal of Clinical Child Psychology, 23*, 249–259.

Shelton, K. K., Frick, P. J., & Wootton, J. (1996). Assessment of parenting practices in families of elementary school-age children. *Journal of Clinical Child Psychology, 3*, 317–329.

Shimkin, D. B., Shimkin, E. M., & Frate, D. A. (Eds.). (1978). *The extended family in Black societies.* The Hague, The Netherlands: Moutin.

Sibbison, V., & McGowan, J. (1978). *New York State children in foster care: Executive summary.* Albany, NY: Welfare Research, Inc.

Siegler, R. S. (1986). *Children's thinking.* Englewood Cliffs, NJ: Prentice-Hall.

Sigelman, C. K., Budd, E. C., Spanhel, C. L., & Schoenrock, C. J. (1981). Asking questions of retarded persons: A comparison of yes-no and either-or formats. *Applied Research in Mental Retardation, 2*, 347–357.

Silverman, A. R., & Fiegleman, W. (1990). Adjustment in interracial adoptees: An overview. In D. M. Brodzinsky & M. D. Schechter (Eds.), *The psychology of adoption.* New York: Oxford University Press.

Simon, R. J., & Alstein, H. (1977). *Transracial adoption.* New York: Wiley.

Simon, R. J., & Alstein, H. (1981). *Transracial adoption: A follow-up.* Lexington, MA: Lexington Books.

Simon, R. J., Alstein, H., & Melli, M. S. (1994). *The case for transracial adoption.* Washington, DC: American University Press.

Skolnick, A. S. (1991). *Embattled paradise: The American family in an age of uncertainty.* New York: Basic Books.

Slade, A., & Cohen, L. (1996). The process of parenting and the remembrance of things past. *Infant Mental Health Journal, 17*, 217–238.

Slaughter, D. T., & McWorter, G. A. (1985). Social origins and early features of the scientific study of Black American families and children. In M. B. Spencer, G. K. Brookins, & W. R. Allen (Eds.), *Beginnings: The social and affective development of Black children* (pp. 5–18). Hillsdale, NJ: Erlbaum.

Slobogin, C. (1989). The "ultimate issue" issue. *Behavioral Sciences and the Law, 7*, 259–266.

Slovic, P., Monahan, J., & MacGregor, D. G. (2000). Violence risk assessment and risk communication: The effects of using actual cases, providing instruction, and employing probability versus frequency formats. *Law & Human Behavior, 24*, 271–296.

Small, M. F. (1998). *Our babies, ourselves: How biology and culture shape the way we parent.* New York: Anchor Books.

Smith v. Organization of Foster Families for Equality and Reform, 431 U.S. 816 (1977).

Smith, A. M., & O'Leary, S. (1995). Attributions and arousal and predictors of maternal discipline. *Cognitive therapy and research, 19,* 459–471.

Smith, D., & Dumont, F. (1995). A cautionary study: Unwarranted interpretations of the Draw-a-Person test. *Professional Psychology: Research and Practice, 26,* 298–303.

Smith, J. R., Brooks-Gunn, J., & Klebanov, P. K. (1997). The consequences of living in poverty for young children's cognitive and verbal ability and early school achievement. In G. J. Duncan & J. Brooks-Gunn (Eds.), *Consequences of growing up poor* (pp. 132–189). New York: Russell Sage Foundation.

Smith, C., & Nylund, D. (Eds.). *Narrative therapies with children and adolescents.* New York: Guilford.

Snyder, D. K. (2000). Computer-assisted judgment: Defining strengths and liabilities. *Psychological Assessment, 12,* 52–60.

Solis, M. L., & Abidin, R. R. (1991). The Spanish version Parenting Stress Index: A psychometric study. *Journal of Clinical Child Psychology, 20,* 372–378.

Somer, E., & Braunstein, A. (1999). Are children exposed to interparental violence being psychologically maltreated? *Aggression & Violent Behavior, 4,* 449–456.

Souldice, A. & Stevenson-Hinde, J. (1992). Coping with security distress: The Separation Anxiety Test and attachment classification at 4.5 years. *Journal of Child Psychology and Psychiatry, 33,* 331–348.

South Carolina Department of Social Services v. Broome, 307 S.C. 48, 413 S.E.2d 835 (1992).

South Carolina Department of Social Services v. Brown, 317 S.C. 332, 454 S.E. 2d 335 (Ct. App. 1995).

South Carolina Department of Social Services v. the Father and Mother; In the Interest of the Child, 294 S.C. 518, 366 S.E.2d 40 (App.1988).

South Carolina Department of Social Services v. Humphrey, 297 S.C. 118, 374 S.E. 2d 922 (S.C. App. 1988).

Southall, D. P., Plunkett, M. C. B., Banks, M. W., Falkov, A. F., & Samuels, M. P. (1997). *Pediatrics, 100,* 735–760.

Spearly, J. L., & Lauderdale, M. (1983). Community characteristics and ethnicity in the prediction of child maltreatment rates. *Child Abuse & Neglect, 7,* 91–105.

Spaeth, H. J., & Smith, E. C. (1991). *The Constitution of the United States* (13th ed.) New York: Harper Collins.

Spanier, G. B. (1989). *Dyadic Adjustment Scale: A manual.* North Tonawanda, NY: Multi-Health Systems.

Spar, K. (1997). *CRS Report for Congress: Foster care and adoption statistics.* Washington, DC: Congressional Research Service.

Sparrow, S. S., Balla, D. A., & Cicchetti, D. V. (1984). *Vineland Adaptive Behavior Scales.* Circle Pines, MN: American Guidance Services.

Spence, J. T. (1985). Achievement American style: The rewards and costs of individualism. *American Psychologist, 40,* 1285–1295.

Sperling, M. B., & Berman, W. H. (Eds.). (1994). *Attachment in adults: Clinical and developmental perspectives.* Guilford: New York.

Sroufe, L. A. (1979). Socioemotional development. In J. D. Osofsky (Ed.), *Handbook of infant development* (pp. 462–516). New York: Wiley.

Sroufe, L. A., & Waters, E. (1977). Attachment as an organizational construct. *Child Development, 48,* 1184–1199.

Stack, C. (1974). *All our kin.* New York: Harper & Row.

Stahl, P. M. (1994). *Conducting child custody evaluations: A comprehensive guide.* Thousand Oaks, CA: Sage.

Starr, R. H. (1982). A research-based approach to the prediction of child abuse. In R. H. Starr (Ed.), *Child abuse predictions: Policy implications* (pp. 105–134). Cambridge, MA: Ballinger.

State v. Brovold, 477 N.W.2d 775 (Minn.Ct.App.1991).

State v. Crandall, 120 N.J. 649, 655, 577 A.2d 483, 485 (1990).

State v. Crossland, 820 S.W.2d 72, 76 (Mo.Ct.App.1991).

State v. Evans, 171 Wis.2d 471, 492 N.W.2d 141 (1992).

State v. Feltrop, 803 S.W.2d 1 (Mo.1991).

State v. Haseltine, 120 Wis. 2d 92, 98, 352 N.W.2d 673, 677 (Ct. App. 1984).

State v. Hollingsworth, 160 Wis.2d 883, 467 N.W.2d 555 (Wis.Ct.App.1991).

State v. Hudnall, 293 S.C. 97, 359 S.E.2d 59 (1987).

State v. Hunt, 406 P.2d 208 (Ariz.1965).

State v. Hussey, 521 A.2d 278 (Me.1987).

State v. Jarzbek, 204 Conn. 683, 705, 529 A.2d 1245, 1255 (1987).

State v. Jensen, 141 Wis. 2d 333, 415 N.W.2d 519 (Ct. App. 1987).

State v. Jensen, 147 Wis. 2d 240, 432 N.W.2d 913 (1988).

State v. Jones, 95 N.C. 588 (1986).

State v. Kaimimoku, 9 Haw. App. 345, 841 P.2d 1076 (1992).

State v. Michaels, 136 N.J. 299, 642 A.2d, 1372 (1994).

State v. Moran, 151 Ariz. 378, 380, 728 P.2d 248, 250 (1986).

State v. Myers, 359 N.W.2d 604 (Minn.1984).

State v. R. W., 104 N.J. 14, 514 A.2d 1287 (1986).

State v. Superior Court, 149 Ariz. 397, 401, 719 P.2d 283, 287 (Ariz.Ct.App.1986).

State v. Thorpe, 429 A.2d 785 (R.I.1981).

State v. Vincent, 159 Ariz. 418, 432, 768 P.2d 150, 163 (1989).

State v. Vosika, 85 Or.App. 148, 735 p.2d 1273 (1987).

State v. Ward, 619 N.E.2d 1119 (Ohio.App.1992).

Steadman, H. J., Silver, E., Monahan, J., Appelbaum, P. S., Robbins, P. C., Mulvey, E, P., Grisso, T., Roth, L. H., & Banks, S. (2000). A classification tree approach to the development of actuarial violence risk assessment tools. *Law & Human Behavior, 24,* 83–100.

Steele, B. (1987). Psychodynamic factors in child abuse. In R. E. Helfer & R. S. Kempe (Eds.), *The battered child* (4th ed., pp. 81–114). Chicago: University of Chicago Press.

Steele, B. F. & Pollack, C. B. (1968). A psychiatric study of parents who abuse infants and small children. In R. E. Helfer & C. H. Kempe (Eds.), *The battered child* (pp. 89–133). Chicago: University of Chicago Press.

Stephenson, M. (2000). Development and validation of the Stephenson Multigroup Acculturation Scale (SMAS). *Psychological Assessment, 12,* 77–88.

Steele, B. (1976). Violence within the family. In C. H. Kempe & A. E. Helfer (Eds.), *Child abuse and neglect: The family and the community* (pp. 3–24). Cambridge, MA: Ballinger.

Steinberg, L., Lamborn, S. D., Darling, N., Mounts, N. S., & Dornbusch, S. M. (1994). Over-time changes in adjustment and competence among adolescents from authoritative, authoritarian, indulgent, and neglectful families. *Child Development, 65,* 754–770.

Steinberg, L., Mounts, N., Lamborn, S., & Dornbusch, S. (1991). Authoritative parenting and adolescent adjustment across varied ecological niches. *Journal of Research on Adolescence, 1,* 19–36.

Stern, D. N. (1985). *The interpersonal world of the infant: A view from psychoanalysis and developmental psychology.* New York: Basic Books.

Stern, D. N. (1994). One way to build a clinically relevant baby. *Infant Mental Health Journal, 15,* 36–54.

Stern-Bruschweiler, N., & Stern, D. (1989). A model for conceptualizing the role of the mother's representational role in various mother-infant therapies. *Infant Mental Health Journal, 10,* 142–156.

Sternberg, K. J., Lamb, M. E., Hershkowitz, I., Yudilevitch, L., Orback, Y., Esplin, P., & Horay, M. (1996). Effects of introductory style on children's abilities to describe experiences of sexual abuse. *International Journal of Behavioral Development, 19,* 627–637.

Steward, R. & Marvin, R. S. (1984). Sibling relations: The role of conceptual perspective-taking in the ontogeny of sibling caregiving. *Child Development, 55,* 1322–1332.

Stolorow, Robert D., Brandshaft, B., & Atwood, G. (1987). *Psychoanalytic treatment: An intersubjective approach.* Hillsdale, NJ: Analytic Press.

Stovall, K. C., & Dozier, M. (1998). Infants in foster care: An attachment theory perspective. *Adoption Quarterly, 2,* 55–88.

Stovall, K. C., & Dozier, M. (2000). The development of attachment in new relationships: Single subject analyses for 10 foster infants. *Development & Psychopathology, 12,* 133–156.

Strand, P. S., & Wahler, R. G. (1996). Predicting maladaptive parenting: Role of maternal object relations. *Journal of Clinical Child Psychology, 25,* 43–51.

Strand, S., & Belfrage, H. (2001). Comparison of HCR-20 scores in violent mentally disordered men and women: Gender differences and similarities. *Psychology Crime & Law, 7,* 71–79.

Straus, M. A. (1983). Ordinary violence, child abuse, and wife beating: What do they have in common? In D. Finkelhor, R. J. Gelles, G. T. Hotaling, & M. A. Straus (Eds.), *The dark side of families.* Beverly Hills, CA: Sage.

Straus, M. A., Gelles, R. J., & Steinmetz, S. K. (1980). *Behind closed doors: Violence in the American family.* Garden City, NJ: Anchor Books.

Strickland v. State, 550 So.2d 1042 (Ala.1988).

Studer, L. H., Clelland, S. R., Aylwin, A. S., Reddon, J. R., & Monro, A. (2000). Rethinking risk assessment for incest offenders. *International Journal of Law & Psychiatry, 23,* 15–22.

Suarez-Orozco, D., & Suarez-Orozco, M. M. (1994). The cultural psychology of Hispanic immigrants. In T. Weaver (Ed.), *Handbook of Hispanic cultures in the United States: Vol. 2 Anthropology* (pp. 129–146). Houston, TX: Arte Publico Press.

Suiomi, S. J. (1995). Attachment theory and nonhuman primates. In S. Goldberg, R. Muir, & J. Kerr (Eds.), *Attachment theory: Social, developmental, and clinical perspectives* (pp. 185–201). Hillsdale, NJ: Analytic Press.

Swanson, A. J., Pantalon, M. V., & Cohen, K. R. (1999). Motivational interviewing and treatment adherence among psychiatric and dually diagnosed patients. *Journal of Nervous & Mental Disease, 187,* 630–635.

Swire, M., & Kavaler, F. (1978). Health of foster children. *Child Welfare, 57,* 563–569.

Tague, R. G., & Lovejoy, O. C. (1986). The obstetric pelvis of AL 288-I (Lucy). *Journal of Human Evolution, 15,* 237–255.

Tallent, N. (1993). *Psychological report writing* (4th ed.). Upper Saddle River, NJ: Prentice-Hall.

Tappin, D. M., McKay, C., McIntyre, D., Gilmour, W. H., Cowan, S., Crawford, F., Currie, F., & Lumsden, M. (2000). A practical instrument to document the process of motivational interviewing. *Behavioural & Cognitive Psychotherapy, 28,* 17–32.

Tarter, R. E., Blackson, T., Martin, C., Loeber, R., & Moss, H. B. (1993). Characteristics and correlates of child discipline practices in substance abuse and normal families. *The American Journal on Addictions, 2,* 18–25.

Tasker, F. L., & Golombok, S. (1995). Adults raised as children in lesbian families. *American Journal of Orthopsychiatry, 65,* 203–215.

Tasker, F. L., & Golombok, S. (1997). *Growing up in a lesbian family: Effects on child development.* New York: Guilford.

Taylor, C. G., Norman, D. K., Murphy, J. M., Jellinek, M., Quinn, D., Poitrast, F. G., & Goshko, M. (1991). Diagnosed intellectual and emotional impairment among parents who seriously mistreat their children: Prevalence, type, and outcome in a court sample. *Child Abuse & Neglect, 15,* 389–401.

Taylor, R. J., Chatters, L. M., Tucker, M. B., & Lewis, E. (1990). Developments in research on Black families: A decade review. *Journal of Marriage and the Family, 52,* 993–1014.

Taylor, R. D., & Roberts, D. (1995). Kinship support and maternal and adolescent well-being in economically disadvantaged African-American families. *Child Development, 66,* 1585–1597.

Terr, L. C. (1991). Childhood traumas: An outline and overview. *American Journal of Psychiatry, 148,* 10–20.

Teti, D., & Ablard, K. (1989). Security of attachment and infant-sibling relationships. *Child Development, 60,* 1519–1528.

Theonnes, N., & Pearson, J. (1999). Supervised visitation: A profile of providers. *Family & Conciliation Courts Review, 37,* 460–477.

Thomas, V. H., Melchert, T. P., & Banken, J. A. (1999). Substance dependence and personality disorders: Comorbidity and treatment outcome in an inpatient treatment populations. *Journal of Studies on Alcohol, 60,* 271–277.

Thomas, W. I., & Znaniecki, F. (1918). *The Polish peasant in Europe and America: Monograph of an immigrant group.* Boston: G. Badger.

Thompson, R. A. (1983). The father's case in child custody disputes: The contributions of psychological research. In M. E. Lamb & A. Sagi (Eds.), *Fatherhood and Family Policy* (pp. 210–235). Hillsdale, NJ: Erlbaum.

Thompson, R. A. (1990). *Socioemotional development: Nebraska Symposium on Motivation 1988* (Vol. 36). Lincoln, NE: University of Nebraska Press.

Thompson, R. A. (1993). Socioemotional development: Enduring issues and new challenges. *Developmental Review, 13,* 372–402.

Thompson, R., & Laible, D. (1999). Noncustodial parents. In M. E. Lamb (Ed.), *Parenting and child development in "nontraditional" families* (pp. 103–124). Mahwah, NJ: Erlbaum.

Thompson, W. C., Clarke-Stewart, K. A., & Lepore, S. J. (1997). What did the janitor do?: Suggestive interviewing and the accuracy of children's accounts. *Law and Human Behavior, 21,* 405–426.

Thomson, E. (1994). "Setting" and "development" from a demographic point of view. In A. Booth & J. Dunn (Eds.), *Stepfamilies: Who benefits? Who does not?* (pp. 89–96). Hillsdale, NJ: Erlbaum.

Thornton, A., & Camburn, D. (1987). The influence of the family on premarital sexual attitudes and behavior. *Demography, 24,* 323–340.

Tobey A. E., & Goodman, G. S. (1992). Children's eyewitness memory: Effects of participation and forensic context. *Child Abuse & Neglect, 16,* 779–796.

Tolson, T. F. J., & Wilson, M. N. (1990). The impact of two- and three-generation Black family structure of perceived family climate. *Child Development, 61,* 416–428.

Tome v. United States, 513 U.S. 150, 115 St.Ct. 696 (1995).

Tonigan, J. S., Miller, W. R., & Connors, G. J. (2000). Project MATCH client impressions about Alcoholics Anonymous: Measurement issues and relationship to treatment outcome. *Alcoholism Treatment Quarterly, 18,* 25–41.

Townsend v. State, 103 Nev. 113, 734 P.2d 705 (1987).

Tracy, L. R., Lamb, M. E., & Ainsworth, M. D. (1976). Infant approach as related to attachment. *Child Development, 47,* 571–578.

Trevathan, W. R. (1987). *Human birth: An evolutionary perspective*. New York: Aldine de Gruyter.

Triandis, H. C., Marin, G., Betancourt, H., Lisansky, J., & Chang, B. H. (1982). *Dimensions of familism among Hispanic and mainstream Navy recruits* (Tech. Rep. No. 14). Champaign: Department of Psychology, University of Illinois.

Trickett, P. K., & Kuczynski, L. (1986). Children's misbehaviors and parental discipline strategies in abusive and nonabusive families. *Developmental Psychology, 22*, 115–123.

Trickett, P. K., & Susman, E. J. (1988). Parental perceptions of child-rearing practices in physically abusive and nonabusive families. *Developmental Psychology, 24*, 270–276.

Trimble v. Gordon, 430 U.S. 762 (1977).

Trimble, J. E. (1990). Application of psychological knowledge for American Indians and Alaska natives. *The Journal of Training & Practices in Professional Psychology, 4*, 45–63.

Troxel v. Granville, 530 U.S. 57 (2000).

Tucker, A., Merton, P., & Luszcz, M. (1990). The effect of repeated interviews on young children's eyewitness memory. *Australian and New Zealand Journal of Criminology, 23*, 117–123.

Umberson, D. (1986). Sociobiology: A valid explanation of child abuse? *Social Biology, 33*, 131–137.

Unger, D. G., & Wandersman, A. (1985). The importance of neighbors: The social, cognitive, and affective components of neighboring. *American Journal of Community Psychology, 13*, 139–169.

U.S. Advisory Board of Child Abuse and Neglect. (1995). *A national shame: Fatal child abuse and neglect in the U.S.* (5th Report). Washington, DC: U.S. Government Printing Office.

U.S. Bureau of Census. (1992). *Marriage, divorce, and remarriage in the 1990s* (Current Population Reports, pp. 23–180). Washington, DC: U. S. Government Printing Office.

U.S. Bureau of Census. (1992). *1990 Census of population, 1990 CP-1–4, General population characteristics*. Washington, DC: U.S. Government Printing Office.

U.S. Bureau of Census. (1993). *Current populations reports, Hispanic Americans today*. Washington, DC: U.S. Government Printing Office.

U.S. Bureau of Census. (1996a). *Poverty in the United States: 1995* (Current Population Survey, No. P60–194). Washington, DC: U.S. Government Printing Office.

U.S. Bureau of Census. (1996b). *Statistical abstract of the United States*. Washington, DC: U.S. Government Printing Office.

U.S. Conference of Mayors. (1993). *A status report on hunger and homelessness in America's cities: A 26-city survey*. Washington, DC: Author.

U.S. Department of Health and Human Services. (1988). *Study findings: Study of national incidence and prevalence of child abuse and neglect: 1988*. Bethesda, MD; Westat.

U.S. General Accounting Office. (1991). *Foster care: Children's experiences* (GAO/HRD-91–64). Washington, DC: Author.

U.S. General Accounting Office. (1993). *Foster care: Services to prevent out-of-home placements are limited by funding patterns* (GAO/HRD-93–76). Washington, DC: Author.

U.S. General Accounting Office. (1995). *Child welfare: Complex needs strain capacity to provide services* (GAO/HEHS-95–208). Washington, DC: Author.

Valentine, D. P. (1990). Double jeopardy: Child maltreatment and mental retardation. *Child & Adolescent Social Work Journal, 7*, 487–499.

Van Horn, D. H., & Box, D. A. (2001). A pilot test of motivational interviewing groups for dually diagnosed inpatients. *Journal of Substance Abuse Treatment, 20*, 191–195.

van IJzendoorn, M. H. (1995). Adult attachment representation, parental responsiveness, and infant attachment: A meta-analysis on the predictive validity of the Adult Attachment Interview. *Psychological Bulletin, 117*, 387–403.

van IJzendoorn, M. H., & Kroonenberg, P. M. (1988). Cross cultural patterns of attachment: A meta-analysis of the Strange Situation. *Child Development, 59*, 147–156.

Vane, J. R., & Motta, R. W. (1987). Basic issues in psychological evaluation. In V. B. Van Hasselt & M. Hersen (Eds.), *Psychological evaluation of the developmentally and physically disabled* (pp. 19–39). New York: Plenum.

Vasek, M. E. (1986). Lying as a skill: The development of deception in children. In R. W. Mitchell & N. S. Thompson (Eds.), *Deception: Perspectives on human and non-human deceit.* Albany: State University of New York Press.

Vasta, R. (1982). Physical child abuse: A dual-component analysis. *Developmental Review, 2,* 125–149.

Vega, W. A. (1990). Hispanic families in the 1980s: A decade of research. *Journal of Marriage and the Family, 52,* 1015–1024.

Verdugo, M. A., Bermejo, B. G., & Fuertes, J. (1995). The maltreatment of intellectually handicapped children and adolescents. *Child Abuse & Neglect, 19,* 205–215.

Viswesvaran, C. & Ones, D. (1999). Meta-analyses of fakability estimates: Implications for personality measurement. *Educational & Psychological Measurement, 59,* 197–210.

von Hahn, L., Harper, G., McDaniel, S. H., Siegel, D. M., Feldman, M. D., & Libow, J. A. (2001). a case of factitious disorder by proxy: The role of the health-care system, diagnostic dilemmas, and family dynamics. *Harvard Review of Psychiatry, 9,* 124–135.

Wahler, R. G., & Dumas, J. E. (1986). "A chip off the old block": Some interpersonal characteristics of coercive children across generations. In P. Strain, M. Guralnick, & H. Walkee (Eds.), *Children's social behavior: Development, assessment, and modification* (pp. 49–86). San Diego, CA: Academic Press.

Wakschlag, L. W., Chase-Lansdale, L., & Brooks-Gunn, J. (1996). Not just "Ghosts in the Nursery": Contemporaneous intergenerational relationship and parenting in young African-American families. *Child Development, 67,* 2131–2147.

Wald, M. (1977). 1977 Juvenile Justice Standards Project. In M. Wald, *Standards Relating to Abuse and Neglect.* Cambridge, MA. Ballinger.

Walker, A. G. (1999). *Handbook on questioning children: A linguistic perspective* (2nd ed.). Washington, DC: American Bar Association.

Walker, A., & Warren, A. (1995). The language of the child abuse interview: Asking the questions, understanding the answers. In T. Ney (Ed.), *Allegations in child sexual abuse: Assessment and case management.* New York: Bruuner/Mazel.

Walker, L. E. A. (1990). Psychological assessment of sexually abused children for legal evaluation and expert witness testimony. *Professional Psychology: Research and Practice, 21,* 344–353.

Ward, M. J., & Carlson, E. A. (1995). Associations among adult attachment representations, maternal sensibility, and infant-mother attachment in a sample of adolescent mothers. *Child Development, 66,* 69.79.

Warren, V., & Cairns, R. (1972). Social reinforcement satiation: An outcome of frequency of ambiguity. *Journal of Exceptional Child Psychology, 13,* 249–260.

Warren, A., Hulse-Trotter, K., & Tubbs, E. C. (1991). Inducing resistance to suggestibility in children. *Law and Human Behavior, 15,* 273–285.

Waterman, J. (1986). Family dynamics of incest with young children. In K. MacFarlane, J. Waterman, S. Conerly, L. Damon, M. Durfee, & S. Long (Eds.), *Sexual abuse of young children* (pp. 204–219). New York: Guilford.

Waters, E., & Deane, K. (1985). The Home Behavior Q-set. In I. Bretherton & E. Waters (Eds.), New directions in attachment research. *Monographs of the Society for Research in Child Development, 50* (Serial No. 209). 41–65.

Watson, D., & Clark, L. (1992). On traits and temperament: General and specific factors of emotional experience and their relation to the five-factor-model. *Journal of personality, 60,* 441–476.

Watt, B. D., & Howells, K. (1999). Skills training for aggression control: Evaluation of an anger management programme for violent offenders. *Legal and Criminological Psychology, 4*, 285–300.

Wauchope, B., & Straus, M. A. (1990). Physical punishment and physical abuse of American children: Incidence rates by age, gender, and occupational class. In M. A. Straus & R. J. Gelles (Eds.), *Physical violence in American families: Risk factors and adaptations to violence in 8,145 families.* New Brunswick, NJ: Transaction Books.

Webster, C. D., Douglas, K. S., Eaves, D., & Hart, S. D. (1997). Assessing risk of violence to others. In C. D. Webster, & M. A. Jackson (Eds.), *Impulsivity: Theory, assessment, and treatment* (pp. 251–277). New York: Guilford.

Webster-Stratton, C. (1985). Comparison of abusive and nonabusive families with conduct-disordered children. *American Journal of Orthopsychiatry, 55*, 59–69.

Webster-Stratton, C., & Hammond, M. (1997). Treating children with early-onset conduct problems: A comparison of child and parent training interventions. *Journal of Consulting and Clinical Psychology, 56*, 93–109.

Weiner, I. B. (1985). Preparing forensic reports and testimony. *Clinical Psychologist, 38*, 78–80.

Weiner, I. B. (1992). The future of psychodiagnosis revisited. In E. I. Megargee & C. D. Spielberger (Eds.), *Personality assessment in America: A retrospective on the occasion of the fiftieth anniversary of the Society for Personality Assessment* (pp. 139–144). Hillsdale, NJ: Erlbaum.

Weiner, I. B. (1993). Clinical considerations in the conjoint use of the Rorschach and the MMPI. *Journal of Personality Assessment, 60*, 148–152.

Weiner, I. B. (1995). Psychometric issues in forensic applications of the MMPI-2. In Y. S. Ben-Porath, & J. R. Graham (Eds.), *Forensic applications of the MMPI-2: Applied psychology* (Vol. 2: Individual, social, and community issues, pp. 48–81). Thousand Oaks, CA: Sage.

Weiner, I. B., Exner, J. E., & Sciara, A. (1996). Is the Rorschach welcome in the courtroom? *Journal of Personality Assessment, 67*, 422–424.

Weinfield, N. S., Sroufe, L. A., Egeland, B. (2000). Attachment from infancy to early adulthood in a high-risk sample: Continuity, discontinuity, and their correlates. *Child Development, 71*, 695–702.

Weintraub, M., Brooks, J., & Lewis, M. (1977). The social network: A reconsideration of the concept of attachment. *Human Development, 20*, 31–47.

Weiss, L. H., & Schwarz, J. C. (1996). The relationship between parenting types and older adolescents' personality, academic achievement, adjustment, and substance use. *Child Development, 67*, 2101–2114.

Weithorn, L. A. (1984). Children's capacities in legal contexts. In N. D. Reppucci, L. A. Weithorn, E. P. Mulvey, & J. Monahan (Eds.), *Children, mental health, and the law* (pp. 25–58). Beverly Hills, CA: Sage.

Wekerle, C., & Wolfe, D. A. (1996). Child maltreatment. In E. J. Mash & R. A. Barkley (Eds.), Child Psychopathology (pp. 492–537). New York: Guilford.

Welch-Ross, M. K., Diecidue, K., & Miller, S. A. (1997). Young children's understanding of conflicting mental representation predicts suggestibility. *Developmental Psychology, 33*, 43–53.

Werner, J. S., & Perlmutter, M. (1979). Development of visual memory in infants. In H. W. Reese & L. P. Lipsitt (Eds.), *Advances in child development and behavior* (Vol 14, pp. 1–56). New York: Academic Press.

West, C. M., Williams, L. M., & Wiegel, J. A. (2000). Adult sexual revictimization among Black women sexually abused in childhood: A prospective examination of serious consequences of abuse. *Child Maltreatment: Journal of the American Professional Society on the Abuse of Children, 5*, 49–57.

Westcott, H. L., & Jones, D. P. H. (1999). Annotation: The abuse of disabled children. *Journal of Child Psychology & Psychiatry & Allied Disciplines, 40*, 479–506.

Western Industries v. Newcor Canada Ltd, 739 F.2d 1198 (1984).

Weston, K. (1991). *Families we choose: Lesbians, gays, kinship.* New York: Columbia University Press.

Wheeler v. United States, 159 U.S. 523 (1895).

Whipple, E. E., Fitzgerald, H. E., & Zucker, R. A. (1995). Parent-child interactions in alcoholic and nonalcoholic families. *American Journal of Orthopsychiatry, 65*, 153–159.

Whitcomb, D. (1992). Use of expert witnesses. In *When the victim is a child* (2nd ed.). National Institute of Justice: Author.

White v. Illinois, 502 U.S. 346, 112 S.Ct. 736 (1992).

White, T., Voter, K., & Perry, J. (1985). Surreptitious warfarin ingestion. *Child Abuse & Neglect, 9*, 349–352.

Whitehurst, G. (1976). The development of communication changes with age and modeling. *Child Development, 47*, 473–482.

Whiting, J. B. (2000). The view from down here: Foster children's stories. *Child & Youth Care Forum, 29*, 79–95.

Whiting, J. W. M. (1981). Environmental constraints on infant care practices. In R. H. Munroe, R. L. Munroe, & B. B. Whiting (Eds.), *Handbook of cross-cultural human development* (pp. 155–180). New York: Garland.

Whitten, M. R. (1994). Assessment of attachment in traumatized children. In B. Jones (Ed.), *Handbook for treatment of attachment trauma problems in children.* New York: Lexington Books.

Wiche, V. R. (1992). Abusive and nonabusive parents: How they were parented. *Journal of Social Service Research, 15*, 81–93.

Widom, C. S. (1989a). Child abuse, neglect, and adult behavior: Research design and findings on criminality, violence, and child abuse. *American Journal of Orthopsychiatry, 59*, 355–367.

Widom, C. S. (1989b). Does violence beget violence? A critical examination of the literature. *Psychological Bulletin, 106*, 3–28.

Wigmore, J. H. (1935). *Evidence in trials at common law* (Vol. 6). Boston: Little, Brown.

Wilentz, A. (1989). *The rainy season: Haiti since Duvalier.* New York: Simon and Schuster.

Williams, E., Radin, N., & Allegro, T. (1992). Sex role attitudes of adolescents reared primarily by their fathers: An 11-year follow-up. *Merrill-Palmer Quarterly, 38*, 457–476.

Williams, L. M., Siegel, J. A., & Pomeroy, J. J. (2000). Validity of women's self-reports of documented child sexual abuse. In A. A. Stone & J. S. Turkkan et al. (Eds.), *The science of self-report: Implications for research and practice* (pp. 211–226). Mahwah, NJ: Erlbaum.

Wilson, W. J. (1987). *The truly disadvantages: The inner city, the underclass, and public policy.* Chicago: University of Chicago Press.

Wimmer, H. Gruber, S., & Perner, J. (1984). Young children's conception of lying: Moral intuition and the denotation and connotation of to lie. *Developmental Psychology, 21*, 993–995.

Winnicott, D. (1965). *Ego distortions in terms of true and false self.* New York: International Universities.

Winnicott, D. W. (1971). *Playing and reality.* London: Tavistock.

Wise, E. A. (2001). The comparative validity of MCMI-II and MMPI-2 personality disorder scales with forensic examinees. *Journal of Personality Disorders, 15*, 275–279.

Wojtkiewicz, R. (1993). Simplicity and complexity in the effects of parental structure on high school graduation. *Demography, 30*, 701–717.

Wolfe, D. A. (1985). Child-abusive parents: An empirical review and analysis. *Psychological Bulletin, 97*, 462–482.

Wolfe, D. A. (1987). *Child Abuse: Implications for child development and psychopathology:* Newbury Park, CA: Sage.

Wolfe, D. A. (1988). Child abuse and neglect. In E. J. Mash & L. G. Terdal (Eds.), *Behavioral assessment of childhood disorders* (2nd ed. pp. 627–669). New York: Guilford.

Wolfe, D. A., McMahon, R. J., & Peters, R. D. (Eds.). (1997). *Child abuse: New directions in prevention and treatment across the lifespan.* Thousand Oaks, CA: Sage.

Wood, R. M., Grossman, L. S., Fichtner, C. G. (2000). Psychological assessment, treatment, and outcome with sex offenders. *Behavioral Sciences & the Law, 18,* 23–41.

Woodall, J. (1998). The nature of memory: Controversies about retrieved memories and the law of evidence. *Journal of Psychiatry & Law, 26,* 151–218.

Wu. D. Y. H. (1985). Child training in Chinese culture. In D. Y. H. Wu & W. S. Tsent (Eds.), *Chinese culture and mental health* (pp. 113–132). Orlando, FL Academic Press.

Wu, L. (1996). Effects of family instability, income, and income instability on the risk of a premarital birth. *Demography, 61,* 386–406.

Wu, L., & Martinson, B. (1993). Family structure and the risk of a premarital birth. *American Sociological Review, 58,* 210–232.

Yates, A. (1987). Current status and future directions of research on the American Indian child. *American Journal of Psychiatry, 144,* 1135–1141.

Yuille, J. C., Hunter, R., Joffe, R., & Zaparniuk, J. (1993). Interviewing children in sexual abuse cases. In G. S. Goodman & B. L. Bottoms (Eds.), *Child victims, child witnesses: Understanding and improving testimony* (pp. 95–115). New York: Guilford.

Zahn-Waxler, C., Radke-Yarrow, M., & King, R. A. (1979). Childrearing and children's prosocial initiations toward victims of distress. *Child Development, 50,* 319–330.

Zaragoza, M. S., & Lane S. M. (1994). Source misattributions and the suggestibility of eyewitness memory. *Journal of Experimental Psychology: Learning, Memory, and Cognition, 20,* 934–945.

Zaragoza, M. S., & Mitchell, K. J. (1996). Repeated exposure to suggestion and the creation of false memories. *Psychological Science, 7,* 294–300.

Zayas, L. H., & Solari, F. (1994). Early childhood socialization in Hispanic families: Context, culture, and practice implications. *Professional Psychology: Research and Practice, 25,* 200–206.

Zill, N. (1994). Understsanding why children in stepfamilies have more learning and behavior problems than children in nuclear families. In A. Booth & J. Dunn (Eds.), *Stepfamilies: Who benefits? Who does not?* (pp. 97–106). Hillsdale, NJ: Erlbaum.

Ziskin, J., & Faust, D. (1988). *Coping with psychiatric and psychological testimony* (Vols. 1–3, 4th ed.). Marina Del Ray, CA: Law & Psychology Press.

Zitelli, B., Seltman, M., & Shannon, R. (1988). Munchausen's syndrome by proxy and video surveillance. *American Journal of Disorders in Childhood, 14,* 918.

Zuravin, S. J. (1988). Fertility patterns: Their relationship to child physical abuse and child neglect. *Journal of Marriage and the Family, 50,* 983–993.

Zuravin, S. J. (1989a). The ecology of child abuse and neglect: Review of the literature and presentation of the data. *Violence and Victims, 4,* 101–120.

Zuravin, S. J. (1989b). Severity of maternal depression and three types of mother-to-child aggression. *American Journal of Orthopsychiatriy, 59,* 377–389.

Zuravin, S. J. (1991a). Research definitions of child physical abuse and neglect: Current problems. In R. H. Starr & D. A. Wolfe, et al. (Eds.), *The effects of child abuse and neglect: Issues and research* (pp. 100–128: New York: Guilford.

Zuravin, S. J. (1991b). Unplanned childbearing and family size: The relationship to child neglect and abuse. *Family Planning Perspective, 23,* 155–161.

Zuravin, S. J., & DiBlasio, F. A. (1996). The correlates of child physical abuse and neglect by adolescent mothers. *Journal of Family Violence, 11*, 149–166.

Zuravin, S. J., & Grief, G. (1989). Normative and child-maltreating AFDC mothers. *Social Casework: The Journal of Contemporary Social Work, 74*, 76–84.

Zuravin, S. J., McMillen, C., DePanfilis, D., & Risley-Curtiss, C. (1996). The intergenerational cycle of child maltreatment: Continuity versus discontinuity. *Journal of Interpersonal Violence, 11*, 315–334.

Index